Schizophrenia

Cognitive Theory, Research, and Therapy

Aaron T. Beck

Neil A. Rector

Neal Stolar

Paul Grant

THE GUILFORD PRESS
New York   London

Paperback edition 2011

Printed in the United States of America

This book is printed on acid-free paper.

Last digit is print number: 9   8   7   6   5   4   3   2

The authors have checked with sources believed to be reliable in their efforts to
provide information that is complete and generally in accord with the standards
of practice that are accepted at the time of publication. However, in view of the
possibility of human error or changes in medical sciences, neither the authors,
nor the publisher, nor any other party who has been involved in the preparation
or publication of this work warrants that the information contained herein is in
every respect accurate or complete, and they are not responsible for any errors
or omissions or the results obtained from the use of such information. Readers
are encouraged to confirm the information contained in this book with other
sources.

Library of Congress Cataloging-in-Publication Data

Schizophrenia: cognitive theory, research, and therapy / Aaron T. Beck . . .
[et al.].
     p. ; cm.
  Includes bibliographical references and index.
  ISBN 978-1-60623-018-3 (hardcover: alk. paper)
  ISBN 978-1-60918-238-0 (paperback: alk. paper)
  1. Schizophrenia—Treatment. 2. Cognitive therapy. 3. Cognition.
4. Cognition disorders. I. Beck, Aaron T.
  [DNLM: 1. Schizophrenia—therapy. 2. Cognitive Therapy.
WM 203 S337223   2009]
  RC514.S33468   2009
  616.89′8—dc22

                                                        2008034198

The characteristics of patients in the case examples are composites so as to
prevent identification, and the details of the case histories and the dialogue were
modified without detracting from their significance.

To my wife, children, and grandchildren
—A.T.B.

To Debora and Zoe
—N.A.R.

In memory of Cyrell and Craig,
and to Kyler, Eden, Brady, and Shannon
—N.S.

To Amy, Leone, and Greg
—P.G.

About the Authors

Aaron T. Beck, MD, is University Professor Emeritus of Psychiatry at the University of Pennsylvania and President of the Beck Institute for Cognitive Therapy in Philadelphia. Dr. Beck developed cognitive therapy in the early 1960s as a psychiatrist at the University of Pennsylvania. He has published over 500 articles and 19 books and has lectured throughout the world. Dr. Beck is the recipient of many honors from professional and scientific organizations, including "America's Nobel," the Lasker Clinical Medical Research Award.

Neil A. Rector, PhD, is Director of Research in the Department of Psychiatry at the Sunnybrook Health Sciences Centre in Toronto and Associate Professor of Psychiatry at the University of Toronto. He is a Founding Fellow of the Academy of Cognitive Therapy, an editorial board member of several cognitive therapy journals, and a Canadian Institutes of Health Research and Social Sciences and Humanities Research Council of Canada-funded investigator for the study of cognitive mechanisms and cognitive therapy treatments for psychiatric disorders. In addition to having an active cognitive therapy practice, Dr. Rector is involved in the training and supervision of cognitive therapists.

Neal Stolar, MD-PhD, is a Medical Director and Director of the Cognitive Therapy for the Treatment of Psychosis Special Project at Project Transition in the Philadelphia area; a psychiatric consultant for Creative Health Services and Penn Behavioral Health; a researcher at the University of Pennsylvania's Psychopathology Research Unit and Schizophrenia Research Center; and is in private practice. Dr. Stolar is a Founding Fellow of the Academy of Cognitive Therapy. He has lectured on cognitive therapy of schizophrenia in the United States, China, and Brazil.

Paul Grant, PhD, is Director of Schizophrenia Research and a Fellow in the Psychopathology Research Unit in the Department of Psychiatry at the University of Pennsylvania. Dr. Grant's research interests include cognitive psychopathological models of positive and negative symptoms as well as cognitive therapy of schizophrenia. He is the author of several journal articles and book chapters.

Preface

The disorder or disorders labeled "schizophrenia" have historically posed many questions and offered a number of challenges. Is it possible to make sense out of the varied, often fantastic, beliefs of the patients? Are there any principles that apply to all patients? Is it possible to treat them with psychotherapy? What is the relationship of organic findings to the clinical picture? Our attempt to answer these questions provided the impetus for preparing this volume. The material evolved from our clinical experience and investigations at the universities of Pennsylvania and Toronto. We have all treated many cases of schizophrenia, supervised other professionals, and engaged in systematic research in this area.

Initially, the success in the application of cognitive therapy (CT) to schizophrenia in the United Kingdom prompted us to conduct randomized controlled trials of CT, first in Toronto and most recently in Philadelphia. As we indicate in our summary of the controlled trials of CT (or cognitive-behavior therapy, as it is frequently called), the results of the previously reported clinical trials are promising—but there is still much room for improvement. Indeed, the fact that a psychological intervention could substantially improve clinical outcomes beyond usual care (generally including pharmacotherapy) has been, of course, a surprise to many investigators and clinicians engaged in the study and treatment of schizophrenia.

We should note at the outset that the preparation of a treatment for a complex disorder such as schizophrenia requires far more than the description of specialized strategies and techniques. Successful treatment depends on an in-depth understanding of its phenomenology and causes. Further, the therapist needs a conceptual framework to serve as a guide, just as a builder needs a blueprint. In this volume we have attempted to provide, first, an understanding of the origin, development, and maintenance of the symptoms (delusions, hallucinations, thinking disorder, and negative symptoms). Second, we have used our understanding of the symptomatology and our therapeutic experience fortified by the research in this area to present our suggestions for the treatment of this disorder. Finally, we have attempted to integrate the vast amount of research on the biology of schizophrenia with the relatively sparse work on its psychological aspects into a comprehensive psychobiological model of schizophrenia.

Following an overview of schizophrenia in Chapter 1 and a review of the disorder's complex and intriguing neurobiology in Chapter 2, we provide a broad survey of the clinical and psychological aspects of delusions (Chapter 3). What struck us are the commonalities across all types of delusions. Most crucially, the hypersalient beliefs (whether paranoid or grandiose) usurp the information processing of the afflicted individuals. Further, the patients' capacity to view their aberrant thoughts, interpretations, and beliefs as mental products subject to evaluation is attenuated. They view their paranoid or grandiose ideas as facts and perceive their fantasies as reality. A number of biases are present in all of the delusions. When the patients slip into the paranoid mode, for example, all their experiences are subjected to the triad of egocentric, externalizing, and internalizing biases: they are the object of other people's investment, their unexpected or unusual experiences are caused by external entities, and these entities are motivated to affect their well-being or autonomy.

Chapter 4, on hallucinations, indicates how these experiences are related to the patients' own thoughts and ideas, which are transformed into auditory images. The key problem is the patients' delusion that the voices are externally produced (often by some inimical entity) and that they are omnipotent, omniscient, and uncontrollable. The hallucinatory experience is often embedded in paranoid delusions and indeed is on a continuum with delusions of mind control (thought insertion, thought capture, and mind reading).

Chapter 5, on negative symptoms, addresses the problem of why impairments in attention, memory, and mental flexibility are related to loss of productivity, anhedonia, and social withdrawal. The missing link, as we describe it, is the patients' negative attitudes about their abilities, expectations of pleasure, and interpersonal competencies—all resulting from a history of frustrations related to actual neurocognitive dysfunction. Our formulation of formal thought disorder (Chapter 6) explains the rambling characteristics as a function of deficient inhibitory mechanisms and the alogia as an attempt to spare resources. The disorganized thinking is triggered when highly charged cognitions are activated and consequently disrupt the normal flow of ideas. We present data from our own studies to support the hypotheses regarding negative symptoms and thought disorders.

The section on treatment begins with a comprehensive discussion of the various techniques used in assessment (Chapter 7). Chapter 8 deals with problems in fostering the therapeutic relationship and provides guidelines for dealing with patients' reticence, poor attention span, many deficits, and suspiciousness. Specific problems in the assessment and therapeutic approaches to delusions are described in Chapter 9, and concrete examples for dealing with them are provided. Similarly, Chapter 10, on assessment and therapy of hallucinations, describes a variety of strategies to help the patient reduce the distress associated with voices and, in some cases, eliminate them completely. The therapy of negative symptoms is described in Chapter 11, and various approaches to neutralize the defeatist attitudes and negative expectancies are detailed. In particular, the goal of improving the quality of life is formulated, and strategies for achieving it are reviewed.

Because thought disorder can be a rate-limiting factor on interpersonal efficacy and engagement, Chapter 12 describes a therapeutic approach that helps patients to better assess their communicative difficulties and, importantly, to decrease stress-inducing thinking and behavior that leads to the disorganization of speech. Questions are often raised regarding the relation of psychotherapy to the pharmacotherapy of schizophrenia. Chapter 13 describes these two approaches as blended. The final chapter (Chapter 14) attempts to present a broad model of schizophrenia, integrating constitutional, stress, and psychological factors. In particular, it attempts to show the role of cognitive biases in producing excessive reactions to life experiences and as the missing link between neurological impairments and clinical symptoms. The reduction of cognitive resources is postulated as a major factor leading to the disruption of the coordination of brain functions essential for reality testing and other complex processes.

The various chapters in this volume represent the combined efforts of each author. Typically, one or more of us assumed the responsibility for preparing an outline for a specific chapter. After discussions with the other authors, the designated authors proposed a preliminary draft. We all reviewed and made suggestions for successive drafts. Thus, the final version of each of the chapters include contributions from all of us.

ACKNOWLEDGMENTS

We wish to acknowledge with gratitude the advice and suggestions of various individuals who read portions of the manuscript: Matthew Broome, Daniel Freeman, Steve Moelter, Steve Silverstein, and Elaine Walker. We also are indebted to Debbie Warman and Eric Granholm, who contributed their wisdom and expertise to the various conceptualizations in this volume. Additionally, we would like to thank Mary Seeman and Zindel Segal for their encouragement and support of cognitive therapy developments in psychosis in the Department of Psychiatry, University of Toronto. Finally, we want to express our gratitude to Barbara Marinelli for overall organization of the project, and to Michael Crooks, Brianna Mann, and Letitia Travaglini for their tireless help in typing and editing the manuscript and conducting literature searches.

ADDENDUM FOR THE PAPERBACK EDITION (2011)

Since the publication of the hardback edition of *Schizophrenia*, there have been several notable research developments related to the formulations on negative symptoms (Chapter 5). There is growing empirical evidence of the important contribution of negative beliefs to the development and maintenance of negative symptoms. Further, these beliefs have been shown to be amenable to change, thus improving the negative symptoms. First, Grant and Beck's (2009b) finding that defeatist beliefs about performance (e.g., "If you cannot do something well, there is little point in doing it at all") mediate the relationship between neurocognitive impairment and both negative symptoms and functional outcome has been replicated twice in chronic patients with schizophrenia (Horan et al., 2010; Quinlan & Granholm, 2009). Granholm and colleagues have, further, demonstrated that defeatist beliefs contribute significantly to the diminished task-related pupillary response (an index of effort) of negative symptom patients (Gallegos, Link, Fish, & Granholm, 2009)—thus, empirically establishing the crucial link we have predicted between defeatist attitudes and deficient behavior in this group. In support of our developmental formulations, individuals at high risk of psychosis have shown elevated defeatist beliefs relative to controls, and these beliefs were associated with greater negative symptom severity (Perivoliotis, Morrison, Grant, French, & Beck, 2009). Grant and Beck (2010) have additionally reported that asocial beliefs (e.g., "I prefer hobbies and leisure activities that do not involve other people") predicted both concurrent and future asocial behavior better than neurocognitive impairment or emotion recognition in patients with schizophrenia. And, patients with the deficit syndrome, which is characterized by persistent primary negative symptoms, have greater defeatist beliefs, asocial attitudes, and lower expectations of future pleasure than nondeficit patients with negative symptoms (Beck, Grant, Huh, Perivoliotis, & Chang, under review), suggesting psychosocial treatment targets for patients who have heretofore been regarded as having a strictly biological pathology.

Finally, our cognitive behavior therapy for low-functioning patients with schizophrenia (Perivoliotis, Grant, & Beck, in press) is being evaluated in an ongoing randomized controlled clinical trial. Preliminary data indicate that patients having prominent negative symptoms who are treated with cognitive behavior therapy are showing clinically significant improvements—that are between one half and a full standard deviation greater than patients receiving their usual care (medications, partial programs, etc.)—on social and vocational functioning, negative symptoms, and neurocognitive impairment (Grant & Beck, 2009a).

Cognitive insight (the ability to reflect on experience and not be overconfident in judgments; see Chapters 3, 4, and 14) is another area of active study. Riggs et al. (in press), in a review of this emerging literature, observe that cognitive insight has been linked to psychotic symptoms, poor functioning, metacognition, and neurophysiological activity (amygdala). Of particular note, in an uncontrolled study in a London cognitive therapy for schizophrenia clinic, patients with better cognitive insight at the beginning of treatment, showed greater improvement in their delusions and hallucinations after six months of therapy; moreover, change in cognitive insight was associated with change improvement in hallucinations and delusions (Perivoliotis et al., 2010). Poor cognitive insight appears to be a mechanism in the development and maintenance of psychotic symptoms, and a natural treatment target of psychosocial treatment (Riggs et al., in press).

There have also been a number of new studies relevant to the pharmacological treatment of schizophrenia. First, there have been new medications introduced; chapter 13 has been updated to reflect this new information. Second, there is emerging research on cognitive therapy without medications. While we originally stated that cognitive therapy for schizophrenia requires concurrent medication, the new literature suggests that cognitive therapy may be effective without medication for individuals with schizophrenia (Morrison, 2010). Finally, Stolar (in preparation) has developed a novel neurocognitive model of schizophrenia.

REFERENCES FOR THE ADDENDUM

Beck, A. T., Grant, P. M., Huh, G. A., Perivoliotis, D., & Chang, N. A. (under review). Dysfunctional attitudes and expectancies in deficit syndrome schizophrenia. *Schizophrenia Bulletin.*

Gallegos, Y., Link, P., Fish, S., & Granholm, E. (2009, April). *Defeatist performance beliefs and diminished motivation in schizophrenia.* Paper presented at the International Congress on Schizophrenia Research, San Diego.

Grant, P. M., & Beck, A. T. (2009a, May). *Advances in the cognitive therapy of schizophrenia.* Paper presented at the Minisymposium—Emotion Regulation, Neuroscience, and Psychological Treatments, Lund, Sweden.

Grant, P. M., & Beck, A. T. (2009b). Defeatist beliefs as mediators of cognitive impairment, negative symptoms and functioning in schizophrenia. *Schizophrenia Bulletin, 35*(4), 798–806.

Grant, P. M., & Beck, A. T. (2010). Asocial beliefs as predictors of asocial behavior in schizophrenia. *Psychiatry Research, 177,* 65–70.

Horan, W. P., Rassovsky, Y., Kern, R. S., Lee, J., Wynn, J. K., & Green, M. F. (2010). Further support for the role of dysfunctional attitudes in models of real-world functioning in schizophrenia. *Journal of Psychiatric Research, 44*(8), 499–505.

Morrison, A. P. (2010, May). *Cognitive therapy in persons not taking antipsychotic medications.* Paper presented at the International CBT for Psychosis Conference, Edinburgh.

Perivoliotis, D., Grant, P. M., & Beck, A. T. (in press). *Cognitive therapy for schizophrenia: A comprehensive treatment manual.* New York: Guilford Press.

Perivoliotis, D., Grant, P. M., Peters, E. R., Ison, R., Kuipers, E., & Beck, A. T. (2010). Cognitive insight predicts favorable outcome in cognitive behavioral therapy for psychosis. *Psychosis, 2*(1), 23–33.

Perivoliotis, D., Morrison, A., Grant, P., French, P., & Beck, A. (2009). Negative performance beliefs and negative symptoms in individuals at ultra-high risk of psychosis: A preliminary study. *Psychopathology, 42*(6), 375–379.

Quinlan, T., & Granholm, E. (2009, September). *Defeatist performance attitudes mediate relationships between neurocognition and negative symptoms and functioning in schizophrenia.* Paper presented at the Society for Research in Psychopathology, Minneapolis.

Riggs, S. E., Grant, P. M., Perivoliotis, D., & Beck, A. T. (in press). Assessment of cognitive insight: A qualitative study. *Schizophrenia Bulletin.*

Stolar, N. (in preparation). Locus of agency: A neurocognitive model of schizophrenia.

Contents

CHAPTER 1

Overview of Schizophrenia

As the most well-known person to be afflicted with schizophrenia, John Forbes Nash serves as a natural starting point to a volume on the disorder. Nash was 30 years old when his difficulties became apparent to others. Until then, he may have appeared odd and socially awkward, but he was professionally successful, having recently been offered a full professorship at MIT. However, Nash himself describes experiencing disappointment that his career was not living up to his own expectations (Beck & Nash, 2005). The emergence and profound disruption of Nash's psychotic disorder has been captured by schizophrenia researcher Michael Foster Green (2003):

> His colleagues recall how, in 1959, he walked into a common room at MIT one day and commented that the story on the cover of the *New York Times* contained cryptic messages from inhabitants of another galaxy that only he could decipher. For the next three decades, Nash was in and out of psychiatric hospitals. When he was not in a hospital, he was described as a "sad phantom" who haunted the halls of Princeton "oddly dressed, muttering to himself, writing mysterious messages on blackboards, year after year." (p. 87)

Nash presents a tragic scenario: an eccentric, intellectually brilliant individual beset with extravagant psychiatric symptomatology that wreaks personal, social, and vocational havoc, leading to decades of cyclical encounters with psychiatric services. Highlighting the link between symptoms and functional disability, Nash's pervasive difficulty in day-to-day living appears rooted in the positive symptoms of schizophrenia (Andreasen, 1984b; Cutting, 2003), which include hallucinations (he hears "voices"[1]), delusions (he believes that the *New York Times* contains special codes sent to him from space), bizarre behavior (he is disheveled and behaves inappropriately), and positive formal thought disorder (his language is difficult to understand). Nash does not appear to have suffered from the negative symptoms of schizophrenia, which include reduced verbal (alogia) and nonverbal expressivity (affective flattening), as well as limited engagement in constructive (avolition), pleasurable (anhedonia), and social (asociality) activity (Andreasen, 1984a; Kirkpatrick, Fenton, Carpenter, & Marder, 2006). Ultimately, Nash's story is one of hope:

> Without warning, Nash started to show signs of recovery in the late 1980s. The reasons for his recovery are still unclear; he was neither taking medications nor seeking help. He started to interact more with mathematicians at Princeton, including several who were old friends. Then in 1994 he won the Nobel Prize in economics. . . . (Green, 2003, p. 87)

In the face of florid symptomatology, behavioral disorganization, and disability, Nash regained much of his lost interpersonal and work-related functioning. Recovery from schizophrenia has been described as an ongoing process of managing symptoms and establishing a sense of purpose (Ralph & Corrigan, 2005); in this respect, Nash certainly has recovered. While Green characterizes Nash's turnaround with the evenhanded caution of a veteran schizophrenia researcher, Nash attributes his own improvement to several factors, the primary cause being acts of reasoning (Beck & Nash, 2005). To illustrate this point, Nash has described, first, convincing himself that the hallucinated voices he was hearing were a product of his own mind, and, later, persuading himself of the improbability and ultimate grandiosity of many of his most cherished beliefs. By adjusting his thinking regarding hallucinations and delusions, Nash diminished symptomatic disruption and brought about considerable improvement in everyday functioning. Nash, thus, exemplifies the cognitive approach to schizophrenia that we advocate in the current volume.

---

[1] Nash reports that "voices" were a prominent aspect of his experience of schizophrenia beginning in 1959 (Beck & Nash, 2005).

Pioneered in the 1960s (Beck, 1963), cognitive-behavioral models that explain emotional and behavioral responses as products of thoughts, interpretations, and beliefs have proven highly successful in the understanding and treatment of a variety of psychiatric psychopathology—for example, mood disorders, anxiety disorders, substance abuse, and eating disorders (Grant, Young, & DeRubeis, 2005)—as well as somatic pathology—for example chronic pain (Winterowd, Beck, & Gruener, 2003). Furthermore, hundreds of studies now support the basic cognitive model in which beliefs precede and, to a large degree, determine emotional and behavioral reactions (Clark, Beck, & Alford, 1999). Building on preliminary work in the United States (Beck, 1952; Hole, Rush, & Beck, 1979), investigators in the United Kingdom successfully extended the cognitive model into schizophrenia in the 1980s and 1990s (Chadwick, Birchwood, & Trower, 1996; Fowler, Garety, & Kuipers, 1995; Kingdon & Turkington, 2005), producing promising adjunctive psychosocial treatment protocols targeting delusions, hallucinations, and medication compliance (Rector & Beck, 2001).

Cognitive approaches to schizophrenia, of this sort, have certainly advanced the treatment of this very serious condition. We believe that it is important to adapt our knowledge of nonpsychotic conditions to the understanding and treatment of schizophrenia. In a way, the formulation and treatment strategies we advocate are an extension of those that have been successfully applied to depression (Beck, Rush, Shaw, & Emery, 1979), anxiety disorders (Beck, Emery, & Greenberg, 1985), and personality disorders (Beck, Freeman, Davis, & Associates, 2003). However, one size does *not* fit all, and there are important revisions that we must make in the way we approach patients with schizophrenia. Basically, it is crucial to understand the neurocognitive and psychological–cognitive aspect of schizophrenia as well as the uniqueness of schizophrenia as a psychiatric condition. Perhaps there is a continuum in terms of neuropathology and cognitive distortions as we move from the neuroses to the psychoses. But just as water changes character when it goes below the freezing point into ice, so the usual neurotic phenomena do evidence a kind of "deep change" when they become frozen into schizophrenia.

The current volume is intended as an elaboration of the cognitive approach to schizophrenia. We believe that the best psychotherapeutic practice derives from cognitive theory that is grounded in the existing scientific evidence base (Beck, 1976); therefore, the volume is organized into theoretical (Chapters 2–6) and treatment sections (Chapters 7–13), each containing chapters that address the four primary psychopathological dimensions of the disorder (delusions, hallucinations, thought disorder, and negative symptoms). Additionally, as we also aim to advance the cognitive model of schizophrenia, the final chapter (Chapter 14) presents an integration of the cognitive framework with neurobiological models of schizophrenia. The present chapter provides a brief overview of schizophrenia and our cognitive approach.

BRIEF HISTORY

In this section we focus on the contributions of three pioneers of modern schizophrenia research: John Hughlings Jackson, Emil Kraepelin, and Eugen Bleuler. To a first approximation, Hughlings Jackson's symptom clusters have been superimposed upon Kraepelin's illness category, with causal explanations derived from a Bleulerian cognitive mediational framework. Notably, each theorist grants importance to negative symptoms, despite their differences in defining the disorder.

Hughlings Jackson: Positive–Negative

A highly influential approach to insanity is to be found in the writings of Victorian-era neurologist John Hughlings Jackson (Andreasen & Olsen, 1982; Barnes & Liddle, 1990; Brown & Pluck, 2000). Hughlings Jackson observed (1931):

> Disease is said to "cause" the symptoms of insanity. I submit that disease only produces negative mental symptoms, answering to the dissolution, and that all elaborate positive mental symptoms (illusions, hallucinations, delusions, and extravagant conduct) are the outcome of activity of nervous elements untouched by any pathological process; that they arise during activity on the lower level of evolution remaining. (as cited in Andreasen, 1990b, p. 3)

Composed in the 1880s, Hughlings Jackson's formulation succinctly sums up the theoretical framework that still guides most schizophrenia research (Andreasen, Arndt, Alliger, Miller, & Flaum, 1995; Meares, 1999). At least three points bear mention. First, Hughlings Jackson classifies insanity as a brain disease that is caused by a particular pathology localized in highly evolved (i.e., cortical) neurological centers. Second, he codifies the maddeningly varying symptomatology of insanity into a bicameral and heuristic framework vis-à-vis normality. Elaborations and distortions of normal perception, belief, and behavior are brought together under the umbrella term *positive mental symptoms*; these symptoms are embellishments of normal experience. Likewise, deficits in speech, motivation, emotion, and pleasure are grouped as *negative mental symptoms*; these symptoms represent losses relative to normal experience. Third, and perhaps most important, Hughlings Jackson proposes an intuitive causal interface of biology and manifest symptomatology: Negative symptoms are deficit states and naturally suggest underlying, disease-compromised brain structures (i.e., neuropathology); positive symptoms are elaborations on what is normal and naturally suggest an underlying cognitive process (i.e., failure of inhibition). Although Hughlings Jackson didn't speculate regarding prognosis and outcome of insane patients, it might be inferred that the "broken brain" disease process he postulated for negative symptoms might augur particularly unfavorably.

Crow's (1980) highly influential type I/type II model of schizophrenia, which is essentially a modern elaboration of Hughlings Jackson's framework, sparked renewed interest in the negative symptoms of schizophrenia (Morrison, Renton, Dunn, Williams, & Bentall, 2004). Compelled by new findings in the neurobiology of schizophrenia emerging at the time, Crow proposed splitting schizophrenia into two distinct disorders. Individuals collected under type I schizophrenia manifest marked positive symptoms, respond well to psychoactive medication, and have an illness course characterized by sudden onset and favorable long-term outcome. Individuals grouped as having type II schizophrenia, by contrast, manifest predominantly negative symptomatology, do not respond well to medications, and have an illness course characterized by insidious onset and poor long-term outcome. Crow argued, further, that neurochemical imbalance related to the neurotransmitter dopamine underlies type I schizophrenia, whereas structural brain abnormality such as reduced cerebral volume underlies type II schizophrenia.

The impact of Crow's model has been considerable (Bentall, 2004), as the Hughlings Jackson-inspired conceptual parameterization of positive and negative symptom groupings has come to dominate schizophrenia theory and research (Healy, 2002). Of primary importance, investigators developed operationalized rating scales focused upon the positive and negative symptoms of schizophrenia—for example, the Scale for the Assessment of Positive Symptoms (SAPS; Andreasen, 1984c), the Scale for the Assessment of Negative Symptoms (SANS; Andreasen, 1984b), and the Positive and Negative Syndrome Scale (PANSS; Kay, Fiszbein, & Opler, 1987). Andreasen's scales (i.e., SAPS and SANS), in particular, are comprehensive, standardized instruments, in which a sizeable array of symptoms is identified in observable terms (see Chapter 7). Psychometrically, these scales have been shown to be reliable and sensitive to change (Andreasen, 1990a).[2]

Kraepelin's Heterogeneous Category

Whereas Hughlings Jackson produced a framework that guides brain–behavior theory and research, it is the German psychiatrist Emil Kraepelin who devised the modern classificatory system, or nosology, for schizophrenia (Healy, 2002; Wing & Agrawal, 2003). Based upon extensive patient observation, Kraepelin (1971) collected three diverse manifestations of insanity—hebephrenia (aimless, disorganized, and incongruous behavior), catatonia (lack of movement and stupor, on the one hand; agitated, incoherent behavior, on the other), and paranoia (delusions of persecution and grandeur)—and placed them into a single disease category that he termed *dementia praecox*. Characteristic symptoms included some that Hughlings Jackson would have termed positive (i.e., hallucinations, disorganized speech, and delusions). However, dementia praecox was ultimately a deficit state, making symptoms Hughlings Jackson might have termed negative central to the condition, that is, "emotional dullness, failure of mental activities, loss of mastery over volition, of endeavor, and ability for independent action" (as cited in Fuller, Schultz, & Andreasen, 2003, p. 25).

It is this fundamental illness chronicity combined with a progressively degenerative course that led Kraepelin to categorize *dementia praecox* as distinct from cyclical, mood-related psychotic conditions such as mania and melancholia, which he aggregated into a second disease category, manic–depressive psychosis. Course and long-term outcome, in this manner, guided Kraepelin's nosological efforts more than manifest symptomatology (Healy, 2002). Although he believed that patients could recover from manic–depression, Kraepelin was deeply pessimistic regarding recovery from dementia praecox (Calabrese & Corrigan, 2005; Warner, 2004).

---

[2] We note that there is debate regarding the limitations of the SAPS and SANS to capture the symptoms of schizophrenia (e.g., Horan, Kring, & Blanchard, 2006).

Though the term dementia praecox has fallen out of favor, Kraepelin's category is very much evident in the diagnostic criteria of two influential codifications of mental disorders: the American Psychiatric Association's (2000) *Diagnostic and Statistical Manual of Mental Disorders*, 4th edition (DSM-IV-TR) and the World Health Organization's (1993) *International Classification of Diseases*, 10th revision (ICD-10). According to both the DSM-IV-TR and ICD-10 (see Table 1.1), there are five characteristic symptoms of schizophrenia: delusions, hallucinations, disorganized speech (e.g., frequent derailment or incoherence), grossly disorganized or catatonic behavior, and negative symptoms (i.e., affective flattening, alogia, or avolition) (Wing & Agrawal, 2003). The two systems do differ on a few points, such as the amount of time the symptoms need to be expressed to reach criterion (DSM-IV > ICD-10), as well as whether functional disturbance is intrinsic to the diagnosis of schizophrenia (DSM-IV = "yes"; ICD-10 = "no").

However, heterogeneity is built into the definition of schizophrenia: at most, two of the five symptom types need be present to qualify for diagnosis, and under specified conditions of severity (e.g., two voices comment-

---

TABLE 1.1. Diagnosis of Schizophrenia

Symptoms

Two symptoms present for at least 1 month: (positive) delusions, hallucinations, disorganized speech, disorganized or catatonic behavior; (negative) affective flattening, alogia, avolition.

Social dysfunction

One or more areas affected for most of the time since onset (required by DSM-IV): work, interpersonal relations, self-care; if during adolescence, failure to reach level of interpersonal, academic, or occupational achievement.

Duration

Active symptoms of psychosis must persist in absence of treatment: ICD-10 active symptoms for at least 1 month; DSM-IV active symptoms for at least 6 months, including prodromal and residual (negative or attenuated positive) symptoms.

Exclusion of other disorders

Other diagnoses with psychiatric symptoms must be excluded: schizoaffective disorder; major depression with psychosis; substance abuse disorders; medical disorders such as head injury, cerebral vasculitis, stroke, and dementia.

Note. Adapted from Schultz and Andreasen (1999). Copyright 1999 by Elsevier. Adapted by permission.

ing on behavior), just one symptom needs to be present. The end result is the possibility that two patients who share the diagnosis of schizophrenia might not share any common symptoms. Yet, this heterogeneity of the concept of schizophrenia is by design, as it follows from Kraepelin's assembly of a mental disease category from syndromes characterized by diverse symptomatology (Bentall, 2004; Healy, 2002). Thus, the five-choose-two scheme allows both the DSM-IV and the ICD-10 to include Kraepelin's paranoid, catatonic, and hebephrenic (in DSM-IV, disorganized) subtypes, because diagnosis of each type requires no more than two of the five symptoms of schizophrenia. Additionally, both the current DSM-IV and ICD-10 classifications follow Kraepelin in categorizing schizophrenia separately from affective psychoses (e.g., bipolar disorder).

The inherent heterogeneity of the category *schizophrenia* complicates research efforts, as it naturally leads to conflicting findings. Some researchers have responded to this problem by attempting to define more homogeneous subcategories of schizophrenia (e.g., Carpenter, Heinrichs, & Wagman, 1988), whereas others have abandoned the categorical illness model in place of a disorder defined in terms of severity on a discrete set of symptom dimensions (van Os & Verdoux, 2003). However, difficulty with DSM-IV, and therefore Kraepelinian, classification is not confined to heterogeneity. Critics (Healey, 2002) have observed that the DSM scheme has unsatisfactory reliability, and that the subcategories are not temporally exclusive (i.e., different subtypes can apply to the same patient at different points in time). Further, the symptoms of schizophrenia are not diagnostic or pathognomic. That is, delusions and hallucinations can be found in a variety of neurological and psychological conditions (Wong & Van Tol, 2003), as can disorganized and negative symptoms (Brown & Pluck, 2000). Finally, despite hundreds of studies locating physiological correlates of schizophrenia, no biological marker has been discovered that distinguishes the physiology of someone diagnosed with a psychotic disturbance from normal physiology (Wing & Agrawal, 2003; Wong & Van Tol, 2003). Indeed, Heinrich's (2005) recent quantitative review of biological studies finds considerable overlap between schizophrenia and control samples (see Chapter 2).

Bleuler's Cognitivism

The Swiss psychiatrist Eugen Bleuler (1911/1950) is schizophrenia's other founding father, and, indeed, he is credited with coining the term *schizophrenia* itself. More important, he characterized schizophrenia as a family of mental disorders (Healy, 2002) and thereby expanded the frontiers of inclusion considerably beyond Kraepelin's formulation. Bleuler's formulation was essentially dimensional (Wing & Agrawal, 2003), as it spanned from mild personality dysfunction of the kind that would later be termed schizotypy/schizotaxia to full-blown, chronic *dementia praecox*. Bleuler's model of psychopathology, like that of Hughlings Jackson, characterized the disturbance of schizophrenia in terms of primary (fundamental) and secondary (accessory) symptoms. Primary symptoms—which were necessary for diagnosis, present in every case, and caused by the basic neuropathology— included loss of continuity of associations, loss of affective responsiveness, loss of attention, loss of volition, ambivalence, and autism (Fuller et al., 2003). Secondary symptoms—which did not have to be present for diagnosis and were not caused by the underlying neuropathology—included hallucinations, delusions, catatonia, and behavioral problems (Warner, 2004; Wing & Agrawal, 2003). Quite importantly, from a theoretical standpoint, Bleuler proposed that a cognitive process—loosening of associations— played an intermediary or mediational role between the obscure neuropathology and the expression of symptoms and signs characteristic of schizophrenia. Indeed, it is this very loosening of associations that the term *schizophrenia* (i.e., *schizo* = to split; *phrene* = mind) is designed to capture.

Bleuler's impact upon schizophrenia research is considerable. First, he widened the concept to include what would later be called schizotypal and schizoid traits that are currently included as personality disorders in the DSM-IV. Much genetic, neurobiological, and diagnostic research, moreover, has been devoted to this "schizophrenia spectrum" over the past 40 years (O'Flynn, Gruzelier, Bergman, & Siever, 2003). More important, arguably, is Bleuler's conceptualization of the mechanics of the disorder; he postulated an intermediary cognitive process that links the as-yet unclear neuropathology to manifest symptoms of the disorder (Bentall, 2004). Theorists of all stripes claim this Bleulerian mantle. Thus, neuropsychological (Andreasen, 1999; Frith, 1992; Green, Kern, Braff, & Mintz, 2000), psychodynamic (e.g., McGlashan, Heinssen, & Fenton, 1990), and cognitive-behavioral (e.g., Kingdon & Turkington, 2005) theorists all work within a Bleulerian framework. Our theoretical approach is also Bleulerian (see Chapters 3–6). Indeed, Chapter 14 presents a new model of schizophrenia that integrates developmental, biological, cognitive, and psychological findings within a mediational framework that both motivates the rationale for psychosocial intervention and identifies specific therapeutic targets.

WHAT WE KNOW AND DON'T KNOW
ABOUT SCHIZOPHRENIA[3]

It has now been nearly 100 years since Kraepelin and Bleuler originated the modern concept of schizophrenia, and an enormous amount of research has accrued over this time period, especially in the last 25 years. In 1988, the lead article in the inaugural issue of *Schizophrenia Research* was titled, "Schizophrenia, Just the Facts: What Do We Know, How Well Do We Know It?" (Wyatt, Alexander, Egan, & Kirch, 1988). The literature on schizophrenia has become too vast and unwieldy to tightly summarize in the manner of Wyatt et al.; nonetheless, we intend the current section as a thumbnail sketch of the current state of knowledge about schizophrenia.

Characteristic Symptom Dimensions

As we have seen, schizophrenia has a diverse symptom presentation, and an important research program has been to determine if the symptoms tend to cluster in a particular manner. If, say, hallucinations and delusions tend to co-occur, this might suggest a common, underlying neurobiological pathology. A consensus has now emerged, based upon factor-analytic studies conducted in several cultures, that, at minimum, three dimensions account for the symptoms of schizophrenia (Andreasen et al., 1995, 2005; Barnes & Liddle, 1990; Fuller et al., 2003; John, Khanna, Thennarasu, & Reddy, 2003): (1) psychotic symptoms (hallucinations and delusions), (2) disorganized symptoms (bizarre behavior and positive formal thought disorder), and (3) negative symptoms (flat affect, alogia, avolition, and anhedonia). This consensus has led to a validation of the specific symptom dimensions (Earnst & Kring, 1997) and, correspondingly, has paved the way for the formulation of symptom remission criteria for schizophrenia (Andreasen et al., 2005). Carpenter (2006) has observed that the emerging database on symptom clusters has helped to return the schizophrenia concept to its Kraepelinian and Bleulerian roots, because it corrects the overly narrow definition of schizophrenia as predominantly a psychotic disorder that has enjoyed prominence in psychiatry over the past 40 years.

---

[3] Angus MacDonald and the Minnesota Consensus group are compiling a more complete list of facts about schizophrenia that is to be published in the March 2009 issue of *Schizophrenia Bulletin*. The title of the section has been adapted from their working report, which appeared on the *Schizophrenia Research Forum* website (*www.schizophreniaforum.org/whatweknow/*) in mid-2007.

Epidemiology

As John McGrath (2005) has observed, epidemiology in schizophrenia has undergone a mini-revolution in the past decade. The view that schizophrenia is a catholic illness that inexorably affects 1 in 100 persons regardless of gender (Buchanan & Carpenter, 2005; Crow, 2007) is giving way to a more nuanced perspective. Schizophrenia appears to have a .7% prevalence rate that varies considerably across cultures (a five-fold difference). Men are at greater risk than women to develop the disorder and tend to develop the disorder earlier. The incidence of new cases of schizophrenia is .03% and may be declining (McGrath et al., 2004). Incidence also varies across culture. Being born or residing in an urban setting is associated with greater risk for developing schizophrenia (Mortensen et al., 1999). Migrants, additionally, have an increased risk of developing schizophrenia; this is especially true if the migrants have dark skin and migrate to an area with a light-skin dominant group (Boydell & Murray, 2003). African Americans are 3 times more likely to develop schizophrenia than European Americans (Bresnahan et al., 2007). Schizophrenia is also associated with increased mortality. Individuals with schizophrenia die prematurely (Brown, 1997). Suicide is a major contributor to this discrepancy, and it has been estimated that 5.6% of individuals diagnosed with schizophrenia die by suicide, with the period of greatest risk coming during the early phase of the illness (Palmer, Pankratz, & Bostwick, 2005). While individuals with schizophrenia are 13 times more likely to die by suicide than individuals in the general population, Saha and colleagues (Saha, Chant, & McGrath, 2007) have recently shown that individuals with schizophrenia also have elevated mortality across a wide array of illness categories.

Genetic and Environmental Risk Factors

Genetics

Eighty years of behavior genetics research in the form of twin, family, and adoption studies indicate that schizophrenia is highly heritable. Family studies have consistently shown that schizophrenia runs in families and that the degree of genetic sharing with the affected member predicts the likelihood of developing schizophrenia (Nicol & Gottesman, 1983). A recent quantitative review of 11 well-conducted family studies found that first-degree relatives of persons with schizophrenia are 10 times more likely to develop schizophrenia than nonpsychiatric comparison subjects (Sullivan, Owen, O'Donovan, & Freedman, 2006). Adoption studies provide

more support for the contribution of genetic factors to the development
of schizophrenia. A quantitative review found no difference in the rates
of schizophrenia in the adoptive relatives of individuals with and without
schizophrenia; however, biological relatives of adoptees with schizophrenia
are 5 times more likely to develop schizophrenia than the biological relatives of adoptees who do not have schizophrenia (Sullivan et al., 2006).
In other words, there is little evidence in these studies to support the role
of post-adoption environmental factors in the etiology of schizophrenia,
which stands in contrast to the evidence for genetic influence. In identical
twin pairs, if one twin has schizophrenia, the other twin has nearly a 50%
chance of also developing schizophrenia (Cardno & Gottesman, 2000).
Such high rates of concordance have led many to observe that a great proportion of the liability for schizophrenia is genetic (Gottesman & Gould,
2003; Riley & Kendler, 2005). Indeed, Sullivan, Kendler, and Neal (2003),
in a quantitative review of 12 twin studies, propose a heritability estimate
of 81% for genetic factors in the liability of developing schizophrenia. In
other words, four-fifths of the variability in schizophrenia liability is due to
additive genetic effects.

Although behavior genetics research has established the importance
of genes in the development of schizophrenia, specific genes and the mechanistic details remain unclear. With the exception of Crow (2007), who
believes that schizophrenia is conferred by a single gene related to language
that is to be found on the sex chromosome, the field of schizophrenia genetics now embraces the conclusion that many susceptibility genes contribute
to schizophrenia, each gene having but a small effect in the overall etiology
of the disorder (Gottesman & Gould, 2003; Sullivan et al., 2006). Thus
far, a dizzying array of candidate genes has been identified (Sullivan et
al., 2006). Owen, Craddock, and O'Donovan (2005) propose that case-
control variations in a few of the candidate genes (e.g., neuroregulin 1 and
dystrobervin binding protein 1) have been replicated several times, making
these genes the most likely schizophrenia genes at the present (see Chapter
2). These best candidate genes, further, are present in a fraction of patients
with schizophrenia (between 6 and 15%) and increase the liability by at
most a factor of two (Gilmore & Murray, 2006).

Environment

While lack of perfect concordance between identical twins has been taken
as evidence for the role of nongenetic factors in the etiology of schizo-

phrenia, Sullivan et al. (2003), in their quantitative review of twin studies, express considerable surprise that the analysis also reveals a significant
effect (a heritability estimate of 11%) for nonshared environment in the
etiology of schizophrenia. There is now considerable evidence implicating
environmental factors in the etiology of schizophrenia. Mary Cannon and
colleagues (2002), for example, have conducted a quantitative review that
identified three groupings of obstetric complication associated with schizophrenia: complications occurring during pregnancy (e.g., bleeding, diabetes), complications occurring at the time of delivery (emergency cesarean
delivery, asphyxia), and abnormal fetal growth and development (e.g., low
birth weight). The risk of schizophrenia associated with obstetric complications is double that without such complications, a small effect that is
comparable in magnitude to the risk associated with variation in particular
genes (Gilmore & Murray, 2006). The second trimester of pregnancy is
particularly key for neurodevelopment, and there is evidence that insults
at this phase of development (e.g., the mother acquiring an infection or
being unduly stressed) approximately double the risk of offspring developing schizophrenia (Cannon, Kendell, Susser, & Jones, 2003) .

Environmental factors that occur considerably after birth have also
been implicated. As we have seen, schizophrenia is disproportionately represented in urban environments (McGrath et al., 2004). Because urban
inhabitance and birth are highly correlated, it is not clear whether the
observed elevations are due to prenatal or perinatal factors associated with
an urban birth, or whether urbanicity confers risk at a later point in development in the form of psychosocial stress and social isolation (Boydell &
Murray, 2003). In this regard, a recent prospective study involving more
than 300,000 Israeli adolescents is notable, as the researchers found an
interaction between population density and factors related to the genetic
risk for schizophrenia (poor social and cognitive functioning), suggesting
that the stress of city living might combine with genetic vulnerability to
produce schizophrenia (Weiser et al., 2007). In a similar fashion, a recent
quantitative review of seven studies estimates that cannabis use during adolescence increases the risk of the subsequent development of psychosis by
two to three times (Henquet, Murray, Linszen, & van Os, 2005). Further,
there is evidence of a gene–environment interaction, as individuals who
have a variant of the catechol-O-methyltransferase (COMT) gene, roughly
25% of the population, are the ones who show elevated risk associated
with adolescent cannabis consumption (Caspi et al., 2005). COMT is not,
importantly, associated with elevated cannabis consumption.

Neurobiological Factors

As we have seen, it has been apparent in psychiatry since the mid-19th century that the behavioral, emotional, and cognitive features of schizophrenia ought to be rooted in the brains of affected individuals (Hughlings Jackson, 1931), a position that has been strengthened by the development of effective antipsychotic medications (Healy, 2002). Brain malfunction or abnormality (termed "pathophysiology") could be responsible for schizophrenia in either of two basic ways: (1) the structure of the brains of individuals with schizophrenia could differ from normal (anatomical pathology), or (2) the functional activity of the brains of individuals with schizophrenia could differ from normal (physiological pathology). As simple and obvious as this formulation might appear, 100 years of schizophrenia research has yet to produce a coherent and agreed-upon account of necessary and sufficient neurobiological factors and processes that distinguish individuals with schizophrenia from individuals who do not develop the disorder (Williamson, 2006). In other words, the pathophysiology of schizophrenia remains elusive (see Chapter 2).

Anatomical Abnormality

Nonetheless, considerable advances have been made in the understanding of the neurobiology of schizophrenia. One approach has been to investigate the anatomy of brains of individuals with schizophrenia after they have died. Postmortem research of this sort has produced two important conclusions: (1) Schizophrenia is not a neurodegenerative illness in the manner that Kraepelin (1971) and his followers supposed, and (2) patients with schizophrenia show evidence of abnormal cellular architecture as compared to the brains of healthy controls. As an example of this latter effect, David Lewis and his colleagues have shown in several studies that, relative to controls, individuals with schizophrenia evidence reduced densities in the input layers of pyramidal cells within the dorsolateral prefrontal cortex (Lewis, Glantz, Pierri, & Sweet, 2003).

Structural imaging has been another fruitful avenue for discovering anatomical differences associated with schizophrenia. Indeed, the oldest image of the living brain of an individual diagnosed with schizophrenia is remarkable, not only because the patient endured the replacement of her cerebrospinal fluid with air, but because the enlargement of the lateral ventricles is visible (Moore, Nathan, Elliott, & Laubach, 1935). Larger ventricles are associated with more cerebrospinal fluid and smaller brain size,

and subsequent imaging studies found evidence that ventricular enlargement is a general feature of schizophrenia (Johnstone & Ownes, 2004; Vita
et al., 2000). In a systematic review of 40 studies, Lawrie and Abukmeil
(1998) estimated a 30–40% median increase of lateral ventricle volume
when patients with schizophrenia are compared to controls, as well as a
median reduction in overall brain volume of 3%. In a quantitative review
of 155 structural imaging studies, Davidson and Heinrichs (2003) report
that frontal and temporal structures, especially the hippocampus, tend to
be smaller in patients with schizophrenia relative to healthy controls. More
recent reviews have established that volumetric abnormality is present at
the outset in schizophrenia, as first episode patients already have larger ventricles, reduced brain volume, and reduced hippocampal volume, compared
to matched controls (Steen, Mull, McClure, Hamer, & Lieberman, 2006;
Vita, De Peri, Silenzi, & Dieci, 2006). Indeed, unaffected relatives also
appear to have ventricular enlargement and hippocampal reduction relative
to control individuals (Boos, Aleman, Cahn, Hulshoff Pol, & Kahn, 2007),
suggesting that anatomical differences might be related to the genetic vulnerability for schizophrenia. However, all observed structural differences
are relatively small (0.5 SD between patients and controls, 0.33 SD between
first-episode patients and controls, one-fifth an SD between unaffected relatives and controls), sharing considerable overlap with healthy samples (Heinrichs, 2005). The results of a recent imaging study are consistent with the
conclusion that a complex set of small differences across the entire cortex
characterizes the difference between individuals with schizophrenia and
normal controls (Davatzikos et al., 2005).

Functional Abnormality

Having patients engage in a task while measuring regional brain activation
is a promising means of determining physiological differences associated
with schizophrenia. Early studies, utilizing positron emission tomography (PET), evidenced abnormal activation patterns across many regions
of the brain in response to a task (Gur & Gur, 2005). Quantitative review
of this literature suggests that the strongest difference is a lack of task-
related activation of the frontal lobes (so-called hypofrontality) in individuals with schizophrenia as compared to healthy controls (Davidson &
Heinrichs, 2003). More fine-scaled analysis of 12 studies suggests that the
brain-activation pattern during working memory tasks is more complex
than the hypofrontality hypothesis might lead one to believe, involving
both hypoactivation and hyperactivation of a variety of structures (Glahn

et al., 2005). Many other differences in task-related activation have been identified (Belger & Dichter, 2005; Gur & Gur, 2005) across a variety of cognitive, behavioral, and emotion-based tasks. Most of the differences are small, many not replicated—factors that inhibit generalized conclusions regarding functional differences in schizophrenia (see Chapter 2).

Neurocognitive Factors

Both Kraepelin and Bleuler observed difficulties in schizophrenic patients' cognitive processes of attention, memory, and problem solving, and systematic tests were developed by the 1940s; however, much of what is known regarding the cognitive impairment in schizophrenia has accrued since a concerted research effort began in the 1980s (Goldberg, David, & Gold, 2003). Reichenberg and Harvey (2007) report a review of quantitative reviews from 12 domains, including general intellectual ability, verbal memory, nonverbal memory, recognition, executive functions, motor skills, working memory, language, attention, and processing speed. The main finding, consistent with the older reports, is that patients perform more poorly than healthy controls across *all* 12 of the neurocognitive domains, the patient–control difference averaging between a 0.5- and 1.5-standard-deviation shift. In a much cited quantitative review of 204 studies, Heinrichs and Zakzanis (1998) found that patient performance is inferior across all cognitive domains, by nearly a standard deviation on average. There was much variability across tasks, with verbal memory showing the largest difference (nearly 1.5 *SD* shift in the average patient mean relative to the control mean across studies). Heinrichs (2005) has observed that the patient–control differences on neurocognitive tasks are much larger than differences found for neurobiological factors, such as those measured in structural imaging studies. However, there is still a fair amount of overlap between the two groups, leading to the possibility that a proportion of patients is neuropsychologically normal (Palmer et al., 1997)—a position that has not gone unchallenged (Wilk et al., 2005).

Nonetheless, the large patient–control differences have led several authors to refer to cognitive impairment as a central feature of schizophrenia, as well as an important key to understanding its pathophysiology (Gur & Gur, 2005; Heinrichs, 2005; Keefe & Eesley, 2006; MacDonald & Carter, 2002; Marder & Fenton, 2004). Cognitive impairment, indeed, emerges prior to the onset of the first psychosis. Longitudinal studies provide the best evidence. For example, poorer test scores in childhood have been found to predict the development of adult schizophrenia in an English sample (Jones, Rodgers, Murray, & Marmot, 1994). Similarly, lower test scores on IQ subtests in adolescence predicted the later development of schizophrenia in Swedish (David, Malmberg, Brandt, Allebeck, & Lewis, 1997) and Israeli (Davidson et al., 1999) conscripts. In this later study, the intellectual decline was shown to start during childhood and continue through adolescence and to be independent of gender, socioeconomic status, and the occurrence of nonpsychotic psychiatric disorders (Reichenberg et al., 2005).

These same researchers readministered the IQ subtests to the 44 individuals who developed schizophrenia and found that, though a few tests showed a decline in performance, there was little change on a majority of the tests, suggesting that a substantial proportion of the intellectual decline occurred prior to the onset of the first psychosis (Caspi et al., 2003). And, it appears that the severity of the cognitive impairment in first-episode schizophrenia is indistinguishable (i.e., on the order of an SD shift, on average, in performance) from the impairment seen in individuals with chronic schizophrenia (Gold & Green, 2005; Keefe & Eesley, 2006), suggesting that neurocognitive deficiency is one of the stabler aspects of schizophrenia. Adding to this perspective, quantitative reviews suggest that cognitive impairment is one of the best predictors of the poor social and vocational outcomes that are characteristic of a vast majority of individuals with schizophrenia (Green, 1996; Green et al., 2000).

An interesting development in the understanding of neurocognition in schizophrenia is the well-replicated finding that genetic relatives of individuals with schizophrenia show an attenuated cognitive impairment that is more severe than healthy controls (Reichenberg & Harvey, 2007). On average, unaffected relatives differ from controls between 0.2 to 0.5 a standard deviation across domains. Raquel and Ruben Gur and their colleagues have reproduced this same pattern of data in a multigenerational family study, demonstrating that neurocognitive domains may be genetic markers for schizophrenia (Gur et al., 2007).

Treatment and Outcome

As seen in the previous section, the modern image of schizophrenia is that of a complex syndrome caused by a variety of genetic and environmental factors, each making a small contribution to the development of a disorder that entails three basic symptom dimensions, pervasive neurocognitive impairment, and many small neuroanatomical and neurophysiological deficits. The present section addresses one of the great revolutions of modern psychiatry—the advent of antipsychotic treatment, which couples naturally with a discussion of short- and long-term outcomes achieved by individuals with schizophrenia.

Antipsychotic Medications

It seems hard to believe that antipsychotic medications have been around for just one-half of a century. One of us (Beck) recalls rather vividly a residency rotation in a psychiatric hospital in which patients with schizophrenia were treated with hydrotherapy (some of them drowned) and insulin coma therapy (some of them died). Other patients, quite famously Tennessee Williams's sister, were given frontal lobotomies, a treatment that created as many problems as it solved. In Paris in 1952, Denker and Delay found, quite by accident, that chlorpromazine (brand name Thorazine), the first neuroleptic medication, reduced hallucinations and delusions (Healy, 2002), a finding that would ultimately transform the treatment of schizophrenia, leading to the elimination of the dubious somatic therapeutic regimes that had dominated the treatment of the disorder since the turn of the 20th century. Chlorpromazine was introduced in the United States in 1954, and many sister compounds (family name *phenothiazine*) were soon synthesized and introduced, including haloperidol (Haldol) and perphenazine (Trilafon). With the vast majority of individuals with schizophrenia in the developed world currently taking antipsychotic drugs, it can be hard to appreciate the skepticism that first greeted the reports of the efficacy of neuroleptic medications. However, by the early 1960s, two facts had emerged. First, the National Institute of Mental Health (NIMH) sponsored a collaborative randomized control trial that demonstrated the efficacy of antipsychotic drugs to reduce psychotic symptoms in patients with acute schizophrenia (Guttmacher, 1964). Second, researchers had determined that the mechanism of action of neuroleptic medications was a blockade of postsynaptic receptors of the neurotransmitter dopamine (Healy, 2002; Miyamoto, Stroup, Duncan, Aoba, & Lieberman, 2003). But neuroleptic drugs are "dirty" in that they also affect other neurotransmitter systems in the brain, causing side effects such as sedation, weight gain, and extrapyramidal side effects (see Chapters 2 and 13 for more detail regarding pharmacodynamics of antipsychotic medicines).

Since the mid-1970s, evidence has accrued that antipsychotic medications help to prevent relapses: Patients who discontinue medication are three to five times as likely to relapse as patients who do not discontinue medication; patients switched to placebo show an elevated relapse rate as compared to patients maintained on antipsychotic medication (Marder &

Wirshing, 2003; Stroup, Kraus, & Marder, 2006). The introduction of clozaril (Clozapine) in the 1980s kicked off the second-generation of antipsychotic medication (Healy, 2002). These agents, which include risperidone (Risperdal) and olanzapine (Zyprexa), are the most prescribed medicines for schizophrenia in the United States and Europe, and currently dominate the treatment of the disorder. Second-generation drugs have a different mechanism of action (they antagonize serotonin in addition to dopamine) and were touted as a breakthrough in terms of efficacy (better), side-effect profile (more favorable), and cognitive impairment (reduced) (Healy, 2002). However, research findings have been disappointing in this regard, as well-conducted studies have shown little difference in efficacy between first- and second-generation antipsychotic medications (Lieberman et al., 2005). Neither have the drugs been found to have a better effect on neurocognition (Keefe et al., 2007), leading some researchers to question the greater cost of the newer medicines, especially given the elevated risk for metabolic side effects such as diabetes (Rosenheck et al., 2006). Harrow and Jobe (2007) have recently reported on the result of a 15-year prospective study in which they identify a subgroup of individuals with schizophrenia who discontinue antipsychotic medication and experience periods of recovery. The authors propose that their results suggest that there is subgroup of individuals with schizophrenia who do not need to remain continuously medicated in order to achieve a good outcome.

Outcome

Disagreement regarding prognosis in schizophrenia can, like much else, be traced to Bleuler and Kraepelin. As we have already seen, Kraepelin was deeply pessimistic about the possibility of significant improvement, let alone recovery (Kraepelin, 1971). Indeed, Kraepelin argued that any patient manifesting the symptoms of *dementia praecox* who subsequently improved must have been misdiagnosed originally (Rund, 1990). Bleuler (1911/1950), by contrast, observed that a majority of his patients improved enough to maintain employment and self-sufficiency. Warner (2004) has suggested that Bleuler's more optimistic perspective on outcome in schizophrenia may have resulted from his superior treatment model, as well as the more favorable economic conditions characteristic of Switzerland at that time.

Calabrese and Corrigan (2005) observe that, in addition to the profound impact of his nosological work, Kraepelin's pessimistic view of outcome in schizophrenia has had a long-term impact upon psychiatry, particularly in terms of treatment expectations. As we have seen, research has failed to support Kraepelin's central claim that *dementia praecox* is neuro-degenerative; however, evidence is more equivocal regarding rates of recovery. Kraepelinian pessimism has tended to prevail within American psychiatry, in particular. Thus, when discussing outcome in schizophrenia, the authors of the DSM-III (American Psychiatric Association, 1980), echoing the pioneer, caution that "remission of symptoms or return to premorbid functioning is so rare that it would likely result in the clinician questioning the original diagnosis" (p. 64). The DSM-IV-TR (American Psychiatric Association, 2000) is not much more encouraging on the subject of outcome in schizophrenia: "Complete remission (i.e., a return to full premorbid functioning) is probably not common in this disorder" (p. 309).

There is some disagreement as to whether the introduction of antipsychotic medication has improved the outcomes achieved by individuals with schizophrenia. Hegarty and colleagues (Hegarty, Baldessarini, Tohen, Waternaux, & Oepen, 1994) report results from a meta-analysis showing that the proportion of good outcomes improved between 1950 and 1980, a period in which the medications became readily available, as compared to 1930–1950. Warner (2004) and others (e.g., Healy, 2002; Peuskens, 2002) have argued, conversely, based upon reviews of the outcome literature, that functional outcomes have not changed dramatically since the introduction of antipsychotics. Either way, a large proportion of patients continue to experience poor long-term outcomes. Hafner and an der Heiden (2003) estimate that the proportion of first-episode patients who demonstrate symptom improvement and have no relapses over 5 years varies from 21 to 30%, suggesting that the majority of patients experience recurrence or continual symptomatology. Hegarty et al.'s (1994) meta-analysis estimated that a clear majority of patients across studies achieve "unfavorable" or "chronic" outcomes. Robinson et al. (2004), in perhaps the best study of this kind, found that 50% of their first-episode patients achieved 2 years of symptom remission (no moAvre than "mild" positive symptoms, as well as no more than "moderate" negative symptoms) over a 5-year follow-up period, while 25% achieved 2 years of adequate social and vocational functioning, and, importantly, just 12% met full recovery criteria for 2 years or more. Given the high quality of treatment delivery and compliance in this study, the result is a sobering portrait regarding the efficacy of existing medication and ancillary treatments to improve social and vocational functioning.

Calabrese and Corrigan (2005) report on the 10 published studies of the long-term course of schizophrenia in which the average time to follow-up assessment was 15 years or more. While these studies differ in terms of the nationality of participants (e.g., German, Japanese, Swiss, American), the definition of schizophrenia (i.e., wide or narrow), the definition of recovery/improvement (e.g., symptom-based or functioning-based), and the time to follow-up (the average follow-up assessment in this group of studies is 27 years, and the range is 15–37 years), the findings appear to be relatively consistent: That is, roughly 50% of the patients are classified as "recovered or improved." Correspondingly, roughly half of the patients were "not improved or chronic," meaning that, on average, this set of patients experience more than two and a half decades of disability. The World Health Organization International Study of Schizophrenia (Harrison et al., 2001) illustrates this point poignantly. Involving 18 international research centers and 1,633 patients with a psychotic illness, the authors report that outcomes were favorable for more than 50% of the sample followed up. However, this conclusion is based upon a clinical rating made on a 4-point scale, and Harrison et al. (2001) argue that more restrictive definitions of favorable outcome that include explicit functioning requirements are more meaningful. When they set a minimal functioning cutoff (i.e., Global Assessment of Functioning rated 60 or above, indicating "mild, minimal or no difficulty in social functioning"), the percentage of favorable outcomes is 38%. If they require, additionally, that patients have not had a flareup requiring treatment within 2 years, the percentage of favorable outcomes is 16%. This latter number resembles the results of Robinson et al. (2004), discussed above.

The available evidence warrants the conclusion that a significant proportion of individuals diagnosed with schizophrenia achieve poor outcomes. Importantly, whether assessed over shorter (e.g., 5–10 years) or longer (i.e., 15 years and more) durations, the functional outcomes of most individuals with schizophrenia appear particularly impaired, a result that occurs even when optimal psychopharmacological treatment has been administered over the entire follow-up period. To improve the outcomes achieved by these individuals, it stands to reason that factors must be identified that are causative of the observed social and occupational dysfunction. These factors, then, might serve as targets of interventions designed explicitly to improve outcomes and quality of life for individuals diagnosed with schizophrenia.

COGNITIVE THERAPY OF SCHIZOPHRENIA

Antipsychotic medications, while efficacious, have important limitations: Many patients continue to experience distressing residual symptoms despite taking appropriate doses, and, as we have seen, several of the most disabling features of schizophrenia are relatively unaffected by the medications (neg-

ative symptoms, functional impairment, and poor neurocognitive performance). These limitations, combined with the poor quality of life of most
individuals with schizophrenia, led to the development of cognitive therapy
as an adjunctive treatment for individuals diagnosed with schizophrenia
(Chadwick et al., 1996; Fowler et al., 1995; Kingdon & Turkington, 1994).
While this approach to schizophrenia shows the influence of early psychiatric pioneers such as Adolph Meyer, Henry Stack Sullivan, and Sylvano
Areti, larger and more proximal influences are Beck's model of depression
(Beck et al., 1979) and David Clark's approach to anxiety disorders (1986).
In this section, we first consider the evidence base that has emerged, largely
in the United Kingdom, in support of cognitive therapy for schizophrenia.
Next, we briefly sketch the cognitive formulation and therapy for each of
the major symptoms of schizophrenia that we will describe in greater detail
in this volume.

Efficacy Research

Review of Reviews

Over the past 15 years an evidence base has accrued supporting the efficacy of cognitive therapy for individuals diagnosed with schizophrenia and
schizoaffective disorder (Gould, Mueser, Bolton, Mays, & Goff, 2001; Pilling et al., 2002; Rector & Beck, 2001). In a recent quantitative review of
13 randomized controlled trials involving 1,484 patients, Zimmermann,
Favrod, Trieu, and Pomini (2005) conclude that cognitive therapy confers,
on average, compared to control treatments, 0.33 of a standard deviation
more symptom reduction for patients in the chronic phase of schizophrenia, 0.5 of a standard deviation more improvement in psychotic symptoms
during acute inpatient application, and 0.33 of a standard deviation more
improvement across posttreatment follow-up periods. Cognitive therapy
produces enduring changes in the positive symptoms of schizophrenia. By
2007, more than three dozen outcome trials had been published on cognitive therapy for schizophrenia.

Standout Studies

Perhaps the best study published to date was conducted by Sensky and colleagues (2000). In a single-blind, randomized controlled trial, cognitive therapy was compared to an active control treatment that was termed *befriending*. The results show that psychotherapy contact produces improvement in
patients with schizophrenia, as both treatments produced significant and

equal changes in symptoms at the end of 9 months of active treatment. However, the results also illustrate that psychotherapy must confer skills to produce enduring change, as the patients treated with cognitive therapy maintained or improved upon their gains from baseline over the 9-month follow-up period, while the befriending-treated patients lost their gains and returned, as a group, to baseline levels of symptomatology. Indeed, patients treated with cognitive therapy had significantly lower negative symptoms for a full 5 years after treatment was completed (Turkington et al., 2008), evidencing considerable durability of treatment gains with regard to a symptom domain that has defied traditional treatment.

In the Sensky et al. (2000) trial, negative symptoms were not the focus of treatment. However, one of us (N. R.) has shown that important treatment gains can be achieved when negative symptoms are targeted directly by cognitive therapy (Rector, Seeman, & Segal, 2003). As compared to an enriched treatment-as-usual condition, patients treated with cognitive therapy showed improvement in negative symptoms over a 9-month follow-up period. Andrew Gumly and colleagues have shown that cognitive therapy can, additionally, reduce the likelihood of psychotic relapse effectively: Adding cognitive therapy to treatment as usual resulted in a 50% reduction in the relapse rate over a 12-month period (Gumley et al., 2003). Finally, a team lead by Tony Morrison at the University of Manchester has demonstrated that cognitive therapy can delay or reduce the onset of schizophrenia in individuals assessed to have "ultra-high" risk for developing schizophrenia. Morrison's group reported that 6% (2 of 35) of high-risk individuals treated with cognitive therapy developed a psychotic disorder over a 12-month period, as compared to 26% (6 of 25) in the nontreatment group (Morrison, French, et al., 2004). Cognitive therapy, additionally, is well tolerated; less than a quarter of high-risk participants dropped out of treatment. This finding is especially notable given the tolerability, ethical difficulties, as well as unsatisfactory results of antipsychotic medications in the prevention of schizophrenia (McGlashan et al., 2006).

Literature's Limitations

As the foregoing review illustrates, cognitive therapy is clearly a promising treatment for schizophrenia. However, we believe that it is important to point out that there is considerable room for improvement of the treatment. For example, most of the literature and theorizing has focused upon medicated outpatients experiencing residual psychotic symptoms. Negative symptoms have rarely been targeted, and patients with thought disorder have tended to be screened out of the clinical trials. Also, the assessment of whether cognitive therapy can produce reductions in symptoms in individuals who refuse or cannot tolerate antipsychotic medications awaits systematic study. A related concern involves the flexibility of the existing protocols. Most of the studies (e.g., Kuipers et al., 1997; Sensky et al., 2000; Tarrier et al., 1998) involve a mean number of 20 sessions delivered over a 6- to 9-month period. Given the diversity of both symptom presentation and course in individuals with schizophrenia, we suspect that the existing protocols will work best for a subset of the patients, and, further, that more sessions delivered more often might be warranted for more severe patients. In this regard, we acknowledge the work of Robert DeRubeis and Steve Hollon, who report finding significantly improved rates of remission when medicines and cognitive therapy are combined to treat major depression over the course of a year (Hollon, 2007). Anecdotally, Turkington has reported successfully treating entrenched delusions with cognitive therapy delivered over a 12-month period, a pattern that we have observed in some of our patients, as well.

Cognitive Approach to Schizophrenia

Despite these limitations, cognitive therapy is a promising intervention in the treatment of schizophrenia. The present section introduces the cognitive approach that we take to schizophrenia in the present volume. The discussion follows the four primary symptom categories that comprise schizophrenia: delusions, hallucinations, negative symptoms, and formal thought disorder. For each symptom type, the cognitive formulation is described, and then a sketch of the therapy is outlined.

A few general principles can be articulated at the outset. First, we have found that the recovery model works best. We collaborate on setting long-term goals with the patients, which generally fall into three categories: forming relationships, getting a job or returning to school, and living independently. When delusions or hallucinations interfere with these goals, we deal with them directly. Second, in most cases of patients experiencing prominent delusions and hallucinations, we find that we do have to use our cognitive techniques to reduce the distress. Third, in adapting the general formulation for an individual patient, we need to have a conceptual formulation based on the patient's symptomatology, history, and neurocognitive functioning. Patients with a good premorbid history and a higher level of functioning can be approached with some of the usual cognitive techniques; those with significant neurocognitive impairment are treated somewhat differently. In those cases, the therapist is far more directive and needs to spend considerably more time engaging the patient in individual sessions and providing explanations in fairly simple terms that the patient can remember.

Delusions

As defining characteristics of schizophrenia, delusions are beliefs that produce considerable distress and behavioral dysfunction in individuals with schizophrenia, often resulting in hospitalization. Factors that distinguish delusions from nondysfunctional beliefs (Hole et al., 1979) include how much the person's moment-to-moment stream of consciousness is controlled by the belief (pervasiveness), how sure the patient is that the belief is true (conviction), how important the belief is in the patient's meaning system (significance), and how impervious the belief is to logic, reason, and counterevidence (inflexibility, self-certainty). In Chapter 3, we present a cognitive model of delusions formulated within a phenomenological analysis of the characteristics and development of delusions. Cardinal features of the model are information-processing biases (e.g., egocentricity, externalizing bias, poor reality testing) and antecedent belief systems (e.g., self as weak and others as strong) that we propose may, in tandem, enhance psychological vulnerability for the development of paranoia and delusions. We apply the model to persecutory and grandiose delusions, as well as delusions of being controlled. This cognitive framework provides an understanding of delusions in terms cognitive distortions, dysfunctional beliefs, and attentional biases that are amenable to cognitive therapeutic interventions. Chapter 9, building on the formulation of Chapter 3, describes the assessment and therapy of the delusions of schizophrenia. Primary assessment foci include developing an understanding of the development of the delusional beliefs, specifying the supporting evidence, and determining the degree of moment-to-moment distress. Techniques are then marshaled to question the supporting evidence and test out adaptive alternative explanations. A final phase of the treatment entails addressing nondelusional cognitive schemas that render patients vulnerable to recurrence and relapse.

Hallucinations

Typically defined as perceptual experiences in the absence of external stimulation, hallucinations can occur in any sensory modality. Hallucinations occur during the waking state and are involuntary. The experience of hallucination is not, of necessity, pathological, as the beliefs about their origin (i.e., my own mind vs. a computer chip) distinguish "normal" from abnormal. Auditory hallucinations are diagnostically the most significant modality and have, accordingly, been the subject of considerable theory and research. In Chapter 4, we present a cognitive framework that explains the most vexing questions regarding auditory hallucinations: How does the hallucinator come to hear his or her own thoughts in a voice other than his or her own? Why is the content of hallucinations primarily negative? Why do patients tend to attribute the hallucinations to an external source? Building on biological constructs, the cognitive formulation characterizes hallucination-prone patients as liable, in the face of isolation, fatigue, or stress, to experience involuntary auditory imagery. Primary mental candidates for this process of perceptualizing are emotion-laden or "hot" cognitions such as negative automatic thoughts (e.g., "I'm a loser"). We propose, additionally, that information-processing biases, especially a propensity to externalizing, lead to the development of dysfunctional beliefs about the "voice" experiences that reinforce the sense of the external origin. Patient beliefs that the "voices" are omnipotent, uncontrollable, and externally generated drive both the experience of distress and their behavioral appeasement strategies. Thus, a combination of dysfunctional beliefs and poor coping behaviors maintain auditory hallucinations. Chapter 10 presents cognitive-behavioral strategies, rooted in the formulation of Chapter 4, designed to reduce the distress and neutralize the behavioral impact of auditory hallucinations. The patient is encouraged to develop distance from the "voices" and to question inaccurate "voice" statements. Delusional and dysfunctional beliefs about the voice are elicited and questioned, as well, via behavioral experiments. Specifically, the patient comes to see that he or she has control over the voice, an efficacy that undermines much of the cognitive structure supporting emotional and behavioral reactions. As with the treatment of delusions, maladaptive, nondelusional beliefs such as those that result in a sense of worthlessness and powerlessness, which determine much of the distressing "voice" content, are elicited, tested, and replaced with more adaptive beliefs.

Negative Symptoms

The negative symptoms of schizophrenia—including reduced verbal (alogia) and nonverbal expressivity (affective flattening), as well as limited engagement in constructive (avolition), pleasurable (anhedonia), and social (asociality) activity—respond poorly to antipsychotic treatment and are, accordingly, associated with considerable disability. Putting the existing research literature together with clinical examples, Chapter 5 describes a cognitive model of negative symptoms. Our approach emphasizes the process by which neurobiological challenges, such as those indexed by cognitive impairment, can, in turn, give rise to cognitive content, in the form of dysfunctional beliefs, negative expectancies, and pessimistic self-appraisals, that precipitate and maintain withdrawal from meaningful endeavors and diminish quality of life. Specifically, we propose that social-aversion beliefs, defeatist beliefs regarding performance, negative expectancies regarding pleasure and success, as well as self-stigmatizing illness beliefs and the perception of limited cognitive resources can all contribute to the negative symptoms of schizophrenia. Given that negative symptoms can arise from varying causes, assessment is a critical first phase of the treatment, described in Chapter 11. Negative symptoms that are found to be secondary to positive symptoms (e.g., not going outside because others will hear the "voices") will resolve by addressing beliefs related to the root cause. More generally, the therapeutic effort has two goals with regard to negative symptoms: (1) Help patients develop resources and enthusiasm for engaging in social, vocational, pleasurable, and other meaningful activity; and (2) guide patients to determine what sorts of factors lead them to disengage and then to develop less disruptive coping strategies. Because many patients with negative symptoms also have cognitive impairment, a variety of additional aids needs to be utilized, such as the hand-held computer to remind the patient of therapy-based homework assignments (e.g., going to bed at a reasonable time, engaging in social activities). In helping patients with predominant negative symptoms, we advocate abandoning Socratic questioning in favor of declarative statements made in definite, concrete terms, such as "Tell me what was upsetting during the past week" rather than "What was upsetting during the past week?" In addition to the memory aids, we enlist the family as a way of reinforcing our general approach in the homework assignments and reducing conflict and misunderstandings.

Formal Thought Disorder

Comprising a subset of the language disturbance found in individuals with schizophrenia, formal thought disorder can present considerable communicative challenge to individuals with schizophrenia and their interlocutors. Positive formal thought disorder, on the one hand, includes loosening of associations (various forms of getting offtrack in conversation as well as tangential responses) and idiosyncratic language use—neologisms (creating new words) and word approximations (employing actual words in a novel manner)—whereas negative thought disorder symptoms, on the other hand, consist of blocking (interruption in the flow of ideas), poverty of speech (conversation is restricted and responses often unelaborated), and poverty of content (normal flow of ideas with a reduced range of denotation). In Chapter 6 we develop a cognitive model of formal thought disorder that takes as its starting point the observation that speech becomes more disordered as patients prone to thought disorder experience stress. Seen in this light, thought disorder becomes, analogous to stuttering, a stress response to "hot" topics and situations. Because the patients have cognitive impairment, they have limited cognitive resources. Specific thoughts (e.g., "they will think I am stupid") triggered by particular situations sap these resources, exacerbating communicative difficulty. The patient develops defeatist beliefs regarding interlocutory efficacy, as well as a general sense of social aversion—cognitive structures that lead to avoidance of social situations and increased stress when such situations are encountered. In Chapter 12 we delineate the treatment approach for thought disorder based on the cognitive model. After an assessment of the topics that lead to thought disorder, the therapeutic interaction can be used as an opportunity to demonstrate to the patient that he or she can be understood. Later the relationship between stress and thought disorder can be illustrated, and beliefs regarding communicative efficacy elicited, tested, and modified.

Integrative Model

In addition to chapters detailing conceptualization and therapy for the four symptom categories, chapters focus on neurobiology (Chapter 2), general assessment issues (Chapter 7), creation and maintenance of engagement in therapy (Chapter 8), and collaborative pharmacotherapy (Chapter 13). The final chapter presents an integrative model of schizophrenia that pulls together concepts from the chapter on neurobiology and the conceptualization chapters (Chapters 3–6). The model features cognitive impairment and moves beyond domain-specific deficits to consider the global integrative capacity of the brain as a means to describe the genesis of schizophrenia. Stress and cognitive insufficiency combine to set up a hyperactivation of dysfunctional schemas and resource sparing that lead to the early negative symptoms that precede psychosis, as well as the reduced reality testing of florid psychosis and the semantic fragmentation of formal thought disorder. Dysfunctional beliefs and assumptions implicated in the development and maintenance of the three symptom dimensions are, moreover, targets for therapeutic interventions (Chapters 9–12). By activating alternate networks and brain structures, cognitive therapy, we propose, helps patients tap into their cognitive reserve to reduce distressing symptomatology and other factors that impede goal-oriented activity and the achievement of an improved quality of life.

SUMMARY

In this chapter we have introduced the concept of schizophrenia, reviewed the essential historical context, painting a thumbnail sketch of the currently known facts, and considered the development of cognitive therapy in the context of antipsychotic treatment and outcome research. Additionally, the cognitive approach to schizophrenia was introduced and described for each of the major symptom dimensions of schizophrenia.

CHAPTER 2

Biological Contributions

There are several reasons why the biological aspects of schizophrenia can be important to understanding and utilizing cognitive therapy principles and techniques in the conceptualization and treatment of this condition. First, recognizing the multiple factors in the etiology of schizophrenia can alert a clinician to limitations in the use of cognitive therapy for its management. Miswirings based on genetic disposition, alterations in neurochemical transmission, and changes in activity of certain brain regions may limit the degree to which attempts at changing beliefs can be accomplished without other means of intervention, such as medication. Second, understanding what specific brain systems may contribute to symptoms of schizophrenia can lead to innovative cognitive approaches based on the functions of these systems. Third, the chasm between those researchers and practitioners in the biological world and those in the psychological world may be bridged by improved communication as each sect learns the other's principles, concepts, and information. Fourth, an examination of all aspects of this condition—psychological, neurological, social, and others—can lead to a more comprehensive appreciation of its complexity. Answering the questions of what schizophrenia is and how its symptoms occur will likely depend on integration of data from multiple disciplines.

The neurobiological underpinnings of schizophrenia have remained elusive despite decades of extensive research. This elusiveness is partly due to the heterogeneity of the condition in a number of realms. In the etiology realm, both genetics and environment (gestational, perinatal, and postnatal) play a role in the development of schizophrenia. Examining each influence separately does not simplify matters, for the genetic component has not proved to be clear-cut, as in the discovery of a single gene, nor have environmental effects been reduced to a virus, toxin, trauma, or some other unknown influence. In the pathophysiology realm, many brain regions have been shown to be altered in some way in those diagnosed with schizophrenia. Pharmacological treatment of schizophrenia has implicated the involvement of a number of neurotransmitters in this disorder. Several pathophysiological models of the neurophysiological processes producing the symptoms of schizophrenia have been suggested, based on these multiple findings of brain region and neurotransmitter contributions. In the phenomenology realm, the search for neurobiological underpinnings of schizophrenia is complicated by the multiple clusters of symptoms observed in clinical presentations, leading some to believe that the disorder is really a set of disorders, each potentially having a different etiology and pathophysiology. Yet no one has been able to reliably delineate and describe what these discrete disorders might be. Related to the symptomatology realm is the neuropsychology realm in which reliable and specific disease markers, utilizing tests of cognitive functions such as attention, memory, and/or executive function, have yet to be discovered.

Despite the enigmatic nature of this condition, the hope is that there will be a neurobiological explanation for schizophrenia that describes the entire, complex process: from the polygenetic and gestational/perinatal etiological factors that yield developmental alterations, to the neurophysiological abnormalities in specified systems of the brain that produce the clinical and neuropsychological features. For now, what follows is an introduction to what is known about the etiology and neurophysiology of schizophrenia. The former consists of genetic findings, environmental influences during pregnancy, and alterations during development; the latter addresses the areas of neuroanatomy, neurochemistry, and neuropsychology/psychophysiology. Finally, theoretical models integrating some of the findings are presented.

ETIOLOGY

Why might it matter to a clinician how schizophrenia originates? After all, the effects of therapy and/or medication can be examined and improved without ever delving into primary causes of the condition. There are a number of answers to this question. First, learning more about the development of schizophrenia can lead to preventive measures such as cognitive therapy, which could then be initiated prior to the onset of schizophrenia with high-risk individuals. Second, isolating the genetic contribution can be useful information in working with family members who might present with less severe, yet pertinent, forms of symptoms. Third, recognizing potential biological causes and informing patients and family members of these can help reduce self-blame. Fourth, as we learn more about the neuronal processes underlying development of psychiatric disorders, we also learn more about neuronal processes underlying physiological changes produced in the course of psychotherapy (see Cozolino, 2002). The notion that there are changes in the brain accompanying the use of psychotherapy can provide hope to patient, family, and clinician alike. Finally, processes involved in the development of schizophrenia (such as the effect of stress-induced cortisol release on cell death) might also be involved in its overall persistence as well as in the onset of specific psychotic episodes.

Although schizophrenia first manifests as overt symptoms in adolescence and early adulthood, it is generally believed that the condition starts prenatally with genetic origins complicated by trauma during pregnancy and/or delivery, exacerbated by further neurological alterations that occur developmentally during adolescence, and aggravated by psychological stressors prior to the clinical onset. Although it would seem that biological contributions to the development of schizophrenia would be easier to determine than would psychological ones, there is considerable confusion in attempts to establish the physiological determinants of schizophrenia (see Bentall, 2004). Schizophrenia is referred to as a disorder, not a disease, because there has not been any clear, reliable, and specific etiological factor or even a set of such factors. Arguments have been made that this lack of conclusive evidence for its biological genesis supports the notion that schizophrenia is not a neurological disorder but rather a psychologically determined condition. However, there are also no clear findings that specific psychological or social stressors lead to the onset of schizophrenia in a manner similar to the case for posttraumatic stress disorder. Most commonly accepted is the stress–diathesis (or stress–vulnerability) model indicating that there is a combination of biological roots and psychological forces combining to produce the schizophrenic condition.

Genetic Factors

Although there is evidence of a genetic component for schizophrenia, there is no simple Mendelian genetic configuration helping to predict the familial frequency of schizophrenia. Even when ignoring the environmental contributions to the etiology, the genetic aspects are still complex and have yet to be determined.

What has led to the belief that genes do play an important role is the higher occurrence of schizophrenia in those that have relatives with schizophrenia. Having a second-degree relative with schizophrenia increases the rate from 1% in the general population to 3–4%; having a first-degree relative increases it to 9–13%. Most striking is that the concordance rate (i.e., the rate of co-occurrence) for schizophrenia in monozygotic twins (twins developed from one fertilized egg; presumably having identical genes) is 48%, whereas in dizygotic (fraternal) twins it is 17% (Gottesman, 1991). However, it is noteworthy that having an identical set of genes does not guarantee complete concordance. This implies that either environment makes a substantial contribution and/or that there is incomplete penetrance (i.e., the degree to which the presence of a gene leads to its outward manifestation [phenotype], as measured by the proportion of carriers of the gene that are affected) or expressivity (i.e., the magnitude of the effect produced by the gene). An argument for the impact of environment includes the findings that better quality of family relationships is associated with high genetic risk individuals developing schizotypal personality disorder or no psychiatric condition rather than schizophrenia (Burman, Medrick, Machon, Parnas, & Schulsinger, 1987), and that the presence of significant problems in families adopting children with a high genetic risk of schizophrenia is associated with a greater chance of developing schizophrenia as compared to children with high and low genetic risk in adoptive families with fewer problems and low-risk children raised in adoptive families with problems (Tienari et al., 1987).

Further evidence for schizophrenia as an inherited disorder comes from adoption studies. In these, the greatest risk of developing schizophrenia is associated with having relatives with schizophrenia (the genetic component); this risk does not change as a result of adoption (the rearing/family component), whether it be nonaffected individuals raised by parents with schizophrenia or affected individuals raised by nonaffected parents (Heston, 1966; Kety, Rosenthal, Wender, & Shulsinger, 1968; Rosenthal et al., 1968). However, the upbringing component is still pertinent, as shown by an increase in risk in an affected individual if raised by affected parents (Gottesman, 1991; Ingraham & Kety, 2000).

Despite strong evidence for the presence of a genetic contribution to the development of schizophrenia, the search for the specific genes associated with schizophrenia has been elusive. Models incorporating single-gene transmission have not explained the pattern of inheritance (O'Donovan & Owen, 1996)—probably due to a number of factors. The lack of homogeneity in the presentation of schizophrenia makes it possible that multiple disorders are being investigated together as one disorder, confounding the results. Some of these disorders may even be ones that do not have genetic components. Indeed, despite the findings in favor of a genetic contribution, 80% of people with schizophrenia do not have a first-degree relative with schizophrenia, and 60% do not have any known relative with the disorder (Gottesman, 1991). For those who do, there may be polygenic transmission, that is, multiple genes contributing to aspects of the disorder that synergistically produce the clinical presentation (Cardno & Gottesman, 2000). Complexities arise as well when considering variability due to penetrance and expressivity.

In an effort to find the genes responsible for the presentation of schizophrenia, genetic studies have focused on linkage analysis in which neurobiological characteristics that appear to run in families of those with schizophrenia are examined for their inheritance pattern in the belief that the genes associated with these marker traits are located near those associated with vulnerability to schizophrenia. The assumption is that these linked genes will be inherited in a pattern similar to the genes for schizophrenia but that environmental factors (e.g., medication, institutionalization, social isolation) will affect the linked genes' phenotypes much less so than the phenotypes of genes for schizophrenia. Therefore, it should be easier to find the genes responsible for these marker traits and then apply those findings to the genes responsible for vulnerability to schizophrenia.

As an example, Freedman et al. (1997) found that inhibition of P50 (the diminished response of a type of brain wave to the repeated presentation of a stimulus) is lacking in nonaffected relatives as well as in those with schizophrenia. Linkage was found to chromosome locus 15q13-14, the site of the gene for the a2 nicotinic receptor (Adler, Freedman, Ross, Olincy, & Waldo, 1999). Other chromosomes containing genes thought to be associated with schizophrenia include 1, 2, 4, 5, 6, 7, 8, 9, 10, 13, 15, 18, 22, and X. Thus 14 out of a possible 24 chromosomes are candidates as loci for these genes. There is no conclusive evidence yet in favor of any one specific locus.

In summary, there is good evidence for a polygenetic contribution to the etiology of schizophrenia, but which specific genes (and phenotypic expressions) are involved is not known. In addition, environment must play an important role, given that when an affected individual has an identical twin (having an identical genetic constitution), only about half of the time will the twin develop schizophrenia as well.

Gestational and Perinatal Influences

The first environmental influences are not what are generally referred to as nurture factors; rather, they are the factors that occur during the 9 months prior to birth that could potentiate the genetic diathesis. Although genetics can account for as much as 85% of the variance of the presentation of schizophrenia (Cannon, Kaprio, Lonnqvist, Huttunen, & Koskenvuo, 1998; Kendler et al., 2000), it is known that there is a higher frequency of gestational and perinatal (around the time of delivery) events in those having schizophrenia. Events of this sort (for which there are no consistent findings directly implicating any single one as a contributing cause of schizophrenia) include maternal starvation during the first trimester (Susser et al., 1996); influenza infection in the second trimester (Mednick, Machon, Huttunen, & Bonett, 1988); rhesus (Rh) and ABO blood-type incompatibility (Hollister, Laing, & Mednick, 1996); and perinatal anoxic (lack of oxygen) brain injury (T. D. Cannon et al., 2002), often associated with prematurity, preeclampsia, and low birth weight. It is thought that gestational and perinatal complications (in particular, neonatal anoxia) accompanying a genetic loading set the stage for the emergence of schizophrenia. The affected twin of discordant monozygotic twins has a score for neonatal anoxia that is two to four times greater than the nonaffected twin (Nasrallah & Smeltzer, 2002). (In contrast, Torrey, Bowler, Taylor, & Gottesman, 1994, found equal frequency of obstetric complications in affected and non-affected twins. However, twins with at least one affected member had more obstetric problems than twins who are both nonaffected.)

Heinrichs (2001) conducted a large series of meta-analyses of various findings related to schizophrenia reported between 1980 and 2000. After removing studies with serious flaws, such as significant confounding factors, his group calculated average effect size (d; the degree to which the averaged results from the various studies differentiate control from experimental group) and confidence interval (CI; the consistency of the results among the studies). Regarding obstetric complications and schizophrenia, they calculated an effect size of $d = 0.32$ (modest), suggesting an overlap of 76% between those with schizophrenia and those without. In other words, obstetric complications can be important but are not necessary factors in determining the etiology of schizophrenia. However, the CI was .20–.44, prompting Heinrichs to note that this is a more consistent finding than many others related to schizophrenia. (A narrower CI indicates more consistent, stabler findings across studies.)

The notion that an influenza virus might be a factor came from noticing that there is a slightly increased risk of developing schizophrenia if born in the late winter or early spring, meaning that the second trimester (when brain development is believed to be altered in schizophrenia) would have occurred during winter when infections with the virus would be most common. However, there are no consistent findings indicating that mothers of people with schizophrenia are more likely to have had an influenza virus (Cannon et al., 1996; Selten et al., 1999). According to Bentall (2004), there may be a confounding factor of schizophrenia occurring more frequently in urban areas, where there is more likelihood that a virus would spread. Other possible explanations for the association of the second trimester (i.e., late-winter or early-spring births) with the development of schizophrenia include decreased maternal nutrition in the winter, genetic protection from intrauterine dangers during winter being associated with genes contributing to the production of schizophrenia (i.e., more people with schizophrenia survive intrauterine complications in winter, thus more winter births for this condition), and seasonal variation in the risk of obstetric complications (Warner & de Girolamo, 1995). Of note, Heinrichs (2001) found that the average effect size for winter births and schizophrenia was $d = 0.05$ (i.e., very low).

In addition to biological stressors, psychological stressors during pregnancy have also been associated with schizophrenia in the offspring. Schizophrenia is more likely to be found in those whose father had died between conception and birth compared to during the first year of postnatal life, independent of any obstetric complication (Huttunen & Niskanen, 1973). The diagnosis was also more prevalent in those whose mothers were pregnant in the Netherlands when it was invaded by Germany in 1940 compared to pregnancies in other years from 1938 to 1943 (van Os & Selton, 1998). One possibility is that stress in the mother was greater for these groups and may have affected the fetus. However, without having direct measures of stress level in these mothers, these studies are only suggestive.

Evidence provides support for obstetric complications as contributing to the etiology of schizophrenia in some, but not all, cases. It would be informative if those individuals with schizophrenia and with known obstetric complications could be differentiated as adults in some significant and consistent way from those with schizophrenia known to not have been exposed to any obstetric problems. Perhaps such an endeavor would allow us to begin distinguishing types of schizophrenia (as with any similar study that divides groups according to other findings such as genetic disposition, specific brain region disruption, and so forth).

Neurodevelopmental Alterations

The combination of genetics and gestational complications may lay the groundwork for the development of schizophrenia with its myriad presentations of various symptoms. However, the path from genes and early insults to the neurophysiological underpinnings of fully developed schizophrenia is as uncharted as are the points of departure and destination. There are some hypotheses, however, related to neurodevelopmental changes during two important time periods: the second trimester of pregnancy and adolescence. In addition, the contribution of stress to neurophysiological changes throughout the years prior to the onset of schizophrenia has been examined, with the implication that there may be other critical developmental periods with neural aberrations (e.g., the neonatal period).

Before exploring these mechanisms of neuronal modification, it should be noted that there is physical and behavioral evidence that schizophrenia does not lie dormant between conception (when the genetic makeup is determined) and late adolescence and early adulthood (when clinical symptoms emerge). There are some signs that neurodevelopment is not progressing in a typical fashion. Complications in delivery, rather than being viewed as a determinant of schizophrenia, may reflect aberrant neurodevelopment. In addition, the increased likelihood of minor physical anomalies at birth, such as reduced head circumference, low-set ears, and abnormal palate height have tended to be associated with abnormal central nervous system development (McNeil, Cantor-Graae, & Cardenal, 1993; McNeil, Cantor-Graae, Nordstrom, & Rosenlund, 1993; O'Callaghan, Larkin, Kinsella, & Waddington, 1991).

Early childhood development can include delayed and abnormal motor, language, intellectual, and social progress compared to siblings and peers, as evident from detailed analyses of retrospective home movies and school records (Davidson et al., 1999; Jones et al., 1994; Walker, 1994). In addition, studies have found more negative emotions and less positive emotions (in girls) in those who later developed schizophrenia (Walker, Grimes, Davis, & Smith, 1993). Prospective studies of those at higher risk for developing schizophrenia (i.e., those with a first-degree relative having schizophrenia) have been found to have motor abnormalities early in life, poor social adjustment in middle childhood, and poor attention/cognitive skills in adolescence (reviewed by Bentall, 2004). In one study, those who went on to develop schizophrenia were more likely as adolescents to have a more external locus of control (Frenkel, Kugelmass, Nathan, & Ingraham, 1995). Cohort studies in which subjects are followed longitudinally have shown that compared to those who did not later develop schizophrenia, those who did walked 1.2 months later, showed more clumsiness at 7 years of age, showed slightly lower IQs at 7–16 years old, and evidenced speech difficulties at 7–11 years (Jones & Done, 1997).

Heinrichs (2001) determined that the mean effect sizes of studies of high-risk populations were modest for intellectual, social, emotional, and behavioral problems ($d = 0.26$–0.42) and high for specific cognitive ($d = 0.68$–3.23) and motor ($d = 1.35$) deficits. However, the larger mean effect sizes for the latter two groups were due to the presence of single studies with large effect sizes that inflated the mean effect sizes showing attention deficits (Cornblatt, Lenzenweger, Dworkin, & Erlenmeyer-Kimling, 1992) and motor deficits (Erlenmeyer-Kimling et al., 1998). Heinrichs suggests the need for replication of these studies to determine if they are representative, or not, of the deficits in these high-risk groups.

The neurobiological changes thought to accompany these early signs of altered functioning have been suggested by postmortem studies of brains of those having had schizophrenia. In these studies, changes in neuronal configurations are not associated with the presence of gliosis, which would have indicated neural degeneration (Heckers, 1997). Therefore, these neuropathological disruptions are believed to have originated during prenatal development, most likely during the second trimester (Arnold & Trojanowski, 1996; Bunney, Potkin, & Bunney, 1995). This is when the cell bodies of many neurons migrate from the walls of the ventricles (fluid-filled cavities within the brain) to the cortical plate (the location of what is to become the cortex) to establish distant cortical connections. The cortical connections are guided by a temporary embryonic template called the *cortical subplate* (Allendoerfer & Shatz, 1994). Disrupted neuronal architecture related to cells of the subplate has been found in brain regions such as the frontal and temporal lobes and the hippocampus (Akbarian, Bunney, et al., 1993; Akbarian, Vinuela, et al., 1993; Anderson, Volk, & Lewis, 1996). These disruptions could alter the connectivity of the cortical neurons as they migrate to the cortical plate during the second trimester.

Heinrichs (2001) again found large mean effect sizes ($d = 0.87$–1.12) accompanied by large CIs, indicating the lack of consistency in findings, which Heinrichs attributes partly to differences in the specific brain subregions examined. Most of the studies he reported explored the hippocampus (in terms of cell orientation) and prefrontal cortex (in terms of poor migration of cells from lower to higher levels).

An alternate explanation for the subplate disturbances is abnormalities in the process of programmed cell death (Margolis, Chuang, & Post, 1994). Mainly during the third trimester, about 80% of subplate cells normally die off. Alterations in the degree of cell death (in either direction) could result in abnormalities in the cortical subplate and therefore disrupted cortical connectivity.

Abnormal amounts of cell destruction might also occur at another critical period of development—adolescence—when pruning (i.e., elimination of some connections) of cortical neurons is completed, especially in the prefrontal area. Connectivity increases greatly during early development, but then synaptic density (i.e., the concentration of points of communication between neurons) gradually decreases to 60–65% of the maximum amount (Huttenlocher & Dabholkar, 1997). This pruning may be even greater in those who develop schizophrenia (Bunney & Bunney, 1999; Feinberg, 1982/1983, 1990; McGlashan & Hoffman, 2000), possibly accounting for the typical onset of clinical presentations of schizophrenia during this developmental period.

Cell death may also occur throughout life as a result of stress via the hormone cortisol, which is at greater levels in the bloodstream in response to stressful situations (or the perception of situations as being a threat). The hippocampus and possibly the prefrontal lobe are particularly sensitive to cortisol released upon stimulation of the hypothalamus–pituitary–adrenal (HPA) axis (Sapolsky, 1992). There is evidence that some people with schizophrenia have had a greater physiological response to stress, such as increased levels of cortisol (Dickerson & Kemeny, 2004; Walder, Walker, & Lewine, 2000). If greater cortisol levels are present before clinical onset of schizophrenia, they may result in gradual degeneration of the hippocampus and the prefrontal lobe during preadolescent development as well as during adolescent and postadolescent development.

To sum up, a genetic predisposition to schizophrenia and/or gestational influences lead to neurodevelopmental changes that include abnormal cell death in the cortical subplate causing abnormal migration of cortical neurons and, hence, miswiring of cortical circuitry. Further excessive cell death in the hippocampus and frontal lobe can occur as a result of inordinate sensitivity to stress, in particular greater cortisol release, and during adolescence, as a result of overactive pruning. These neurodevelopmental modifications contribute to the cognitive, motor, and behavioral disadvantages seen in childhood and early adolescence. Again, there is no concrete evidence that this process occurs in every, or even most, cases of schizophrenia.

NEUROPHYSIOLOGY

Neuroanatomical Findings

A substantial number of brain regions have been implicated as disrupted in individuals with schizophrenia. These include the frontal, temporal, and parietal lobes, the hippocampus, amygdala, thalamus, nucleus accumbens, cerebellum, basal ganglia, olfactory bulbs, and corticocortical connections. This assortment of candidate regions does not leave many areas of the brain beyond suspicion. Of these, the ones most attended to are the frontal cortex and the temporal lobes, including the hippocampus. The frontal cortex (layers of cell bodies in the front portion of the brain behind the forehead) is thought to be responsible for executive functions, including attention, decision making, working memory (storing information for imminent use), and inhibition of emotional reactions. The hippocampus (part of the temporal lobe that is located beneath the temple area of the head) is thought to be involved in memory consolidation for both verbal and spatial material, context updating, episodic memory (memory of experienced events), and regulation of mood. The temporal lobe also includes the amygdala, involved in emotional responses and fear conditioning. Of note also are some of the structures that are subcortical (beneath the wrinkled surface of the brain). The thalamus is a relay station for sensory and motor information reaching the cortex. The basal ganglia (which include the nucleus accumbens) seem to be involved in coordinating motor and cognitive activity. The multiple interactions between these areas (both anatomically and functionally) give a hint as to why schizophrenia might involve any or all of them.

Some factors complicating interpretations of neuroanatomical findings (as well as findings in other areas of neurophysiology) are the heterogeneity of symptom presentations (both between subjects and temporally within an individual), accuracy of symptom reporting (in studies relating neuroanatomical findings to presence of specific symptoms), effects of duration of illness, medication effects, and selection biases with regard to the type of subject who will agree to, and be able to participate in, studies. In addition, some findings of altered functioning in certain brain regions depend on the performance of specific tasks that elicit differences in individuals with schizophrenia from controls. Differences in brain activity during performance of cognitive tasks can be confounded by differences in strategies used between those with schizophrenia and those without this condition as well as by statistical problems inherent in including any task that differs in difficulty between the two groups (Chapman & Chapman, 1973b). It should be noted as well that increased brain activity in a certain region can reflect better performance by that region or it may reflect increased work by that region to compensate for deficits in that (or another) region's abilities. Finally, the actual neurophysiological differences between controls and those with schizophrenia may not be accurately and consistently measured by even our modern imaging techniques. If differences lie at the level of diffuse firing patterns of neuronal systems spread throughout the brain, it is unlikely that our current methods of measuring brain activity (relying on regional activity or animal studies of individual neurons) would give us a clear and consistent picture. It is analogous to trying to determine why one soccer team performs better than another one simply by measuring how far each member can kick the ball and how fast each member can run. Although significant differences in these measures could provide the answer, it is more likely that the *interactions of the players* are most important. To appreciate the difficulties in the field of neuroscience, imagine the players being millions in number, greatly reduced in size, and interacting in multiple permutations. This is where research into the neurophysiology of schizophrenia is at an impasse. As of yet, there is no method for measuring the individual activities and interactions of large numbers of neurons of the brain within short time spans in living human beings.

Despite these caveats and limitations, some findings have emerged, although none has been both robust and consistent (Heinrichs, 2001). Early use of structural imaging techniques, such as computerized tomography (CT) that displays detailed anatomical information about the brain, demonstrated the presence of enlarged sulci (valleys on the surface of the brain) and lateral ventricles in some people with schizophrenia (reviewed by Bentall, 2004; Bremner, 2005). Enlarged lateral ventricles can be present even in premedicated conditions and may be more specific for those demonstrating the negative symptoms (Andreasen, Olsen, Dennert, & Smith, 1982) as well as for those with poor social adjustment, poor outcome, and cognitive dysfunction. However, as noted by Bentall (2004), this structural state can also be present in those with other psychiatric disorders as well as in those without a psychiatric diagnosis. In addition, he explains that there are less differences in large, well-controlled studies and that many factors influence ventricle size, including sex, age, head size, and water retention. Furthermore, ventricular enlargement is not very specific in that it may be due to atrophy of adjacent structures such as the hippocampus, amygdala, thalamus, striatum (a part of the basal ganglia), and corpus callosum (the connection between the two sides of the brain).

More focused approaches have examined individual brain regions such as the frontal lobe. The use of functional imaging techniques (such as positron emission tomography [PET], single photon emission computed tomography [SPECT], and functional magnetic resonance imaging [fMRI] that demonstrate the degree of activity of brain regions) led to the discovery of decreased frontal activity (hypofrontality) in persons with schizophrenia, particularly when engaged in tasks, such as the Wisconsin Card Sorting Test (requiring detection of changes in the rule by which cards are being sorted; Heaton, Chelune, Talley, Kay, & Curtiss, 1993) and N-back tasks (requiring recall of items a given number of places back in a series), that seem to require frontal activation in controls (Ingvar & Franzen, 1974; Weinberger, Berman, & Zec, 1986). However, this hypofrontality has not been present in other studies (Gur et al., 1983; Mathew, Duncan, Weinman, & Barr, 1982) and seems to disappear upon recovery from the acute illness (Spence, Hirsch, Brooks, & Grasby, 1998) or if trained on the eliciting task (Penades et al., 2000). Additional findings in support of a frontal involvement include postmortem studies that have demonstrated abnormal neuron numbers, reduced neuronal size, and decreased dendritic spine density in the prefrontal cortex (reviewed by Gur & Arnold, 2004). As well, structural imaging has demonstrated reduced gray matter in the dorsolateral prefrontal cortex (Gur et al., 2000), although others have found higher right orbitofrontal volume (Szeszko et al., 1999). Investigations using magnetic resonance spectroscopy (MRS; a technique that measures specific neuronal molecules) have discovered markers of decreased neuronal integrity as well as signs of neuronal pruning in the frontal cortex (reviewed by Bremner, 2005).

Using meta-analyses, Heinrichs (2001) challenges the imaging findings supporting frontal lobe dysfunction in schizophrenia. Among those studies reporting frontal lobe dysfunction, imaging studies had the lowest average effect sizes ($d = 0.33$–0.80), corresponding to a maximum non-overlap of those with schizophrenia and those without of about 50%, this despite the studies having used activation tasks rather than "at rest" conditions. However, Heinrichs's analyses do not include more recent studies, in particular, the now widely used functional MRI techniques.

Another area demonstrating differences associated with schizophrenia, the temporal lobes, is also beset by inconsistencies (reviewed by Gur & Arnold, 2004). Hippocampal volume reduction and shape alteration have been reported (Csernansky et al., 1998; McCarley et al., 1999), but not in all studies. There is reported loss of gray matter in the superior temporal gyrus (Bremner, 2005; Pearlson, Petty, Ross, & Tien, 1996; Zipursky, Lim, Sullivan, Brown, & Pfefferbaum, 1992). Postmortem studies of the hippocampus have identified reduced numbers, sizes, or orientations of certain types of neurons (Arnold, 1999; Benes, Kwok, Vincent, & Todtenkopf, 1998), altered neuronal fiber connections (Heckers, Heinsen, Geiger, & Beckmann, 1991), changed synaptic organization (Eastwood, Burnet, & Harrison, 1995), decreased dendritic spine density (Rsoklija et al., 2000), and abnormal cytoskeletal protein expression (Cotter, Kerwin, Doshi, Martin, & Everall, 1997). As with the frontal cortex, the hippocampus and associated areas show differences in activity (Kawasaki et al., 1992), in this case, increased activity in those with schizophrenia, most notably during hallucinations (Silbersweig et al., 1995). There is less activity during recollection of semantically encoded words (Heckers et al., 1998). However, temporal lobe activity at rest has been shown to be increased (Gur et al., 1995), reduced (Gur et al., 1987), or unchanged (Volkow et al., 1987). Decreased neuronal integrity, as determined by MRS findings, has also been found in the temporal cortex (reviewed by Bremner, 2005).

As with the frontal lobe, Heinrichs (2001) surveyed the literature on neurophysiological studies of the temporal lobe and did not find strong, consistent evidence demonstrating significant separation of those with schizophrenia from controls on the basis of temporal lobe abnormalities. Imaging studies did not generate average effect sizes any greater than 0.59 and revealed greater inconsistencies (including variation in the direction of change for volume and activation of temporal lobe structures). In contrast, postmortem studies (which were too few in the frontal lobe literature to be analyzed in this way) had more robust average effect sizes (d = 0.86 and 0.92), the former referring to reduced hippocampal pyramidal cell numbers and densities and the latter to reduced hippocampal volume and corresponding to about 50% non-overlap. Along with differences in cortical structure and function, there is also some evidence for subcortical involvement. This finding is not surprising, given the extensive communication between cortical and subcortical structures in the service of cognitive, emotional, and behavioral functions. Decreased thalamic volume (especially of the medial dorsal thalamic nucleus) due to cell loss (Heckers, 1997; Pakkenberg, 1990), decreased number of neurons in the anteroventral nucleus (Danos et al., 1998), and decreased blood flow (Hazlett et al., 1999) have all been described, but again the findings are not consistent (Portas et al., 1998). Basal ganglia volume has been shown to be decreased, increased, or normal (Heckers, Heinsen, Geiger, & Beckmann, 1991; Keshavan, Rosenberg, Sweeney, & Pettegrew, 1998) and sensitive to medication use (Chakos et al., 1994); its activity has been shown to be increased or decreased (Liddle et al., 1992). Postmortem studies have indicated an increase in the number of neurons in the striatum (Beckmann & Lauer, 1997), a reduced number of neurons in one part of the striatum (the nucleus accumbens; Pakkenberg, 1990), or a change in the synaptic organization of the striatum (in particular, the caudate; Kung, Conley, Chute, Smialek, & Roberts, 1998).

There have been some attempts to elucidate neuroanatomical findings by dividing subjects according to symptomatology. Liddle (1992) determined that positive symptoms are associated with temporal lobe volume reduction and increased blood flow, whereas negative symptoms are associated with decreased prefrontal cortical blood flow. However, Carpenter, Buchanan, Kirkpatrick, Tamminga, and Wood (1993) found that although patients with extensive negative symptomatology (i.e., the deficit syndrome) had more frontal lobe abnormalities, both those with the deficit and non-deficit syndromes had temporal lobe abnormalities. Liddle (2001) later compiled a review of findings of regional brain activity associated with three symptom clusters he determined from factor analysis (Liddle, 1992). He found associations of (1) *reality distortion* with increased activity in the medial temporal lobe, left lateral frontal cortex, and ventral striatum, and decreased activity in the posterior cingulate cortex and left lateral temporoparietal cortex; (2) *disorganization* with increased activity in the right anterior cingulate cortex, medial prefrontal cortex, and thalamus, and decreased activity in the right ventrolateral frontal cortex and parietal cortex; and (3) *psychomotor poverty* with increased activity in the basal ganglia and decreased activity in the frontal cortex and left parietal cortex. Thus even dividing subjects along symptom types does not easily clarify the picture.

To quote a prominent researcher in this area (Gur, 1999) in relation to laterality, but which may be applied to schizophrenia in general: "One may vacillate . . . between being overwhelmed by the amount of data that have converged on the issue . . . and feeling some exasperation at the paucity of solid answers for questions that seem quite rudimentary" (p. 8).[1]

Neurochemical Findings

At one point, it seemed that there was a physiological finding that could account for schizophrenia in a parsimonious way, similar to finding that deficits in insulin account for the myriad presentations of diabetes. This was the discovery that the earliest medications used in the treatment of

[1] We thank Bentall (2004) for pointing this quote out to us.

schizophrenia worked by blocking the receptors for the neurotransmitter dopamine (Carlsson & Lindqvist, 1963, as cited in Bentall, 2004) and subsequent findings that efficacy of antipsychotic medication is tied to the affinity for dopamine receptors (specifically D_2 receptors; Creese, Burt, & Snyder, 1976; Seeman, 1987). Additional support for excessive dopamine activity as a cause of schizophrenic symptoms is the observation that amphetamine (which stimulates dopamine receptors) leads to psychosis, including paranoid ideation and visual hallucinations (Angrist & Gershon, 1970; Connell, 1958, as cited in Bentall, 2004). Psychosis can also develop from the use of other dopamine agonists, including those used to treat Parkinson's disease (Jenkins & Groh, 1970). Other support for the hypothesis includes a finding, using a radioactive form of a precursor of dopamine, of increased dopamine synthesis in the striatum (see Bremner, 2005).

Dopamine-producing neurons are found in four main pathways in the brain, most originating in the brainstem (the stalk at the base of the brain connecting to the spinal cord). Of most importance here are (1) the nigro-striatal tract, which runs from the substantia nigra (a brainstem structure involved in movement) to the dorsal striatum; (2) the mesolimbic tract, which runs from the ventral tegmental area (also in the brain stem) to the ventral striatum (including the nucleus accumbens), the entorhinal cortex (that provides input to the hippocampus), and the amygdala; and (3) the mesocortical tract, which runs from the ventral tegmental area to the cortex, particularly the frontal cortex. Some putative functions of dopamine include reinforcing behavior via reward mechanisms (Fibiger & Phillips, 1974; Lippa, Antelman, Fisher, & Canfield, 1973) and increasing the signal-to-noise ratio of stimuli so as to increase the importance or salience of particular stimuli (Kapur, 2003). Many of these areas receiving dopaminergic input are ones that have been implicated in their own right as being altered in schizophrenia. In fact, there have been findings of altered dopaminergic innervation of frontal and temporal cortices (reviewed by Gur & Arnold, 2004).

There is not universal support for the dopamine hypothesis. Some arguments against it include the fact that many patients do not get better with the use of antipsychotics, despite confirmation of dopamine blockade (Coppens et al., 1991). Postmortem studies (van Kammen, van Kammen, Mann, Seppala, & Linnoila, 1986) and examination of dopamine metabolites in cerebrospinal fluid (Post, Fink, Carpenter, & Goodwin, 1975) have not demonstrated reliably the finding of increased dopamine in those with schizophrenia (McKenna, 1994). Postmortem studies have found increases in dopamine receptors, but this finding might be due to the use of medications. (The brain reacts to a blockade of receptors, which is the effect of antipsychotic medications, by producing more receptors.) Imaging of dopamine receptors has disclosed an increase in the density of D_2 receptors (including in the striatum; Abi-Dargham et al., 2000) in people with schizophrenia unexposed to medication (Wong et al., 1986), but others have not found this occurrence (Fadre et al., 1987). Heinrichs's (2001) meta-analyses confirm the lack of consistent findings for dopamine abnormalities, in particular, receptor counts. However, he found a large, consistent average effect size ($d = 1.37$) for D_2 receptor densities in medicated subjects. The caveat is that medication can produce increases in receptor densities as a confounding factor. He notes that one study (Seeman et al., 1984) uncovered a bimodal distribution in which one group had receptor densities that completely distinguished them from controls in a manner deemed to be independent from medication use.

Another argument against the dopamine hypothesis is that dopamine receptor blockade occurs within hours of medication usage, but antipsychotics typically take weeks to exert their clinical effects (Johnstone, Crow, Frith, Carney, & Price, 1978). This argument has been countered by Bunney (1978), who determined that dopamine neurons compensate for the blockage of dopamine receptors by increasing their firing rate. However, this overexcitation leads to a state in which it is difficult to produce action potentials (i.e., the electrical activity along the axon leading to signal transmission by the neuron). This phenomenon is known as the *depolarization block* and occurs over the course of weeks, equivalent to the time needed for the clinical effects of antipsychotic medications to appear.

The lack of beneficial effects of the earlier antipsychotic medications on negative symptoms suggested that excessive dopamine activity is not connected to schizophrenia, in general, but only to its positive symptoms. Weinberger (1987) countered this view with the hypothesis that in schizophrenia, there may be decreased dopaminergic activity in projections to the cortex (in particular, the frontal cortex), resulting in decreased inhibition by the cortex of subcortical structures, thus leading to an increase in subcortical dopaminergic activity.

Disruptions in other neurotransmitter systems have been proposed as candidate causes of symptoms of schizophrenia. Glutamate is a common excitatory neurotransmitter, and gamma-aminobutyric acid (GABA) is a ubiquitous inhibitory neurotransmitter. One type of glutamate receptor, the N-methyl-D-aspartate (NMDA) receptor, is blocked in part by phencyclidine (PCP), producing a syndrome very similar to schizophrenia with features of both positive and negative symptoms. Some findings support the model of NMDA hypoactivity in schizophrenia (Goff & Wine, 1997; Javitt & Zukin, 1991), including brain imaging and postmortem studies (reviewed by Hirsch, Das, Garey, & de Belleroche, 1997; Tamminga, 1998). Postmortem studies have also implicated GABA in that there is an increase in GABA-A receptor binding in the cingulate cortex as well as altered GABA receptors in the prefrontal cortex, hippocampus, and basal ganglia (reviewed by Bremner, 2005; Gur & Arnold, 2004). One difficulty in trying to point to one neurotransmitter over another as a cause of symptoms is that neurotransmitter systems often interact in ways that make it difficult to determine cause and effect (e.g., see West, Floresco, Charara, Rosenkranz, & Grace, 2003 for interactions of dopamine and glutamate).

Serotonin (5-hydroxytryptamine, 5-HT) and acetylcholine (ACh) are two more neurotransmitters implicated in the manifestations of schizophrenia. Like dopamine, their sources are located in circumscribed areas of the brain, but they project widely to sites throughout the brain. Serotonin-containing neurons are found in the raphe nuclei in the midline of the brainstem and project to the cortex, the hippocampus, the striatum, the thalamus, and other areas. It is believed that the newer atypical antipsychotic medications have their effects on negative symptoms via blockage of 5-HT_{2A} receptors found on the ends of dopamine neurons. Presumably, blocking these receptors aids in releasing more dopamine and counteracting side effects of antipsychotic medications, such as slowed movement and cognition, resembling the negative symptoms. In addition, the hallucinogenic effects of lysergic acid diethylamide (LSD) are believed to derive from its role as an agonist (stimulator) for 5-HT_{2A} receptors. Postmortem studies have shown decreased $5\text{HT}_{2A/C}$ binding in the frontal cortex and increased 5HT_{1A} in the prefrontal and temporal cortices, although findings have not been consistent. A PET imaging study of drug-naïve subjects demonstrated no changes in $5\text{-HT}_{2A/C}$ receptors but increases in 5-HT_{1A} in the medial temporal cortex (see Bremner, 2005). Meta-analyses of both serotonin and glutamate studies reveal even less consistency than the dopamine studies (Heinrichs, 2001). Studies tended to produce effect sizes in opposite directions.

One other candidate neurotransmitter, ACh, is found in interneurons throughout the brain and in muscles. Groups of ACh-containing cells are found in areas at the base of the brain known as the nucleus basalis, the diagonal brand of Broca, and the septum. These cells project to the cortex. There is a significant inverse correlation between severity of symptoms of schizophrenia and numbers of muscarinic receptors (one type of ACh receptor) in the frontal cortex and striatum. The other type of ACh receptor is the nicotinic receptor. Receptors of this type that contain α_7 subunits have been proposed as the reason for heavy smoking among those with schizophrenia. It is believed that the nicotine in cigarettes serves as self-medication to correct some deficit in the functioning of areas containing this receptor (Adler et al., 1988). The nucleus accumbens has a particularly high density of these types of receptors (O'Donnell & Grace, 1999).

Rather than reducing the number of possible causes of symptoms of schizophrenia, research seems to increase that number. Not only are there many brain regions implicated as being altered in the course of schizophrenia, each region has multiple neurotransmitter systems projecting to them, each of which has a potential role in the pathophysiology of schizophrenia.

Neuropsychological/Psychophysiological Findings

Neuropsychological tests and psychophysiological methods such as measuring eye tracking and scalp potentials are means of assessing cognitive abilities and discovering the physiological underpinnings of these abilities.

Neuropsychological testing bridges the gap between symptoms of schizophrenia and the neurobiological underpinnings. These tests were originally developed to determine the functioning of specific brain regions by noting deficits in individuals with known, localized brain lesions due to stroke, tumors, or physical traumas. However, performance on these tests usually requires the use of multiple brain regions, thus limiting their individual specificity. Additionally, the lesions usually have effects on more than one specific brain region as well as on fibers of passage unrelated functionally to the main area damaged. Nonetheless, as performance on tests became associated with damage to specific brain regions, they were applied to individuals without known localized brain damage (as in schizophrenia) as a way to determine what regions might be affected. With the advent of brain imaging techniques, there seemed to be less need for neuropsychological tests. However, it was soon discovered that brain activity at rest was less useful as a distinguishing factor than was brain activity during performance of a task requiring activation of specific brain regions.

In addition to this purpose for neuropsychological tests, there was the search for neuropsychological/psychophysiological markers. These are tests that measure deficits in cognition (attention, memory, decision making) that might provide clues to psychological (and potentially neurophysiological) processes accounting for the symptoms of schizophrenia. In addition, the markers may be present in family members of those with schizophrenia, thus serving as indicators of vulnerability to schizophrenia (especially if the deficits continue to occur in those with schizophrenia who are not actively symptomatic; Green, 1996). A given test can serve both purposes of eliciting differential brain activity in specific regions and serving as a marker for vulnerability as well as elucidating psychological aspects of neurocognitive processes. In addition, cognitive task performance tends to be a good predictor of functional outcome (even more so than symptoms themselves).

Although people with schizophrenia may show diffuse neuropsychological dysfunction, possibly due to motivational/attentional problems that may or may not be related to medication effects, there are more delineated deficits in executive functions (including motivation and attention) and learning and memory that are typically associated with frontal and temporal regions (Cornblatt & Keilp, 1994; Gold, Randolph, Carpenter, Goldberg, & Weinberger, 1992; Heinrichs & Zakzanis, 1998; Saykin et al., 1991).

Two tests often considered frontal tasks are the Wisconsin Card Sorting Test and the Verbal Fluency Test. In the former, subjects are required to determine the rule governing the placement of cards (with different numbers of different shapes of various colors) into one of two piles. The rule is based on number, color, or shape, but changes without notice after a certain time interval. Subjects with schizophrenia do well on the initial rule but often fail to change responses as the rule is changed. As expected, this performance deficit is associated with decreased frontal regional blood flow (Weinberger et al., 1986). The average effect size ($d = 0.88$) corresponds to a non-overlap of about 50% (Heinrichs, 2001). For the verbal fluency test (requiring production of as many words from a given category as possible), the non-overlap was about 60% ($d = 1.09$). This finding still leaves a large number of people with schizophrenia showing frontal lobe abilities that are within the range of normal. Again, either only certain subtypes of schizophrenia are associated with frontal lobe dysfunction, or a frontal lobe task or imaging technique that is accurate and specific enough to distinguish those with schizophrenia from those without has yet to be developed.

A number of tasks measure types of attention. The digit span distraction test (DSDT) requires focusing on target stimuli while ignoring distractors. Subjects are requested to repeat a series of orally presented numbers while ignoring background orally presented numbers. People with schizophrenia perform poorly on this task (especially if thought disorder is present; Oltmanns & Neale, 1978). The continuous performance test (CPT; (Rosvold, Mirsky, Sarason, Bransome, & Beck, 1956) requires the attentional process of vigilance, that is, sustained attention. Subjects must press a button when a target or specified pattern appears. With time, sustained attention diminishes. Performance is worse in those with schizophrenia, especially when difficult versions are given (Nuechterlein, Edell, Norris, & Dawson, 1986). In the backward masking effect (BME), stimuli presented immediately after target stimuli are presented interfere with perception and recall of the targets (reviewed by Green, 1998). This effect is more pronounced in those with schizophrenia. Average effect sizes for attention tasks ranged from $d = 0.69$ to 1.27, the latter pertaining to the BME and having a large non-overlap of 65% (Heinrichs, 2001).

Nuechterlein and Subotnik (1998) have proposed a partial explanation for the attentional deficits elicited by these tasks. They posit two types of attentional problems. One concerns very early, automatic stages of information processing as represented by poor performance on tests of the BME and the CPT (versions utilizing blurred stimuli). This deficit continues even without the presence of symptoms, indicating a vulnerability that may lead, under conditions of stress, to clinical symptoms. The second type of attentional problem is the inability to use active memory (working memory) to guide the selection of information. This deficit is associated with poor performance on the DSDT and the CPT (versions with complex targets). This type is more prominent when symptoms are active, so it is more closely tied to symptom onset.

Deficits in eye tracking (another frontal function) have long been observed in people with schizophrenia. In this task, the subject follows a slow moving target. Smooth-pursuit eye movements are more erratic in those with schizophrenia. This abnormality may precede the onset of the disorder and is often found to be present in relatives (even if not present in the person with schizophrenia; Holzman, 1991). Eye-tracking meta-analyses revealed average effects sizes of $d = 0.75$–1.03, the larger effect size being associated with a large CI, thus indicating poor consistency.

Neuropsychological tests for temporal lobe functioning are plentiful because memory has been tested in a multitude of ways. Global verbal memory deficits produced an average d of 1.41 with a narrow CI, indicating a large and consistent finding of about 70% non-overlap between those with schizophrenia and controls. However, this deficit may reflect more general brain activity. Selective verbal memory measures, related more directly to left temporal lobe functioning, examine specific features such as intrusion rate, forgetting, recall and recognition rates and showed a lower average $d = 0.90$ with a wider CI, corresponding to an overlap of about 50%.

In addition to neuropsychological tasks is a set of techniques aimed at assessing cognitive functioning by recording event-related potentials

(ERPs). ERPs are multiple scalp recordings of brain electrical activity averaged to reveal characteristic responses to stimuli consisting of "bumps" on a waveform. The potentials are named by their direction (positive or negative) and latency (in milliseconds) following onset of the stimulus. This psychophysiological technique provides a means of determining the nature of the sequence of cognitive processes in response to stimuli. Although it excels in temporal resolution, this method is not good at localizing the cognitive functions to any specific brain region. When used in conjunction with brain imaging techniques, however, we can open the door, eventually, to illuminating the time course of activation in specific brain regions.

An early-occurring brain potential is the P50 (i.e., positive, and 50 milliseconds following onset of the stimulus). Two stimuli (such as tones) presented close together will result in a P50 response to the first tone only. This is the phenomenon of sensory gating in that the first tone hampers response to the second one. In those with schizophrenia, the gating is faulty and there are two P50 potentials, one in response to each stimulus. A meta-analysis of the P50 studies produced one of the largest average effect sizes ($d = 1.55$) in Heinrichs's series of meta-analyses of schizophrenia research studies, with a narrow CI (Heinrichs, 2001).

Another common task used to elicit various ERPs is the oddball paradigm, in which a series of two tones is presented, with one tone presented less frequently than the other. A brain wave, the P300, is larger in response to the oddball, infrequent stimulus. There is a lack of activation during the oddball task in the superior temporal gyrus, the thalamus, and the cingulate, parietal, and frontal cortices in those with schizophrenia. Heinrichs (2001) reports relative low average effect sizes ($d = 0.70–0.80$) for P300 studies.

As noted by Bentall (2004), most of the above findings are not specific to people with schizophrenia, but may be present, in some degree, in those with other conditions—mostly bipolar disorder, but also psychotic depression. The deficits are not often associated with the positive symptoms of hallucinations and delusions, so they may not provide much information about the pathophysiology of these symptoms. However, they have been shown to correlate with severity of negative symptoms and thought disorder (reviewed by Green, 1998) and may aid in elucidating the neurocognitive processes underlying these sets of symptoms.

In comparing the findings of neurophysiological studies to those of neuropsychological (cognitive) and psychophysiological ones, it is useful to examine a meta-analysis by Heinrichs (2001). He compared effect sizes and CIs for findings that met the criteria of (1) stemming from more than one study and (2) having at least 100 patients and controls per study, with the patients having a diagnosis of schizophrenia. He determined that the cognitive (neuropsychological) tasks were best at distinguishing those with schizophrenia from controls, with psychophysiological methods following next, and biological studies trailing in last place. (Overall, the most powerful and consistent finding was the P50 sensory gating deficit.) Heinrichs provides a few possible explanations for his conclusion. Heterogeneity in the presentations of schizophrenia could account for discrepancies in findings. However, one would expect this factor to affect the cognitive findings as well. Another possibility presented by Heinrichs is that our methods of measuring biological correlates are not sufficiently advanced yet to yield robust, consistent results. Finally, we may need to shift our general way of thinking about biological correlates. Unlike strokes and tumors that result in aphasia or unilateral neglect, schizophrenia may not be caused by any localized lesion and may not be characterized by any specific deficit related to that lesion, but instead may involve a breakdown in the functioning of parallel distributed processes that are not easily captured by current brain imaging devices. He believes that such techniques as computer modeling (Cohen & Servan-Schreiber, 1992; Hoffman & Dobscha, 1989) may be necessary to determine how these processes lead to symptoms.

THEORETICAL MODELS

The neurophysiological, neuropsychological, and psychophysiological findings of biological correlates of schizophrenia, even if they were straightforward and consistent, would offer a meaningless matching between psychological entity (disorder or individual symptom) and brain part if it were not for the theoretical models. Such models are constructed to describe distinct functional roles of systems of structural components that interact to produce a mechanism by which psychological processes, and their malfunctioning, occur. Without these theoretical models, it would be similar to describing where different parts of an automobile are located, and what their individual purposes are, without explaining how they interact. Describing that the radiator, which stores coolant, is in front of the motor, which produces rotational energy and which is next to the battery that supplies electrical energy, does not illuminate *how* the radiator cools the engine, the motor turns the wheels, and the battery provides a spark to ignite combustion in the motor pistons (as well as to power various lights, the radio, and other components). Localization of function also does not reveal how the individual parts produce their functions.

The models proposed to explain schizophrenia vary from general illustrations of how some symptoms may be produced to more detailed descriptions attempting to account for the diverse presentations of this disorder by depicting disruptions of complex interactions between multiple components (brain structures, neurotransmitter systems, parallel distributed processes).

Meehl: Schizotaxia Model

Meehl's (1962, 1990) basic premise is that vulnerability to schizophrenia arises from a single schizotaxia gene and that the full expression of schizophrenia depends on numerous other genes and the social environment with its inherent rewards and punishments. The gene produces a schizotypal personality that develops into schizophrenia only if genes such as those for introversion, anxiety, low energy, passivity, or others are also present in the context of a typical, yet challenging, social milieu. The single schizotaxia gene itself produces what Meehl calls "hypokrisia," hypersensitive nerve conduction in response to stimulation occurring throughout the central nervous system. The hypokrisia results in "cognitive slippage" in which information is not channeled through distinct pathways but instead gets jumbled. Although the phenomenon affects all brain regions, only certain cognitive functions—those involving integration of information—are noticeably affected. General intelligence can continue virtually unhampered, whereas loosening of associations with random connections of ideas (as seen in thought disorder) is a prominent feature of cognitive slippage. As this cognitive deficit interferes with social functioning, there is an "aversive drift" whereby adverse social experiences lead to withdrawal and the negative symptoms. Cognitive slippage can also produce unusual sensations leading to hallucinations and delusions, the latter being viewed as explanations for the sensations. These explanations are not considered to be very different from commonly found cognitive biases, errors, and distortions seen in the general public (e.g., beliefs in horoscopes, expectations of winning the lottery). However, some delusions can be more directly tied to cognitive slippage if they involve making connections between unrelated events (e.g., a stranger on a bus coughing, while a person with schizophrenia is thinking of leaving home, is interpreted as signaling that he or she should leave home).

Phillips and Silverstein: Cognitive Coordination Model

In addition to the localization of some functions of the brain to specific brain regions, there are extended connections within and between regions that help integrate these functions. According to Phillips and Silverstein (2003), when these connections are impaired, there is a breakdown in cognitive coordination, leading to the symptoms of disorganization such as that seen in thought disorder in schizophrenia. Cognitive coordination is necessary to achieve such functions as grouping items into units, managing selective attention (i.e., maintenance of separation between units), and utilizing contextual information to disambiguate information and thereby constrain potential interpretations of the meaning of a stimulus to those that are relevant to the current context, based on their past co-occurrences. Improper operation of these cognitive processes is associated with disorganized thought. Disruption in the connecting fibers responsible for cognitive coordination between and within cortical brain regions is thought to be due to reduced ion flow in NMDA receptors. This model does not dismiss the many studies that suggest the potential involvement of dopaminergic systems in schizophrenia, but rather focuses on the possible contribution of glutaminergic systems throughout the cortex. The authors note that although glutaminergic receptors are ubiquitous in the cortex, they are especially dense in the prefrontal cortex, the hippocampus, and the basal ganglia.

Hoffman: Parallel Distributed Processing Model

Computer simulations have been used to test models of the brain in terms of cognitive functions. One general model of brain functioning is that of neuronal networks interacting across brain regions in a multidirectional fashion. Hoffman and associates (Hoffman & Dobscha, 1989; Hoffman & McGlashan, 1993) have used this approach to support the idea that the neurological dysfunction associated with symptoms of schizophrenia involves poor communication between cortical regions resulting from excessive pruning of axonal collateral fibers, particularly in the prefrontal cortex, during adolescence. The computer simulation associated with pruning of connections between cortical areas produced "parasitic foci"—that is, areas in the cortex where information is generated repeatedly in a manner that disregards input from other cortical areas. The activity of these foci produces the sense that thoughts, images, and ideas are being created involuntarily in a manner similar to how involuntary movements during seizures are produced by uncontrolled brain activity in cortical motor areas. Delusions of control, delusions in general, and hallucinations are the result of the activity of these parasitic foci. If the repetitive activity of the parasitic foci produces meaningless output, there may be thought blocking, thought withdrawal, and negative symptoms such as avolition.

Kapur: Salience Model

Kapur (2003) presents a model in which excess dopaminergic release leads to an exaggeration of its hypothesized "central role . . . to mediate the 'salience' of environmental events and internal representations" (p. 13). This means that the individual with schizophrenia assigns more significant meaning to stimuli in the outside world as well as thoughts from within than is typically warranted. This ubiquitous weighting of meaning creates confusion because there are too many items of interest in the mind to effectively handle. The individual then creates explanations (in the form of delusions) to account for this strange subjective experience. Hallucinations may be caused by the "direct experience of the aberrant salience of internal representations" (p. 13).

Walker and Diforio: Stress Response Model

According to Walker and Diforio's (1997) model, vulnerability to schizophrenia arises from three components: (1) an overactive dopamine (and possibly) glutamate system; (2) an overactive HPA response to stress, leading to excess glucocorticoids that accentuate the overactivity of the dopamine system; and (3) a pre-/perinatally damaged hippocampus resulting in a lack of inhibitory feedback to the glucocorticoid release. These three systems interact such that each disruption leads to the worsening of the other. Normal life stressors are all that are needed to cause exacerbations of these abnormal hormonal and neurotransmitter responses. Positive symptoms might result from the increase in dopaminergic activity, whereas negative symptoms may be adaptive responses to reduce stress. The typical increase in cortisol release during adolescence may account for the onset of full symptom expression around this time.

Weinberger: Neurodevelopmental Model

Weinberger (1987) postulates that schizophrenia results from a pre-/perinatal brain lesion (genetically and/or environmentally produced) that is not evident until normal neurological development and common stressors (especially those during young adulthood) result in its full expression. The lesion is present in the prefrontal lobe (although other locations could be involved instead). In normal development, the dorsolateral prefrontal cortex reaches maturity in early adulthood, with an accompanying increase in dopaminergic activity that controls the contemporaneous increase in limbic (including medial temporal) dopaminergic activity. In those with schizophrenia, this maturational level interacts with the dormant lesion to produce a deficit in dopaminergic activation of the frontal cortex by midbrain structures. The underactive frontal cortex is unable to inhibit the excessive dopaminergic activity in the medial temporal lobe. Environmental stressors contribute to the surplus limbic activity and insufficient frontal activity. The former leads to the positive symptoms, and the latter leads to the negative symptoms.

Grace: Nucleus Accumbens Model

Grace and associates (O'Donnell & Grace, 1998, 1999; West & Grace, 2001) describe a complex model centered on a basal forebrain structure, the nucleus accumbens. This small brain region is located at an intersection of projections from the hippocampus, the prefrontal cortex, the amygdala, and the mesolimbic dopaminergic tract—areas implicated as possible loci of alteration in schizophrenia. According to this model, prefrontal glutaminergic input to the nucleus accumbens modulates the dopaminergic input in a manner that influences the activity of frontal-subcortical circuits. In addition, the hippocampus and amygdala control gates in the nucleus accumbens that allow the frontal-subcortical circuits to activate. In schizophrenia, frontal dysfunction leads to a lack of glutaminergic modulation of the dopaminergic influence over the frontal-subcortical circuits. A decrease of tonic dopaminergic activity leads to decreased activation of the circuits. In addition, less hippocampal input to the accumbens results in fewer open gates allowing for transmission of the circuit flow in frontal-subcortical circuits. This hypoactivation results in decreased behavior, thought, and emotion manifested as the negative symptoms of avolition, alogia, and flattened affect.

The positive symptoms (in particular, reality distortion) are due to altered hippocampal firing, leading to either fewer gates being opened in the accumbens with a shift toward more preponderance of amygdala-controlled gates in the accumbens being open (and hence more attention to fear-related items as in paranoia) or to inappropriate-controlled gates being opened, leading to incorrect contextual cues being incorporated into the attended situation.

Thought disorder is believed by Grace and associates to be due to diminished accumbens activity (lower tonic dopaminergic levels), leading to decreased inhibition of the globus pallidus, which normally inhibits the reticular thalamic nuclei. Thus there is increased inhibition of the reticular thalamic nuclei, diminishing its role in filtering sensory input to the thalamus, leading to difficulties in maintaining focus and organization of thought.

Frith: Willed Intention Model

Frith (1992) explains that actions can occur in response to external stimuli (stimulus intentions) or as a result of internal decisions based on goals and plans (willed intentions). A central monitoring system distinguishes between the two when actions are made. In schizophrenia, there is a deficit in this central monitoring system such that actions from willed intentions are mistaken as being derived from external sources. This misperception produces delusions of control (the belief that one's actions are caused by others) and, by considering thoughts as a type of action, thought insertion (the belief that one's thoughts are caused by others). Hallucinations are also a consequence of perceiving that one's thoughts are produced externally. An inability to correctly assess the intention of others leads to delusions of reference and paranoid delusions. Negative symptoms involve a different mechanism: a deficit in producing willed intentions, which leaves actions more heavily dependent on stimulus input (e.g., a person with avolition needing someone else to prod him or her to get out of bed and take a walk).

The brain correlates of this model include frontal structures (the dorsolateral prefrontal cortex, the supplementary motor area, and the anterior cingulate cortex) that activate basal ganglia (striatal) structures, which then produce actions. The frontal structures also send corollary discharges to the posterior brain regions responsible for perception, which makes the action seem self-generated. Disconnections here produce the misperception that willed intentions are produced by external sources; consequently, delusions and hallucinations occur. When the frontal-striatal connections are disrupted, negative symptoms evolve.

Cohen: Cognitive Control Model

Information processing can be hampered if there is inadequate cognitive control of the functions involved, according to Cohen and associates (Braver, Barch, & Cohen, 1999; Braver & Cohen, 1999). In their model, cognitive control is "the ability to properly maintain and update internal representations of task-relevant context information" (Braver, Barch, & Cohen, 1999, p. 312). Disorganization in thought and action, as well as deficits in cognitive tasks, can result from poor cognitive control (Cohen & Servan-Schreiber, 1992).

Cognitive control is mainly the function of the prefrontal cortex. Impairments in attention, executive functions, and working and episodic memory can all be traced to a common deficit in "the internal representation and use of context information in the service of exerting control over behavior" (Braver et al., 1999, p. 314). The prefrontal cortex is central to this function of context updating and maintenance.

Dopaminergic input to the prefrontal cortex influences the activity of the prefrontal cortex by gating contextual information in order to allow updating of this information while avoiding interference by irrelevant information. In general, dopaminergic systems in the brain serve the task of "[providing] the means for the organism to learn about, predict, and respond appropriately to events that lead to reward" (Braver et al., 1999, p. 317). Contributions to this overall task vary depending on the various recipients (limbic, striatal, cortical) of dopaminergic input. Specifically, the dopaminergic input to the prefrontal cortex provides for updating of contextual information and protection against interference. In schizophrenia, there are disturbances in the activity of the dopamine projections to the prefrontal cortex, leading to either perseveration (due to a lack of updated information to guide behavior), the insertion of irrelevant information that can disrupt the use of important information, or impairment in the maintenance of information. Cognitive deficits and disorganization result from these disruptions.

Gray and Hemsley: Motor Program Model

Gray, Feldon, Rawlins, Hemsley, and Smith (1991) propose a complex neurophysiological model to explain the psychological hypothesis of Hemsley (1987a) as well as integrate this with the models of Frith (1987) and Weinberger (1987). Hemsley postulates that a "final common pathway" may be a "failure to integrate contextually appropriate stored material with current sensory input and ongoing motor programs" (Hemsley, 2005, p. 43). This concept is used by Gray to develop a model to explain the positive symptoms of schizophrenia as a disruption in the smooth operation of planned "motor" programs (including thoughts, focused attention, and speech as well as physical actions).

Motor programs require (1) maintenance of a given step until it is completed (corticothalamostriatal loops), (2) monitoring whether the actual outcome of a step matches the intended outcome (septohippocampal system), (3) termination of a step (dopaminergic input to the nucleus accumbens), and (4) switching to the next step in the program (nucleus accumbens). In addition, the specific content of each step needs to be determined (caudate) based on reinforcement contingencies (amygdala). Irrelevant associations need to be inhibited (striatum), whereas important unexpected intrusions need to be noticed (septohippocampal system). Finally, coordination of these activities is required for its proper operation (prefrontal cortex).

In schizophrenia, irrelevant stimuli intrude into the process of a motor program due to dysfunction in the connection from the hippocampus via the subiculum to the nucleus accumbens and/or due to excess dopamine causing termination of the planned motor program, leaving it open for intrusion by novel/irrelevant stimuli. Thought disorder and attentional problems can occur when there is overattention to stimuli that are irrelevant to the current motor program. These stimuli can include thoughts that divert a speech program from its intended goal (e.g., derailment, clanging). Delusions arise as a way to account for events that are given inappropriate significance due to their intrusion into awareness. Hallucinations involve an intrusion by items in long-term memory that are misinterpreted as being generated externally (Hemsley, 1987b).

Summary and Commentary

The first four models describe an alteration in cognitive processing as a basis for the symptoms of schizophrenia. Cognitive slippage, lack of cognitive coordination, parasitic foci, and hypersalience each lead to disorganized thought and unusual sensations/experiences (that are rationalized in a delusional manner and/or form hallucinations) and either directly limit functional output (in speech, affect, activity) or produce accommodation reactions of withdrawal and passivity. These models do not attempt to explain anatomically localized disruptions in schizophrenia but rather postulate that the dysfunction arises from problems in the basic circuitry of the brain (which is basically similar across all cortical regions), such as in neuronal density, neuronal organization, or abnormal communication between cells due to alterations in excitatory and/or inhibitory neurotransmitter activity. That is, there may be a problem in one or more basic cognitive algorithms or operations carried out by the brain that affect information processing in multiple brain regions (and therefore sensory and higher-order integrative processes). These models do not all give a clear sense of how the cognitive aberrations lead to hallucinations and delusions, but focus primarily on basic disorganization of cognitive processes. In some of these models, hallucinations, delusions, and negative symptoms are seen as compensatory phenomena arising in response to network abnormalities.

Walker and Diforio's model does not attempt to explain how the symptoms of schizophrenia arise but rather how increased dopaminergic activity results from stressors and malfunctioning cortisol systems. Their supporting evidence, however, is limited to some people with schizophrenia, so it may not be an all-inclusive explanation. (However, see Chapter 14, this volume.)

The remaining models introduce more anatomical detail to the picture. Although Weinberger's and Grace's do not give sufficient speculation about the transition from physiological dysfunction to psychological dysfunction, the others do make this endeavor. A difficulty with these two models is that they do not completely complement each other. Grace's model involves frontal-subcortical systems for both positive and negative symptoms, whereas Weinberger's designates the frontal system as relating to negative symptoms and the subcortical system as corresponding to positive symptoms. Nonetheless, there is some overlap, and future models would likely incorporate aspects of each of these two.

The remaining three models—those of Frith, Cohen, and Gray and Hemsley—assign psychological tasks to various brain regions and describe how these structures interact when performing their respective functions. The latter two, in particular, present similar psychological models of the intrusion of irrelevant stimuli into the process of stored information, thereby influencing willful activities. The brain structures involved are similar in the two models, but the functions of each structure and the specific interactions among them differ. What is important about these three models is the attempt to relate hypothetical psychological processes to physiological processes.

We use this same approach in our own model, presented in Chapter 14, but we postulate a deficiency in the total integrative capacity of the brain, rather than interactions of localized dysfunction, as a cause for schizophrenia. In this model, schizophrenia originates with cognitive insufficiency and hypersensitivity to stress. These deficits lead to hyperactivation of dysfunctional schemas (responsible for the positive symptoms) and resource sparing (partly responsible for the negative symptoms).

As all these models are tested, modified, and updated, with differences resolved by empirical confirmation or refutation, a clearer picture of the current enigma that is schizophrenia will emerge.

SUMMARY

Unlike Type I diabetes, Huntington's disease, or posttraumatic stress disorder, schizophrenia has not revealed itself to be caused predominantly by any single physical malfunction, genetic disturbance, or environmental event. More akin to irritable bowel syndrome, fibromyalgia, and major depression, schizophrenia is a cluster of symptoms that may turn out to be one disease or a group of related diseases. It may be a categorically distinct entity, occurring only in those with the factors necessary for its appearance, or it may be discovered to be one end of a spectrum on which all of us can find a locus.

What we do seem to know is that there is a polygenetic component to the etiology of schizophrenia; that obstetric complications and environmental stressors add to the probability of acquiring the disorder; that there are disruptions in parts of the brain—most notably the frontal cortex, the temporal lobe (including the hippocampus and amygdala), subcortical areas (e.g., the nucleus accumbens), and neurotransmitter systems (e.g., the dopaminergic and glutaminergic systems)—that probably arise in early neural development yet do not cause much noticeable difference until further neural maturation transpires in adolescence; and that an atypical interaction of these brain regions results in an atypical interaction of the person with society due to a constellation of symptoms and cognitive alterations.

The task ahead for neurobiologists is mainly twofold: to determine (1) what factors truly contribute to the etiology of schizophrenia, either as a single disorder or as multiple disorders, and (2) how these factors interact to bring about the outward manifestations of schizophrenia. The task ahead for cognitive therapists is to apply the findings of neurobiology to the psychotherapeutic treatment of schizophrenia. This can be useful in a number of ways: (1) the development of new cognitive therapy techniques based on neurophysiological findings; (2) support for the use of specific, current cognitive therapy techniques; (3) assistance in deciding between different cognitive approaches; (4) appreciation of the potential limits of cognitive therapy interventions; and (5) a more comprehensive understanding of the complexity of schizophrenia.

CHAPTER 3

A Cognitive Conceptualization of Delusions

A 20-year-old man dropped out of college because he believed that there was a conspiracy among the students to disparage him and spread ugly rumors about him. Wherever he went, he believed that he could pick up snatches of conversations that were derogatory toward him and also that the other students were looking at him. He became increasingly agitated and finally had to leave school. He was hospitalized and received antipsychotic medications, which seemed to take the edge off of the delusions but did not eliminate them. When he returned home, he continued to perceive other people as talking about him. He believed that TV characters and commentators were talking directly to him. At times, he thought that other people were taking his thoughts away from him and that they were putting strange ideas in his head. He was particularly concerned about sexual thoughts being transmitted to him. Sometimes at night he would feel one of the female characters from a television show enter his room and have sex with him. Although this tryst apparently occurred in a dreamlike state, he nonetheless believed that it was true. He became more and more secluded because of fears that if he went outside the house, people would not only talk about him, but might attack him.

This patient's experiences illustrate the central features of delusions: a combination of *egocentricity* and *external locus of control*. The patient relates irrelevant events (other people's conversations and observations, the statements of television broadcasters) to him- or herself and at the same time ascribes internal experiences (thoughts, erotic feelings) to the intrusion of external entities. The classical features of schizophrenia (e.g., "thought capture" and "thought insertion") indicate this patient's experience of his mind as permeable. He also fails to discriminate between daydreams about sex and the actual occurrence because he interprets sexual feelings and fantasies as originating from the outside. This case illustrates the patient's basic beliefs in his vulnerability, helplessness, and powerlessness and his image of other people as powerful, controlling, and intrusive. Therapy addresses these basic beliefs by empowering the patient, building up self-confidence, and teaching him or her strategies for reality testing the delusional ideas (as described in Chapter 9).

Delusions are defining characteristics of schizophrenia and delusional disorder (paranoia). They are also observed in the context of a number of other psychiatric disorders such as depression, obsessive–compulsive disorder, and body dysmorphic disorder, but delusions are not defining characteristics of these disorders as they are of schizophrenia (American Psychiatric Association, 2000). It is an open question as to whether delusions in other disorders are formed in the same way as those observed in the context of schizophrenia. Nonetheless, delusions share many common characteristics irrespective of the specific disorders in which they occur. In this chapter, we focus primarily on delusions in schizophrenia. According to DSM-IV (American Psychiatric Association, 2000) a delusion is defined as:

> A false belief based on incorrect inference about external reality that is firmly sustained despite what almost everyone else believes and despite what constitutes incontrovertible and obvious proof or evidence to the contrary. The belief is not one ordinarily accepted by other members of the person's culture or subculture (e.g., it is not an article of religious faith). (p. 821)

Like many definitions, this definition in DSM-IV leaves a number of unresolved problems. How can we be certain that an idea is false when we know from history that many ideas deemed to be false by an individual's contemporaries at the time were eventually shown to be correct? Moreover, many beliefs such as telepathy, thought transmission, and alien possession that sophisticated individuals consider false are entertained by a large segment of the population (Lawrence & Peters, 2004). Paranormal beliefs like these, which are often central parts of the delusions, may be prevalent in the patient's subculture (contrary to the DSM-IV definition).

In order to resolve the question "When is a belief delusional?", it is helpful to start by examining the nature of delusions within the context of what we know about the role of specific beliefs in nonpsychotic conditions. The same dimensions of the beliefs observed in these disorders are also present in delusions (Hole et al., 1979; Garety & Hemsley, 1987). Among these are the dimensions of *pervasiveness* (how much of the patient's consciousness is controlled by the belief), *conviction* (how strongly the patient believes), *significance* (how important the belief is in patient's meaning assignment system), *intensity* (to what degree it displaces more realistic beliefs), *inflexibility* and *self-certainty* (how impervious the belief is to contradictory evidence, logic, or reason), *preoccupation*, and *impact* on behavior and emotions. For example, a patient who believed totally (conviction) that everyone was an FBI agent (pervasiveness) could not entertain the possibility that the belief might be wrong (inflexibility and self-certainty), and, as a result, hid in his room (behavioral impact). High levels of endorsement of these variables distinguish patients with schizophrenia from those individuals who may be at risk for the disorder.

A test of patients' inflexibility is their response to the hypothetical contradiction of the delusions (Hurn, Gray, & Hughes, 2002). Patients' willingness to consider contradictory information has been found to improve their prognosis (Garety et al., 1997). It is important to recognize that the patients' degree of conviction of the validity of a delusion and their delusional interpretations of events fluctuate from time to time. Many patients acknowledge that they do not totally believe in their delusions (Strauss, 1969). Nonetheless, their *delusional interpretations* tend to control their affect and behavior.

Because the content of schizophrenic delusions may be compatible with that of the beliefs of normal members of patients' subgroups, it would be helpful to clarify what characteristics of a "compatible" belief would lead other group members to consider it a delusion. If the delusional belief is strong enough to produce "weird" behavior, then other group members might start to wonder about the individual's state of mind. Unusual behavior, such as muttering to oneself or striking a stranger without provocation, for example, might be driven by a socially acceptable belief in receiving messages from God—considered normal in many religious denominations. But if behavior is aberrant, the underlying belief becomes suspect. If the individual clings steadfastly to his belief that God has sent him a message to attack certain individuals whom he identifies as sons of Satan, other people would probably be inclined to regard him as delusional. It should be noted that specific supernatural beliefs advocated by certain religious groups may be considered delusional or dangerous by psychiatrists if they are unaware of the connection with the religious faith. Sometimes a patient's delusion is reinforced by close relatives. The mother of a woman who believed her actions were controlled by spirits believed that this was true and held to the belief even after the daughter no longer believed it. In other cases, the content may be so extreme or bizarre—for example, that the individual is manipulated by aliens on a distant planet—that others would have no problem in labeling it as delusional.

The criteria for labeling an unusual, even bizarre, idea as delusional may be difficult to determine simply by its content. Delusions can be best understood in terms of abnormalities of thought processes rather than simply in terms of their specific content (irrational ideas are not necessarily delusions). First, the pathogenic belief has taken control of the information processing so that the *interpretations of events show a systematic bias* that is refractory to the evidence or to logic. Second, the biased interpretations are idiosyncratic—the individual attaches highly *personal meanings* to events that clearly are irrelevant to him or her. These biased and incongruous interpretations seem rational to the patient but not to others in his group. These cognitions are "ego-syntonic" as distinct from obsessive cognitions in obsessive–compulsive neurosis, which are "ego-alien." The patient with delusions and the one with obsessions are similar, however, insofar as their distress and disability are instigated by their intrusive thoughts (Morrison, 2001). Importantly, the salience of delusional interpretations is so powerful that the delusions are regarded by patients as *reality* rather than as interpretations of reality or as beliefs.

Finally, the individual's holding steadfastly to the belief, despite overwhelming evidence to the contrary, would lead to the diagnosis of a delusion. The degree of self-certainty about the validity of patients' strange experiences has been demonstrated in a number of studies utilizing the Beck Cognitive Insight Scale (see Beck & Warman, 2004; see also Chapter 14). Thus, several factors, including bizarre content, strange behavior, and resistance to disconfirmation (see Woodward, Moritz, Cuttler, & Whitman, 2006), constitute criteria by which a belief may be labeled a delusion.

A marker that distinguishes paranoid delusional from nondelusional thinking is the integration of three extreme biases: *preemptive self-centered focus, external locus of causation*, and *attribution of intentionality*. The nature of these cognitive aspects and their specific role in the formation of different delusions are addressed in this chapter. Kimhy, Goetz, Yale, Corcoran, and Malaspina (2005) factor-analyzed the scores of 83 patients on the Scale for the Assessment of Positive Symptoms (SAPS). They extracted

three factors: Delusions of Being Controlled (including "anomalous" delusions, described in this chapter), Self-Significance factor (grandiose, religious, and sinful delusions) and Delusions of Persecution. This and other
studies found Delusions of Persecution to be the most common. In formulating the psychological mechanisms involved in the formation of the content of these delusions, we describe the kind of biases and reasoning aberrations that are specifically intrinsic to paranoid delusions but are found,
to some degree, in grandiose delusions. Because there is an overlap in the
content of the different kinds of delusions, there is also an overlap in their
psychological determinants.

OVERVIEW OF THE COGNITIVE MODEL
OF DELUSIONS

The psychology of delusions is discussed first in the context of an analysis of the phenomenology of this disorder. The biases intrinsic to these
phenomena are obvious in all forms of delusional beliefs. These biases
are reflected in the interpretations (actually, misinterpretations) of experiences. The patients' difficulty in evaluating these erroneous interpretations
as inferences rather than factual representations of reality is an aspect of
this impaired reality testing. Further, confirmatory bias and compensatory
behaviors tend to reinforce the delusional beliefs. This section formulates
the development of delusions in terms of the impingement of multiple stressors on preexisting vulnerabilities; then we apply this module of biases,
erroneous thinking, and stress vulnerability to persecutory, grandiose, and
control delusions, respectively.

Biased Thinking

A wealth of clinical observations of the phenomenology and accumulated
experimental data provides the foundation for a conceptual analysis of
delusions. Drawing on this body of knowledge, we have developed a cognitive model of delusions that is applicable to paranoid, interference, and
grandiose delusions. We propose first that skewed information processing
plays a central role in delusional thinking, and that this skewing is driven
by a system of dysfunctional beliefs maintained by a variety of biases and
behaviors. We describe the profound *egocentric orientation* that preempts
normal information processing in favor of self-referential attributions of
irrelevant events. This *self-referential bias* reflects patients' underlying

views of themselves as at the vortex of their social environment. Depending on the content of this self-centered orientation, these patients unrealistically perceive themselves as the central focus of others' attention (be those others human or supernatural) and the objects of their malevolence, intrusiveness, or benevolence. Concomitantly they perceive themselves as vulnerable or superior, weak or omnipotent. Patients also attach personal significance to impersonal and irrelevant events, seizing on random events and coincidences to detect signs of the intentional work of external entities.

A closely related and particularly powerful bias is the attribution of an *external causation* for their subjective experiences. Contingent on the nature of the delusional belief, patients ascribe certain normal physical, mental, or emotional experiences to the manipulation or intrusion of other animate or inanimate entities. They explain unpleasant somatic sensations, anxiety, dysphoria, or intrusive thoughts as being caused by the actions of these agents. The central feature of the biased thinking is the indiscriminate attribution of *negative or positive intentions* to other people. The self-referential, external causation, and intentionality biases together form a composite of patients' worldview that involve "they vs. me" internal representations.

Errors

Cognitive functions at each level of delusional information processing are biased in such a way that they lead to errors that culminate in distorted, unrealistic, and self-defeating appraisals of experience. Although biased appraisals may be adaptive in responding to certain life situations, such as threats from a real enemy, they are obviously dysfunctional when they occur in delusions that essentially create a pseudo-threat. These specific interpretations of a situation are not only unrealistic but also lead to excessive distress and maladaptive behavior.

The cognitive biases resulting from this pathogenic orientation provide the content of the delusional inferences and conclusions, and they inevitably lead to a variety of errors in information processing. Cognitive errors such as *selective abstraction, extreme judgments*, and *overgeneralization* are especially prominent in delusional thinking. The biased assimilation of data (selective abstraction) is particularly salient as a consequence of patients' excessive focus of attention on particular internal and external stimuli. The *loss of context* typical of delusional thinking may be due, in part, to this exclusive and selective focus. The processing of the selected data is further distorted by *inferential biases* (e.g., perceiving connections between irrelevant events), *"catastrophizing,"* and making *absolute judg-*

ments. Other mental mechanisms related to the formation of the delusional interpretations include *inadequate data gathering*—not examining the available evidence sufficiently—and disproportionately favoring easy interpretations (that fit their delusions) in preference to more complex but correct judgments. Patients also have *difficulty in inhibiting* the easy (but incorrect) automatic responses and consequently are more prone to accept them without further reflection.

Impaired Reality Testing

In the prodromal period, patients experience "inferential confusion" manifested by uncertainty regarding whether some of their strange experiences are real or misinterpretations. As the delusional beliefs become stronger, however, patients stop questioning their validity. Given that patients' unreasonable or bizarre interpretations are often questioned by other people and lead to interpersonal difficulties, the question arises: Why don't patients respond to corrective feedback, as do other individuals when the invalidity or negative consequences of their cognitive errors are apparent? Patients with delusions are able to see the flaws and distortions in other people's reasoning but don't recognize these in their own delusional thinking. They are especially oblivious to their own illogical and unreasonable thinking when it is related to their underlying delusional beliefs.

An important factor contributing to the maintenance of delusions is *attenuated reality testing*—that is, the impaired capacity to distance oneself from one's beliefs and interpretations, to consider that they could be erroneous and to correct the errors. Delusional individuals do not regard their interpretations as mental constructions but as reality itself. Reality testing one's own interpretation is a resource-demanding task, and patients with schizophrenia have a cognitive reserve that may be too limited to meet the demands of reflection and reappraisal of misinterpretations. A number of cognitive, motivational, and behavioral factors contribute to patients' refractoriness to corrective feedback from others once the delusions have formed fully. Certain cognitive biases reflect patients' deficiencies in evaluating the contradictory evidence against their delusional interpretations. Their *confirmatory bias* selects evidence that supports their own conclusions, and the *disconfirmation bias* rules out any consideration of inconsistent evidence. Because of this mechanism, as well as other factors, patients become overconfident of the truth value of their conclusions.

Motivational factors also contribute to the relative impermeability of delusional thinking. Patients with persecutory delusions, for example, are disinclined to relinquish their disposition to attribute negative motives to other people because they believe this strategy provides a margin of safety from being deceived, manipulated, or attacked; if they relinquish their suspiciousness of others' motives and their hypervigilance, they believe they will become more vulnerable. Grandiose patients are reluctant to examine their self-inflating ideas because they regard them as a source of pleasure and a bolster to their self-esteem. They also attempt to ward off any suggestions that their grand ideas are wrong because the alternative explanation may be that they are "crazy." *Safety-seeking behaviors*, such as avoidance of situations that trigger their paranoid thinking, also prevent patients from testing their fears against the reality of the feared situation.

Clinical observations and experimental data can be organized to describe the steps in a hypothesized pathway to the delusional experience (see Figure 3.1).

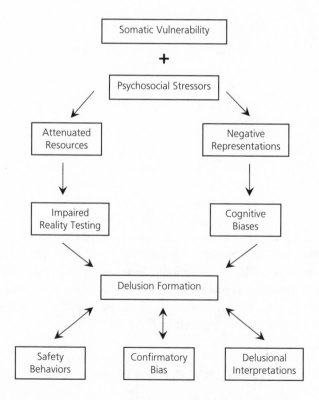

FIGURE 3.1. Hypothesized pathway from diathesis (vulnerability) to formation of delusion.

Stress–Vulnerability Model

In the stress–vulnerability model a variable range of interacting genetic and experiential factors are seen as producing distorted internal representations that constitute the *somatic and cognitive vulnerability* to schizophrenia. These representations reflect patients' fundamental orientation (e.g., "they vs. me"). Concurrently, the stressors impinging on somatic vulnerability *attenuate the resources* necessary for adequate self-reflection and responsiveness to feedback—crucial elements in reality testing. These elements lead to the following pathological process:

1. The representations make patients vulnerable to experiencing non-psychotic reactions such as suspiciousness, depression, and anxiety, and they provide the substrate for the formation of delusions.
2. The trigger for activation of dysfunctional thinking involves some type of impingement on life situations (e.g., defeat, rejection, isolation) on patients' specific cognitive vulnerabilities (negative internal representations).
3. Under acute or prolonged stress, these distorted representations become hypersalient, influence the information-processing system, and produce distorted interpretations of experiences. Patients do not reality-test these misinterpretations, which reinforce the distorted representations.

The delusional constructions consequently influence the information-processing system and shape the interpretation of experiences. When fully activated, the delusions swamp and supersede normal information processing. Once formed, the delusions are maintained by confirmation and antidisconfirmation biases, safety behaviors, and feedback from repeated unrealistic cognitions. The delusional beliefs coexist with more realistic or adaptive beliefs. When the delusions are not active, patients can engage in normal activities, make accurate judgments, and even reality-test and correct some of their erroneous ideas (i.e., those not connected with the delusions). During periods of recovery, the delusional beliefs become latent but are still susceptible to reactivation by life circumstances.

THE EGOCENTRIC PERSPECTIVE

The Self as Object: Self-Referential Bias

During delusional episodes patients are locked into an *egocentric perspective*. They see themselves as at center stage in a drama in which all the happenings are relevant to them. Whirring motors, muffled conversations, billboard advertisements, television commercials all take on a special meaning; they convey overt or hidden messages directed specifically to the patients. For some patients, threats are everywhere. A tall man with a bulge in his pocket is perceived as an armed undercover agent who wants to kill the patient. A bitter taste in a cup of coffee is a sign that it has been poisoned. Although people ordinarily dismiss such ideas readily, they take on the force of reality for patients with schizophrenia. Moreover, these patients may attach personal significance to the most mundane, irrelevant events. One patient, for example, interpreted a sign on a bus as a message from God. Another assumed that a yellow-colored car conveyed a message from the Mafia that he was "yellow" (a coward). Patients may also attach positive, self-enhancing meanings to irrelevant stimuli (a smiling face on a billboard indicated to a patient that the person in the image liked him).

For many patients, self-referential thinking is activated only in highly specific situations. One of our patients, Ms. G., had a 9-year delusion of being persecuted only in the workplace. She perceived virtually all events taking place in the office as self-relevant: She was convinced that people were telling her, by the absence of their smiles, that she was "incompetent" and "hopeless." In addition, she interpreted the smile from another colleague, accompanied by "Good morning," as an expression of ridicule and also an indication that "my days [in the office] are numbered." The egocentric bias also extended to distant sounds. For instance, when a colleague slammed her door at the opposite end of the hallway, the patient perceived this as a covert communication: "You're incompetent" and "You should leave."

Many other patients experience arousal of their persecutory beliefs only in a specific locale (e.g., in the workplace but not in restaurants) in which they have an expectation of a personal threat. The *activating situations* are highly specific, just as they are for patients with specific phobias such as claustrophobia and agoraphobia. For other patients with delusions, the activating circumstances are more generalized. They may experience paranoid reactions whenever they are in public situations. A patient watching a baseball game, for example, overheard a player mutter "Damn!" after making an error. The patient immediately concluded that the player was swearing at him. The self-references may be even more bizarre. Several patients, for example, asserted that the anchor persons on television news programs were talking to them. Others conclude that various items in newspapers, in books, or on the Internet contain coded messages intended for them. The common element of all of these examples is that the patients perceive themselves as the passive objects of others' influence, whether demeaning or uplifting.

A striking feature of delusional thinking is the act of focusing on a particular aspect or detail of a situation that "feels" relevant to patients and then *taking it out of the context* of the total situation. As a result, patients distort the meaning of the situation. An example of taking material out of context and conjuring up a fantastic interpretation was the experience of a young woman who, absorbed in reading a romantic novel, decided that a particularly erotic passage represented the author's expression of love for her.

Safety Behaviors

Patients with persecutory delusions often resort to a number of "safety behaviors" in an attempt to avoid or neutralize danger. One patient, for example, believed that she had been targeted for elimination by the Mafia. When she would see strangers loitering outside her house, she would run to her room, lock the door, and hide under the bed. To her, any unfamiliar people were members of the mob. Other patients may simply stay indoors because they believe that various and sundry enemies are waiting for them outside. Still others may lower their heads in an attempt to foil television cameras that they believe are trained on them. Patients may utilize a number of rituals (e.g., making hand movements or praying) to ward off the influence of "evil spirits." These safety behaviors, which play an important role in maintaining delusions, need to be targeted in any therapy aimed at reducing delusional conviction (see Chapter 9).

Although people generally are inclined to accept their factual interpretations of events as reasonable, patients with delusions seem to lack the normal capacity to distance themselves from their "factual" interpretations and to correct them in response to contradictory evidence. The combination of (1) consistent self-referential meanings attached to irrelevant situations, (2) the loss of context, and (3) the relative imperviousness to correction defines the important boundaries of delusional thinking.

Causal Explanations of Internal States:
The Externalizing Bias

Just as patients are strongly invested in attaching personal meanings to irrelevant external events, they also tend to attribute external causes to internal psychological or somatic events. Patients with paranoid schizophrenia are especially prone to conceiving extraordinary explanations for their ordinary physical, mental, or emotional experiences. Because of a powerful *externalizing bias*, they forgo plausible explanations in favor of unlikely or impossible external attributions. Thus, they may attribute difficulty in performing manual tasks to interference by alien forces, blame a headache on beams from a satellite, and mistake command hallucinations for orders from God. Unlike most individuals with hypochondriasis, for example, who ascribe normal somatic sensations to medical illness, paranoid patients may ascribe their subjective experiences such as aches or fatigue to the manipulation of an external entity. They focus their attention particularly on external (usually social) stimuli for signs of potential danger, instructions, or (in some cases) rewards. Like a soldier in a combat zone, they are hypervigilant to any environmental event that could signify danger. They misread danger when there is none, and they perceive enemies when there are none.

Some patients are inclined to believe that unusual feelings or thoughts— pleasant or unpleasant—are the products of manipulations by an external agent (animate or inanimate). One patient, for example, concluded that a good feeling—occurring either spontaneously or after a pleasant event— was due to God's benevolent intervention. Conversely, a bad feeling was produced by God's disfavor. Other patients have assumed that a stomachache is produced by the penetration of a magnetic field, that anxious sweating is due to intrusion by radar, and that a lump in the throat is caused by a computer chip implanted during an imagined surgical operation. Although these patients are able to conjure scientific-sounding explanations for distress, they generally believe that human or supernatural entities or some vague but powerful force is ultimately responsible for producing these experiences. Their concern about being influenced is so strong that it overrides common-sense explanations of the purely somatic origin of their sensations. With their fixation on extreme causes, they draw upon their knowledge of the latest technology to explain how their persecutors (or benefactors, in some cases) are controlling their feelings. These beliefs in external sources of control reach the ultimate in so-called *passivity delusions*, in which patients assume that external forces manipulate their behavior. Various "anomalous" experiences, such as auditory hallucinations and intrusive thoughts, are similarly attributed to external sources.

A common example of external attributions is the image or feeling of being observed or even stared at by people in public places. This experience is often accompanied by somatic sensations: a prickly sensation on the skin, a heaviness in the body, a blurring of vision. Patients "read" these sensations as indications that others are observing them—an example of *somatic-based reasoning*. As they enter public situations, these patients expect to be singled out for scrutiny; they then feel the self-conscious sensations and interpret these feelings as proof that people are watching them. The intensity of self-conscious feelings is proportional to the degree to which they believe that they are the center of attention. Their acute awareness of themselves as the object of others' attention is akin to the self-focus in patients with social phobia upon entering social situations; patients with delusions, however, feel exposed to scrutiny even when they are at the periphery of a social gathering. Powerful beliefs about being closely observed may progress to ideas of being followed by other people or tracked by radar. These patients consequently may seclude themselves as a safety strategy.

Social situations may activate a variety of beliefs about thoughts or actions as controlled by others. One patient tended to experience social anxiety when she was in a group. She interpreted her anxious feelings (rapid heart rate, sweating) as indicating that she was being mentally assaulted by the group members. Such patients take their emotional reactions as *direct* proof that they are in danger. Their *emotion-based reasoning* takes a form: "Since I feel anxious, it means that *they* are preparing to attack me." For many patients, their feeling states preempt rules of logic or evidence. They will say, "If I feel something, it means it's true." Although the thoughts and images that paranoid patients experience in a "hot" situation are similar to those reported by patients with social anxiety problems, paranoid patients carry the fears to the extreme. A socially anxious patient who experienced anxiety in crowded situations interpreted her anxiety as a sign that others were talking about her. Another patient reported that when she became anxious in groups, she would begin to think, "If I stay, I'm going to lose control. . . . If I lose control, then others will take advantage of me. . . . They will think I'm crazy and try to have me hospitalized." She would accept these fears as absolute reality and would run out of the room (a safety behavior). Research has demonstrated the disposition of these patients to engaging in extreme thinking (Garety et al., 2005; Startup, Freeman, & Garety, 2007).

Patients may simply blame other people for influencing their well-being without any consideration of how these others might accomplish this feat. One of our patients, for instance, believed that other people had removed his ability to enjoy music, his most important leisure pleasure. Whenever he became anxious, both in his home and in public, for example, his enjoyment of listening to music was reduced. Although it was obvious that social concerns were responsible for his anxiety, he concluded that other people intentionally made him anxious in order to remove his ability to enjoy this important source of satisfaction. On one occasion, he feared being arrested after passing a police station while listening to the radio, then interpreted his anxious feelings as a sign that officers in the station were trying to "steal" his enjoyment of music. In this way, the power of the externalizing bias overrode his awareness at another level that the real reason for his anxiety was his concern about being arrested.

It is interesting to note that many patients include pictures of eyes in their drawings and paintings. This image may fit in with their egocentric beliefs about being watched and also their perceived necessity to observe others for signs of hostile intentions. The fixation on eyes is illustrated by a patient who reported that when he looked at other people in a group, he could perceive a steel band extending from their eyes to his. We discovered that this experience was based on a tension he felt in his eyes just prior to making eye contact with other people. He would then have a visual image of the steel band connecting both sets of eyes. This image had the intensity of a visual hallucination and produced a further distressing tension in his eyes. As a result, he usually looked away from other people to avoid their staring at him and his staring at them. Of course, his obvious eye aversions often made people stare at him—the very consequence that he wanted to avoid.

Almost any sensations can be attributed to an external entity. A number of patients, for example, have reported a variety of imagined experiences based on their attribution of sexual sensations to an external agent. A woman believed that genital sensations experienced when she was lying (alone) in bed were caused by having intercourse with the president. A man believed that his erections were caused by the distant manipulations of a movie actress. In these cases, the experiences and attributions were found to be based on vivid fantasies and woven into a story.

The tendency to attribute normal physical or psychological sensations to the manipulations of an external agent can be contrasted with the biased attributions in other forms of psychopathology. In panic disorder, for example, chest pain is attributed to a realistic life-threatening medical condition such as a coronary attack, whereas for a patient with schizophrenia, it might be explained as the result of death rays aimed at him or her from a nuclear plant by an enemy. A number of patients who have experienced symptoms of posttraumatic stress disorder prior to the onset of their psychosis, or as a result of forced hospitalization after its onset, are prone to attribute symptoms such as depersonalization, flashbacks, or spotty amnesia to the work of an external agent such as an enemy or the devil.

Patients with nonpsychotic disorders, moreover, recognize that their distress is generated within themselves—that their own reactions to situations or to subjective experiences constitute a large part of their problem. In contrast, patients with schizophrenia are prone to locate the source of their symptoms as outside themselves and generally ascribe their distress to the work of a specific agent or agents. They construe the cause of their symptoms in terms of a definable entity that can be assigned to a concrete category—in preference to "natural" but less-defined constructs, such as emotions or beliefs.

The nature of the agent or agents and the kind of influence or harm attributed to them vary substantially from patient to patient. For some, the agent is supernatural or mystical (God, the devil, spirits); for others, the agents may be strangers, neighbors, or members of the family. For still others, they are organized groups such as the Mafia, the FBI, or ethnic or political groups. Occasionally, the agent is presumed to be a dead person, an animal, or a vague, ill-defined force. In some cases, the influence may be benign or may fluctuate between benevolent and malevolent. The kind of inimical action may range from simple observation (by video cameras or spies) to active persecution or lethal attack. What are common fears in normal people are transformed into actual events in these patients' minds. Malevolent influences range from control or intrusion to manipulation of the mind or body. The presumed methods often draw on recent technology: radar, microwave, computer chips, rays from satellites. The attributed mechanism of influence is invisible, almost by necessity, since there is generally no obvious sign of how the agents are carrying out their intentions. In some cases the influence is audible: noises, banging on the walls, or voices.

The image of the external agent may vary from the supernatural (God, devil, spirits) to powerful authorities or groups (FBI, police, Mafia, gangs) to ordinary individuals (neighbors, strangers, coworkers). The presumed powers of the agent are expressed in any combination of control, manipulation, interference, intrusions, harassment, disparagement, active persecution, and even lethal attack. The degree of power of the agents varies from omnipotent and omniscient (God) to no more than that possessed by any person—but because many patients believe in paranormal phenomena, for example, they may believe that anyone can read their minds.

Intentionalizing Bias

An important component of patients' explanations for their experiences is their focus on the presumed negative or positive intentions of the putative agent: the *intentionalizing bias*. With their profound egocentric orientation, patients not only attach personal meaning to irrelevant events but they also believe that the events are motivated by others' attitudes and feelings toward them. With their simplistic reasoning style, they exclude irrelevance, randomness, and coincidence as possible explanations for certain events or experiences. For them, accidents are never accidental. A patient stumbles as he passes a stranger; the patient's explanation is that the stranger deliberately tripped him. We have found that when presented with a series of ambiguous scenarios, patients will consistently explain the problematic event as a conspiracy. Examples include: "You notice that a car is parked outside your apartment all day; your phone rings but nobody responds when you answer; your food has a funny taste." Given the broad range of possible causes, these patients are drawn to interpret the scenario in a paranoid way.

Since persecutory fears are based on the assumption that other people are malevolent, patients with schizophrenia are suspicious of others' motives. They continually look for signs of hostility and read hidden meanings into innocuous or irrelevant events. Interestingly, despite their hypervigilance, patients' actual perception of potential persecutors is often fuzzy. What they seem to perceive is a projection onto others of their own mental images of persecutors. For example, one woman believed that most of the people on her psychiatric ward were members of the Philadelphia police force. They all had the appearance (to her) of tough, aggressive individuals. (After responding to cognitive therapy, she began to see them as distinct individuals—and not members of the police force.) In a sense, she had "homogenized" their characteristics, in a way similar to negative stereotyping.

The perception and expression of intentionality have been demonstrated to be intrinsic to human interactions (Clark, 1996). The meanings we attach to other people's communication and behavior integrate the apparent purpose of other people's verbal utterances or actions (Grice, 1957). Other people's intentions toward us become crucial when they are concerned with our well-being or survival. Because patients with schizophrenia are particularly suspicious of others, they tend to focus on possible negative motives embedded in people's verbal and nonverbal behavior to the exclusion of the broader context. Thus, they overinterpret or misjudge negative meanings. Further, because of their penchant for jumping to conclusions, these individuals do not ordinarily reappraise and correct negative interpretations.

Although studied separately, the various biases represent different aspects of the same mental construction. The content of the delusional mode is organized into a story or plot consisting of a triad of internal representations. These include the *subject*: an active agent or agents; the agent's *motivations*: malevolent or benevolent; and the *object*: the patient. (The basic scenario and its components may appear in different ways depending on external circumstances.) For example, the subjects may change or their motivations may get worse or better. External stimuli such as traffic, conversations, or television programs are interpreted as signals from entities to the patient (internalizing bias), and these entities are represented as having a malevolent (or benevolent) motivation (intentionalizing bias). Also, internal experiences such as hallucinations, obsessive thoughts, or somatic sensations are attributed to an external agent (externalizing bias). As long as the mode is activated, the delusional plot is played out and leads to relevant affective (anger and/or anxiety) and behavioral (attack/flee) consequences.

Like the overgeneralization bias of the depressed patient, who experiences a downward spiral following a life event, or the catastrophic bias of the anxious patient, who experiences an escalation of fear and arousal, the egocentric and externalizing intentionality biases serve to maintain the delusional patient's sense of personal threat and vulnerability. These biases may also consolidate fundamental dysfunctional beliefs the patient has about him- or herself, others, and the world, which in turn shape the idiosyncratic form and content of delusions.

In a thinking disorder, the patient's metaphorical descriptions of an experience become reified. A patient with a variety of dissociative symptoms, including a pervasive sense of unreality, initially described these in metaphorical terms as a "numbness of the brain." Later when he transitioned into psychosis, he believed that his brain was literally dead. Also, many patients who think their food tastes differently than previously perceive the sensation as poisonous. The materialistic model applied by psychotic patients to their perceptual experiences contrasts with the medical model used generally by nonpsychotic patients and normal individuals. Patients with hypochondriasis, for example, view their somatic sensations (pain, stiffness, fatigue) as signs of a medical illness. Individuals with anxiety, depression, or obsessive–compulsive disorders, on the other hand, describe their symptoms in psychological terms. They could be said to use a mental model. The more normal models help define the problem and point to solutions. The materialistic model used by many patients with schizophrenia simply intensifies existing problems.

Empirical Investigations

A number of empirical studies have confirmed the clinical observation of an intentionalizing bias for ambiguous distressing events in patients with paranoia. Some people (e.g., depression-prone individuals) may attribute the cause to their own personal deficiency; others attribute distressing events to circumstance (external–situational); but paranoid patients have an exaggerated tendency to blame other persons' intentions (external–personal; Kinderman & Bentall, 1996; Kinderman & Bentall, 1997). Experimental studies comparing patients with paranoia to depressed and nonpsychiatric controls find that patients with paranoia exhibit an excessive bias for making external–personal attributions rather than external–situational attributions for negative events (see Garety & Freeman, 1999, for review). These individuals find it difficult to make situational attributions—that is, acknowledging that an aversive event could be due to circumstances, chance, or accident (unintentional). Interestingly, the tendency to formulate explanations in terms of external factors, even when internal explanations are more obvious, seems to be almost reflexive for normal individuals—the *fundamental attribution error* (Heider, 1958; Gilbert & Malone, 1995).

In a review of the literature on the cognitive psychology of delusions, Miller and Karoni (1996) found substantial support for the role of the externalizing bias. Patients with persecutory delusions were found to make excessive personal attributions for negative events (Bentall, Kaney, & Dewey, 1991). Patients with paranoid delusions were prone to offer an external attribution in explaining a negative outcome with transparent test items (Lyon, Kaney, & Bentall, 1994). Words with a paranoid content created greater interference in the emotional Stroop task (naming the color of the ink in which the words had been written) than other kinds of words for subjects with persecutory delusions (Bentall & Kaney, 1989). When asked to recall vignettes with either threatening or neutral themes, patients with delusions recalled more threatening propositions than did depressed controls (Kaney, Wolfenden, Dewey, & Bentall, 1992). The bias in memory tasks was confirmed by Bentall, Kaney, and Bowen-Jones (1995), who asked subjects to recall words that were threat-related, depression-related, or neutral. As compared to normal controls, the deluded group was more prone to recall both threat- and depression-related words, whereas a depressed group showed a bias toward depression-related words only. Phillips and David (1997) found that patients with paranoia spent less time looking at pictures with threatening poses than did nonparanoid patients. This avoidant pattern is typical of the safety behaviors adopted by patients with delusions to reduce their distress (actual or anticipated). Avoidant behaviors interfere with effective processing of the data, thus leaving these patients' delusional beliefs uncorrected.

An interesting theoretical challenge is to determine what mechanisms or deficiencies mediate the crossover from nonpsychotic experiences, such as extreme self-consciousness, to delusional beliefs, such as those about being observed or followed. Considerable research has also focused on the patient's problem of understanding other people's thinking when in a psychotic episode. Generally labeled *theory of mind* deficits, these have been used to explain schizophrenic symptoms, specifically the external attributional style (Taylor & Kinderman, 2002; Frith & Corcoran, 1996). Presumably, problems in understanding other people's motivations, combined with the negative bias, feed into beliefs that have malevolent themes. McCabe, Leudar, and Antaki (2004), however, dispute the laboratory-based findings and provide data that in real-life interactions, patients with schizophrenia are able to tune into and discern other people's beliefs and feelings.

Impaired Reality Testing

Why do patients with schizophrenia seem to disregard the more obvious, common-sense explanations for their experiences and sensations (e.g., medical explanations for pain, psychological explanations for anxiety)? The answer seems to lie partly in the power of the delusional beliefs in preempting more reasonable explanations. Thus a mystical, magical explanation "feels" more real than a realistic explanation because it is more vivid as a result of the hypersalient belief. It should be noted that much of patients' thinking can appear rational. These individuals may be perfectly logical in the way they formulate their inferences and make decisions based on their irrational assumptions. But they are lacking the capacity to distance themselves from these inferences and to reflect on them.

Compared to the dysfunctional beliefs in nonpsychotic disorders, the delusions in schizophrenia do not yield readily to reality testing. Patients with schizophrenia have greater difficulty distancing themselves from their delusional thinking and beliefs or even considering that they might be wrong. In psychiatric terms, they have "impaired insight." In contrast, patients with depression are generally amenable to examining their negative interpretations and, when questioned skillfully, can acknowledge that their negative thinking might be erroneous or exaggerated (Beck et al., 1979). The capacity to recognize cognitive distortions, evaluate or test them, and consider more realistic interpretations of events has been termed "cognitive insight" (Beck & Warman, 2004). The Beck Cognitive Insight Scale (BCIS), developed to measure this construct, consists of two subscales: (1) Self-Reflection and Receptivity to Corrective Feedback, and (2) Overconfidence. Scores on this scale discriminate schizophrenia and other psychotic disorders from nonpsychotic disorders (Beck, Baruch, Balter, Steer, & Warman, 2004). The Overconfidence (self-certainty) subscale, in particular, is correlated with the "jumping to conclusions" (Warman, Lysaker, & Martin, 2007; Pedrelli et al., 2004). Patients receiving cognitive therapy for schizophrenia showed more improvement on this scale than did those receiving treatment as usual (Granholm et al., 2005).

Some of the items on the Self-Certainty subscale of the BCIS are (1) "My interpretations of my experiences are definitely right" (item 2); (2) "If something feels right, it means that it is right" (item 7); and (3) "When people disagree with me, they are generally wrong" (item 10). Items on the Self-Reflectiveness subscale include: (1) "If someone points out that my beliefs are wrong, I am willing to consider it" (item 12) and (2) "My unusual experiences may be due to my being extremely upset or stressed" (item 15) (see Appendices A and B for complete scale and scoring instructions).

As noted earlier, a major question in understanding the phenomenology of delusions is: Why do patients continue to adhere to these delusional beliefs despite their bizarre, or at least improbable, nature and the lack of consensual validation? Why don't patients with psychosis draw on their life experiences and accepted notions of cause and effect and probability, as well as correctional feedback from other people, to question their unreasonable and frequently distressing ideas? Moreover, why can't patients with psychosis draw on the same important cognitive skills that they use to challenge the delusional beliefs of other patients to question their own?

An approach to resolving this question is to consider that the generation and maintenance of beliefs (as opposed to the reality testing of beliefs) represent two different psychological domains. In contrast to the automatic, reflexive, parsimonious function of the primal level of information processing, the self-questioning mode is reflective, deliberative, less automatic, and effortful (Beck, 1996). Interpretations based on highly charged beliefs such as delusions are generated by the primal processing system. Questioning beliefs—an important function of the secondary corrective system—

requires distancing from the automatic interpretations (recognizing them as mental products rather than reality), evaluating them, examining the evidence, and considering alternative explanations—all of which draw on the individual's resources. If the underlying beliefs are highly charged (and consequently carry a high level of conviction), they tend to swamp the information processing. The relative inaccessibility of corrective information is partly the result of reduced cognitive resources. If resources are strained or attenuated, it is difficult to activate the self-questioning mode and allow for reality testing. Therapeutic interventions, whether pharmacological or psychological, appear to reduce the intensity of the highly charged beliefs and, in the case of cognitive therapy, mobilize the cognitive resources necessary for reality testing the delusional thinking.

COGNITIVE DISTORTIONS IN SCHIZOPHRENIA

A *thinking disorder* has been observed in psychiatric patients ever since Beck's (1963) description of it in depression and then in other common psychiatric disorders (Beck, 1976). The term is used to denote errors (distortions) in the formal cognitive processing of experiences, in contrast to the kinds of bizarre, disorganized thinking described as *thought disorder* in psychosis. Patients with schizophrenia show the same types of cognitive distortions as other patients.

Patients with schizophrenia are known to make very far-fetched interpretations of personal events. Those interpretations associated with a self-referential or persecutory content generally produce anxiety, or less frequently, sadness or depression. Given that previous studies of anxiety have indicated that a variety of cognitive errors or distortions can lead to anxiety and other types of distress (Beck, Emery, & Greenberg, 1985), it would be expected that patients with delusions who have excessive or inappropriate anxiety would show the same kind of errors. In fact, we have found that these patients' experience of anxiety frequently is preceded by cognitive distortions. Of course, this anxiety may, at times, be based on realistic worries, such as the fear of rehospitalization or rejection by other people.

Catastrophizing

Anxiety has been observed at all stages of delusion formation and maintenance (Startup, et al., 2007). Prospective and retrospective studies indicate that symptoms of anxiety, depression, and irritability precede the onset of delusions and hallucinations by 2–4 weeks (Birchwood, Macmillan, & Smith, 1992). Catastrophizing (anticipating or imagining unrealistically bad outcomes of present concerns) is a thinking problem characteristic of patients with acute or chronic anxiety (Ellis, 1962; Beck, 1963; Beck et al., 1985). Since many patients with schizophrenia show a high level of anxiety (Steer, Kumar, Pinninti, & Beck, 2003), Startup et al. predicted that they would show this cognitive error. In a study of patients with schizophrenia, compared to normal control-group participants, Startup et al. found that a high proportion (68%) of the patients had elevated levels of worry and anxiety. On a catastrophizing test similar to the "downward arrow" technique, the "worst outcome" of the test was more likely to occur in patients with delusions than in controls. Also, there were "greater leaps between each of their steps" and "incorporat[ion of] a greater number of extraordinary possibilities" (Startup et al., 2007, p. 533) in the patient group when compared to normal controls. Further, the patient group assigned a greater likelihood to the catastrophic events' ever occurring. The degree of these patients' distress as well as the persistence of their delusions were related to their catastrophizing.

Clinical cases illustrate not only that catastrophizing but also that *elaboration of exaggerated fears* differentiate delusional from nondelusional thinking. A socially phobic person may feel conspicuous or even self-conscious in a crowd. She thinks that others direct their attention toward her because of, say, some presumed oddity in her appearance, and she has a negative image of how others perceive her (Clark & Wells, 1995). For the patient with persecutory delusions, however, these circumstances are more catastrophic because he believes that others have malicious intentions toward him. He not only attributes malice to others, but he believes he has been singled out—that others have a preexisting bias against him. Indeed, they have a plan to watch him, send coded signs, and torment him (*personalizing* and *intentionalizing biases*). In succession, the catastrophizing proceeds from "They *may* be watching me" to "They *are* watching me." The believability that this individual attaches to this interpretation increases as the probabilities increase from "possible" to "likely" to "definite." Also, he expects the worst possible outcome to other threats such as his actions being monitored and manipulated. This progression in the degree of conviction is enhanced by the various biases: emotion-based reasoning, confirmation bias, bias against disconfirmation, selective abstraction, and overgeneralization. The delusional catastrophizing is more distressing than in generalized anxiety disorder because of the egocentric bias and attribution of negative intention.

Thinking Out of Context

Thinking out of context is a component of various cognitive errors such as *selective abstraction, overgeneralization,* and *dichotomous (extreme,* or *all-or-nothing) thinking.* Recognition of this thinking problem has a long history dating back to clinical observations and further documentation in experiments by Chapman and Chapman (1973a). In selective abstraction and overgeneralization a conclusion is based on a salient (to the person) detail or event to the exclusion of overall characteristics of the situation that would lead to a different conclusion. For example, a patient with schizophrenia received a critical comment from her supervisor. Even though the rest of the supervisor's comments were favorable and the critical comment was very clearly intended to help the patient, she took the comment out of context and concluded, "She wants to get me fired."

Thinking out of context also occurs in an ahistorical perspective, such as when an individual bases a broad conclusion on an immediate event without taking into account other *previous* events that would contradict it: Words such as *never* and *always* are symptomatic of this error (as well as an expression of dichotomous thinking). A patient with schizophrenia who heard static in a telephone conversation on one occasion, for example, concluded, "They are *always* interfering with my calls." Abnormal out-of-context reasoning is also obvious in self-referential thinking. A patient with psychosis heard the sound of a loud horn in busy traffic and concluded that somebody was sending him a message. The search for threats or other kinds of relevant signs in the environment prompts patients to focus on the specific detail, refer it to themselves, and disregard the setting. Thinking out of context may be a survival mechanism at times. When a specific event that could be a real threat occurs, it is better to focus on it, mobilize now, and then correct a false impression when there is time later to review the entire situation. In persecutory delusions, however, patients' sense of danger is so generalized that they misidentify safe situations as threatening *and* do not review the misidentifications and make the necessary corrections.

The general tendency of patients with schizophrenia to jump to conclusions is also related to thinking out of context. As indicated by clinical observations and experiments, patients simply do not take in sufficient data to arrive at reasonable conclusions, possibly reflecting a lack of motivation to make a sustained effort: These patients "run out of steam" and give up rather than looking for more data. Alternatively, since these patients have an accentuated self-certainty set, they are overconfident in their conclusions at an earlier stage than are other people. Another cognitive error is dichotomous (or all-or-nothing) thinking, especially in emotionally charged situations. It may be easier to think in extreme terms than to carefully parse out the mitigating or moderating aspects of a situation.

Chapman and Chapman (1973a) have shown that patients with schizophrenia make inappropriate responses to test instructions by selecting the more familiar but incorrect options in preference to the less salient but correct response. When asked to select a word that is similar to a stimulus word, for example, they are prone to choose incorrectly a word that is a strong associate, but not similar, to the stimulus word. For example, they are likely to select a common (i.e., dominant) but wrong associate such as "fish" in response to the stimulus word "gold" instead of the weaker but correct associate "steel." They appear to have difficulty in "disattending" to a strong (common) but inappropriate association when presented with several response alternatives. The authors concluded that patients with schizophrenia show an accentuation of normal biases; that is, normals may make the same errors (particularly under cognitive load) but to a much lesser degree. Patients' responses in these experiments also can be related to jumping to conclusions—they selected the first response that came to mind and failed to consider the rest of the data. Because these patients evidently do not reflect on the validity of their responses, they consequently don't correct them. Alternatively, they have difficulty in inhibiting the easy response that might occur first but is rapidly corrected by normals before they provide their answer to the question. Jumping to conclusions may be related to poor attention span—patients may have difficulty in keeping the instructions "online" and searching for alternative (correct) words (Broome et al., 2007a).

Taken together, the clinical and experimental findings identify the factors involved in the patients' compromised decision making. In the experiments, patients with schizophrenia show a "normal bias," such as incorrectly selecting the more salient associates. But unlike normals, these patients have difficulty in inhibiting this initial spontaneous response. Their responses, both experimental and clinical, can be attributed to "resource sparing." In the experiments, patients do not make the effort to inhibit and examine their initial impression, take into account the total context, and consider alternatives. With coaching, however, patients do show the capacity to search for a more appropriate response.

Inadequate Cognitive Processing

The literature has shown that patients with schizophrenia do not process information adequately and also fail to correct erroneous interpretations. As pointed out by Gilbert and Gill (2000), there is a universal tendency to make practically instantaneous interpretations that are subsequently evaluated and corrected if they appear to be false—without the individuals being very much aware of the appraisal and correction. However, this normal falsification process (which Gilbert labels the "Spinoza Effect") is nullified under cognitive load; thus, a false interpretation remains accepted (as though it were true). Patients with delusions react to everyday situations like normal patients under cognitive load. The biased interpretations remain unevaluated and therefore accepted. These patients cannot integrate all of the relevant information in a situation. Moreover, they do not have sufficient cognitive resources to review an initial erroneous response and to process additional information relating to the context and consider alternative explanations. Furthermore, the hypersalient delusional beliefs tend to fixate their holders' attention on the initial delusional interpretation. This phenomenon may be analogous to the experience of patients with panic disorder, who can consider alternative explanations for their catastrophic misinterpretations with relative ease within the security of the therapist's office; in situations that trigger anxiety, however, their attention becomes fixated on danger (e.g., having a heart attack, losing control, fainting) and their ability to consider alternative explanations for their symptoms is severely compromised.

Another factor leading to the acceptance of faulty conclusions is a defective "self-monitor" (Frith, 1987, 1992), whereby the patient is less aware of his or her interpretations and actions. In support of this possibility, an experimental study (Frith & Done, 1989a) observed that patients with schizophrenia were less likely to correct errors on a tracking task, suggesting an impairment in their ability to monitor and modify their judgments.

Categorical Thinking

The homogeneous image of "the enemy" reflects a more general disposition to engage in categorical thinking. Patients create an imaginary category to define the persecutory agents and then apply it vigorously to "suspicious" individuals. The paranoid category may be broad with loose boundaries (e.g., Philadelphia police) or narrow and well defined (e.g., coworkers, family members). Once the category is created, however, the individual characteristics of the identified persecutors are blended into the category. The same categorical thinking extends to invisible entities such as the devil, spirits, or dead relatives. When the image of the defined entity has been created, patients either "see" them or feel their invisible influence.

BELIEF SYSTEMS

As indicated previously, patients with paranoid delusions have a "they versus me" orientation, which is expressed in the content of their delusions, their biased explanations of specific and generally innocuous events, selective focus on presumably hostile external sources, hypervigilance, and suspiciousness. People normally are keyed into situations by a master plan that signifies either "good for me" or "bad for me" (Clark et al., 1999), but in paranoid states this orientation is fixed on misidentifying adverse external influences (just as in mania, patients are oriented to reward and in depression, to loss). The internal representations of the self and others consist of beliefs such as "Everyone is against me" or "I am controlled by external forces." When the belief is activated, it shapes the interpretation of stimuli according to its content. Thus, a patient's interpretation of a yellow car could be "The Mafia is following me."

Patients' internal representations of the self can vary from weak, helpless, and powerless to powerful (as in patients with grandiose paranoia). Patients who believe that their minds are permeable, however, may feel vulnerable to anyone, powerful or not. The common denominator across patients' paranoid delusions is a belief in the negative intentions of the external agent *and* their own vulnerability. Because any external stimulus could be a sign of threat, it needs to be surveilled. False negatives are dangerous, and maximizing false positives through overattention to details and over-interpreting minimizes false negatives. To the degree that the delusional beliefs control information processing, they direct the focus of attention and provide patients with explanations for their adverse experience. The resulting external focus leads patients to search for and "discover" signs that are coherent with their specific delusional schemas—the *confirmation bias*. A belief that other people are hostile to them, for example, will focus their attention on indistinct stimuli such as other peoples' conversations, whereupon the patients will "hear" disparaging comments (self-referential bias).

These ideas of reference are apparently on a continuum with auditory hallucinations (see Chapter 4). Highly charged beliefs are resistant to change, even when decisive disconfirming evidence (antidisconfirmatory bias) is presented (Woodward et al., 2006). The hypersalient beliefs also provide the explanations for (or, actually, misinterpretations of) various undesirable, unexpected, or unintentional physical, emotional, or mental experiences. The precise nature of the explanations depends, to some extent, on the specific power attributed to the agent. Patients' focus on their mental and bodily sensations maintains the malevolent explanations. Thus, a vicious cycle is experienced. The more a patient focuses on a lump in his or her throat, for example, the more he or she thinks of the agent using electromagnetic power to produce the lump—leading, of course, to increased attention to the sensation.

DEVELOPMENT AND FORMATION OF PERSECUTORY DELUSIONS

Delusions may arise through a number of different mechanisms. First, a persecutory delusion may represent the progressive elaboration of a fear of being observed or harmed in some way. Most of the persecutory delusions originate this way. Second, the delusion may represent the transformation of the self-image developed prior to the onset of the overt psychosis. A patient who had previously regarded himself as defective and weak, for example, developed the delusion that he was subhuman. Third, a grandiose delusion may develop as a compensation for an underlying sense of loneliness, unworthiness, evil, incompetence, or powerlessness.

Many clinical and behavioral signs may be apparent prior to the development of persecutory delusions. The changes in behavior, such as withdrawal from other people and avoiding certain situations, are often a manifestation of a patient's increasing suspiciousness of other people's motives and the assumption that these people are, in some way, disposed to harm him or her.

Suspiciousness

Detecting the earliest signs of others' harmful intentions is a crucial survival strategy that becomes exaggerated in suspicious individuals. These individuals actively scan other people's expressions or behavior for signs of malevolent intent, may read signs of ill will or deception in other people's bland or benign expressions, and may even project a prefabricated malevolent image onto their faces or entire personage. Driving the suspiciousness is an intense concern about being diminished, manipulated, or physically harmed. Accompanying this negative anticipation is an aggressive vigilance for any evidence of hostile intentions in other people's actions.

These individuals also have a confirmatory bias—that is, they search for and integrate evidence that will confirm their belief in others' negative intensions and ignore or dismiss contradictory evidence. As pointed out by Dudley and Over (2003), searching for confirmatory rather than disconfirmatory cues is generally the safest (and preferred) strategy when faced with *real* danger. But imaginary dangers will invoke the same biases. Chronic suspiciousness and the ultimate progression into paranoid thinking represent the exaggeration of this strategy for coping with perceived malevolence.

Suspicious individuals may be contrasted with socially anxious individuals, whose main fear is that their own supposed inadequate or socially unacceptable characteristics will be exposed. Thus, the main focus of people with social phobias is on their presumed inadequate self-presentation, and their goal is to relieve their social anxiety. If they do look at others, it is to find a friendly face, to *disconfirm* that they are in danger of being diminished in some way.

Similarly, obsessive checkers (who have obsessive–compulsive disorder) will check repeatedly to disconfirm that they have made a serious error, such as having left the oven on. Individuals with a suspicious mindset, in contrast, look for signs to *confirm* their belief that others are hostile to them. They believe they need to be hypervigilant because missing the signs of malevolence would endanger them. Although suspicious and socially anxious people are hypersensitive to the *possibility* of being watched, disparaged, or ridiculed, suspicious individuals may extend their worry to being physically harmed. Consequently, suspicious persons cope with the supposed danger by preparing to defend themselves and possibly counterattack, whereas the socially anxious individuals attempt either to compensate for, or to disguise, their supposed social inadequacies (see Table 3.1).

As the suspiciousness spreads, it may progress into a paranoid delusion. Patients no longer think that other people *may* have hostile motives; now they *know* they have hostile motives. The prototype of malevolent others may include only a few individuals (e.g., coworkers) or may extend to an entire group (e.g., foreigners, aliens). Suspiciousness about being observed, manipulated, or harmed may crystallize into delusions of being followed, controlled, or persecuted.

TABLE 3.1. Comparison of Suspiciousness and Anxiety

	Suspiciousness	Socially anxious
Focus	Others' intentions	Self-presentation
Internal representation	Others as hostile	Self as inadequate
Vigilance	Malevolent signs	Signs of acceptance
Bias	Confirm hostility	Disconfirm hostility

Formation of a Persecutory Delusion

Although it may be difficult to determine the remote antecedents of persecutory delusions, we can frequently pinpoint the proximal factors. The sequence typically starts with a fear or worry. A common fear is the anticipation of retaliation for having done something that might offend another person or group. For example, a patient reported observing a rash of illegal gambling to the authorities. She subsequently had the thought: "Suppose the Mafia finds out that I made the report." She then began to imagine scenes of the Mafia attacking her. She started to look for (and find) evidence to support this notion. She decided that cars honking their horns, shady-looking characters outside her apartment, and unexplained noises in the apartment were signals from the Mafia that they were out to get her. When she saw a yellow car, it meant to her that the Mafia regarded her as "yellow" (cowardly). Her ideas changed from "This *could* happen" to "This *is* happening."

A similar sequence was established more precisely in the case of a man who reported drug dealers to the police. He subsequently saw a news article implicating several policemen as members of a drug ring. He had the thought: "The crooked cops could have spread the word around [about me] to the other cops." He then started to speculate that the entire police force was in cahoots with the drug dealers. He became increasingly worried about this possibility and began to focus on police cars in town to ascertain whether they were following him. He stared at the policemen in the vehicles, and they apparently returned the stare. If he saw the same person in two different places, he decided that he was a plainclothes man observing him. Eventually he had enough (supposedly) confirmatory material to formulate a conspiracy theory. By this time he believed that many ordinarily appearing vehicles were unmarked police cars.

The steps in the formation of this delusion can be outlined as follows:

1. *Fear* that police would retaliate against him for reporting the drug dealers.
2. *Intentionalizing bias:* Elaboration of conspiracy theory after the news of police involvement in the drug dealing; projection of hostile intent onto police generally.
3. *Attentional bias:* Selective focus on police cars and individuals in his environment.
4. *Self-referential (personalizing) bias:* Interpreted irrelevant events as indicators of police animosity.
5. *Confirmatory bias:* Integrated each supposed example of the police following him into his theory, ignored the context, and was oblivious to alternative explanations (antidisconfirmatory bias).
6. *Capitalizing on coincidence:* The patient saw the same individual initially when shopping at a grocery store and later when attending a reception at his church. This coincidence indicated to him that the person was a police officer who was observing him.
7. *Enhancing the similarity of "persecutors":* As the patient developed a mental representation of the "conspirators," an increasing number of individuals began to fit this image.
8. *"Connecting the dots":* Putting together all this evidence, the patient became convinced that he was surrounded by police who intended to harass him and, perhaps, to harm him. The delusion was consolidated.

The various strategies that patients employ in order to reduce their anxiety—for example, avoiding "hot situations" that might provoke their fears—deprive them of the possibility of receiving corrective feedback. The fact that neutralizing these avoidances (safety behaviors) through therapy can substantially undercut the delusional thinking indicates that these patients' have some capacity for reality testing.

GRANDIOSE DELUSIONS

In contrast to patients with persecutory delusions, patients with grandiose delusions are focused on *self-fulfillment* and, for the most part, detachment from others' input, often in a solipsistic way. Some of these patients, however, may feel persecuted when others challenge or refuse to accept their claims to specialness. Unlike the defensive orientation of patients with paranoid delusions ("they vs. me"), these patients are oriented to inflating their self-esteem (Smith, Freeman, & Kuipers, 2005). The content of their self-centered beliefs consists of unrealistic self-inflation: "I'm king of the universe"; "I'm the richest man in the world"; "I'm the greatest scientist"; "I have universal power." Many of these patients are so wrapped up in their grandiose ideas that they are oblivious to negative feedback or reframe it as confirmation of their delusions (Smith et al.).

Typically, these patients do not process environmental cues that are discrepant with their presumed status (Moritz & Woodward, 2006). When confronted with such discrepancies, they may provide a plausible-sounding rationalization. A patient, for example, believed that he was the richest man in New York. When asked what he was doing in a mental hospital, he responded, "Why, I own the hospital." These patients do pay attention to the external world to the extent that it supports their grandiose belief and frequently believe that others share their view of themselves. Although patients with paranoia generally maintain their premorbid identity, patients with grandiose delusions frequently assume a grand identity that is the opposite of their real self: omnipotent in place of weak; rich instead of poor; popular rather than socially isolated. A homeless woman, for example, believed that she was a royal princess. A shy, withdrawn bookkeeper believed that he was a famous rock star. A mentally retarded patient pictured himself as a great mathematician. The new identities are often bizarre. An African American man thought that he was President Carter. A woman believed that she was Jesus.

In many cases, the new identity seems to be the expression of a previous wish-fulfilling fantasy. A pre-psychosis Walter Mitty–type daydream is expanded and refined: A poor man imagines himself to be wealthy. The daydream or image gradually becomes transformed into a delusion as the patient increasingly believes in its reality. Sometimes a grandiose delusion may progress quickly from a *thought* that the patient finds reassuring or gratifying to a *belief* that maintains this level of relief. A patient had a thought: "I have suffered a great deal" (painful), "therefore, I *am* Jesus" (satisfying). The progression of "I think, therefore I am" was automatic, without reflection. The patient remained unaware of the implausibility of this notion. The content of the delusions often reflects patients' predelusional beliefs. Belief in paranormal phenomena, for example, leads to delusions about mind reading, telepathy, and alien possession. Strongly held religious beliefs, likewise, provide the substrate for delusions about God and the devil. One patient, Simon, for example, initially experienced a wish-fulfilling fantasy of being the Good Lord as a way of relieving his sense of guilt over past "sins" and also to compensate for a sense of total powerlessness. He then began to reify the fantasy, that is, to accept it as reality. Thus, the original fantasy or daydream became a delusion.

The formulation of the stages in the development of the grandiose delusion, for the most part, is based on retrospective accounts from patients. Typically, the precursor of the delusion is the formation of the patient's self-image as socially undesirable, demeaned, powerless. Of course, the development of this image may be facilitated by the negative response of the patients' social group to his or her atypical withdrawal and peculiar behavior. The patient next begins to have wish-fulfilling daydreams of being the extreme opposite of how he perceives him- or herself. He or she places the highest value on being powerful, admired, and perfect. Thus, the individual who regarded him- or herself as defective, rejected, and powerless starts to daydream of being perfect, universally worshipped, and omnipotent—say, as God or Jesus. Because of the tendency of these individuals to reify their dreams and fantasies, the idealized self-image becomes a reality to them.

Many of the delusions are so grandiose that they appear to set patients apart from the rest of their social group. Interestingly, these extravagant self-images of being God, Jesus, a royal princess, or president of the United States are generally not accompanied by the feelings of excitement or power that would be generated by such an elevated status. In fact, gentle questioning often reveals feelings of loneliness and distress.

Consider the following condensed interview with Simon:

THERAPIST: Can you tell me your name?

PATIENT: I'm the Lord, king of the universe.

THERAPIST: How do you feel—being God?

PATIENT: Pretty powerful, I guess.

THERAPIST: Any downside to being God?

PATIENT: I guess I'm so high up, I don't have anyone to talk to.

THERAPIST: How does that make you feel?

PATIENT: Sort of lonely, I guess.

THERAPIST: How long have you felt lonely?

PATIENT: I suppose—all my life.

Although the patient's delusions may be drawn from beliefs that are current in his or her own subculture, the other members of the group generally label the thinking as delusional because of its exaggerated egocentricity and idiosyncratic features as well as the totality of the patient's behavior, which is considered odd or strange. Although members of the patient's group may strongly believe in God or the devil, they regard the patient's claim that he or she is God as a sign that the person is "crazy."

It is not surprising that some patients who enhance their sense of power or importance through grandiose delusions find that other people do not show them the kind of respect to which they believe they are entitled, or may even oppose their influence. Typically, these patients have fantasies of creating great works of poetry or art, inventing important innovations, or acquiring high status. When they do not get the positive feedback that they expect, their shaky self-esteem is threatened and they are driven to find face-saving explanations for these rebuffs. If they are expecting admiration, they may latch onto the notion that certain individuals are jealous of them and, for example, are spreading malicious lies about them, or they may jump to the conclusion that a specific individual or group of individuals has stolen their ideas. Of course, the more they accuse others of conspiring against them, the more they are dismissed as "crackpots" or "crazy." This negative response, of course, only confirms their belief that others are plotting against them. Sometimes, the explanations have a bizarre twist. Kingdon and Turkington (1994) describe a patient passed over for a promotion who concluded that other employees had conspired to influence him through rays directed at him by satellite.

ANOMALOUS EXPERIENCES
AND DELUSIONS OF CONTROL

The anomalous symptoms in psychosis, such as thought insertion, thought capture, and thought broadcasting, are often considered pathognomic features of schizophrenia (American Psychiatric Association, 2000). Other beliefs concerning external control of the body or mind (passivity or control delusions) are also related to this group of symptoms (American Psychiatric Association). Hallucinations, which are included in the group of first-rank symptoms (Schneider, 1959) and share many features with anomalous symptoms, are covered in detail in Chapter 4. In particular, hallucinations appear to be on a continuum with thought insertion. In recognition of the common features of the anomalous symptoms, Linney and Peters (2007) have assigned them the label of *interference symptoms*—the imagined influence of paranormal phenomena on the workings of the mind. They also include mind reading, which is not included in the Schneiderian list.

Interference symptoms also include the belief that an inhibition of speech or action is due to outside influences.

Maher (1988) considered these symptoms to be the products of patients' efforts to make sense of anomalous mental experiences, such as thought blockage, and he explained these symptoms as the result of *normal explanations for anomalous experiences*. A different formulation is based on the thesis that these symptoms result from the *anomalous interpretation of normal experiences*. Patients provide paranormal explanations to account for unwanted, unexpected, or puzzling mental, emotional, or physical experiences.

In thought insertion, one of the more common interference phenomena, a thought seems different in quality and content from the patient's usual stream of consciousness and thus is perceived as alien. These patients have been found to experience an unusual number of intrusive thoughts (Linney & Peters, 2007) and at times the intrusions are believed to originate elsewhere. Often the thought is similar to the obsessions in obsessive–compulsive disorder. In that disorder, the intrusion is recognized as internally generated, however. In schizophrenia, because the thought is intrusive—that is, seemingly *forced* into patients' minds and often of an unusual or aversive content ("I could never have thoughts like that")—an external explanation is given (i.e., an invasion from an external source). Similarly, thought blockage, which occurs when there is interference with the flow of ideas, may seem strange and consequently is attributed to "thought capture" by outside individuals or obscure powers. Mind reading, or thought projection, may occur when a patient hears another person say something similar to what the patient has been thinking (a word, a subject, or a theme). Because these patients appear to be predisposed to make connections among random events, they interpret coincidences as having special meaning—in this instance, as due to the other person reading his or her thoughts. Alternatively, patients may conclude that other people put thoughts in their head or that they have projected their thought into other people's heads.

One common denominator in these anomalous symptoms seems to be the experience that, when feeling self-conscious and/or socially anxious, these patients feel not only vulnerable but also exposed: Their thoughts seem to be discernable by other people or may be broadcast to them. A few patients believe generally that others can read their minds in all situations. One patient, for example, giggled when questioned by doctors. He believed that they were playing a game with him since they "obviously" knew what he was thinking without having to ask. Patients are likely to experience the symptoms when they are in situations that they consider threatening. A patient, for example, believed that other people could read his mind only when he was in a crowded place, such as a subway, where he felt he was under close observation. Patients are especially vulnerable when their resources are low due to insufficient sleep, stress, or anxiety. A series of overwhelming challenges may produce the same effect. Thus, the summation of stressors or exposure to a situation that impinges on a particularly sensitive vulnerability can suffice to activate these symptoms.

An important mechanism in the generation of most anomalous symptoms is the patient's reliance on subjective states (or "internal signals") to determine the meaning and origin of feelings, thoughts, and actions. If a feeling (e.g., a sense of depersonalization or a feeling of depression or anxiety) or a thought seems strange, unfamiliar, or unwanted, it is not recognized as "mine" and therefore is believed to originate elsewhere. It is as though the threshold for identifying an experience as "not me" or "not mine" is very low. Similarly, if a behavior feels as though it is unintended, it is similarly disowned.

Many of these patients generally experience an "external locus of control." They are prone to draw on beliefs of external control to explain involuntary or apparently unintended movements ("psychokinesis"). A patient, for example, had a startle reaction when a door slammed. She attributed her sudden stiffening to the power of some hidden person. Another patient who was upset because she was having a problem dressing herself in time for an important appointment had the thought, "My father is hypnotizing me." Similarly, a loss of positive feeling or a surge of anxiety may be attributed to the deliberate manipulation of other individuals. Spontaneous genital sensations may be attributed to sexual advances by a remote individual.

Delusions of being controlled, in general, may be viewed as including the anomalous symptoms, the common denominator being patients' proneness to ascribe the cause of particular unwanted or unfamiliar subjective physical experiences to the manipulations of other individuals or entities. Sometimes the supposed source of control may be a group of individuals or some undefined entity. A patient, for example, ascribed his noneating and nonparticipation in group activities to the work of a "Superior World." When he started to eat again and became more active, he believed that it was due to the intervention by the Superior World. A possible mechanism underlying the control/interference phenomena could be a mismatch between patients' expectancy and their subjective experience. According to this thesis, patients are presumed to have rigid expectations of events *not happening* (insertions, "involuntary" or impaired movements, hallucinations, mental blocking). When they experience a discrepancy between this "null expectation" and the subjective feedback (perhaps a feeling of surprise or puzzlement), the patient experiences the discrepant experience as foreign (Blakemore, Wolpert, & Frith, 2000).

Certain biases that occur in paranormal explanations are essentially the same as in other kinds of delusional thinking:

1. The *egocentric bias*: Patients believe that others' attention is focused on them.
2. The *externalizing or attributional bias*: Patients believe that certain internal experiences are caused by external forces. Thus, intrusive thoughts and thought blocking are attributed to the influence of outsiders. The presumed mechanisms are thought insertion and thought capture.
3. The *intentionalizing bias* is present with delusions of control but not always in mind reading. This external explanatory bias is so strong in these cases that it overrides (displaces) more normal (internal) explanations. In addition, reality testing for hypersalient ideas is defective.

Origin of Anomalous Delusions

These patients are prone to explain certain experiences, such as loss of train of thought, mental blocking, or coincidences, in terms of paranormal processes in preference to the more obvious normal explanations. Some of these paranormal explanations (e.g., mind reading, psychokinesis) are based on beliefs entertained by a significant segment of the population (Lawrence & Peters, 2004). Others seem to be idiosyncratic to patients with schizophrenia (e.g., thought capture). Many of the anomalous symptoms are simply explanations drawn from patients' repertoire of premorbid paranormal beliefs and superstitions. The more popular of the paranormal beliefs are included under the lists of "magical" beliefs (Eckblad & Chapman, 1983) or "delusions" (Peters, Joseph, & Garety, 1999; Stefanis et al., 2002).

Individuals who receive the diagnosis of "positive schizotype" (i.e., have a number of attenuated positive symptoms of schizophrenia) endorse a large percentage of these magical or paranormal beliefs. Because a proportion of these transition into psychosis (see Kwapil, Miller, Zinser, Chapman, & Chapman, 1997), this group of individuals can provide some insight into the relation of paranormal ideas to delusions. Magical and paranormal beliefs are common among schizotypal individuals, and when they lapse into psychosis, they draw on these beliefs to explain what seems to them to be mental or physical aberrations—and they do so in the same logical way that others may come up with a psychological or medical explanation. They have many features in common with patients with psychosis who have the anomalous or control symptoms. They engage in making causal connections between random events and coincidences, show similar loosening of associations on various tests, and seem to have a predilection for looking for hidden meanings in random events. The crucial common characteristic is that these meanings refer to themselves. The fixation on paranormal explanations shows self-referential thinking, vulnerability, and externalized explanations.

There probably is no sharp dividing line between the paranormal thinking of individuals with severe schizotypal personality disorder and those who have transitioned into schizophrenia. Patients with schizophrenia lack insight or awareness that these explanations are unreasonable and thus adhere to them despite confrontation with normal explanations for their experiences. Their paranormal explanations have an adverse impact on the patients' behavior and emotion. These interpretations occur far more frequently in the patients with schizophrenia and cause more distress than in the schizotypal group and are more frequently woven into a persecutory delusion. They resort to safety behavior such as avoiding the provocative situations or engaging in ritual behavior to ward off the influences of paranormal or mystical forces. Examples of interference beliefs are provided in Table 3.2.

TABLE 3.2. Examples of Explanations in Anomalous and Control Delusions

Event	Explanation
Thought: "You are bogus."	"Someone put it there."
Mind goes blank.	"They are messing with my mind."
Thinks of a word and then somebody says it.	"He is reading my mind."
Trouble lifting heavy object.	"Spirits have drained my strength."
Sudden dysphoria.	"They removed my pleasure."
Feeling anxious.	"They are controlling my feelings."

Patients' underlying self-representation is an image of being the vulnerable object of the intrusions, control, and interference by outside individuals or forces. These external entities generally are viewed as *intentionally* encroaching on patients' vital functions. But sometimes, as in mind reading, the supposed transparency of patients' thinking may be sufficient to expose them to whomever is nearby. An example is the patient who believed that other passengers on the subway train knew what he was thinking.

Linney and Peters (2007) showed that patients with schizophrenia with one or more of these interference symptoms had more symptoms than did other patients with psychosis who did not experience interference: increased cognitive intrusions, more negative interpretations of cognitive intrusions, and lower cognitive control. Moreover, on a card trick thought interference was significantly associated with appraisals regarding permeability of the mind and conspiracy. Patients with thought interference were also more likely to attribute self-generated words to an external source than were patients with psychosis but no thought interference.

Freeman, Garety, McGuire, and Kuipers (2005) examined paranormal beliefs in the context of biases in decision making. In an analog study of college students, they found that individuals who showed a confirmation rather than a disconfirmation style in arriving at a solution to an arithmetic-type problem also showed haste in data gathering (i.e., jumping to conclusions), diminished consideration of alternative solutions, and *greater endorsement of paranormal beliefs*. A recent study by Broome et al. (2007a) showed that the jumping-to-conclusions style was associated with impaired attention span. Brugger (2001) examined paranormal thinking within a broader framework that incorporated neurophysiological dysfunction. First, he attributed the tendency of human beings to see order when there actually is disorder (or randomness) to a bias of the perceptual–cognitive system. He demonstrated that the exaggerated tendencies to see patterns where there are none and to accept paranormal beliefs are characteristic of individuals whom he labeled as "believers." These individuals are also more likely than controls to attribute paranormal causation to coincidences. Ultimately, he attributed the detection of meaning-laden patterns to a functional asymmetry of cerebral functions, specifically the right cerebral hemisphere. Also, he found that the loose associative thinking characteristic of right-hemisphere bias is present to a greater extent in the productions of believers in the paranormal and in individuals with acute schizophrenia.

As a clinical documentation for his theory, Brugger (2001) cites the psychotic experiences of the Swedish writer and playwright August Strindberg. Already in the throes of persecutory delusions, Strindberg would see meaningful connections in the placement of furniture in a hotel room, twigs and sticks on the ground, and in hearing a clap of thunder while glancing at the word *thunder* in a section of the Bible. Patients may perceive such connections or coincidences as reflections of some mystical, surreal, or supernatural influence. Finally, Brugger attributes the loose associations of thought disorder to the hyperfunction of the right hemisphere, which is responsible for crude processing as well as creative thinking. (The left hemisphere, on the other hand, has a functional specialization for linguistic processing.) Following Brugger's reasoning, paranormal beliefs and attributions, far-fetched connections, loose and disinhibited associations, and loss of ego boundaries would fit together as correlates of dysfunction.

Anomalous experiences are reported not only by patients with psychosis but also in individuals who have not sought professional help. Brett et al. (2007) analyzed the interviewer-derived reports from both patients with schizophrenia and a group who had anomalous experiences for at least 5 years but did not seek or warrant treatment. This nonclinical group reported the same range of anomalous experiences as the clinical group but with less frequency or intensity. A key differentiating factor was that the patients attributed their experiences to interference by external agents, whereas the nonclinical individuals understood their experiences as part of meaningful spiritual system.

SUMMARY

We have presented a cognitive model of delusions based on a phenomenological analysis of the characteristics of schizophrenic delusions and their development. We have attempted to delineate the information-processing biases and the content of antecedent belief systems, which may act in concert to enhance psychological vulnerability to the development of paranoia and delusions that are compensatory in nature. Construing delusions within a cognitive framework allows them to be understood in terms of familiar concepts, such as dysfunctional beliefs, cognitive distortions, and attentional bias. This conceptualization provides the kind of understanding that facilitates psychotherapeutic interventions and can also be extended to account for other delusions such as thought broadcasting or insertion and still more bizarre beliefs such as those captured in the Capgras and Cotard delusions (Ramachandran & Blakeslee, 1998).

Further systematic study of the phenomenology of delusions as well as experimental approaches are necessary to expand (and validate) the cognitive formulations presented in this chapter. For example, how frequently do specific biases (egocentrism, externalizing, and intentionalizing) occur? What is the natural history of the development of the delusions? Do grandiose delusions always begin with a wish-fulfilling daydream? Tests are needed to assess various biases and also to evaluate the defective reality testing of psychologically meaningful material.

A portion of this chapter is adapted from Beck and Rector (2002). Copyright 2002 by Springer Publishing. Reprinted by permission.

CHAPTER 4

A Cognitive Conceptualization
of Auditory Hallucinations

A 28-year-old white male was referred to the clinic for treatment after having had two hospitalizations. At the time of admission, he was moderately depressed and complained of hearing voices through the ventilator in the office. The period of time leading up to his psychosis was marked by two severe depressive episodes, during which he was suicidal and required hospitalization. During one of these episodes, he thought he heard his father's voice criticizing him and calling him a *fag* and a *queer*. Subsequently, he heard voices wherever he went, and they gradually became transformed into the voice of a 12-year-old and an 6-year-old. These voices commented between themselves on what a weakling he was and also continued to call him names such as *fruit, faggot,* and *queer.* Some clues to the origin of the content of the voices were evident in his past history. His father, who was very large and athletic, disparaged him because of his poor athletic ability. He himself was critical of his awkwardness and general ineptitude. When he was around 6 years old, a cousin of his was given the job of babysitting him. At this point, the older boy seduced him. This experience apparently fixed in the young boy's mind that he was homosexual, although he did not actually experience homosexual feelings or urges. In the hallucinations, the 12-year-old voice and the 6-year-old voice "ganged up" to depreciate the patient. He believed that these unidentified individuals had control over his mind, could read his thoughts, and could control his actions. He also found that the harder he tried to fight against the voices, the stronger they became.

This patient illustrates how early traumatic events may be integrated in such a way as to appear in the form of hallucinations. He developed a negative self-image, based on his father's criticisms, of being inferior, inadequate, and weak. His traumatic experience with the babysitter fixed this notion (and a sense of helplessness). His negative view of himself was expressed in self-demeaning ideas of being a "fag" and a "queer." These thoughts became perceptionalized—that is, they crossed the auditory threshold (as described later in this chapter). The therapist used a variety of strategies to help the patient deal with the voices (as described in Chapter 10). One technique was to demonstrate that the voices are not omnipotent and are controllable. The therapist also demonstrated how the content of the voices reflected the patient's own thoughts and could be dealt with similarly to the "automatic thoughts" in depression.

Hallucinations have been regarded as a sign of mental illness for only the past 200 years. Prior to that time, they were considered to be messages from God (divine intervention) or from the devil (demonic possession). Interestingly, many contemporary patients with schizophrenia also regard them as communications from one or the other of these supernatural entities. Hallucinations are generally defined as perceptual experiences in the absence of external stimulation; they occur in the wakeful state (unlike dreaming) and are not under voluntary control (unlike daydreaming). They are often associated with the use of psychostimulants or with various mental disorders. The auditory hallucinations associated with schizophrenia are distinguished from "normal" hallucinations by the patient's delusional beliefs regarding their origin (e.g., from an external agent or from a device implanted in the brain).

A full understanding of this phenomenon has to contend with the diversity of the opinions regarding its nature and causes. Hallucinations that occur in either a normal or abnormal context may involve any of the sensory modalities: hearing, seeing, touching, smelling or tasting. Auditory hallucinations in the context of schizophrenia have been extensively studied from diverse perspectives: cultural, genetic, anatomical, neurochemical, and psychological. With the enormous advances in neurochemistry and neuroimaging, we have gained new insights into the biological nature of hallucinations (see Chapter 2). The revolution in the biological approaches to schizophrenia has provided additional understanding of its basic neurochemistry. In addition to these advances, however, a *silent revolution* has occurred in the cognitive approaches to the phenomenology of schizophrenia. The success of cognitive interventions, in fact, has provided the major stimulus to understanding the cognitive mechanisms that are involved in the production of hallucinations.

In this chapter, we draw upon current neuropsychology literature as well as the phenomenological accounts from patients in psychotherapy as the basis for formulating a cognitive model of auditory hallucinations. The first part of this chapter focuses on the phenomenological aspects of hallucinations. Next, the precursors and factors contributing to the formation of hallucinations are elucidated. Finally, the cognitive factors contributing to their persistence are outlined.

CONTINUITY OF HALLUCINATIONS: FROM NORMAL TO ABNORMAL

From 4 to 25% of the population report having had auditory hallucinations at some point in their lifetime (Johns, Nazroo, Bebbington, & Kuipers, 2002; Slade & Bentall, 1988; Tien, 1991; West, 1948). Studies have shown that the statistical variation is due in part to the way questions are phrased and to the stringency of the definition. Most people who experience auditory hallucinations would not be regarded as psychiatrically ill by themselves or others. Romme and Escher (1989) found that a sizable proportion (39%) of people who reported experiencing auditory hallucinations regularly was not receiving treatment for them. There is evidence that the prevalence of hallucinations varies according to ethnic groups. Johns et al. reported that 4% of the sample of the general population of England and Wales reported "hearing or seeing things that other people could not" (p. 176), but reports of hallucinations were 2.5-fold higher in a Caribbean sample than in a European American sample, and half as common in the South Asian sample. Of those who reported hallucinatory experiences, only 25% met the criteria for psychosis. The finding in the British sample contrasts with the data from the National Institute of Mental Health Epidemiological Catchment area program, which showed a lifetime prevalence of hallucinations of 10% for men and 15% for women, both from a sample of community residents (Tien). The differences may be related to the wording of the questions about the frequency of voices.

Surveys of college students have shown that from 30 to 71% report having had hallucinations (Barrett, 1992; Posey & Losch, 1983). Interestingly, several studies have found that a substantial proportion of students report the experience of hearing a voice saying their thoughts aloud (Bentall & Slade, 1985; Young, Bentall, Slade, & Dewey, 1987). The attribution of voices to a paranormal or supernatural entity is also consistent with the finding that a relatively large proportion of adolescents and young adults believe in mind reading, thought broadcasting, and witchcraft (van Os, Verdoux, Bijl, & Ravelli, 1999). They also have more grandiose ideas, but not more ideas of a personal relationship with God, than do those in other age groups.

Hearing voices is the most commonly reported symptom of schizophrenia, occurring in approximately 73% of patients with the diagnosis (World Health Organization, 1973). A well-known classification of these hallucinations includes those described as "first-rank" symptoms of schizophrenia by Kurt Schneider (1959). He distinguished three types of hallucinations: (1) patients hearing ongoing commentary on their behavior in the second person, (2) patients hearing voices talking about them in the third person, and (3) patients hearing their own thoughts spoken aloud. Contrary to popular belief, hallucinations are not specific to a diagnosis of schizophrenia. These experiences occur in a wide variety of disorders, including psychotic depression, bipolar disorder, and posttraumatic stress disorder. Auditory hallucinations have also been reported in a very broad range of organic conditions, including neurological disorders, hearing loss, deafness, and tinnitus. Patients with tinnitus generally state their hallucinations are a replay of past memories (Johns, Hemsley, & Kuipers, 2002).

There are evidently substantial cultural differences in the experience of hallucinations both in terms of the frequency with which they are reported by people who regard themselves as normal and also in the specific modality (auditory vs. visual), as reported to clinicians in various countries (Satorius et al., 1986). Moreover, hallucinations have been described in a wide variety of situations that are unrelated to psychosis. A survey of widows and widowers who had recently lost a spouse showed an unusually high incidence of either visual or auditory hallucinations of the dead spouse (Rees, 1971). Close to half of the subjects in that study reported having had hallucinations in either or both the visual or auditory form, and about 10% reported having carried on conversations with the dead spouse. Rees could not find any indication that the subjects were experiencing any psychiatric disorders such as depression. Ensink (1992) studied close to 100 women who were incest survivors. She reported that 28% of these patients had auditory hallucinations and 25% had visual hallucinations either with or without auditory hallucinations.

A comparison of nonpatient voice hearers and psychiatric patients indicates a remarkable similarity in the physical characteristics of the voices. This observation suggests that hallucinations may lie on a continuum with normal experience. The main differentiating features are that the psychotic hallucinations tend to be more negative, are adamantly attributed to external sources, and their content is taken at its face value despite evidence to the contrary (e.g., "You are evil"). Escher, Romme, Buiks, Delespaul, and van Os (2002a) found that although many adolescents hear voices, only those who consistently attribute them to an external entity were prone to develop psychosis at a later date.

Vocal Quality and Content of the Hallucinations

Auditory hallucinations may have a wide range of characteristics. Typically patients report hearing spoken words, but some experience nonverbal hallucinations in the form of a variety of sounds: buzzing, clanging, tapping, and sometimes even music. The spoken words reported by patients consist of a wide variety of comments, criticisms, commands, ruminations, worries, and questions. Many patients report hearing single one-word utterances, usually with a demeaning content such as "jerk," "loser," or "useless." Two-word phrases often have a command quality, such as "Do it," "Die, bitch," or "You're worthless." Some hallucinations may be continuous throughout the day and resemble ruminations. A patient, for example, received commands such as "Pick up the book" and "Write me a song" that persisted continually. These commands may range from innocuous instructions such as "Go for a walk" to commands instructing the person to break the law, to harm him- or herself, or to harm another person. Other patients may hear a running commentary on their behavior.

The voice may also ask a question. As he started his day, a patient would hear the question, "Are you sure you are who you say you are?" and was prompted to look into the mirror. Another heard the reassuring voice of his doctor stating, "You're OK, I'm OK." The voices are in second person ("You are great") or in the third person ("He doesn't know what he's doing") but not in the first person. There may be a "conversation" involving several different voices that may communicate with each other regarding the patient. The third-person voices are more likely to occur in patients who have potent ideas of reference that transition into hallucinations. We have also observed them in patients who are prone to ruminate or to have obsessive thoughts. Many patients report that they hear voices only when they are feeling bad. The voices vary in the degree of loudness and pitch.

Sometimes they may be barely audible and at other times so strong that the patient's entire attention is focused on them. One patient stated, "The voice was so loud it was like you were shouting in my ear. I was certain that people in the next room heard it." The pitch may vary—for example, from low, like a man's voice, to high, like a woman's voice.

The frequency varies considerably, even for a given patient. The hallucinations may continue throughout one waking day and be hardly present or entirely absent on another day. Some patients describe incessant noises coming through the wall (in the absence of positive evidence) or they may magnify the sounds (and their significance) that are normally audible between apartments with thin walls. Often the sounds are attributed to harassment by neighbors. One patient would hear noises coming from his neighbor's apartment when he was rubbing his hands together. He would then interpret this "intrusion" as a deliberate attack on his ability to enjoy the positive sensations he expected from rubbing his hands. Some patients report hearing whirring sounds from a machine supposedly operated by their tormentors. Sometimes patients interpret noises made by other people as meaningful signals; at other times the noises are transformed into voices. A patient, for example, would interpret other people's laughs or grunts as derogatory messages. At other times, she perceived the same kind of nonverbal sounds as voices saying, "You slut."

In other instances, patients hear voices that make comments or criticisms that are frequently heard in their day-to-day lives. A patient heard the voices of different doctors telling her to "quit work" prior to several therapy sessions. In reality, the different staff doctors had recommended that she give up her part-time job due to the stress it created in her life. The *agent* of the voice is sometimes different from the actual people making the comments. For example, one patient heard an unfamiliar voice repeat the phrase, "You bitch," but was unsure of the agent of the voice. In understanding the context of this voice, she noted that her boyfriend had verbally attacked her with the same phrase. Another patient heard the voice of a Chinese warlord stating, "You're useless" and "You're weak"—the same critical comments made by her father throughout her life. Thus, the voices may reflect the content of a remote memory or a current automatic thought about the self. The voice content is often similar to the automatic thoughts that are observed in other psychiatric conditions, such as depression, mania, and social phobia. They may also be similar to the intrusive thoughts in obsessive–compulsive disorder (Baker & Morrison, 1998). Just as the content of the voices may vary from past to present preoccupations, the temporal origin of the voices ranges from the distant past to the most immediate experience. We have found that there appears to be a continuum from intrusive thoughts attributed to an external agent and voices. The content of these "thought insertions" is often similar to that of hallucinations and may have the same impact on the patients' feelings and behavior.

Initial Onset and Reactivation of Voices

In their survey of the heterogeneous group of individuals who had experienced auditory hallucinations, Romme and Escher (1989) found that people who heard voices reported that the experience began quite suddenly, at a moment they remembered well. This event was usually startling and anxiety provoking. One individual reported the following:

> On a Sunday morning at 10 o'clock, it suddenly was as if I received a totally unexpected enormous blow on my head. I was alone and there was a message—a message at which even the dogs would turn up their noses. I instantly panicked and couldn't prevent terrible events from happening. My first reaction was: What on earth is happening? The second was: I'm probably just imagining things. Then I thought: No, you're not imagining it; you have to take this seriously. (p. 210)

Another person stated: "They said all kinds of strange things and they made the things that were important to me look ridiculous. It was a full-blown civil war, but I was determined to win and I continued to ignore everything" (p. 212). In this survey, only 33% of the respondents were able to ignore the voices successfully.

Like other psychiatric symptoms, hallucinations may occur following acute stressors. Many patients report that they first heard a voice or voices after a traumatic experience. The immediate impact of the voices varies. Some individuals regarded the voices as helpful—occurring during a period of rest "after a miserable time" (Romme & Escher, 1989, p. 211). For other individuals, an analogous type of trauma evoked voices that were aggressive and hostile from the beginning. They reported that the voices caused mental chaos and captured so much attention that the individuals "could hardly communicate with the outside world anymore" (Romme & Escher, p. 211). The voices may originate in childhood and continue until adulthood. One of our patients first heard the hallucinated voice of his grandfather in early childhood and continued to hear his voice long after his grandfather died. Not infrequently, voices originate in childhood in response to traumas. For instance, a patient experienced hallucinations for the first time at the age of 9 when he was in the midst of being attacked by other students in the school playground. As he lay on the ground, he saw an image and heard the voice of a guardian angel tell him, "You will be OK and forever protected." A patient who had been called a "goof" by his brother throughout childhood heard the voice of his (absent) brother stating, "You're a goof." Another patient was sexually abused at the age of 6 by a 12-year-old babysitter. Fifteen years later, he heard two voices talking about him in a disparaging way.

Hallucinations are more likely to recur in both nonpatient and patient populations during periods of stress. Indeed, any of the kinds of adverse circumstances that produce dysphoria, anxiety, or exacerbation of current symptoms in nonpsychotic individuals may increase the likelihood of psychotic patients' experiencing hallucinations. Certain specific situations are likely to activate auditory hallucinations in patients with schizophrenia. After the initial hallucinatory experience, the voices may remain latent for varying periods of time, then become active again during periods of distress. Depending on the particular vulnerabilities of the patient, the triggering incidents may vary from increased conflicts with family or neighbors, to financial or housing problems, to problems at school or at work. Delespaul, deVries, and van Os (2002) used the *experience sampling method* to determine the general circumstances that were most likely to trigger the voices. These included being in the presence of a large number of people (generally more than two or three) or, conversely, being by oneself. Sitting alone or watching TV, for example, promotes attention on internal experiences, specifically the train of thoughts. Because there is little distraction from the outside to compete with internal stimuli, the patient's attention becomes focused on thoughts to the point of their becoming audible.

Exposure to a group situation is likely to produce a sense of vulnerability to being rejected, humiliated, or attacked. The specific interaction between the vulnerability to the triggers and life experiences is similar to the sequence observed in patients suffering from anxiety, panic, depressive, or obsessive–compulsive disorder. The fears of being demeaned may activate voices when the patient anticipates entering a situation that involves the potential for being observed. By avoiding the situation, the patient can be relieved of the critical voices. When the hallucinators contemplate encountering situations in which they had previously experienced voices, their recollection can prime the hallucination. For example, one patient became anxious when he visited a shopping mall in which he had previously heard voices telling him to steal. As he walked through the mall, the sight of the merchandise activated the previous symptom, and he again heard the voice commanding him to steal a garment from one of the shelves. Another patient had experienced threatening voices during a panic attack while he was riding a subway train. He heard a voice saying, "You're going to die." When he subsequently approached the entrance to that specific subway station, he heard the same voice again.

Communication and Communicator

Because the voices are regarded as communications, the patient usually (but not always) infers *intent* from them, whether benevolent or malevolent (Chadwick et al., 1996). The assumed source of the hallucinations may vary from known, unknown, or deceased persons, to supernatural entities such as God, the devil, or a guardian angel, to machines such as a radio or satellite, or to esoterica such as an implanted chip in the head or a growth on the finger. In a minority of cases, patients do not attempt to identify a communicator. The voice often resembles that of somebody familiar to the patient: a relative, living or dead; an enemy; a former lover; a stranger. Some patients identify the voice as coming from ancestors, others from supposed conspirators in the workplace. Patients may attribute the communications to a mythical or supernatural entity. When patients recognize the voices as coming from a known person, the message is often consistent with what they recall hearing from that person in the past. One patient heard a voice reproaching him, "Children should be seen and not heard" and "Don't speak until you are spoken to." The voice was that of an aunt, now dead, who would discipline him when he was a child. A patient may not identify the communicator of the voice initially but may discover its origin on exploration with a therapist. Even when the historical antecedent of the voice is discovered, the actual speaker or speakers may remain anonymous.

The content of the voices may be traced to early traumatic episodes such as bullying, rape, or other abuse. One patient, for example, had been called "a mongoloid" by some of the students at school. When he became psychotic, he heard the voices of his fellow students calling him "stupid," "a loser," "a mongoloid," and also, a command, "Kill yourself." There is not always a match between the putative speaker's voice and the kind of statements that the individual would make in real life. For example, a patient heard his father's voice stating, "You are a bum," but he was puzzled because his father never talked to him like that. For some patients the agent of the voice is anonymous. Although most patients try to identify the communicator and may form an elaborate delusion about it, others may question its identity: "Who would be saying such mean things about me?" Over time, the hallucinatory experience may become more complex. Additional voices are experienced, and the patient forms a personal relationship with them and carries on a conversation with them (Nayani & David, 1996).

PSYCHOLOGICAL THEORIES OF HALLUCINATIONS

Three major theories of the psychological mechanisms of hallucination formation revolve around (1) auditory images, (2) source monitoring, and (3) the phonological loop. Mintz and Alpert (1972) and Young et al. (1987) reported that hallucinators were abnormally responsive to suggestions about auditory events. Findings of unusually vivid images in hallucinators, however, have not been substantiated by other writers. Frith and Done (1989b) proposed that auditory hallucinations are the result of a malfunctioning neuropsychological mechanism associated with the monitoring of speech. However, the evidence supporting such a deficit applies to patients with psychosis in general and not exclusively to those with auditory hallucinations. Bentall (1990) proposed that hallucinations are related to problems in monitoring the source of verbal material. The concept of source monitoring is derived from the psychological literature (Johnson, Hashtroudi, & Lindsay, 1993) and can be applied to reality discrimination of external (public) events and internal (private) experiences. Although experiments appear to confirm the application of this theory to hallucinations, other theoretical interpretations seem more parsimonious.

Considerable attention has been directed to the mechanisms of "inner speech." Baddeley (1986) has suggested that inner speech consists of two distinct subcomponents of the working memory system: a phonological input store capable of representing speech for a brief period, and an articulatory loop by means of which information in the phonological store can be refreshed before it fades. Tests of the theoretical application to hallucinations by Haddock, Slade, Prasaad, and Bentall (1996), however, did not support this hypothesis.

A COGNITIVE MODEL OF HALLUCINATIONS

As an alternative to the above unitary theories, which have not proved adequate to account for hallucinatory phenomena, we propose a comprehensive cognitive model of the initial formation and maintenance of auditory hallucinations. The components of this model are listed in Table 4.1.

- *Predisposition to auditory imagery*: Hallucinating patients have a low threshold for imaging, as indicated by a past history of unintended auditory (and visual) images that seemed real or almost real.
- *Hyperactive beliefs and cognitions*: Schemas (formed frequently, but not necessarily, in response to life events) generate "hot cognitions," some of which are transformed into auditory images.
- *Perceptualization*: Certain of these hypervalent cognitions exceed the threshold for unintended imaging and are experienced as identical to externally produced sounds.
- *Disinhibition:* The normal restraints on involuntary imaging are weak and consequently facilitate the perceptualization process.
- *Externalizing bias*: The tendency to ascribe unusual psychological experiences to an external agent reinforces the belief in external origin.
- *Deficient reality testing*: Poor detection and correction of errors, overconfidence in judgment and absence of reappraisal allow initial belief in the external origins of the voices to remain uncorrected (by default).

TABLE 4.1. Hallucinations: Precursors, Formation, and Maintenance

- Precursors
  - Predisposition to auditory imagery
  - Hyperactive cognitive schemas
  - Perceptualization
- Initial fixation
  - Premature closure
  - Overconfidence
  - Externalizing bias
  - Deficient reality testing
- Maintenance
  - Delusional beliefs about agent
  - Beliefs about voices
  - Expectancies
  - Relationship with voices
  - Safety behaviors
  - External stressors
  - Reasoning biases

- *Reasoning biases*: Circular reasoning and conclusions derived from emotion-based and somatic-based reasoning sustains belief in external origin.
- *Progression of hot cognition to voices*: Negative automatic thoughts activated in depression and the intrusive thoughts in obsessive–compulsive disorder are the kind of hot cognitions that are readily transformed into hallucinations.

Predisposition to Auditory Imaging

It is self-evident that hallucinators have a special predilection for *involuntary*, mostly unwanted, auditory imaging. The literature regarding *volitional* auditory imagery is inconsistent, however. Some studies (discussed below) have indicated that hallucinators are more prone than normals to produce vivid auditory images when prompted to do so; other studies have contradicted these findings. In any event, by all definitions, hallucinators are subjected to involuntary auditory images—even if not especially adept at intentional auditory imagery. Further, studies (discussed below) have demonstrated an unusual propensity for unintended imagery in the auditory and visual modalities of hallucinators.

Volitional auditory imaging experiments by Barber and Calverly (1964) provided the prototype for later studies of psychopathological groups. They instructed secretarial students to imagine a record playing "White Christmas" and found that 5% of the subjects actually believed that the music came from a record player. Mintz and Alpert (1972) repeated the experiment with people with schizophrenia, both hallucinating and nonhallucinating, and found that 95% of the hallucinators reported hearing at least "a vague impression" of the record playing as compared with 50% of the nonhallucinators. Of particular interest, 10% of the hallucinators (and none of the nonhallucinators) believed that the record had actually been played.

Young et al. (1987) replicated the Mintz and Alpert (1972) study with a nonclinical sample using "Jingle Bells" as the assigned song. The Launay–Slade Hallucinations Scales (LSHS) have been used in several studies as a measure of predisposition to hallucinations. Sample items include "Sometimes my thoughts seem as real as actual events in my life" and "I often hear a voice speaking my thoughts aloud." The authors asked subjects to imagine that they were hearing a recording of the song through an actual headset connected to a tape recorder that was switched off during the experiment. In the first experiment, the 5% highest scorers on the LSHS reported that they heard music, compared to 0% of the low scorers. The high scorers also obtained higher scores on several tests of suggestibility. The authors repeated this experiment with patients with schizophrenia, both hallucinating and nonhallucinating. Although these hallucinators showed a significantly higher degree of imaging (30% compared with 0%) than the nonhallucinators), Young et al.'s finding was not as striking as in the "White Christmas" experiment of Mintz and Alpert. The hallucinators also scored significantly higher on one test of suggestibility.

Despite these dramatic findings, several more recent studies have failed to substantiate the notion that individuals prone to auditory hallucinations or patients who hallucinate have more vivid (volitional) auditory imagery. For instance, Slade (1976) found that although psychotic patients reported more vivid imagery than a control group, there were no differences between patients with and without hallucinations. Brett and Starker (1977) also found no significant differences in various measures of volitional imagery between groups of hallucinating patients with schizophrenia, nonhallucinating patients with schizophrenia, and controls. Interestingly, hallucinators had significantly *lower* vividness scores for emotional interpersonal items and significantly decreased controllability compared to the other two groups. Starker and Jolin (1982) found no evidence of increased vividness in volitional auditory imagery in hallucinating patients with schizophrenia, but found *less* vivid imagery in this group for items with neutral image content. Further disconfirmatory evidence was reported by Böcker, Hijman, Kahn, and de Haan (2000) and Aleman, Böcker, and de Haan (2001). In summary, the early indicators of increased vividness of *volitionally* produced auditory hallucinations have not been borne out in later studies.

However, since the hallucinations for psychosis are unintended, it is more appropriate to study involuntary rather than volitional hallucinations. It is more fruitful, for instance, to address the question of whether *unintended* hallucinations can be evoked in hallucination-prone individuals and hallucinators in laboratory experiments, given that activated involuntary hallucinations would most closely approximate the phenomena experienced by the patient. Several studies have supported the hypothesis that hallucination-prone subjects and hallucinating patients have an unusual propensity for unintended or *involuntary imaging* in the auditory and visual domains. Bentall and Slade (1985) administered an auditory signal-detection task using white noise and periodic intrusions of a voice to high scorers and low scorers on the LSHS. They found that the high scorers were significantly more likely to perceive a voice when it was not present (false alarm). The same experiment administered to hallucinating and nonhallucinating people with schizophrenia found that the hallucinators showed significantly more erroneous perceptions of a voice than did the nonhallucinators. A similar study reported by Rankin and O'Carroll (1995) also found that subjects scoring high on hallucination proneness (as measured by LSHS) overestimated the presence of a verbal signal. A study by Margo, Hemsley, and Slade (1981) indicated that hallucination-prone individuals were more likely than controls to experience spontaneous auditory hallucinations when exposed to white noise. In a somewhat different vein, Feelgood and Rantzen (1994) found that hallucination-prone individuals were more likely than controls to perceive distorted words as real words.

In sum, these studies indicate that compared to nonhallucinators, patients who are predisposed to hallucinate are prone to respond with auditory hallucinations to ambiguous auditory stimuli. Because hallucinators are prone to focus excessive attention on auditory stimuli, their hypervigilance may be reflected in an expectancy for the occurrence of a voice. This expectancy may lead to their misinterpretation of sounds as voices. Also, the directed focus on ambiguous auditory stimuli, whether voices or nonvocal sounds, may stimulate auditory imagery sufficiently to exceed the threshold for auditory verbal perception. In contrast, the exposure to "white noise" may lower the threshold for auditory imaging by eliminating other distracting stimuli—similarly to isolation experiments. Patients appear to go into a "listening mode" before they enter a situation in which they expect to hear voices. One patient, for example, anticipated that his neighbors would start talking about him when he came home from a walk. He would start to listen for voices at that time, and then would begin to hear them. This example illustrates how hypervigilance and expectancies combine to activate the voices (see Arieti, 1974).

Hallucinators are also especially susceptible to auditory hallucinations when deprived of external auditory input. Starker and Jolin (1983) obtained periodic thought samples from patients who were left to daydream with limited external stimuli (participants faced a blank wall in a quiet room) for 15 minutes. The researchers found a greater occurrence of auditory imagery in hallucinating patients with schizophrenia (as compared to nonhallucinators), but no evidence that their imagery was more vivid than nonhallucinators. This experiment supports the notion that the absence of competing stimuli lowers the threshold for auditory perception of internal stimuli.

Studies have also shown the relationship of inner speech to hallucinations. Gould (1950) and Inouye and Shimizu (1970) demonstrated a relationship between hallucinations and activation of the organ of covert speech production. McGuigan (1978) showed the same findings in normal thinking. The fact that verbal tasks could block both subvocalization and auditory hallucinations was demonstrated by Margo et al. (1981) and later by Gallagher, Dinan, and Baker (1994).

Aleman (2001) suggested that imagery and perception are closely related in hallucination-prone subjects and thus more difficult to distinguish from one another. He also presented evidence that when volitional imaging is more salient than a real perception, a patient is more likely to hallucinate actively. Thus, it is the relative balance between imagery and perception that contributes to the formation of hallucinations. The findings that auditory imagery relies on auditory areas in the temporal lobe and that neuroimaging studies of hallucinations show activity in these areas are consistent with the thesis that imagery processes play a role in the formation of hallucinations. Kosslyn (1994) also observed that imagery and perception basically share the same processing structures in the brain. The functional overlap of imagery and perception increases the possibility that, under certain conditions, an image can be mistaken for a perception.

The physiological relation between volitional imagery and unintended hallucinations has also been demonstrated. Shergill, Cameron, and Brammer (2001) utilized functional MRIs on hallucinating patients and concluded that auditory hallucinations may be mediated by distributed networks in cortical and subcortical areas. They also pointed out that the pattern of activation observed during auditory hallucinations was remarkably similar to that seen when healthy volunteers imagine another person talking to them (auditory verbal imagery). This finding provides support to the hypothesis that auditory hallucinations are an expression of "internal speech." The authors also pointed out that there is a paucity of activation of the supplementary motor area during auditory hallucinations; they speculated that this lack of activation might be related to a lack of awareness that inner speech has been generated.

Hyperactive Cognitive Schemas

Understanding the mechanisms involved in the formation of hallucinations requires consideration of the role of cognitive organization in providing the matrix for the phenomena. Cognitive organization, in general, consists of suborganizations of representations embedded in cognitive schemas that concern individuals' relations with the outside world and with themselves (see Beck, 1996). The content of the schemas varies from the concrete (e.g., a person) to the abstract (e.g., justice) representation and include episodic and procedural memories and systems of formulas and rules. Externally oriented representations extract relevant data regarding individuals' relationships and integrate them into meaningful information. In contrast, internally oriented representations provide essential data relevant to patients' relationship to themselves. When one of the schemas (representations) is activated, it elicits a derivative cognition: a memory, a rule, an expectation. Externally oriented cognitions present as fears, predictions, and projected evaluations by others. Internally oriented cognitions assume the form of self-evaluations, self-control, self-commands and prohibitions, self-criticism, and self-praise. These kinds of cognitions occur normally in individuals but tend to be accentuated in people with psychopathology. They also often provide the content of hallucinations.

When activated, schemas provide meaning to experiences. When hyperactive, they can preempt the central information processing and produce interpretations (cognitions) that are congruent with their own content rather than with external reality. When psychopathology is present, certain idiosyncratic schemas become dominant and drive the cognitions typical of the disorders: self-degrading cognitions accompany depression; self-enhancing cognitions, mania; danger-related cognitions, anxiety; cognitions regarding specific dangers, phobias; persecutory cognitions, paranoia; warnings and doubts, obsessive–compulsive disorder; flashbacks, posttraumatic stress disorder. These specific cognitions are often prominent in psychosis as well as in the nonpsychotic disorders. Whether normal or abnormal, the schemas may also contain memories or fragments of memories. The perpetual communicator may be extracted from a remote memory schema or from a contemporaneous entity.

The specific rules that patients apply to themselves may also influence the specific content of voices. A patient followed the rigid rule, "If it's not perfect, then you've failed." Whenever she perceived a mistake in her performance, critical voices would be triggered, stating "You can't do anything right" and "You're a complete failure." Another patient, who maintained the rule, "It is not acceptable to disappoint your parents," would hear the voices of his dead relatives chastising him whenever he conjured up a memory of having skipped school or taken drugs.

Specific events trigger the schemas typical of a particular disorder and lead to the kind of cognitions described above. However, even in the absence of triggers, certain schemas remain hyperactive and guide the content of the stream of consciousness. Thus, many depressed patients continue to ruminate about their failures, whereas anxious patients perseverate about their fears and worries. Less dramatic cognitions such as commands, evaluations, and reflections are also derived from activated schemas. Any or all of these types of cognitions may be transformed into perceptions in the form of verbal hallucinations. Not infrequently, several activated schemas that would normally appear as an internal dialogue become perceptualized: one aspect as a thought, the other as a voice. Patients may experience their self-observations as an auditory commentary about themselves. The crucial feature of the hallucinated cognitions is that the self is perceived as the object (receiver) rather than the generator of the voice. Since the message is intended for the patient, it takes the second or third person form: *you* or *he/she*.

Progression of Hot Cognitions to Voices

A considerable body of clinical observation, as well as experimental findings, indicate that hallucinations are representative of the "inner voice," thoughts that occur in the stream of consciousness, "pop up" spontaneously, or are responses to stimulus situations—and become audible. Hallucination-prone patients may have the same sequence of thoughts as other people, but their ultimate thought or conclusion may be transformed into an external voice. A woman, for example, was working on a manual project and became frustrated when she ran into difficulties. She thought, "I can't do anything right. I'm stupid." Following this highly charged cognition, she heard a voice saying, "You can't do anything right." Because thoughts like these trigger an emotional response, they are often labeled *hot cognitions*.

Thoughts in the first person (e.g., "I am a loser") may transition into a *voice* in the second person (e.g., "You are a loser"), but critical automatic thoughts are frequently formulated in the second person. Many automatic thoughts are directed at the patient as an object: for example, "You are dumb." Third-person voices frequently develop from ideas of reference. A patient noticing people looking at him thought, "They are talking about me" and then heard their voices saying, "He's a slob." He projected onto them what *he* thought they were thinking about him. A hallucination may evolve from a fear. A patient was afraid that other people thought he was gay and heard a voice saying "He's a queer." Third-person voices may also consist of mundane observations about the patient: "Now he's getting dressed . . . washing his face . . . brushing his teeth." This type of hallucination tends to occur in obsessive ruminating individuals and reflects their automatic self-observations.

Sometimes a particular cognition is experienced as an automatic thought and sometimes as a hallucination. If the cognition happens to be particularly salient at the time or the threshold for perceptualization is low, a hallucination may be formed. It also should be noted that certain ideas occur only as hallucinations and seem alien and incomprehensible to the patient. A hallucinating man, for example, at times would hear a little girl crying and at other times he would hear the voice of an adolescent calling him "creep" or "faggot." The content of both hallucinations was derived from memory schemas that incorporated previous traumatic experiences (watching a little girl being abused and not intervening; being verbally abused by classroom bullies). In the majority of cases, the content of voices and automatic thoughts is similar except for the transformation from first person to second or third person. But although the content of cognitions and voices may be similar or even identical, the experience of the automatic thoughts and that of hallucinations is totally different. Not only is the sound quality different, but the voices are experienced as actual happenings external to the self.

When patients engage in an internal debate or dialogue, the more salient side may be transformed into a hallucination. In one kind of internal dialogue, the "voice of authority" in the form of commands, criticisms, or evaluations frequently prevails and may become audible. A patient approached a vending machine and had the thought, "Should I get a Coke or a cup of water?" He then heard the command, "Get the water." At other times, the self-indulgent response may be vocalized. Sometimes the more permissive cognition is dominant. The same patient, sitting in the group room, thought, "I shouldn't eat another snack," and then heard the indulgent voice state, "You can eat the snack."

Not infrequently, patients' day-to-day difficulties trigger critical responses. A patient was rushing to get ready for school and was getting more and more distressed as she thought, "I'm going to be late and my friends will be disappointed." She next heard a voice say, "You think too much . . . you are too rigid." Discouraged, she withdrew, turned on the stereo, and went to bed. In contrast, other patients experience grandiose hallucinations when confronted with problems that reflect on their adequacy or social desirability. A student, thwarted in his effort to solve an arithmetic problem, thought, "I'll never get it." He then heard a voice, "But you're a genius." The positive image was evidently a compensation for his sense of failure. If patients are depressed, the train of thoughts in psychosis may be similar to depressive cognitions (Beck, 1976): for example, "You are scum,"

"Nobody loves you," "You are a total failure." A relevant study by Waters, Badcock, Maybery, and Michie (2004) indicated a high correspondence between depressotypic hallucinations and the presence of depression.

These voices frequently make statements that are on a thematic continuum with other people's comments, as are the consequent automatic thoughts. A patient, for example, was out for a walk with her father when he said to her, "You're not ill, you're just frail." Her automatic thoughts were "I can't do anything right" and "I'm so weak." She began to feel sad and hopeless. Upon returning home, she isolated herself in her room and heard the voice (identified as her father's) state, "You get sick all the time," "You're ungrateful," and "You're such a burden." In this instance, the combination of the lowered threshold for perceptualization (discussed in the next section) as a result of social isolation and the hyperprimed recall of her father's criticism coalesced into the formation of the hallucination. Many patients, especially if in a depressed mood, experience voices when they are alone and ruminating. A young man who had recently lost his father lay in bed, thinking about his father and missing him greatly. He thought, "Dad did so much for me, but I was ill and couldn't do anything in return." As he thought to himself "I'm completely useless," he heard the voice of his father say "You let me down." Again, the lowered threshold due to his isolation permitted the highly charged cognition to be hallucinated.

The content of the voices may be similar to the thoughts found in other psychiatric disorders. Disgusting, blasphemous ego-alien thoughts such as those found in obsessive–compulsive disorder may take on a hallucinatory form in patients with schizophrenia, such as "Sleep with your mother," "God sucks," and "Clean the toilet." Patients with a more paranoid orientation may experience aggressive thoughts that activate voices expressing a fear of retaliation. A patient walking down the bicycle path saw a bicycle approaching and had this thought about the rider, "If you don't move over, I'll give you a slap in the head." He then heard a loud male voice, "Do YOU want a slap in the head?" Patients with characteristics of social phobia may have automatic thoughts similar to those of nonpsychotic patients with social phobias, and they may have hallucinations that seem to broadcast other people's unfavorable thoughts about the patient: "You're weird," "You sound so stupid," "Don't you know, you make everyone uncomfortable," and the like. Patients subjected to earlier trauma, such as bullying or rape, may retain an audible memory of statements made by their victimizer. One patient, for example, heard the voices of his tormentors calling him a "freak." He continued to have thoughts with the same contents as the hallucinations after they disappeared following pharmacotherapy.

Perceptualization

Auditory and visual perceptualization is generally regarded as a complex process that converts externally originated sound or light waves received by sensory organs into mental images. A perception, however, is not a reliable mirror of external reality. What we perceive as real can be a gross distortion of the actual patterns of external stimuli. Certain mental processes can imitate the kind of signals ordinarily transmitted to the organs of sensation. Hallucinations, for example, are experienced as though they are due to sensory stimulation from external sources. It is obvious that the formation of a perception is not necessarily dependent on the stimulation of the sensory organs.

How can internally originated phenomena be experienced as identical to externally derived phenomena? The answers would seem to point to some kind of central processing system that is receptive not only to signals from the senses but also from purely endogenous sources. Recognition of an external object, for example, requires not only the stimulus from that object but a match-up with the relevant representation (schema) in the cognitive organizations. If a particular schema is overactive, it may intrude on the processing system and produce a false match. If, for example, I expect a phone call, I may hear the ring even though the telephone is silent. The perception represents a match with the expectancy rather than with an external stimulus.

We can observe a progression from a sporadic pseudomatch to the more serious distortions in clinical cases. Patients with ideas of reference may misperceive other peoples' talk (and other sounds, e.g., a cough or sneeze) as commentary about them. The inner verbal representation of "What people think of me" overrides the actual external stimulus and produces an auditory image (e.g., "He's a loser") just as real as the transmission of actual sound. When the internal representations co-opt the cognitive-processing system, they create a false reproduction of the external world of sight and sound—a visual or auditory hallucination.

The most baffling characteristic of patients' auditory hallucinations is not their content, which is generally an extraction from memory or the stream of consciousness, but the quality and identity of the voices. These voices, which rarely resemble patients' own voices, are identified by them as familiar or unfamiliar, male or female (or both), single or multiple, young or old, or supernatural (demons, Satan, or God). To some degree, the same creativity manifested in dreamwork is expressed in the formation of hallucinations. In most cases, patients identify the speakers as either contemporaries or from the past, but in some cases their identity is completely unknown. The versatility in the identity of voices may be likened to the novelty in the choice of characters and action in a dream.

Seikmeier and Hoffman (2002) have presented persuasive evidence that neural connectivity is reduced in schizophrenia due to the excessive pruning of neurons during adolescence in schizophrenia-prone individuals. They postulate that the neural hypersalience resulting in hallucinations may be a consequence of the reduction in connectivity. Hoffman and Cavus (2002) and R. E. Hoffman (personal communication, August 26, 2002) also report (see also Hampson, Anderson, Gore, & Hoffman, 2002) preliminary evidence that

> Broca's and Wernicke's area are excessively coupled in voice-hearers (i.e., that the time course of their activations are more highly correlated than in normals). It is like these two areas of the brain are feeding each other information and are less reliant on other parts of the brain for inputs—in essence that they compose a (semi-) autonomous circuit. . . . [We speculate] that Broca's area (as a language production area) is "dumping" language representations into Wernicke's area as a speech perception [auditory] area, thereby creating hallucinated percepts of spoken speech. (R. E. Hoffman, personal communication, August 26, 2002)

It is conceivable that the hyperpriming proposed by Hoffman and his group may be mediated by excessive dopamine transmissions (as well as other neurochemicals). Kapur (2003) provides evidence that "abnormal salience of the internal representations of percepts and memories" (p. 16) may be the result of excessive dopamine transmission. For support of this thesis he notes that the dampening of dopamine production is one of the mechanisms that mediates the effectiveness of antipsychotics. The abnormal salience that Kapur describes is very similar to the hypersalient (hot) cognitions described in this chapter.

The variability in the experience of hallucinations suggests a corresponding variability in the *threshold* for perceptualization. Patients do not describe a step-by-step ratcheting up of thoughts to hallucinations. The apparent on–off character of voices suggests the functioning of a threshold for perceptualization that may vary considerably depending on endogenous and exogenous factors. The threshold is lowered, for example, by fatigue, stress, reduction in external stimulation, and emotional factors such as anxiety, anger, and depression (see also Slade & Bentall, 1988). The other major contribution to the perceptualization of cognitions is the pressure from the hypersalient cognitions. Thus, the combination of a lowered threshold for perceptualization and an increased activation of the underlying beliefs may result in a hypersalient cognition "crossing the sound barrier."

Disinhibition

As pointed out by Behrendt (1998), external stimuli ordinarily impose a constraint on such false perceptions. When an individual is asleep, however, these constraints are absent and the internal representations take over the perceptual system. The formation of dreams shares some similarities with the production of waking-state hallucinations. Dreams demonstrate how endogenous events are experienced as though they are actually occurring in the real world. They also show the versatility of the perceptual processes in creating novel auditory and visual images. Hallucinations, however, are narrower in scope and repetitive, whereas dreams are unlimited in their creative utilization of images and narrative.

Patients with schizophrenia also show deficiencies in the ability to appropriately inhibit a number of mental processes. This phenomenon has been observed clinically but also has been demonstrated experimentally. There evidently is a deficit in both conscious and automatic inhibition in these patients (Badcock, Waters, Maybery, & Michie, 2005; Waters, Badcock, Michie, & Maybery, 2006). In a seminal paper, Frith (1979) proposed that deficient cognitive inhibition leads to a "hyperawareness" that becomes manifest in hallucinations and delusions. This report, combined with other findings relevant to schizophrenia in general, indicates a special vulnerability of hallucination-prone individuals to disinhibitory processes. Gray et al. (1991) proposed a more complex model that includes a "fail[ure] to inhibit the intrusion of material from long term memory" (p. 3). They implicate dopamine transmission abnormality in this process. Weinberger (1996) proposes that an abnormality in neurological development leads to impairment of inhibitory control of the mesolimbic dopamine system involved in reward and punishment, resulting in hypersalient symptoms. This theory is significant in that the content of hallucinations is generally either rewarding or aversive.

Badcock et al. (2005) and Waters et al. (2006) demonstrated a significant lack of intentional inhibition in patients with schizophrenia who had auditory hallucinations. This deficit was assessed by two different tasks: The first involved suppressing the plausible completing word in a sentence completion test, and the second, inhibiting an appropriate memory in a memories task. Patients performed significantly worse than normal controls and also showed significant positive correlations between an index of auditory hallucination severity and the errors on the two tasks. An increase in auditory hallucination severity was associated with increasingly impaired inhibitory control. These findings, which may be characteristic of schizophrenia in general (because the authors did not include a nonhallucinating schizophrenia group, this is a possibility), may indicate a general difficulty in executing specific effortful tasks related to nonautomatic (or secondary) processing.

Braff (1993) has proposed that the inability to "gate" sensory information leads to sensory overload and the failure to filter incoming information. Sensory gating abnormality in patients with schizophrenia is a specific form of inhibitory disability; it refers to prepulse inhibition: that is, a person's ability to inhibit a startle response to a strong sensory stimulus (e.g., loud sound) in the presence of a preceding weak prepulse stimulus. Peters et al. (2000) have shown a deficit in negative priming; that is, patients with schizophrenia fail to show the normal automatic inhibition of previously primed stimuli following a subsequent exposure. These patients have also shown a deficiency in inhibiting the priming of meanings that were irrelevant to the context of a lexical decision task (Lecardeur et al., 2007).

In summary, two processes may be identified in the formation of hallucinations: *excitation* and *disinhibition*. First, certain internal representations (beliefs), expressed in the form of automatic thoughts, memories, or visual images, are hyperprimed. Next, the usual constraints on the formation of endogenous perceptualization are diminished (disinhibited). The combinations of these factors subvert the normal functioning of the internal processing systems and lead to hallucinations.

Externalizing Bias

Although hallucinations are relatively common in young adolescents, they do not generally progress into the typical hallucinations observed in schizophrenia. As pointed out by Escher et al. (2002a), the key factor predictive of later schizophrenia is the attribution of the voices to an external agent. This kind of attribution suggests the early formation of a paranoid delusion, which crystallizes into a full-blown delusion at a later date. The attribution of certain specific internal experiences to an external origin is characteristic of the paranoid schizophrenic disorder and also applies to the phenomenon of thought insertions, thought capture, and thought control: the belief that one's thoughts have been inserted, taken away, or controlled by an external agent (generally included along with hallucinations in Schneider's 1959 formulation of primary symptoms). The tendency to ascribe unusual or discomforting mental experience to an external agent is an expression of an externalizing bias. Similarly, paranoid delusions and ideas of reference are based on an external focus of attention. The same biased information-processing system operating in paranoid thinking reinforces the patient's intractable conclusion that the voices are indeed external.

This externalizing bias has been well documented in patients with paranoid delusions (Bentall, 1990; Young et al., 1987; Beck & Rector, 2002), and this bias in the attributions of hallucinations has been demonstrated by Johns et al. (2001), who found that hallucinators were prone to attribute feedback of their own voice to an external source. Other studies by Rankin and O'Carroll (1995) and by Morrison and his colleagues (Morrison & Haddock, 1997; Baker & Morrison, 1998) found that hallucinators with schizophrenia, compared to nonhallucinators with schizophrenia, were significantly more likely to misattribute the source of self-generated speech to an external source. Further, the persistent experience of hallucinations may condition patients to attribute an external, non-self locus of control for particular hypersalient thoughts.

This specific bias may be a manifestation of the *fundamental attributional error* (Heider, 1958). Described at some length by Gilbert and Malone (1995) as the *correspondence bias*, this mechanism consists of an automatic external attribution of the cause of an unpleasant experience. According to this concept, an individual may initially interpret an internal stimulus as originating externally. Ordinarily, one would detect and correct an incorrect external attribution. Under stress, however, even normal people may fail to make the correction. Individuals such as those with schizophrenia, who are already under stress, are not only especially susceptible to this bias but maintain it because of poor reality testing. Consequently, when the correcting mechanism is inactive, psychological processing remains stuck in the default condition—that of making externalizing attributions.

A number of studies (e.g., Brébion, Smith & Gorman, 1996; Franck et al., 2000; Morrison & Haddock, 1997) demonstrated a tendency of hallucinators to misattribute some of their own spoken words to the experimenter. The patients also had a tendency to misclassify words that they had actually read silently as having been read aloud (Franck et al., 2000). They were prone to recall certain categories (e.g., fruit) that had been presented to them previously in verbal form as having been presented in pictorial form (Brébion et al., 1996). Following Johnson et al. (1993), the authors of these various studies have proposed defective source monitoring as the cause of the errors.

The proposal of defective source monitoring as a primary explanation for the attributional error in hallucinations is problematic for several reasons. First, most of the evidence on which it is based involves the exclusive unidirectional misattribution of *internal* events to *external* sources. There was no evidence that the subjects attributed external stimuli to internal sources. Logically, deficiencies in a particular mental mechanism such as source monitoring should result in patients' unsureness about, or at the least inconsistency in, their attributions. Second, the experimental situations described in the studies are very different from the clinical phenomena they attempt to explain. The voluntary reading of words, for example, is different from the involuntary production of hallucinations. Third, the content of the stimulus words is far removed from the dramatic content of the voices (e.g., "Die, Bitch!"). Fourth, the utilization of recall methodology is inconsistent with the immediate experience of hallucinations. Fifth, and perhaps most important, these experiments involve auditory stimulation, whereas the sine qua non of hallucinations is that there is no sensory stimulation. Finally, a study by Versmissen et al. (2007) failed to confirm the earlier findings. These researchers propose that the studies demonstrate a top-down processing bias rather than defective self-monitoring.

If we disregard the experimental problems and discrepancies, we can offer a more parsimonious explanation of the findings; namely, that these patients have a *bias* toward attributing certain internally generated events to external sources. Thus, the misattribution of their own words to the experimenter, for example, reflects their cognitive processing, which biases their recall toward external attributions. Moreover, the misattribution of read words to spoken words could perhaps be due to a tendency to form auditory images of the read words and consequently to recall the images rather than the words. Similarly, incorrect conversion (on recall) of verbally produced words to pictorial images could be explained as a manifestation of the tendency to create visual images of exemplars (e.g., apple) and consequently to recall the image rather than the verbally presented category. This explanation is consistent with patients' unique predilection for visual (as well as auditory) images. Because this kind of perceptualizing implies an external source, patients' disposition to imagine the presented stimuli converges with their externalizing tendency. Their failure to correct their misattributions, because of their lax criteria for making decisions regarding the source of their hallucinatory experiences, contributes to the distortions (see disruptions in source monitoring; Johnson et al., 1993).

The technical problem posed by the dependence on recall of internally or externally generated stimuli was remedied in a study by Johns et al. (2001), who found that patients with schizophrenia tended to attribute distorted feedback of their own voice to an external source. This finding also was consistent with the concept of an externalizing bias in patients with hallucinations or delusions. Further, the hallucinators were particularly prone to error in response to distorted negative words. The utilization of negative words makes the study more consistent with the clinical observations of a predominance of negative cognitions in these patients. Bentall, Baker, and Havers (1991) found that hallucinators attributed more self-generated high-cognitive-effort words to the experimenter than did psychiatric or normal controls. This finding is consistent with the hypothesis that when cognitive resources are strained, these patients are biased toward attributing certain perceptions to an external source.

Deficient Reality Testing

In evaluating the meaning of events, individuals are faced with a wide variety of possibilities. A smile may represent mirth, sarcasm, or disbelief. We often decide on one meaning and then quickly revise it as contradictory information becomes available. For example, when experiencing certain sensations, we may attach erroneous meanings—a headache = a brain tumor; pain in chest = heart attack; faint feeling = a stroke. Certain hyperactive beliefs or formulas distort the kind of interpretation we make. Under stress, it is more difficult to reconsider the initial interpretation, or if the belief is particularly salient, we hyperfocus attention on normal sensations and as a result experience an increased physiological discharge—we feel weak, faint, and sweaty, all of which tends to confirm in our minds the supposed pathology (e.g., heart attack, stroke). Patients with psychosis not only attach erroneous meanings to their experiences but have the additional disability of weaker reality-testing functions than normal controls (perhaps because of hypoconnectivity, as described by Hoffman & Cavus, 2002). To make it worse, the same deficiencies of resources that weaken the reality-testing functions also favor "easy" (but erroneous) methods of processing information. As shown by Chapman and Chapman (1973a), these patients will select easy answers to problems even though the context clearly calls for a different but harder answer. Consequently, patients are drawn to the energy-sparing types of reasoning described below (e.g., emotion-based reasoning). To override the "easy solution" bias requires not only extra effort but sophisticated forms of self-correction—strategies that are often poorly developed in patients with schizophrenia. Other reality-testing functions, such as the ability to consider alternate explanations, suspend judgment pending the accumulation of more information, withdraw attention from the hallucinations and delusions, and view reasoning biases objectively, are also weak.

These reality functions are not totally absent, but they are hypoactive during accentuated psychotic episodes and specifically when patients are in stressful situations. When their psychotic episodes have subsided, patients frequently recognize that their erstwhile hallucinations were internally generated—actually, they are their own thoughts. However, even in periods of complete remission, the reality-testing abilities function on a thin margin of safety. Stressful situations may not only exacerbate symptoms but also soak up the resources requisite for effective reality testing (Chapter 14). Fortunately, cognitive therapy has been shown to be effective in reinforcing reality testing. In fact, it seems to be particularly effective with relatively naive patients who have never developed good cognitive skills (e.g., gathering all the data, suspending judgment, making alternative explanations).

People generally are surprised by extraordinary sensory experiences such as hearing music or voices when there is no apparent source. When they do not discover evidence that the music or voices originate externally, they attribute them to their imagination or some medical problem. If they hear the voice of a distant or deceased relative, they conclude they are imagining it and disregard the experience. As pointed out by Johns, Hemsley, et al. (2002), people who hear sounds as a manifestation of tinnitus or hear music or voices related to the aging process may check the radio or television set or test their perceptions with others. In this study, when patients with tinnitus did not find an external cause for their musical hallucinations, they wondered about their origin and were then, for the most part, able to come up with a ready-made medical explanation, because they already knew that they had a medical disorder. In contrast, patients with schizophrenia do not reality-test their beliefs about voices and thus maintain their convictions regarding external origins. Also of importance is the cognitive bias of patients with "anomalous" symptoms, such as thought insertions and thought capture, to attribute their baffling mental experiences to an external agent. Thus, they already have in place a ready-made explanation for these experiences as a result of their cognitive biases (see Chapter 3). Moreover, patients with psychosis are prone to accept, without question, the *reality* of an unusual experience, such as hearing voices, and generally do not check or seek others' opinions regarding the validity of their interpretation. If the voice *seems* to be real (i.e., from an external agent), then it *is* real (i.e., it does not originate internally). These patients seem to lack the normal propensity to question the reality of these experiences and, indeed, have a difficult time questioning the veridicality of the voices even at a hypothetical level. They are often disinclined to consider alternative explanations for the source of the voices because of the negative significance to them if the voices are not real. This resistance may be illustrated by a patient's statement (ironic, from the psychiatric perspective): "If the voices are not real, it means I'm mad." That thought—with all its implications of being out of control, alienated from the human race, and so forth—is intolerable.

When the content of the voices matches the vocal quality of a deceased person, the patient identifies the voice as that of the decedent and does not attempt to evaluate how he or she could be receiving a message from the grave. A patient who believed that he heard his dead mother say "I told you that you shouldn't have married her," explained, "That's what she always said . . . and besides, I recognized her voice." He did not question the incongruity of this explanation with his disbelief in an afterlife. Another of our patients heard a number of different voices from deceased family members, including his grandfather's, uncle's, and aunt's. When asked how he knew they were real, he explained, "The voices *are* real—they're identical to my dead relatives." He reasoned that because he had heard their voices when they were alive and the voices had not changed after they died, they were consistent over time and they had to be real. Moreover, because he had heard the voices during church services, which he used to attend with his relatives, the voices had to be real. In both these examples, the similarity of the voices overrode the implausibility of the explanation.

Reasoning Biases

Patients with schizophrenia show a variety of illogical processes in reaching conclusions about the source of the voices and accept their conclusions as undeniable fact. Not infrequently patients use *circular reasoning* to explain or justify their belief in the veridicality of the voices. For instance, a patient heard a voice state "God is a goof." Because he recognized the voice as that of a neighbor, he concluded that the neighbor was a sinner for having said such a thing. Thus, since he was a sinner, it was logical that he had to be the source of the blasphemous statement. Another patient, Hank, heard voices that he attributed to the knights of King Arthur's round table. Since these were voices from the past, he inferred that he must have lived in the past.

Consequently, since he had lived in the past, he could be certain that the voices came from people in the past and were real.

Circular reasoning about circumstances can be taken by the patient to provide further support for the belief about the voice. For instance, one of our housebound patients believed that his neighbors were constantly ridiculing him and conspiring to have him removed from the apartment complex. Just prior to their returning home from work, he would go into the "listening mode." As they entered their apartments, he would hear the creaking of the stairs and would start to hear the persecuting voices. When asked in a session how he knew the continually derogatory voices were those of his neighbors, he stated that because he only heard the voices when the neighbors came home, the voices had to be real. Also, the extraordinary loudness of the voices was taken as proof that they were external. In reality, there were several solid walls separating his living quarters from those of the neighbors.

The specific emotional and behavioral *consequences* of the voices not only serve to validate the beliefs about the voices but also shape the ongoing relationship that the patient has with the voices. Some patients use a kind of *emotion-based reasoning* to confirm the veridicality of the voices: The occurrence of an emotional response to the voice indicates that the voice is real. Hank responded to the "friendly voices" of the ancient knights and his ancestors with a feeling of comfort and relaxation; the fact that the voices could make him feel so good proved that they were real, and at the same time, demonstrated that he was better off living in the past than in the present. The emotions created by the voices also served to reinforce Hank's beliefs about the voices originating in the past. Because the voices often spoke to him when he was lonely, offering comfort and friendship, the positive feelings created by the voices further validated his belief that the past was a better place to be in and that he should continue to watch for and welcome the voices. Jack would become enraged when he "heard" his old school buddy call him bad names. He believed that he could not have gotten that upset if the message wasn't real. Another patient, who felt a warm glow when she heard comforting voices, explained, "I wouldn't feel this way if the voices weren't real." These emotion-based inferences are examples of *consequential reasoning*—the true value of an inference is based (by the patients) on the consequences of an experience. Arntz, Rauner, and van den Hout (1995) have demonstrated experimentally the propensity for this kind of reasoning.

Because their auditory images are especially vivid and seem identical to actual voices, patients are especially likely to regard them as real; that is, as originating from the outside. Furthermore, the voices are repeated frequently and the commands, criticisms, and comments are the kind of utterances that one would expect from outside. Tom was convinced of the reality of the voices of his dead relatives because he could "feel them in my heart" when they spoke. The context of the voices also provided compelling confirmatory evidence. The voices had to be real because he "heard them in church," a place where he used to spend time with his relatives.

Patients may draw not only on their emotional reactions but also on their somatic sensations to validate their interpretations and expectations. A patient believed that he heard the voice of a guardian angel. When he heard the voice, he would also experience a warm, pleasant feeling in his chest. These feelings were taken, in turn, as evidence that it must be the voice of a guardian angel because only an angel could influence his bodily sensations. In a more dramatic example, a patient reported hearing the voice of God as a form of punishment for having sexual fantasies. She reported experiencing being "slapped, kicked, and spanked" at times when the voices were activated. Because these sensations occurred only when the voice was activated, and because only God could know her inner thoughts, she then concluded that this was direct evidence that God was speaking to her.

Even mental dysfunctions may be taken as evidence that the voices are real. A patient heard a voice, which she recognized as coming from another planet, telling her that, "We will make you forget." She decided that her difficulties with concentration and memory were direct evidence for the veridicality and perceived agency of the voice. Another patient interpreted painful tactile and olfactory hallucinations as signs that he should comply with command hallucinations. He interpreted these sensations as evidence that the voices were torturing him and would kill him if he did not comply with their commands to steal certain objects from his shop. He complied with the commands in order to achieve the goal of saving his life. He considered his illegal behavior justified because the stakes were obviously so high.

Because these patients are susceptible to *premature closure* in their judgments, they stick to the belief that the voices are "real"; that is, external in origin. They follow the easier route of accepting real-seeming perceptions as veridical rather than undertaking the more taxing task of experience reconsidering and possibly discounting their reality. However, even when they do not identify a particular agent, they do believe that the voices are coming from "somewhere." The belief in the external origin of the voices hardens as patients begin to accumulate supporting evidence (e.g., consequential reasoning). For example, a patient heard a command hallu-cination telling her that she must run errands or she would regret it. If she did not comply, she would hear a voice scolding her and she would feel bad and indeed regret not complying. If she did comply, the voice would praise her, thus reinforcing the notion that the voice must be real. Also, the mere repetition of the experiences impressed on the patient that they must be real and should be taken seriously. Further, if a particular experience is "real," there is no motivation to question it—a wasted effort.

Some patients may validate the reality of the voices on the basis that other people behave as though they hear the same voices. A patient, Jim, heard a voice calling him "a wimp" while he was standing in line at a the-ater. He noticed that other people turned their heads toward him, indicat-ing to him that they had heard the voice and could tell that it was directed toward him. At other times, he believed that he could hear their critical thoughts, which assumed the form of voices.

It may appear puzzling that although the voices appear to reflect the patient's own thoughts, they do not sound like their own voices to patients. It seems that many of the hallucinators experience an activation of the stored memory of other people's voices—voices of people with whom they have had contact. In some instances, they may recognize the voice as that of the person who originally spoke to them. Even when the content is different from the statements made by these individuals, the perceived high fidelity of the vocal reproduction indicates to patients that they are real.

Close and Garety (1998) postulate that the negative content of hallu-cinations tends to produce a self-devaluation that is manifested in the low self-esteem. We propose an alternative hypothesis; namely, that patients already have negative beliefs regarding themselves, and it is these beliefs that are reflected in the negative hallucinations. Since the content of the negative hallucinations (punitive and persecutory) is taken seriously, as though stated by an omniscient authority, they tend to further depreciate the person's self-esteem (a vicious cycle).

An important question relevant to the *formation* of hallucinations should be addressed: What characterizes the thoughts that are normally per-ceived as originating internally (e.g., positive or negative automatic thoughts and intrusive thoughts) but become audible and are perceived as uncontro-vertibly external in origin? When we interview a patient with depression or obsessive–compulsive disorder, for example, we try to elicit the salient or hot cognitions that are externally triggered by any event that impinges on his or her specific vulnerability. These cognitions generally are an extreme or distorted interpretation of the situation and influence the patient's affect and behavior. Similarly, patients with schizophrenia usually can identify a fairly coherent sequence of thoughts that also culminates in an extreme or distorted content. Examples of these salient thoughts are self-evaluations, self-criticisms or self-congratulations, imperatives (shoulds/musts), fears, flashbacks, and other significant memories. These cognitions have in common the characteristics of being automatic, highly charged, and seeming plausible and realistic to the patient. Under certain circumstances, the same kinds of cognitions experienced by hallucination-prone individuals acquire sufficient potency (or charge) to trip the perceptualization mechanism.

Although the process of transformation into auditory images can be described in terms of neurophysiological mechanisms, analysis at the phenomenological level can provide valuable insights. Although only a proportion of the hot cognitions are transformed into auditory hallucinations, the vocalization of the thought may be triggered by an intensively charged cognition and also by a qualitative change in content. A *jump* from a negative automatic thought (e.g., "I've ruined this meal") to a salient condemnation ("You're a slob"), or a *switch* from a negative evaluation ("I'm a loser") to its opposite ("You're a genius") may be sufficient to activate the perceptualization so that the second thought is experienced as a voice. At times the hallucinations may be transformed into an aversive intrusive thought (e.g., "God sucks") or a fearful expectation ("They are thinking 'He's a wimp' "). In fact, any of the hot cognitions may, under certain circumstances, trip the mechanism and be imaged in the auditory domain.

Patients' fixation on the potential activation of voices may have a similar effect. Certain conditions tend to generate or intensify salient cognitions (e.g., being observed by a large group) and thus amplify them above the perceptual threshold. It should also be noted that a variety of nonverbal sounds may be hallucinated as voices. Patients report hearing voices emanating from the sounds produced by automobile engines and other traffic sounds, whirring electric fans, and even shuffling of feet on a staircase. For instance, one of our patients believed that noises from different cars on his street represented different voices, and he could hear them speak to him as they passed by. The sound of one engine, for example, was heard as the disgruntled voice of a man.

In addition to the clinical data, there is accumulating empirical evidence of the correspondence between the content of automatic thoughts and that of hallucinations. Csipke and Kinderman (2002), for example, found that a self-report questionnaire consisting of items relevant to depressive, conscious, and hostile automatic thoughts (Automatic Thoughts Questionnaire; ATQ) could be reasonably converted to a questionnaire concerning the content of hallucinations by changing the form of the item from the first to second person (ATQ-V). Thus, the standard item "I am a loser" for the ATQ would be represented in the ATQ-V as "You are a loser." The investigators found a significant correlation between item scores on the ATQ and the ATQ-V, which also correlated significantly with the clinical diagnosis of hallucinations. A shortcoming of the study was the lack of items relevant to positive automatic thoughts and positive hallucinations. Of tangential interest was the finding of the significant relationship of positive voices to grandiosity and negative voices to depression.

Close and Garety (1998) showed a correspondence between the content of the hallucinations and the patient's self-esteem. A significant percentage of negative hallucinations was associated with negative beliefs about the self, thus confirming the continuity between beliefs and the content of hallucinations. It is apparent that in those cases in which there are negatively worded hallucinations, there is a core belief about the self that corresponds to the hallucinations ("You are useless," "You are a fat slob").

Early core beliefs and assumptions about the self influence both the content and the appraisal of the voices. An underlying belief regarding oneself as worthless, for example, may lead to automatic thoughts of being a failure and demeaning hallucinations in response to a failure at school or work. Many patients who hear critical, demeaning, and insulting comments report having had similar automatic thoughts pertaining to worthlessness. For example, the content of the automatic thoughts of one patient who saw herself as incompetent, "I can't do anything right," mirrored that of her critical voice, "You can't do anything right." Another patient, who had overprotective parents, thought of herself as "dependent" and "weak." Her voices would become activated when she felt afraid of, or perceived herself to be failing at, a task. Her voice content directly reflected her self-view as weak and vulnerable: "You're afraid of everything" and "You can't even manage yourself, let alone the problem."

Patients who report voices that reflect their perceived interpersonal inadequacy often see themselves as unlovable and unworthy. For instance, when she passed couples on the street, a patient would hear a voice intone "You'll always be alone." Another patient, who believed he was unattractive, would hear a critical voice state "Why would she be interested in you? You're just a bum" when he saw an attractive woman. At times, positive voice content seems to compensate for overly developed negative self-views. For instance, the patient who viewed herself as unattractive and socially awkward would also hear the voices affirming "You're beyond reach" and "Just let them wait and see" when she saw couples together.

THE MAINTENANCE OF HALLUCINATIONS

The persistence of hallucinations and the belief that they are externally caused is facilitated by a number of factors, which are also outlined in Table 4.1. The formation of delusional beliefs about the purported agent weaves the hallucinatory experience into a delusional belief system. Further, the interaction between underlying *dysfunctional beliefs* and external stressors helps to prime hypersalient cognitions that are transformed into voices. The *maladaptive beliefs about the voices*, affirming that they are omnipotent and omniscient, enhance their credibility, and consequently, their durability. *Dysfunctional coping* and other "safety behaviors" confirm (for the patient) the veridicality of the hallucinations. The relationship with the voices and *expectancies* regarding them promote vigilance toward any indications of their arousal. If voices are perceived as friendly, the patients are likely to try to engage them. These processes tend to fixate attention on precursors of hallucinations and consequently activate them.

Beliefs about Voices

Patients have a variety of beliefs regarding the nature of the voices, the supposed communicator, and the nature of their relationship with the voices. The importance of these beliefs is documented in a study by Escher et al. (2002a). As mentioned earlier, these authors found that the experience of hallucinations alone did not generally lead to psychosis but that the development of *delusions* about the hallucinations (e.g., attributing them to an external source and attributing special personal significance to them) predicted the development of psychosis. These beliefs are also responsible for the maintenance of the voices. Chadwick et al. (1996) suggest that the content of these beliefs, which are generally delusional by nature, may have a greater impact on affect and behavior than the content of hallucinations. The activation of the voices triggers these beliefs, which then intensify the importance of the voices. The particular beliefs activated by the voices are not necessarily evident from the content of the voices. The content, for example, may be negative ("You always mess up") and yet, because patients have a benevolent belief about the voices, they may put a positive twist on them: "The voice wants to help me." It is clear that *both* the content of the voices and the beliefs about them influence affect and behavior.

Vaughan and Fowler (2004) refined previous findings by Birchwood and Chadwick (1997) in a study that specifically investigated the relationship between the dominant style of the voice and patients' perceptions of voice malevolence and powerfulness. The authors found that how patients perceived the dominance of the voice was more strongly related to the level of distress they experienced than their beliefs about the malevolence of the voice. Specifically, the more the voice was perceived as dominant, the more distressed the patient felt. In addition, previous findings regarding the relationship of perceived powerfulness to distress were refined by the new finding that the way the voice is perceived to *use* its power is most important. Finally, the authors found that, contrary to expectations, there was a negative correlation between patients' submissiveness to the voice and their distress. Specifically, the more distressing the voice-hearing experience, the less likely that the patient's relationship to the voice was submissive.

When the voices are frequent, particularly intrusive, or unpleasant, patients may react to them as they might to any continuous or upsetting symptom, such as pain or shortness of breath. Beliefs such as "I can't cope with them," "I can't stand it," and "They are ruining my life" become activated and can produce anxiety, anger, or depression. These patients also have beliefs about the communicator (or agent) that may take a paranoid form (e.g., "They are after me"), a depressive form (e.g., "God is unhappy with me"), or a fearful form (e.g., "The doctors want to poison me"). As with many other aspects of the hallucinations, these beliefs themselves prompt the patient to focus on the voices in an effort to block them or damp them down. However, this increased attention to the voices tends to accentuate their potency and frequency and, consequently, to confirm the validity of the belief that they are intolerable.

The experience of hearing voices stirs up other distressing beliefs. Because patients believe the voices are uncontrollable, they assume that they also have no control over their own lives. In addition to the distress caused by this belief, the threats or criticisms contained in the voices may produce anxiety, anger, and sadness. Another concern elicited by hearing voices is the thought "I am going mad." This worry encompasses all the presumed consequences of being considered crazy: commitment to a hospital, mandated medication with distressing side effects, separation from the family, stigmatism, and possibly ostracism.

The extent to which patients appraise the voice activity itself as a sign of impending danger, distraction, or interference is directly associated with the level of distress experienced following their activation. Morrison and Baker (Baker & Morrison, 1998; Morrison & Baker, 2000) have examined whether patients with hallucinations have a greater tendency than those without hallucinations to experience their cognitive products as unwanted and unacceptable. Morrison and Baker (2000) found that, in comparison to patients with schizophrenia but without hallucinations, and nonpsychiatric controls, patients hearing voices report experiencing more intrusive thoughts, and they experienced these intrusive thoughts as more distressing, uncontrollable, and unacceptable than did participants in the comparison groups. Patients who hear voices tend to appraise the voices in the same way as the obsessional patient appraises intrusive thoughts: as a sign of danger and future harm. This appraisal process contributes to the emotional and behavioral reactions to the voices and possibly to the maintenance of voice activity—just as similar appraisals have been shown to maintain the distress associated with intrusive thoughts in the obsessional patient.

Baker and Morrison (1998) found that hallucinators could be distinguished from nonhallucinating psychiatric controls on the basis of their beliefs regarding their automatic thoughts. Specifically, hallucinators showed a greater degree of perceived uncontrollability and dangerousness in their automatic thoughts. In a follow-up to this study, Morrison and Baker (2000) reported that hallucinators have a greater number of intrusive thoughts that they perceive as more distressing, uncontrollable, and unacceptable in comparison to normal and nonhallucinating psychiatric controls. Lowens, Haddock, and Bentall (2007) administered the Inventory of Beliefs Regarding Obsessions (IBRO; Freeston, Ladouceur, Gagon, & Thibodeau, 1993), an instrument that measures a variety of beliefs regarding automatic thoughts, such as their degree of intrusiveness, patient's degree of responsibility for them, and a variety of methods for counteracting these intrusive thoughts. They found that hallucinating patients scored just as highly on the measure as did obsessive–compulsive patients and significantly higher than normal controls.

Patients with strong paranormal beliefs interpret the voices within the framework of these beliefs, which then form a delusional system. For instance, one of our patients first started hearing voices after watching a television program about telepathic powers. Following a period of 6 weeks at home and total seclusion, the patient began to hear male and female voices offering a running commentary on his daily movements. He interpreted the emergent voices as "telepaths" from the show. Similarly, a teacher had a well-developed interest in the paranormal and visited a psychic on a weekly basis. Subsequently, she began to hear the voices of her students and interpreted these voices as the students' ability to communicate with her telepathically. The delusional beliefs about the voices not only accentuate their importance but serve to provide further proof to the patient of their validity.

Research by Chadwick and Birchwood (Birchwood & Chadwick, 1997; Chadwick & Birchwood, 1994) suggests that a person's idiosyncratic beliefs about the voices' power and authority, and the consequences of not complying with their requests or commands, are especially important. For instance, Chadwick and Birchwood (1994) found that patients generally resist severe commands (i.e., those insisting on dangerous behavior), whereas their compliance with mild commands was influenced primarily by the nature of their beliefs about the voices. Patients were far more likely to comply with voices commanding them to harm themselves or to refuse medication than to harm others. Beck-Sander, Birchwood, and Chadwick (1997) divided command hallucinations into short imperatives (e.g., "Shut up!"), day-to-day directions (e.g., "Make a cup of tea"), antisocial commands (e.g., "Shout at Freddie"), commands to commit minor illegal offenses, commands to commit major crimes, and commands to self-harm. The important findings were that patients were more likely to comply with voices they believed to be benevolent, whereas they were more likely to resist voices deemed malevolent. Patients who believed that they had subjective control over the voices were less likely to act on their commands.

Some patients complied with some commands in order to "appease" the voices for having transgressed other commands (Beck-Sander et al., 1997). For example, a participant noted that in order to "ingratiate myself with God," whose voice she believed commanded her to hit other patients, she would "sing his praise, shower him with apologies, and promise to obey him later." Another patient who believed he heard a voice commanding him not to cook sought to appease the voice by cooking his food only partially so that the food still tasted unpleasant.

Patients were more willing to comply with commands to harm themselves than they were to comply with commands to hurt others. Acts of appeasement often involved incidents of self-harm. A patient slashed his own wrists, hoping to satisfy the voice of the devil telling him to attack a member of the staff. Another patient attempted to appease a voice telling him to forcibly perform oral sex on a female patient against her will by swallowing varnish and fishing shot (Beck-Sander et al., 1997).

"Relationship" with the Voices

Patients may build up a relationship with the voices just as they would with other people: a relationship that is positive, ambivalent, or negative (see Benjamin, 1989). The voices seem to take on a life of their own—as though they are entirely autonomous and separate from the patients, who may then complain to the voices that they make them do things they don't want to do. But some patients enjoy the voices ("They are my only friends") and find them entertaining and diverting. At times the voices seem to "give good advice." One patient, for example, claimed that "The voice is keeping me sane." Some patients form an intimate relationship with the voices, just as they would with another person and interact with the voices as they might in a regular conversation. They may use methods to activate the voices in order to fill a void in their lives, but the relationship is not necessarily fulfilling or satisfying.

Patients often build up positive expectations based on the content of the voices, then are disillusioned. For example, the voices may make promises that they don't keep and then patients feel that they cannot trust them anymore. However, patients may also rationalize an unkept "promise." A patient was told by the voices that he would be moved to better living quarters by a specific date. When this did not occur, he decided that something important had intervened (Chadwick et al., 1996).

Maladaptive Coping and Safety Behaviors

Patients who hear voices also engage in behaviors intended to reduce the activation of voices, to neutralize the unpleasant consequences of hearing voices, and/or to appease the perceived agent of the voices. Just as the patient with panic disorder avoids rigorous exercise in fear of producing symptoms of autonomic arousal that mimic panic sensations, or the social phobic sits in the last row of an auditorium to avoid drawing attention to him- or herself, patients who hear distressing voices engage in overt as well as covert behaviors that they believe aid in the management of their voices and reduce attendant distress. Because these actions are intended to ward off anticipated danger or anxiety, Morrison (2001) has referred to them as "safety behaviors." Analogous to the "social phobic patient," the reliance on safety strategies by hallucinators tends to maintain the hallucinations.

Patients who hear voices report staying away from public places and keeping busy with household chores as a way of minimizing them (Romme & Escher, 1989). One patient could anticipate that his voices would get worse in the late afternoon of each day, and so he scheduled a nap at that time. A patient, a musician, would play his guitar to escape from hearing the voices. Another patient jumped off a bridge in flight from tormenting voices; the behavior did not represent suicidal wishes but rather an attempt to escape the menacing presence of the voices themselves. In their study, Romme and Escher found that roughly two-thirds of people who experience voices are not successful in their efforts to escape or ignore the voices. Unfortunately, the effort spent on avoiding or neutralizing the voices curtails the scope of patients' activities—which, in turn, leads to social isolation and then to a paradoxical increase in voice activity.

Patients who hallucinate may use the same kind of strategies reported by obsessive patients in dealing with their obsessions. For instance, one patient whose voices made blasphemous comments would try to think positive thoughts or engage in prayer to cancel out or neutralize the feared consequences of offending God. Similarly, another patient would respond to his "rude" voices by engaging in "positive affirmations," stating to himself "People are good and everything is OK." At the onset of hallucinations, another patient would simply dial the operator on the telephone on the assumption that the telephone operator could make the voices go away. Still another of our patients, who could anticipate hearing voices as he returned home to his apartment, would state aloud "You can't do this to me" as a way of forestalling the voices. Efforts to suppress awareness of the voices may lead to the same rebound effect that has been demonstrated when people attempt to suppress ordinary thoughts (Wegner, Schneider, Carter, & White, 1987). As an example of engaging in safety behaviors in response to the beliefs about voices, one of our patients would put on a headband when the voices became activated because he believed that the headband could not only terminate the voices but would also give him "strength of mind," which the voices threatened to take away if he did not comply with their commands.

Patients also engage in selective attention and hypervigilance as a way of responding to their voices. One of our patients responded to activation of the voices by isolating himself and concentrating on the voices in order to "figure out what the voices were up to." Other patients focus their attention on the voices, as other people would confront a potentially dangerous stimulus or message. Some focus their attention on the positive voices as a way of deflecting attention from the more malevolent and distressing voices (Romme & Escher, 1989). Of significance is the finding that engagement in these coping behaviors prevents patients from disconfirming negative appraisals about the consequences of hearing the voices (e.g., "If I hadn't followed the command, God would have killed me"). Further, the safety strategies deprive patients of the opportunity to determine whether their belief about the source of the voices is true. By foreclosing the process of reality testing, the coping behaviors may make the experience of hearing voices worse. These various safety behaviors are analogous to those employed by patients with panic disorder, obsessive–compulsive disorder, and phobias in general: They may provide temporary relief, but they also maintain the disorder.

One biological factor that contributes to hallucinations in these patients is the *hypoconnectivity* in their brain resulting from excessive priming of neurons during adolescence. This pruning reduces the resources available in patients for higher-level cognitive functioning and reduces their ability to reality-test delusional interpretations. Instead, they rely on low-level dysfunctional reasoning strategies. An additional biological factor, the cerebral flooding with dopamine and other transmitters (possibly in reaction to the neuronal loss), "hyperprimes" the salient cognitions (self-evaluation, intrusive, or obsessive) until they cross the perceptual threshold to hallucinations.

SUMMARY

Auditory hallucinations in patients with schizophrenia can be understood within a cognitive framework that incorporates relevant biological constructs. The formation, fixation, and maintenance of hallucinations is dependent on multiple determinants:

1. Patients have a low threshold for perceptualizing, which is exacerbated by stress, isolation, or fatigue.
2. Hypervalent (hot) cognitions of sufficient energy exceed the perceptual threshold and are consequently transformed into hallucinations.
3. An externalizing bias reinforces the purported external origin of the voices.
4. Resource-sparing strategies and diminished reality testing (detecting and correcting errors, suspending judgment, collecting more data, reappraising, and providing alternative explanations) buttress this bias.

The maintenance of hallucinations is, in turn, determined by a range of beliefs: delusions regarding an external agent, underlying core beliefs, and the perceived "relationship" with the voices. Specific coping responses and safety-seeking behaviors also tend to maintain the faulty beliefs.

CHAPTER 5

A Cognitive Conceptualization of Negative Symptoms

A patient with a history of poor hygiene arrives to see his therapist appearing particularly unhygienic. Upon questioning, the patient, Mike, is quick to explain that his mother has suffered a hand injury that prevents her from doing all of the household chores, including, not insignificantly, his laundry. Further, Mike describes a recent meeting in which his psychiatrist inquired how, in lieu of his mother, he might get some laundry done. This question prompted Mike to explain that he needed to regain his health and intelligence (via an obscure procedure) so that he could get a girl who would do it for him. The psychiatrist responded by asking Mike if he was still taking his medication. Mike later confided in his therapist that he elected not to tell his psychiatrist that he actually planned to get two girls when he cured himself.

Mike is an Irish American in his mid-40s who developed schizophrenia during his high school years. Adherent to his expertly delivered pharmacotherapy, Mike regards his psychiatrist with high esteem. On tasks of attention, memory and executive function, Mike scores at least 2 standard deviations below the healthy control sample mean, suggesting a fairly significant cognitive impairment. Could this mean that he is incapable of doing his own laundry because he cannot marshal the cognitive resources to execute the task? When asked, Mike explains, "I do not like doing laundry." It does not take much more questioning (e.g., "Have you ever done your own laundry? How do you know if you like something without trying it?") before he says, "I cannot operate the machine." However, because he has never tried to do his own laundry, and because he has operated other devices that have equivalent procedural complexity as a laundry machine (e.g., VCR, stereo, and stove), a compelling alternative to cognitive impairment suggests itself: Mike has defeatist expectations regarding his ability to perform unfamiliar tasks, on the one hand, and perfectionist performance standards, on the other. These beliefs have safeguarded Mike against frustration and perceived failure and create the erroneous impression that a whole range of everyday tasks require more effort than he is able to muster.

Patients such as Mike, who manifest prominent negative symptoms, evidence a remarkable attenuation, if not an outright absence, of behavioral responses and internal experiences that typify healthy individuals. The core pathology consists of reduced verbal and nonverbal expressivity, as well as limited engagement in constructive, pleasurable, and social activity (Kirkpatrick et al., 2006). Whereas the clinician must rely on self-report and inference to assess hallucinations and delusions, negative symptoms are directly observable in patients' behavioral repertoire. Thus, *affective flattening* is seen in the "wooden exterior" and absence of mood; *alogia* in the paltry spontaneous speech; *avolition* in the passivity of going days without activity; *anhedonia* in the lack of engagement in pleasure; and *asociality* in the interpersonal isolation (McGlashan et al., 1990). Not observable in such patients are psychological states that accompany the behavioral and expressive diminution. What could such withdrawn and unresponsive individuals be thinking and feeling? McGlashan et al. speculate that their patients' lack of outward manifestation is mirrored by an equal attenuation of the inner experiences of motivation, emotion, and thought: Patients are described as "experiencing no motivation or purpose," lacking in "creativity and initiative," and possessing a simplified reality. The negative symptoms, finally, are characterized as stable defect or deficit states that form the baseline upon which the "acute, fragmented, and florid" symptoms (i.e., psychotic and disorganized) of schizophrenia are superimposed.

Observed in patients for more than 150 years (Berrios, 1985), the negative symptoms were central to the early definitions of the schizophrenia concept (see Chapter 1). Kraepelin (1971) thus proposed "weakening of the mainsprings of volition" and "the destruction of personality" (p. 74) as the two fundamental processes underlying *dementia praecox*; Bleuler (1911/1950), in agreement, suggested that "emotional deterioration stands in the forefront of the clinical picture. . . . Many . . . sit about the institutions to which they are confined with expressionless faces, hunched-up, the image of indifference" (p. 40). Yet, despite nearly 100 years of centrality, negative symptoms were neglected during the middle decades of the 20th century. It has been suggested (Carpenter, 2006) that the emergence of effective antipsychotic medications, combined with the popularity of Schneider's formulation of first-rank symptoms, produced a redefined concept of schizophrenia that emphasized episodic disruption of reality over stable emotional and behavioral deterioration.

In the 1980s, Tim Crow, Nancy Andreasen, and others spearheaded a revival of the concept of negative symptoms in schizophrenia (Brown & Pluck, 2000). As we saw in Chapter 1, Crow's (1980) type II schizophrenia (characterized by negative symptoms, poor treatment response, insidious onset, poor long-term outcome, and structural brain abnormality) placed negative symptoms into the foreground and reasserted the central formulation of Hughlings Jackson (1931), and others, that stable encephalopathology subtends the stable behavioral deficits of negative symptoms. Andreasen, correspondingly, developed an operationalized scale, the Scale for the Assessment of Negative Symptoms (SANS; Andreasen, 1984b), specifying the negative symptoms in observable terms. Scales such as the SANS, and later the Positive and Negative Syndrome Scale (PANSS; Kay et al., 1987), allowed for reliable ratings of negative symptoms across time and place and thus improved negative symptom measurement (Andreasen, 1990a, 1990b).

EMPIRICAL FINDINGS

Validity, Outcome, and Course

In the ensuing two decades, considerable progress has been made in the understanding of negative symptoms. First, while no more pathognomic than positive symptoms (Brown & Pluck, 2000), negative symptoms do have construct validity in schizophrenia (Earnst & Kring, 1997): Factor-analytic studies conducted in several cultures consistently include a unitary and distinct negative symptom factor in addition to psychotic and disorganized factors (Andreasen et al., 1995; Andreasen et al., 2005; Barnes & Liddle, 1990; John et al., 2003). Although the negative symptom dimension of schizophrenia can be further decomposed (Kimhy, Yale, Goetz, McFarr, & Malaspina, 2006), the singular factor hangs together such that it has a differential relationship, as compared to the other two factors, with course and outcome variables, as well as neurobiological and cognitive dysfunction. The validity of negative symptoms in schizophrenia is assured.

In terms of outcome, longitudinal studies show that degree of negative symptomatology is a prognostic indicator of impoverished social and occupational functioning, as well as inferior quality of life (Fuller et al., 2003). For instance, Andreasen and colleagues report that negative symptom severity—not positive or disorganized—at intake predicts worse quality of life 2 years later (Ho, Nopoulos, Flaum, Arndt, & Andreasen, 1998) and worse social functioning 7 years later (Milev, Ho, Arndt, & Andreasen, 2005). Other research groups have found a similar relationship between negative symptoms and outcome (Breier, Schreiber, Dyer, & Pickar, 1991; Wieselgren, Lindstrom, & Lindstrom, 1996). Long-term (i.e., 10 years or more) outcome studies also identify negative symptoms as a significant predictor of poor functioning (Bromet, Naz, Fochtmann, Carlson, & Tanenberg-Karant, 2005).

Differential relationship with outcome suggests differential course—and, indeed, epidemiological studies have found that negative symptoms differ from psychotic and disorganized dimensions across time. Research confirms, in accord with early theorists, that negative symptoms are relatively trait-like. Stable levels of negative symptoms have been reported prospectively, for example, across a 2-year follow-up (Arndt, Andreasen, Flaum, Miller, & Nopoulos, 1995). Additionally, a large German first-episode study also found stability of negative symptoms across 5 years (Hafner, 2003). Psychotic and disorganized factors were not as stable and did not, accordingly, predict outcome in either study. A recent study of chronically institutionalized individuals suggests that negative symptoms tend to remain stable or increase across the lifespan, whereas positive symptoms tend to decrease, with the best predictor of elevated negative symptoms being onset prior to the age of 25 (Mancevski et al., 2007). Results such as these have led several authors to conclude that for a great proportion of patients, schizophrenia is characterized by relatively enduring negative symptoms embellished with periodic psychotic exacerbation (Andreasen et al., 1995; American Psychiatric Association, 2000).

Carpenter and colleagues have identified a subset of patients with schizophrenia (15–20%) who demonstrate striking stability in a constellation of core negative symptoms (Carpenter et al., 1988). In order to be classified as "deficit syndrome," patients must have, for a period of 12 months, elevated negative symptoms (at least two of the following: restricted affect, diminished emotional range, poverty of speech, curbing of interests, diminished sense of purpose, diminished social drive) that are not secondary to illness-related factors such as positive symptoms, medications, cognitive deficits, anxiety, or depression (Kirkpatrick, Buchanan, McKenny, Alphs, & Carpenter, 1989). A study of first-episode patients illustrates the stability of the deficit syndrome: Deficit patients evidenced more consistently elevated negative symptoms as compared to nondeficit patients over a 2-year period (Ventura et al., 2004).

In addition to stability, negative symptoms also evidence temporal precedence with respect to the other symptom dimensions. Retrospective studies provide evidence that negative symptoms tend to emerge prior to the first onset of psychosis (Cannon, Tarrant, Huttunen, & Jones, 2003; Peralta, Cuesta, & de Leon, 1991). In a prospective design involving a large number of Israeli conscripts, negative-type symptoms (e.g., lack of friends) were the best predictors of later schizophrenia (Davidson et al., 1999). Similarly, individuals identified as being at high risk for developing schizophrenia tend to be characterized by significant elevation of negative-like symptomatology and a relative absence of positive symptomatology (Lencz, Smith, Auther, Correll, & Cornblatt, 2004).

That negative symptoms emerge prior to the other dimensions has led some authors to conclude, in line with Bleuler (1911/1950) and Kraepelin (1971), that negative symptoms are primary rather than secondary aspects of schizophrenia (Hafner & an der Heiden, 2003). Further, the addition of relative stability to early emergence has been interpreted as reflecting a stable underlying brain process in negative symptoms. Indeed, the earliest brain imaging results found enlargement of the lateral ventricle in schizophrenia (Moore et al., 1935), suggesting reduced brain volume, a finding that correlates with negative symptoms, according to later research (Johnstone & Ownes, 2004). Functional imaging, moreover, reveals underactivation of the frontal cortex in schizophrenia (Liddle & Pantelis, 2003; Stolar, 2004), which also correlates with negative symptoms (Wong & Van Tol, 2003). Taken together, this line of epidemiological and imaging research brings us back to Hughlings Jackson and Crow. Whether the mechanism is reduced volume of a specific brain region or hypoactivation of a specific area, researchers assert an isomorphism between observed behavioral deterioration and postulated brain dysfunction.

Neurocognitive Impairment

As we have already seen (Chapters 1 and 2), the information-processing tasks of everyday life present challenges to patients with schizophrenia: They show a reduced capacity to cull information from the environment, as well as an impaired ability to sustain concentration; they are easily distracted by internal and external stimuli and struggle when generating and implementing plans; they also have difficulty solving problems whose solutions are not readily apparent (Goldberg et al., 2003). Heinrichs (2005) reports results of a meta-analysis showing that patient performance on tasks of attention, memory, and executive function are shifted a standard deviation, relative to healthy controls, in the direction of worse performance. Importantly, cognitive deficits tend to be associated with negative symptoms more than with the psychotic or disorganized symptom dimensions (Keefe & Eesley, 2006; van Os & Verdoux, 2003). For example, in a cross-sectional study, O'Leary and colleagues (2000) found that, whereas psychotic symptoms were unrelated to cognitive measures and disorganized symptoms were related to a single cognitive measure, negative symptoms were related to performance on several tasks entailing memory, attention, and motor skills. Similar results have been reported by several international groups (Greenwood, Landau, & Wykes, 2005; Muller, Sartory, & Bender, 2004; Velligan et al., 1997).

Measures of neurocognitive performance not only correlate with negative symptoms but, not surprisingly, with outcome. Indeed, several researchers have found cognitive measures to be the best predictors of poor outcome (Green, 1996; Harvey et al., 1998; Velligan et al., 1997), though null findings have been reported (e.g., Addington, Saeedi, & Addington, 2005). For instance, patient performance on neurocognitive tasks at baseline predicts outcome at 5-year (Robinson et al., 2004) and 7-year (Milev et al., 2005) follow-ups. Green and colleagues (2000), in a widely cited meta-analysis, report small-to-medium effect sizes when measures of functional outcome were related to tests of executive function, secondary verbal memory (e.g., delayed recall of a list of words), immediate verbal recall, and sustained attention.

Diathesis–Stress Model of Negative Symptoms

The emerging research corpus supports a diathesis–stress formulation of schizophrenia (Strauss, Carpenter, & Bartko, 1975). Consistent with the research already reviewed, the genetic contribution to the emergence of negative symptoms is greater than that of positive symptoms, and obstetric complications appear more strongly associated with negative symptoms, as well (Cannon, Mednick, & Parnas, 1990). Certain individuals thus become susceptible to developing negative symptoms during adolescence due to a complex mixture of genetic and environmental risk factors. The genetic and obstetric factors seem to result in structural abnormalities, such as enlarged cerebral ventricles (Vita et al., 2000). Accordingly, Walker, Lewine, and Neumann (1996) have associated brain morphology to childhood motor abnormalities. Ventricular enlargement appears likely to predate the onset of psychosis (Foerster, Lewis, & Murray, 1991). Neuropathology in the form of abnormal cell migration, programmed cell death during gestation (Bunney & Bunney, 1999), and abnormal pruning during adolescence (Feinberg, 1983) may underlie the ventricular abnormality. Connectivity between various brain regions may be compromised by these neuronal insults, leading to poor integrative functioning of the brain (McGlashan & Hoffman, 2000) that, in turn, places limits on neurocognitive performance and processing resources. Indeed, adverse developmental stressors such as social and academic failures (Lencz et al., 2004), related to cognitive deficits and the dearth of processing resources, may comprise the proximal vulnerability to negative symptoms (see Chapter 14 for a further elaboration of these ideas).

That neurobiological and neurocognitive deficits are implicated in the pathogenesis of negative symptoms seems clear. Yet, despite the rich findings of research into the biocognitive substrates of negative symptoms, the psychological aspects of these symptoms remain relatively unexplored (Morrison, Renton, Dunn, Williams, & Bentall, 2004). This poverty of psychological theorizing may be partially due to an assumed isomorphism between lack of behavior and lack of thought. Nancy Andreasen (1984a) famously described the patient with negative symptoms as "an empty shell" who "cannot think" and has, consequently, lost the ability to suffer and hope. In this view, it is the root neuropathology that hollows the patient, limiting engagement in constructive activity as well as the production of expressive and communicative responses.

PSYCHOLOGY OF NEGATIVE SYMPTOMS

First-Person Accounts[1]

The self-reports of affected individuals provide a starting point for articulating the psychology of negative symptoms—and contrast rather poignantly with the postulated "empty shell." The following description comes from a 25-year-old male, 1 year after the onset of his psychosis:

---

[1] These personal accounts of schizophrenia were first collected by Davidson and Stayner (1997).

I can't control my thoughts. I can't keep thoughts out. It comes on automatically. . . . I lose control in conversation then I sweat and shake all
over. . . . I can hear what they are saying all right, it's remembering
what they have said the next second that's difficult—it just goes out of
mind. . . . I try to say something sensible and appropriate, but it is a
strain. . . . I keep talk to a minimum to prevent these attacks coming on.
(Chapman, 1966, p. 237)

The patient has a sense that memory and language are out of control, which
makes conversation with others particularly challenging. Cognitive impairment and thought disorder are evidently related to this patient's alogia and
social withdrawal. However, the effect is not direct; a desire to meet social
expectations of interlocutors combined with a keen sensitivity to rejection,
as well as possible overgeneralization of his difficulties to communicate,
drive this patient's social aversion and, ultimate, asociality. Another link
to social difficulty comes by way of the challenges that work and monetary
concerns present:

Many of us have to learn to cope with little money, or no money from
time to time. It almost always has an effect upon our relationships. If
we lose a job . . . it is difficult to maintain self-respect and relationships
with those we love, no matter what kind of relationship it is. (Seckinger,
1994, p. 20)

Not being able to keep a job or maintain fiscal autonomy has a considerable
negative impact on this patient's relationships with family members, as well
as potential friends and relationship partners. This patient may well anticipate criticism from others and elect to avoid them to reduce his distress.
Yet, it is the psychological factor of his own negative self-regard that mediates this relationship between vocational hardship and social withdrawal.
Warner (2004) has marshaled considerable data charting the impact of
unemployment upon recovery and quality of life in schizophrenia—data
suggesting that this patient's experience is a common occurrence.

The patient's self-perception of his or her own ability to function in
social situations can have a great deal to do with whether or not the patient
engages in social activity:

The largest problem I face—I think the basic one—is the intensity and
variety of my feelings, and my low threshold for handling other people's
intense feelings, especially negative ones. . . . I began to be afraid of people, of my family and friends; not because of what they represented . . .

but because of my own inability to cope with ordinary human contacts. (Hatfield & Lefley, 1993, p. 55)

Notable in this patient's account is the absolute terms in which he describes his social facility; he sees himself as simply lacking in his capacity to deal with the social interactions of everyday life. However, while empathizing with the patient's sense of futility, it also seems likely that he underestimates his ability to learn to cope with others. This is worth noting because of the ambivalent result that withdrawing from social engagement presents. The patient protects himself from aversive social experiences, but at the cost of isolation and acute loneliness. Another patient wrote: "I cannot control what words do to me. My physiology weeps. I hate myself. I am too weak to apologize for hurting the world. I want to love. I envy those who can relate to each other" (Bouricius, 1989, p. 205). In addition to a sense of social inadequacy, social stigma and incumbent threat of rejection also can contribute to the patient's uneasiness with others and, ultimately, to his or her profound isolation:

> Aggravating matters more is the painful knowledge that you can't talk to anybody about these things. Not only are these things hard to talk about, but if you admit to having any of these kinds of problems you are likely to get puzzled looks or face immediate and often final rejection. (Weingarten, 1994, p. 374)

The patient with prominent negative symptoms may feel "walled off" from others at a fundamental level. To the degree that the patient perceives social separation as irrevocable, he or she may be at risk for suicidal behavior.

Taking these self-reports as a starting point and integrating relevant research findings, the following sections articulate a psychology of negative symptoms in which dysfunctional and negative beliefs lead to the avoidance of constructive and pleasurable activity. The relevant factors contributing to loss of motivation and avoidance are low expectancies for pleasure (e.g., "I won't enjoy it"), low expectancies for success at social and nonsocial tasks (e.g., "I'm not going to be good enough"), low expectancies for social acceptance (e.g., "What do you expect? I'm mentally ill"), and defeatist beliefs regarding performance (e.g., "If I'm not sure I will succeed at a task, there's no point in trying"). The negative and overly general beliefs stymie the initiation of action (including speech and emotional expression), and, as such, act as mediators in the causal chains that link cognitive impairment, negative symptoms, and poor functioning in schizophrenia.

Negative Beliefs Activated by Positive Symptoms

Positive and negative symptoms overlap and interact to a considerable degree. The patient who hears denigrating voices in crowds, for example, chooses not to socialize because she fears others will hear the insults. Likewise, a patient who experiences delusions of somatic influence chooses to lie down all day to minimize the pain his tormentors' actions create in his body. Such effects are termed secondary negative symptoms. Ventura and colleagues (2004) have demonstrated, in support of anecdotal reports, that negative symptom exacerbations tend to be contemporaneous with exacerbations in hallucinations and delusions to a greater extent than would be predicted by chance.

These "secondary" behavioral responses are frequently mediated by negative beliefs and attitudes. For example, idiosyncratic delusional beliefs regarding voice omnipotence, uncontrollability, and infallibility determine whether the patient engages with the voices or, alternatively, becomes disengaged and withdrawn (Beck & Rector, 2003). Negative symptoms, additionally, can serve a compensatory protective function for the patient confronted with threatening delusions and hallucinations. For instance, one patient spent the entire day in bed to alleviate his fears of being monitored by government officials outside his home. Another patient withdrew from family and friends because she feared making mistakes that would trigger a voice stating "You're worthless." Idiosyncratic delusional beliefs can also lead to negative symptoms. One patient feared that he would get an erection while speaking to others and thus spoke very little (i.e., reflecting alogia). His concern to control arousal was such that he kept all activity to a bare minimum and spent most of his time trying to control his thoughts (i.e., reflecting anergia and withdrawal).

Social Aversion

Evidence of the role of negative attitudes toward social engagement in schizophrenia can be found on the Social Anhedonia Scale (Chapman, Chapman, & Miller, 1982; Chapman, Chapman, & Raulin, 1976) and its revision, the Revised Social Anhedonia Scale (Eckbald, Chapman, Chapman, & Mishlove, 1982). The values and preferences detailed in the items of this scale appear linked to social withdrawal: for example, "I attach very little importance to having close friends," "People sometimes think I'm shy when I really just want to be left alone," and "I prefer hobbies and leisure activities that do not involve other people." Such negative attitudes toward social affiliation appear to be prominent in biological relatives of individuals diagnosed with schizophrenia (Kendler, Thacker, & Walsh, 1996) and, accordingly, are also characteristic of those prone to developing psychosis (Chapman, Chapman, Kwapil, Eckbald, & Zinser, 1994; Miller et al., 2002). Further, Jack Blanchard and colleagues have found that patients with schizophrenia evidenced greater stability in negative attitudes toward social affiliation than either nonpsychiatric controls (Blanchard, Mueser, & Bellack, 1998) or individuals diagnosed with major depressive disorder (Blanchard, Horan, & Brown, 2001).

We have collected 15 items from the Revised Social Anhedonia Scale that best reflect social aversion. Sample items include "I prefer watching television to going out with other people," "I'm much too independent to really get involved with other people," and "I could be happy living all alone in a cabin in the woods or mountains." Endorsement of these items is related to performance on tasks of executive functioning, verbal memory, as well as to positive, negative, and disorganized symptoms. Indeed, the social aversion attitudes appear to be meditating variables (1) in the relationship between positive and negative symptoms, and (2) between cognitive impairment and negative symptoms (Grant & Beck, 2008b). These results suggest the therapeutic utility of eliciting social aversion attitudes in persons with negative symptoms, because the attitudes could be targeted directly to reduce social withdrawal.

Defeatist Performance Beliefs

Rector (2004) has found that patients with negative symptoms are likely to endorse dysfunctional beliefs and attitudes that reveal overly generalized negative conclusions regarding their own task performance. Sample items include "If I fail partly, it is as bad as being a complete failure," "If you cannot do something well, there is little point in doing it at all," and "If I fail at work, I'm a failure as a person" These items all entail a defeatist set and have been termed "defeatist performance attitudes" (Grant & Beck, in press). Rector found evidence that such beliefs feed into avoidance, apathy, and passivity, as defeatist attitude endorsement rates correlated with negative symptom levels independently from positive or depressive symptom levels. In a replication and extension of Rector's work, Grant and Beck (in press) report that patients who endorse defeatist beliefs show greater cognitive impairment on tasks of abstraction, memory, and attention, as well as worse negative symptoms and poorer social and vocational functioning. Significantly, defeatist performance beliefs mediated the relationship between cognitive impairment and both negative symptoms and functioning, suggesting a causal role in the withdrawal from constructive activity seen in individuals with negative symptoms.

Barrowclough and colleagues (2003) have found a significant negative correlation between patients' evaluation of their own positive attributes and role functioning, on the one hand, and their manifest negative symptom levels, on the other. Presumed deficits appear to determine patients' evaluations of personal worth: for example, their perceived lack of attractiveness, intelligence, and social skills, as well as perceived deficiencies in their role in various domains (e.g., social, interpersonal, occupational). Dysfunctional attitudes and perceived personal and interpersonal inadequacies might well converge to steer patients to a "point of safety" that isolates them socially.

Developmentally, social distancing combined with negative attitudes toward affiliation and defeatist attitudes regarding performance might potentiate negative symptoms at the point of illness onset. In support of this idea, there is preliminary evidence of a relationship between defeatist beliefs and negative symptoms in individuals who are at "ultra-high" risk for developing a psychotic disorder (Perivoliotis, Morrison, Grant, French, & Beck, 2008). More generally, specific attitudes and beliefs mediate the effect of cognitive impairment upon negative symptoms and social and vocational functioning, exacerbating and maintaining withdrawal from constructive activity. The emphasis upon beliefs and expectations for failure in negative symptoms is much in line with conceptualizations of motivated behavior (Eccles & Wigfield, 2002); efficacy beliefs, in particular, have been shown to be important mediators between task resources and task engagement in healthy subjects (Llorens, Schaufeli, Bakker, & Salanova, 2007).

Negative Expectancy Appraisals

In addition to defeatist social and performance beliefs, there is another set of cognitive factors that participates in negative symptoms independent of positive symptoms. Specifically, patients appraise their future experience with diminished expectation for pleasure, success, and acceptance; additionally, they perceive themselves to be lacking in the cognitive resources required for the tasks of daily living (Rector, Beck, & Stolar, 2005). The form and content of each negative expectancy is considered next.

Low Expectancies for Pleasure

Pessimistic and negativistic expectations are also a hallmark of patient cognition regarding engagement in pleasurable activity. As an illustration, consider the patient who tended to spend many hours each day lying in bed. On one occasion, he decided to pick up his guitar and proceeded to play a few chords. He rapidly had the realization, though, that the strings needed tuning, and he quickly had the thought "Why bother? It's more work than it's worth." He turned on the television instead. Patients thus appear to anticipate yielding little enjoyment in exchange for any effort they might muster; further, their attention is keenly fixated on great expectations for displeasure. DeVries and Delespaul (1989), utilizing methodology that samples experiences throughout the day, found that patients with schizophrenia report experiencing more negative emotions and fewer positive emotions in their day-to-day lives than healthy controls, a result that agrees with questionnaire-based studies (Berenbaum & Oltmanns, 1992; Burbridge & Barch, 2007) and might occur because these patients participate in fewer pleasurable activities.

An intriguing contrast has emerged in the experimental literature regarding emotional expression and experience in schizophrenia. Patients consistently evidence significantly fewer positive and negative facial expressions, as compared to nonpatient controls, in response to emotionally eliciting stimuli (Kring & Neale, 1996), an effect which is especially pronounced for patients with enduring negative symptoms (Earnst & Kring, 1999). Patient subjective reports of emotion, on the contrary, reflect the full range, in terms of magnitude (i.e., arousal level) and valence (i.e., positive and negative), found in nonpatient controls (Berenbaum & Oltmanns, 1992; Kring & Neale, 1996), even when the patients manifest chronic and severe negative symptoms. Anhedonia is typically defined as a diminution in the ability to experience pleasure (Andreasen, 1984b; American Psychiatric Association, 2000), yet the emerging research literature suggests that these patients can and do experience pleasure to an equivalent degree as healthy controls.

Rather than reflecting a deficit of emotional experience, anhedonia may reflect incorrect expectancies with regard to engagement in pleasurable activity on the part of individuals diagnosed with schizophrenia (Germans & Kring, 2000). This formulation simultaneously accounts for patients' lower reported pleasure and equal ability to experience pleasure. Specifically, if patients do not anticipate that pleasurable activities will indeed be pleasurable, they may well choose not to engage in them, leading to less pleasurable experiences in their everyday life. In support of this proposal, Gard and colleagues (2007) have found that patients with schizophrenia score lower, relative to healthy controls, on a scale tapping the *anticipa-*

tion of pleasure, while scoring equivalently on a scale that taps the actual experience of pleasure.

Despite their low expectancy for pleasure, patients do experience some enjoyment once engaged in a task. For instance, one patient, whose day-to-day routine had been reduced to sleeping, eating, and attending doctors' appointments, identified a list of activities in which she used to take pleasure but no longer anticipated enjoying, including calling family, vacuuming the house, taking baths, watching television, and praying. Although the initial ratings of *expected* pleasure were close to zero, she subsequently reported experiencing mild satisfaction when vacuuming, moderate enjoyment during the bath and watching television, and high pleasure when speaking with her mother on the telephone. It is important to obtain ratings at the time of the event, because upon recall, patients tend to underestimate their level of enjoyment. Of course, the negatively biased recollections serve to reinforce a negative view of the situation and to minimize the pleasure taken.

Low Expectancies for Success

Patients also show bias in their reported low expectancies for success in a proposed task. They often expect to fail to meet given goals and if they meet the goals, they tend to perceive substandard performance in comparison to their expected performance. This negative outlook affects their motivation to initiate and sustain goal-directed behavior, especially when under stress. The impaired role of executive functioning in maintaining goal-directed thoughts, especially on complex tasks, in schizophrenia (Berman et al., 1997; Stolar, Berenbaum, Banich, & Barch, 1994), does not adequately account for why patients do not complete simple tasks at times or are engaged in making an effort toward a specific goal one day but not the next. Moreover, when sufficiently motivated, these patients can carry out complex tasks that seem to be beyond their capacity.

Many patients show negative expectations that interfere with motivation and action. A socially isolated patient, for example, would pick up a phone to make a call but would then quickly hang up. The patient's thought was "I'm not going to sound right, I'll have nothing to say." He was then able to recognize similar performance-related concerns when he thought about attending day hospital groups ("I'm going to take too long to say everything that I'll want to say"), going to the gym ("I won't be able to get through all the weights"), and playing soccer ("I'm not going to be good enough"), areas that he listed at the beginning of treatment as those in which he is "lacking motivation." As he recognized these deterrents to action, he became motivated to follow through on a given goal.

Because some patients do indeed report having greater difficulties with concentration, fine motor skills, and sustained effort to see things through to the end, the question emerges: Is this negative view of likely success accurate? A core difficulty contributing to negative performance expectation is that patients become easily defeated and consequently disappointed in their performance. In addition to the frustration that follows from failing to meet self-directed goals, patients with prominent negative symptoms also experience considerable guilt in the perception that they have failed to meet other people's past and present expectations of them. The double burden of the persistent recognition of failure to meet their own and others' expectations consolidates core beliefs around themes of being a "failure," "useless," "worthless," "a bum." Patients become hypervigilant and exquisitely sensitive to the perception of criticism. A patient, encouraged by his mother to awaken and get dressed for a doctor's appointment, reported feeling annoyed as he thought to himself, "I'm always being hassled," "I'm too tired," and "They expect too much from me." He responded by going back to bed.

Barrowclough and colleagues (2003) found that the degree of perceived critical comments from family members predicted the presence and severity of negative symptoms but not positive symptoms. Conversely, when relatives were perceived as warm and supportive, patients reported a higher positive evaluation of their own role performance.

Low Expectancies Due to Stigma

The sense of defeat can loom large over the patient with prominent negative symptoms. Such a patient might say, "I have no house. I have no wife. I have no car. I have no friends." These patients poignantly realize that they have not achieved the broader goals of the culture—to work, find a life partner, and enjoy leisurely pursuits—yet they have not abandoned their desire for these goals. The symptoms of schizophrenia can introduce real limitations; however, being given a *diagnosis* of schizophrenia is demoralizing in and of itself. Patients may interpret the diagnosis as confirmation of negative beliefs that they hold about themselves; for example, "I have schizophrenia, and that is why I am incompetent, worthless, and a failure." It might seem natural for patients to see the diagnosis of schizophrenia as a "death sentence." Stigmatizing illness-related beliefs may become integrated into the patient's self-construals, adding to his or her disability. When faced with challenges, these construals can have a deleterious effect on the patient's perception of self-efficacy. Such beliefs are reflected in statements such as "What do you expect, I'm mentally ill," or "It doesn't matter what I do, it's not going to change the fact that I'm just a schizophrenic," or "There's no hope for me—I've got schizophrenia."

For instance, a patient developed a sense that he was being "judged for being crazy" when he played basketball. The patient explained that he would get a "weird sensation" in his stomach while playing, which made it clear to him that he was being criticized. He subsequently avoided playing a game that had been highly pleasurable for him in the past. When presented with a volunteer opportunity, another patient stated, "Why bother? I've already been left behind. It's as if I have a yellow stripe down my back. I'm just a label living in a bubble." A third patient considered himself "walled off" from others because of his condition and committed suicide.

Perception of Limited Resources

Beliefs related to the perceived personal cost of expending energy to make an effort also contribute to the pattern of passivity and avoidance. When the opportunity arises to participate in an activity that they used to engage in and enjoy, patients with prominent negative symptoms will have the thought, "It's not worth the effort" (Grant & Beck, 2005). For instance, one patient referred for treatment complained of "low motivation and low energy," explaining that it "took too much effort" to lift his head from the pillow.

Patient perceptions of limited resources are likely to have more than a grain of truth to them, as a considerable literature has accrued documenting processing decrements in schizophrenia (Keefe & Eesley, 2006). Affected processes include reductions in sustained attention, difficulty maintaining a task set, and a suboptimal level of readiness for processing (Nuechterlein & Dawson, 1984). Moreover, it has been argued that affective flattening, alogia, apathy, and social withdrawal might result from reductions in the nonspecific pool of cognitive resources (Nuechterlein et al., 1986). Yet, patients with prominent negative symptoms are also characterized by a defeatist cognitive set that leads them to exaggerate the extent of their cognitive limitations.

Avoidance of effortful engagement can be seen as a resource-sparing strategy consciously aimed at limiting future harm. When confronted with a challenge, patients will explain that they are "not ready," that it would be "too uncomfortable," and that they have "low energy." These beliefs protect patients from raising the expectations of others; however, the cost is high as they jettison their goals and ambitions for the sake of interpersonal comfort. Indeed, there is evidence that patients with cognitive impairment are quite likely to endorse the statement, "If a person avoids problems, the problems tend to go way" (Grant & Beck, 2008, unpublished data).

SUMMARY

Research over the past 25 years has established negative symptoms as relatively stable features of schizophrenia that are treatment refractory and thereby associated with considerable disability. Based on first-person reports and the existing research literature, we have charted a cognitive model of negative symptoms that provides a link between neurocognitive impairment and emotional and behavioral deficits. Specifically, we have identified several cognitive factors that participate in negative symptoms: social-aversion attitudes, defeatist performance beliefs, negative expectancies for pleasure and success, and perception of limited cognitive resources. Because each of the cognitive factors can be assessed and modified by cognitive-behavioral techniques (see Chapter 11), the present conceptualization of negative symptoms provides a basis for a cognitive therapy of negative symptoms aimed at increasing engagement in constructive and pleasurable activity. This model of negative symptoms is further elaborated and advanced in Chapter 14.

CHAPTER 6

A Cognitive Conceptualization of Formal Thought Disorder

Bill is a 23-year-old single unemployed former college student who presents with delusions of having written novels that have been published but for which he has not been compensated. He exhibits disorganized speech, such that every third sentence is not comprehensible in terms of any intended meaning. The sentences make grammatical sense but utilize words in unique ways. An example of one response that was at least partially understandable was:

THERAPIST: So what would you say you want out of life?
PATIENT: Structurally speaking, I want to remain grounded.

When he was asked by the therapist what he thought of the last session:

PATIENT: I was talking to a guy with brown hair.

Another example when he was interrupted by a family member:

PATIENT: You are going over my feet.

The therapist took this last statement to mean that he was upset with the family member for interrupting him and asked if that was the case. He replied that he was upset, and the family member let him continue first.

The therapist noticed that Bill's disorganized speech got worse when he was angry about something. The therapist decided to not pursue the current topic when the disorganized speech worsened but rather to wait until a later time. Items of speech that were comprehensible were repeated back in the therapist's words to confirm comprehension. Items that were partially understood were examined with queries about their meaning. For example:

THERAPIST: Would you be OK if we had a session with your parents also present?

PATIENT: I want to remain here in a box.

THERAPIST: Do you mean that you want to keep these sessions private, as if we were in a box, or do you mean something else?

PATIENT: Yes.

THERAPIST: You mean that you want to keep these sessions private?

PATIENT: Yes.

THERAPIST: Or did you mean something else?

PATIENT: No.

Repeated use of queries, confirmations, and breaks from certain subjects eventually led to a better understanding between the therapist and the patient, with subsequent examination of the automatic thoughts behind Bill's anger in response to certain situations. He was better able to control his anger, which led to less instances of formal thought disorder, even outside of session.

Formal thought disorder is part of a larger set of symptoms frequently categorized under the term *disorganization* that also includes inappropriate affect and bizarre behavior. Disorganization is one of three categories resulting from a factor analysis of the symptoms of schizophrenia (Liddle, 1987), the other two being reality distortion (hallucinations and delusions) and psychomotor poverty (the negative symptoms). Bleuler (1911/1950) considered disorganized thought to be a fundamental symptom of schizophrenia in that it is present throughout the course of the disorder and as a primary symptom in that other symptoms follow from it. The practical importance of investigating the nature and potential amelioration of this set of symptoms is shown by its correlation with present and future poor performance in work, school, and social functions (Harrow, Silverstein, & Marengo, 1983; Liddle, 1987; Norman et al., 1999).

Most of the work in cognitive therapy for schizophrenia has focused on delusions, hallucinations, and, more recently, negative symptoms. We present here a cognitive model of formal thought disorder both as a way of conceptualizing this set of symptoms through an understanding of its cognitive factors and as a way to enhance the use of cognitive therapy for schizophrenia by including therapeutic approaches to manage these symptoms in addition to the negative and other positive symptoms. Descriptions of the various types of formal thought disorder precedes the presentation of the cognitive model. These are followed by explanations of how information-processing models of thought disorder are compatible with the cognitive model. Finally, the application of these ideas to the use of cognitive therapy for the treatment of formal thought disorder is presented in Chapter 12.

PHENOMENOLOGY OF FORMAL THOUGHT DISORDER

Formal thought disorder is manifested as a language disorder. The language (or speech) presumably reflects disorganized thought in terms of thought *processes* as opposed to thought *content*.

Formal thought disorder is composed of various symptoms. There are positive forms that cluster into two groups—loosening of associations and idiosyncratic use of language (Andreasen & Grove, 1986; Peralta et al., 1992)—and there are negative forms such as poverty of speech and thought blocking.

Loosening of associations consists of various forms of getting off the track of a flow of the conversation—hence the term *derailment* preferred by Andreasen (1979). Individual examples of this category (as defined by Andreasen, 1979) include:

- Derailment (or loose associations): "Ideas slip off the track onto another one that is . . . obliquely related . . . or unrelated" (p. 1319).
- Tangentiality: "Replying to a question in an oblique, tangential or even irrelevant manner" (p. 1318).
- Loss of goal (or drifting): "Failure to follow a chain of thought through to its natural conclusion" (p. 1320).

- Incoherence (or word salad): "A series of words or phrases seem to be joined together arbitrarily and at random" (p. 1319).
- Illogicality: "Conclusions are reached that do not follow logically" (p. 1320).

Idiosyncratic use of language includes:

- Neologisms: "New word formations" (p. 1320).
- Word approximations: "Old words that are used in a new . . . way, or new words that are developed by conventional rules of word formation" (p. 1320).

The negative thought disorder symptoms that are not necessarily part of the psychomotor poverty syndrome (the negative syndrome) include:

- Blocking: "Interruption of a train of speech before a thought or idea has been completed" (p. 1321).
- Poverty of content of speech: "Speech . . . conveys little information. Language tends to be vague, often over abstract or over concrete, repetitive, or stereotyped" (p. 1318). This includes (Marengo, Harrow, & Edell, 1994).
  - Concreteness: "A lack of generalization from an immediate stimulus" (p. 29).
  - Perseveration: "Persistent repetition of words, ideas, or subjects" (p. 29).
  - Clanging: "Sounds rather than meaningful relationships appear to govern word choice" (p. 29).
  - Echolalia: "The patient echoes words or phrases of the interviewer" (p. 29).

In summary, formal thought disorder is divided into loosening of associations, idiosyncratic use of language, thought blocking, and poverty of content of speech.

A COGNITIVE MODEL
OF FORMAL THOUGHT DISORDER

The basic cognitive model is one in which events (or situations) stimulate automatic thoughts (adding psychological meaning to the events), which in turn call forth emotional and behavioral responses (Beck et al., 1979). The automatic thoughts often contain, or are guided by, beliefs and underlying assumptions. The emotions often include physiological responses and the conscious experiencing of emotion (the cognitive element of emotion). These emotions and behaviors can themselves become stimuli for automatic thoughts (and further emotional and behavioral reactions). For example, a person with schizophrenia is admonished by her caretaker for making a mess (event). This experience leads her to believe that an impostor has replaced the caretaker (automatic thought). She gets angry (emotion) about this perceived turn of events and starts yelling (behavior), but when asked why she is angry, she says that the imposter hypnotized her to yell (automatic thought).

The symptoms of schizophrenia correlate with the stages of the cognitive model. Hallucinations are events that may contain automatic thoughts, delusions are beliefs, and bizarre behaviors and negative symptoms are behavioral responses (inactivity, in the case of negative symptoms). Formal thought disorder is viewed here as part of a stress (physiological) response to the automatic thoughts elicited by various events. The process might be similar in certain respects to that of stuttering, in that stressful situations exacerbate both types of symptoms (Blood, Wertz, Blood, Bennett, & Simpson, 1997), and that the phenomena can occur in nearly anyone under certain traumatic conditions. Those with each disorder, however, have a much lower threshold for occurrence of the symptoms than does the general population.

There is evidence that symptoms of formal thought disorder worsen in those with schizophrenia when there is increased stress, as when the topic is emotionally salient (Docherty, Cohen, Nienow, Dinzeo, & Dangelmaier, 2003) or when the person is criticized by family members (Rosenfarb, Goldstein, Mintz, & Nuechterlein, 1995). Lack of familiarity with an interviewer or therapist, increased length of time spent talking in a given session, and "hot" topics can all contribute to increased severity of symptoms.

For example, consider the case of a patient who showed marked formal thought disorder consisting of derailment (loosening of associations) and tangentiality. It appeared that the patient would not be able to engage in therapy, given her lack of focused discourse. She had been seeing a different psychiatrist for medication management for many years and was reluctant to be brought by her mother to the new therapist/psychiatrist. By the very next session, her formal thought disorder had disappeared and has remained latent for the more than 4 years of therapy, which focuses instead on her hallucinations and delusions. It appears that the stress of the first meeting with the therapist contributed to the exacerbation of the formal thought disorder.

Another patient's formal thought disorder was not apparent until the end of 15-minute medication management sessions. Each new session started with normal discourse but evolved into frank disorganized speech after about 10 minutes. Presumably there was a limit to how long this patient could keep her thoughts organized each time.

For yet another patient, short instances of formal thought disorder appeared mainly in sessions in which his mother was invited to attend and when he showed signs of annoyance in response to things she said.

As these examples imply, the process producing the stress response has psychological meaning. This meaning can be determined by exploring the automatic thoughts that precede onset or worsening of the thought disorder symptoms. The occurrence or exacerbation of formal thought disorder can be a signal that the current issue being discussed (or raised by the therapist) is important, and likely distressing, to the patient. Derailment might even be an unintentional means by which patients avoid certain unpleasant items.

As in depression and anxiety disorders, specific types of automatic thoughts and distorted beliefs can lead to the occurrence of the thought disorder symptoms. By examining the upsetting thoughts a person has prior to the moment of disorganized speech, strategies for cognitive therapy are developed for that person and can be applied to other patients as well. This application is important, since it would be very difficult to access the automatic thoughts of more severe cases of formal thought disorder. Assumptions based on the speech of more comprehensible patients facilitate treatment with less intelligible ones until the severity of the formal thought disorder is diminished to the point that formal cognitive therapy can be initiated and idiosyncratic automatic thoughts accessed. To date, there are no studies exploring the content of automatic thoughts that are related specifically to the presence and severity of formal thought disorder. Some automatic thoughts that might be particularly likely to precede the activation of formal thought disorder include:

"I can't handle what is happening right now."
"I don't know what I should say."
"What I say will probably be wrong."

Interviews and questionnaires can be used to determine if these or other automatic thoughts are characteristic of situations involving formal thought disorder.

In addition to determining initial cognitive precipitants of formal thought disorder, it is also useful to explore cognitive responses to the reactions of other people to patients with formal thought disorder (these responses can worsen or at least perpetuate formal thought disorder). In particular, the inability of most people to comprehend what is being related by someone with formal thought disorder can lead the patient to think "I'm not understood," thereby increasing stress and worsening the formal thought disorder. On the other hand, the common occurrence of others' pretending to understand the person with formal thought disorder can lead to automatic thoughts such as "I'm understood [so I can continue to talk the way I am]." These scenarios can transpire despite the fact that patients with formal thought disorder are not usually aware of their disorganized speech. What they notice is that others do or do not seem to understand what they are saying.

Although thought disorder is considered here as part of a stress response, the content of the material uttered often has psychological meaning. This meaning is typically missed by others due to the difficulty of comprehension. A patient who says, "I'm happy to be here—I'm off work, off-site, off meds" may be admitting to poor medication compliance, but the significance is lost in the string of irrelevant phrases. In fact, on the other hand, it may be unemployment that is the real issue for the patient.

As this example illustrates, the specific content of thought disorder can be influenced by the presence of hypersalient cognitions. These are automatic thoughts that have a particular, timely relevance for the patient and tend to have emotional valence. Most people can inhibit the expression of these cognitions if the context calls for such inhibition. In those with thought disorder, the hypersalient cognitions will more often encroach on current discourse—though not in a clear, comprehensible manner but rather via loose associations or idiosyncratic word usage.

INFORMATION-PROCESSING MODELS
OF FORMAL THOUGHT DISORDER

Spreading Activation in Semantic Networks

Since thought disorder manifests in the modality of speech (Salomé, Boyer, & Fayol, 2002), it is useful to outline a model of normal speech production as a template on which to examine disruptions that could account for thought disorder. Levelt's (1989) model of speech production posits a system in which concepts are the starting point and words the end point. In essence, the model hypothesizes a conceptual formulation of the intended message, followed by word choices and grammatical and syntactic planning, then phonological encoding to result in motor output. Words at the conceptual, syntactic, or phonological levels are connected based on degree of similarity (e.g., rhyming, alliteration, categorization) and personal learned associations. Modifications that incorporate ideas from Dell (1986) transform this linear model into one containing feedback loops as well as more interactions and temporal overlaps among the various stages of Levelt's model.

As an example of these models, imagine wanting to tell someone about what happened during your day. At the conceptual level you could decide to give a chronology of the day's events or a review of the most important events. The former would involve a search of memory involving a series of events associated by time. Memory of one event in the morning would connect to the next event. A template of your normal routine would guide your thinking process. The latter might involve a more categorical search, possibly for emotional content, to recall the day's significant events. Once an event is selected, the general concepts (possibly in imagery form) are ready. Now the means of expressing the content must be selected in terms of word choice and grammar. However, as these are being selected, you may edit portions of the general concept of the event (e.g., if you suspect that the listener might get offended by certain parts of the narrative). At times, you may have to decide in what order to give the information, such as leaving the ending as a surprise versus giving the ending and then explaining what led up to it.

In these models, there are many points at which errors of expression can be made. In terms of thought disorder, many errors are related to a lack of linear progression in speech. Levelt (1989), as well as Collins and Quillian (1969) and others, describes how the mind has networks of related items such that activation of one item can lead to activation (recall) of other associated items. These networks operate at the various levels of concept, word choice, pronunciation, and so forth. Collins and Loftus (1975) showed how different items (nodes) are located at various semantic distances from each other, and when one becomes activate, spreading activation to associated nodes commences. The likelihood of an associated node being activated depends partly on its semantic distance from the initially activated node.

As an example of how one word can have multiple associations, consider how the word *rose* can be associated with the flower, the color, people with that name, a song of that name, the sound of the word, other meanings of the word (e.g., "got up"), words that rhyme with it (as when constructing a poem). In thought disorder, controlled selection regarding word or sentence choice is lacking such that related but nonetheless irrelevant paths are taken. These paths include derailment to an oblique but somehow related topic (loosening of associations), use of rhyming words (clanging), repetition of words (perseveration), repetition of what is said by another (echolalia), use of the literal version of an abstract concept (concreteness), and use of conceptually related words that are not used conventionally in that way (neologisms). In other words, most of the formal thought disorder symptoms can be described as verbalizing an associated path in the networks described by Levelt. The term "loosening of associations" may have been chosen rather than "non-associations" because there is probably some connection between the current item and the divergent item, even if this connection is not obvious to the listener.

Returning to the example above, related items come to mind while telling about one's day. For example, telling about the drive to work can bring up thoughts about the car having troubles, a billboard advertising an upcoming event of interest, one's desire to bike to work to lose weight, and so on. These associated thoughts vary in degree of activation and therefore the degree to which one is aware of each associated thought. One might be fully aware of an associated thought and decide to veer the conversation in that direction, or the thought might be held in working memory for later reference after finishing the current topic of one's day. A third alternative when one is aware of the thought is to reject its overt expression. In formal thought disorder, inhibition of these offshoots is lacking, such that topics are switched without warning and may be so loosely associated or associated in such an idiosyncratic way that the listener might not make the connection.

For example, an inpatient with schizophrenia was told that she may need an inhaler for a respiratory condition. She responded by saying, "The model." After the initial confusion, a member of the treatment team remembered that not too long ago, there was a model who died while using an inhaler. The patient confirmed that this is what she meant. Without this information, the tangential remark may have been viewed as having no association to the current item.

In normal speech, similar associative processes and choices occur at the levels of word or sentence choice and pronunciation. Choosing a word, phrase, or sentence activates other associated choices to various degrees. One might be fully aware of another word that could be substituted for the chosen word. The *drive* to work could have been the *route* or *way* just as easily, but *drive* is chosen. In formal thought disorder, there is a breakdown in the word choice, as occurs in neologisms in which related words are used in a meaning not customarily used for that purpose (e.g., *hot glove* for oven mitten), or when associated concrete words are used in place of one of the proper choices (e.g., saying "myself in front of me" in place of "my reflection in the mirror"). In normal discourse, associated pronunciations are activated to some degree, as evidenced by the not uncommon occurrence of slips of tongue with words similar in pronunciation or meaning to the intended word. In formal thought disorder, associated pronunciations can take the form of rhyming words (e.g., "I went to the store, floor, shore") or alliterations (e.g., "I went to the store, stay, stare, star").

Evidence for the increased spread of activation along nodes in a semantic network existed before these terms were used. Payne (as cited in McKenna & Oh, 2005) twice reviewed the literature on tests of *overinclusiveness*, a term coined by Cameron (as cited in Chapman & Chapman, 1973a) but later replaced by *increased spread of activation*. Such tests included (1) sorting cards into word categories, in which those with schizophrenia would make such overinclusive errors as putting vegetables in the fruit category (Chapman & Taylor, 1957); (2) underlining words that were central to the description of target words, in which those with schizophrenia would include related but nonessential words, such as *stewardess* and *luggage* (in addition to the correct answers of *wing* and *cockpit*) as defining words for *airplane* (Moran, 1953; Epstein, 1953). Hawks and Payne (1971) were one of the only researchers at the time to demonstrate the specificity of overinclusiveness for formal thought disorder. They found that the mean of three tests distinguished those with thought disorder from those with schizophrenia but without formal thought disorder (the latter not differing significantly from controls).

Although future theorists eventually dropped the term *overinclusiveness*, Maher (1983) presented a theory similar to the principles of over-inclusiveness. McKenna and Oh (2005) rephrased Maher's theory, using more modern terms, stating, "When a cognitive process activates a node in semantic memory, this increases the probability that some of the nodes with links to it will be activated as well. Normally, most of these associations do not enter consciousness" (McKenna & Oh, 2005, p. 156). In formal thought disorder, this spreading activation is not inhibited so that associations irrelevant to the topic at hand intrude into speech. As further explained by McKenna and Oh (2005), "The problem was not one of abnormal associations, but the inappropriate intrusion of normal associations into speech" (p. 157). (However, we argue here that some of these associations could actually have some psychological significance to the patient.) Maher added, however, that over time repetition of some irrelevant associations could become more solidified, leading to idiosyncratic associations. (Again, we add that the patient's personal history can lead more rapidly to idiosyncratic associations. For example, a person with formal thought disorder who took train rides as a child to go to the dentist might say, as an adult, when seeking help in a station to find a certain train, "I need to find the right train to pull my teeth.")

Maher tested his model using a lexical decision task in which the subject must decide whether a target word is a real word or not (Manschreck et al., 1988). A priming word precedes the target word. In controls, if the priming word is semantically related to the target word, the reaction time to decide if the target word is real or not is reduced. This effect is referred to as semantic priming, and it provides evidence for a spreading activation from nodes to associated words. The idea is that the priming word creates a spread of activation to associated words. When the target is one of these associated words, it has already been activated by the prime words; thus when it appears on the screen, the reaction time for the lexical decision is reduced. In those with formal thought disorder, hyperpriming occurs— that is, even shorter reaction times occur due to an accentuation of the priming effect. This finding was confirmed by others (e.g., Spitzer, Braun, Hermle, & Maier, 1993), but studies have shown contradictory findings, partly due to the lack of using short time intervals between the prime and target words (relating to the time interval in which the importance of increased spreading activation would be most prominent). A meta-analysis (Pomarol-Clotet et al., as cited in McKenna & Oh, 2005) controlled for this factor and found that there is significantly increased semantic priming effects in patients with formal thought disorder (effect size = 0.55; CI = .36/.73).

The associated words mistakenly used in speech by those with formal thought disorder tend to be words that are also predominantly chosen by those without schizophrenia as associated words when there is no contextual constraint (Chapman & Chapman, 1973a). For example, "Father, Son . . . " would most commonly be followed by "Holy Ghost" by most controls as well as by those with schizophrenia. However, if one is listing one's household starting with "Father, son . . . ," one would not continue with "Holy Ghost," as did one of Bleuler's patients (as cited in Chapman & Chapman, 1973a). The task context of listing one's household would normally constrain the word choice. In a series of studies conducted by Chapman and colleagues (Chapman & Chapman, 1973a), it was shown that

the associated words used by those with schizophrenia tend not to be idiosyncratic as much as they are the product of an "excessive yielding to normal
response biases" (p. 119). The normal biases may be based on familiarity, recency effects, similarity, and other factors. People with schizophrenia
tend to choose words based on normal response biases, even if the context requires the choice of a word with a weaker normal response bias. For
instance, *bear* would produce a normal response bias of a type of animal,
but in some contexts, the meaning *carry* is the appropriate choice. People
with schizophrenia tend to choose the animal despite the contextual constraint that leads nonclinical controls to the choice of *carry*.

The studies cited by Chapman and Chapman (1973a) typically con-
sisted of tasks that required associating a target word with one of three
choices: the correct choice (given the context or task demands), an associated choice, or an irrelevant choice. The controls would make more errors
by choosing associated words than by choosing irrelevant words, and the
degree of error increased with increased difficulty of the task. This response
bias was accentuated for those with schizophrenia (Chapman, 1958). Later
studies by this group demonstrated that people with schizophrenia choose
word meanings that are the same as those preferred by nonclinical controls
(Chapman & Chapman, 1965; Chapman, Chapman, & Miller, 1964), further supporting the idea that the key difference is the degree of spreading
activation as opposed to the specific nodes to which activation spreads.
There was some deviation from this general finding, however, when there
was no strong consensus among nonclinical raters for preferred word meanings. In other words, those with schizophrenia would choose nonpreferred
word meanings when there was less agreement among the raters. Although
it has not been tested yet, we predict that, in specific instances, those with
formal thought disorder will experience increased spreading activation to
nodes that are based on more personal associations, as explained earlier.
Nonetheless, on average, the associated words are based on associations
also present in the general population.

Attentional Resources

In normal discourse, an attentional process imparts a general linearity to
the conversation such that a goal is pursued (allowing for some divergence,
but usually with a return to the intended path). The lack of inhibition of
associated words (conceptual or phonological) in formal thought disorder,
leading to nonlinear discourse, can be viewed as an attentional disorder.
(This formal thought disorder difficulty differs from the difficulty associ-

ated with attention-deficit/hyperactivity disorder in that the former involves attention toward internal, cognitive material, such as words, whereas in the latter, the difficulties occur in relation to external stimuli.) Chapman and Chapman (1973) present possible reasons for their findings indicating an accentuation of normal response biases, including a failure to attend to contextual cues and an inability to "disattend from strong stimuli" (Cromwell & Dokecki, as cited in Chapman & Chapman, 1973a, p. 134). Support for the latter process over the former comes from one of Chapman's own studies (Chapman et al., 1964), in which nonpreferred meanings were correctly identified by those with schizophrenia when the preferred meanings were excluded from the possible choices. The presence of a strong (preferred) stimulus creates the difficulty of inhibiting attention to that choice. It is possible that the inhibition process in these circumstances involves properly using contextual cues to divert attention from normal response biases to the correct, but atypical, responses.

A number of models of attention posit that a supervisory attentional system (Norman & Shallice, 1980; Shallice, 1982) or a central executive (Baddeley, 1986, 1990, 1992; Cowan, 1988) "oversees" the selection of items from activated memory or working memory to become the foci of attention. These models are supported by neuropsychological and imaging studies showing the involvement of the dorsolateral prefrontal cortex in tasks requiring selective attention (Smith & Jonides, 2003). The supervisory attentional system keeps the associated thoughts in the network from diverting the direction of the discourse too much or too frequently. In thought disorder, there is a breakdown in the focus provided by this supervisory attentional system, such that associated items may divert the conversation at the conceptual, lexical, and phonological levels.

The central executive is used when a task is difficult or novel, requires planning, or cannot be accomplished with automatic, habitual responses. Conversation would fit a number of these requirements in that even simple conversation requires rapid selections of multiple choices of words, phrases, sentences, and topics in a multitude of possible orders. While speaking, one often has to nearly simultaneously choose what to say, monitor what one actually says, observe nonverbal feedback from the listener, and keep in memory what the listener has already said. Add to this complex task the emotional stress of being in a social situation and that much of social conversation involves emotional topics. Given these attributes, conversation can easily be disrupted due to an overload of the central executive, leading to a reduced capacity to inhibit divergent associated thoughts and to maintain a linear course. The prominence of formal thought disorder within the symptom category of disorganization could be due in part to these features of conversation that make it so taxing, as well as the importance of conversation in our everyday functioning.

One view of the cognitive etiology of formal thought disorder derives from the concept of limited attentional resources. According to this theory, the difficulty of the central executive to maintain attention is due to limited attentional resources or poor allocation of available resources (Nuechterlein & Dawson, 1984). Poor filtering of external stimuli (i.e., sensory gating; Braff, Saccuzzo, & Geyer, 1991) and an inability to inhibit the spreading of semantic and phonological associations (Spitzer et al., 1994) lead to a flood of information that contributes to a depletion of attentional resources that is unmanageable by the central executive. With thought disorder, the central executive has difficulty selecting from a large number of choices for the next word or phrase to be uttered. In normal discourse, there are a limited number of choices because irrelevant choices (e.g., rhyming words) are inhibited at a lower level before processing by the central executive is needed. The context dictates what is relevant—the context being what is being said by others in the conversation as well as what the speaker has already said and is deciding to say. Utilizing the context in deciding on the next word or phrase requires holding the context (the conversation as well as what one has just said) in working memory while selecting from various possible words or phrases. If the context is ignored (as is the case in schizophrenia, as explained below), irrelevant information does not get filtered.

Alternatively, rather than a primary lack of inhibition leading to a resource-depleting overload, there could be a primary malfunction of the supervisory attentional system leading to the attenuated inhibition of associated paths. Both processes can occur synergistically in that the increase in activation of associated paths poses a further strain on an already weak supervisory attentional system. A downward spiral ensues once the process begins in response to a stressor.

Limited resources trigger efforts to spare resources by choosing easier paths of discourse, such as selecting concrete over abstract, ignoring the need for transitional sentences and referential guides (e.g., indicating to whom personal pronouns refer), speaking one's own stream of consciousness rather than relating these items to the social conversation, merely repeating what has been said by another person or already said by oneself, producing simple rhyming or alliteration words, or using whatever word combinations come to mind over conventional words that are hard to access at a given moment.

To summarize the information-processing model, (1) the supervisory attentional system (or central executive) is malfunctioning, leading to insufficient inhibition of irrelevant stimuli and poor choice of appropriate words, sentences, or topics; (2) limited attentional resources contribute to (or are due to, or both) diminished filtering of both external and internal stimuli, thus burdening an already overloaded supervisory attentional system; and (3) resource sparing, by choosing discourse paths of least resistance, leads to the manifestation of formal thought disorder symptoms.

Results from neuropsychological testing of subjects with schizophrenia support the model described above. In general, thought disorder has been shown to correlate most strongly with deficits in neuropsychological functioning, compared to the other factors of distorted reality and negative symptoms, when all three factors are considered (Bilder, Mukherjee, Rieder, & Pandurangi, 1985). This finding is especially pertinent to language and memory functions. In studies that examined only two factors (positive and negative symptoms), thought disorder is the positive symptom most strongly associated with performance on neuropsychological tests (Walker & Harvey, 1986). These findings support the idea that formal thought disorder is particularly associated with limited resources (although negative symptoms also are associated with poor neuropsychological functioning).

The specific performance deficits associated with formal thought disorder can be encapsulated into two basic difficulties: those of (1) selecting between competing responses and (2) suppressing inappropriate responses (Liddle, 2001). This condensation is in line with the model, above, that views thought disorder errors as the products of central executive difficulties in selecting among choices for the next word or phrase—especially when inappropriate possibilities are not filtered out to narrow down the choices.

Specific neuropsychological deficits associated with thought disorder include poorer performance on recall of strings of digits, especially with distracters (Oltmanns, 1978; Walker & Harvey, 1986); distraction performance (Harvey, Earle-Boyer, & Levinson, 1988), Stroop performance (Liddle & Morris, 1991; Ngan & Liddle, 2000), Trails B (Liddle & Morris, 1991); choice reaction time tasks (Ngan & Liddle, 2000); continuous performance test errors of commission (Frith, Leary, Cahill, & Johnstone, 1991); and verbal fluency (Liddle & Morris, 1991), including more inclusions of odd words (Allen, Liddle, & Frith, 1993; Frith et al., 1991).

Cohen and colleagues, using two types of studies, found that the factors of holding contextual information in working memory while choosing what is relevant from a number of choices are pertinent aspects of the difficulties found in schizophrenia. In one study using computer models of cognitive deficits in schizophrenia (Cohen & Servan-Schreiber, 1992), it was shown that task variations most affecting performance were those involving the relative strengths of competing responses and the delay between cue stimuli and response elicitations. In other words, people with schizophrenia would do worse if competing choices of responses were more closely associated and if there was an extended time during which they were required to remember presentations before responding.

Cohen and colleagues (Cohen, Barch, Carter, & Servan-Schreiber, 1999) hypothesized that there is a single function underlying these two dimensions: maintaining task-relevant information in working memory while ignoring irrelevant information. They showed that manipulating dimensions of the continuous performance test and the Stroop task along the lines of these two factors produced a strong correlation between difficulties with response inhibition and difficulties with retention of contextual information. Performance measures combining these two factors were highly correlated with severity of thought disorder. The neuropsychological data support the hypotheses that those with formal thought disorder have limited attentional resources, difficulties in selecting between competing responses, difficulties suppressing inappropriate responses, and difficulties maintaining task-relevant information (including context) in working memory while suppressing irrelevant information. These are all functions of the supervisory attentional system, as described above. The exact sequence of events and the primary neuropsychological source(s) of the difficulties have yet to be determined.

SUMMARY

Formal thought disorder is one of the three symptom types that constitute schizophrenia. It consists of various forms of odd word usage, including loosening of associations, idiosyncratic use of language, thought blocking (an absence of word usage), and poverty of content of speech. Thought disorder fits into the cognitive model as part of the emotional and behavioral response to automatic thoughts. There have been no formal studies of what automatic thoughts are specific to the occurrence of formal thought disorder, and there are likely to be many nonspecific automatic thoughts that contribute to the onset or exacerbation of formal thought disorder. The content of formal thought disorder can consist of psychologically meaningful passages, including automatic thoughts, but detecting them requires careful listening, directed questioning, and creative thinking. Hypersalient cognitions, having timely relevance and emotional significance, are more likely to contribute to the presence of formal thought disorder and could be encrypted into disorganized discourse.

We hypothesize that formal thought disorder arises from a lack of adequate inhibition of spreading activation along associated, but context-incongruent, nodes in a semantic network. This inadequate inhibition is due to a poorly functioning central executive that is then further taxed by an overabundance of unfiltered activation. Limited attentional resources, both absolute and relative to the amount of activated information, lead to resource-sparing processes such as concreteness, clanging, echolalia, poverty of content, and lack of referential and syntactic guides.

CHAPTER 7

Assessment

To accomplish one's work as a detective, scientist, politician, engineer, architect, or most any other professional, one needs first to gather information. Without knowing the facts about the task at hand, one cannot adequately set out to solve problems or make changes. In cognitive therapy, there is a strong emphasis on gathering data—both from the patient to the therapist, and to the patient from the outside world. Socratic questioning, collaborative empiricism, and guided discovery are hallmarks of this type of psychotherapy. Before an automatic thought can be examined for veracity, it must be identified. Before therapy can truly begin, an assessment process is needed, during which information about the person engaging in therapy is obtained in a collaborative, sensitive manner.

Assessment can include collection of information in various manners and from various sources. Clinicians can use clinical interviews; clinical rating scales; hospital records, prior therapy progress notes, laboratory results and school records; consultations with social workers, psychiatrists, family doctors, neurologists and teachers; interviews with parents, siblings, children, and spouses; and neuropsychological testing. In this chapter, we focus on clinical interviews and clinical rating scales in the assessment of patients during cognitive therapy with schizophrenia.

Although assessment is usually thought of as a process that occurs before therapy has begun, it is better to think of it as an ongoing process employed throughout the course of therapy and even after its completion. For one, later stages may elicit important information from a patient (or family member, e.g.) that had not been revealed during the initial interview. The therapist may not have asked the appropriate question, or the patient may have misunderstood the question, forgotten something, been reluctant to admit information before getting to know the therapist better, or been hampered by the presence of psychosis or medication effects during the initial interview. Reliance on the accuracy of patients' reports of their symptoms jeopardizes research in the field of psychosis. The factors presented as potentially distorting responses to interview questions need to be considered in these studies. In therapy, there is the advantage of having an extended relationship with the patient: Information may be more forthcoming as therapy progresses.

Another reason for considering assessment as an ongoing process during therapy and after its completion is the value (emphasized as well in cognitive therapy) of assessing progress during and after therapy. Assessment (1) monitors whether therapy is working, (2) shows the patient the value of continuing therapy (although there may be long lags of "latent progress," in which changes are not yet manifested in an observable manner), (3) guides the course of therapy, and (4) determines the effects of outside events that might occur during the course of therapy.

Our discussion of assessment is divided into the initial assessment interview and the assessment at each session.

THE INITIAL ASSESSMENT INTERVIEW

The initial assessment interview may occur before or following the examination of other sources of information, such as intake interviews (in some agencies); spouses, parents, or other relatives; school counselors or teachers; prior therapists or psychiatrists; hospital, school, or police records; the media, and so forth. There are varying opinions as to whether to examine other information prior to interviewing the patient. Some believe it is best not to have any biases before hearing patients' stories directly; others believe that patients may be offended if they are asked to start from scratch after having just related their story to an intake coordinator within the last week or even that day. In addition, there may be important information in prior records that a patient may not disclose without being asked. Our recommendation is to examine other sources of information when available, but keep an open mind and use the interview to elucidate any data from other sources. Remember that prior diagnoses can be incorrect or need modification as new symptoms arise. Also, prior interviews can contain miscommunications. Discrepancies between the current and past interviews can be addressed directly with the patient in a nonaccusatory manner.

The initial interview is usually the start of therapy. Therefore, the beginnings of establishing rapport and trust occur here, so basic therapeutic techniques of empathy, reflective listening, supportive statements should not be delayed until "the actual therapy" starts later. In the therapeutic setting, the patient needs to feel safe, listened to, and not judged.

Although in the initial interview, the therapist can gather much useful information, there is the danger of asking too many questions in one sitting. Potential negative outcomes of too many questions include the following: The patient feels oppressed or paranoid (which may not be apparent to the interviewer) and then is reluctant to provide information; the patient becomes fatigued (physically and/or mentally) and is not able to recall items as well; the patient forms a habit of passively relying on the therapist to "conduct" the therapy and continues to do so throughout therapy. Some ways to avoid these negative outcomes are to (1) gauge from verbal and nonverbal feedback how well the patient is tolerating the interview process; (2) spread out the interview over a number of sessions, if needed (three is recommended by Fowler et al., 1995); (3) collaborate with the patient from the beginning about the purpose, duration, and content of the upcoming interview (including allowing the patient to refuse to answer questions, which could occur until rapport is established); (4) ask for direct feedback from the patient regarding the need for a break or how it feels to provide such personal information; (5) watch for feedback that the patient is ready to move on to the next item or wishes to continue on current one; (6) provide periodic feedback to the patient; and (7) use open-ended questions as much as possible, followed by direct questions if still needed.

An example of starting with open-ended questions might look like this: a patient reports having bouts of depression; rather than first asking a litany of yes–no questions about problems with sleep, appetite, motivation, and the like, try asking, "How would you describe your depression?" or "How do you know when you are having a bout of depression?" This approach serves the dual purpose of (1) allowing the patient to form the habit of expounding on answers rather than giving short replies, and (2) showing which symptoms are most prominent in the patient's mind—which ones are voiced by the patient and in what order. Following the open-ended response, the therapist may then ask about symptoms not volunteered spontaneously and elicit details about those provided.

Confidentiality rules should be discussed early in the interview in order to establish informed consent before the patient reveals information that may need to be shared later with others. This information includes material that (1) could directly prevent significant harm to the patient and/or others, (2) involves child abuse, (3) is court-ordered to be released, (4) is allowed by the patient to be released, or (5) would be needed in a defense if the patient should sue the therapist.

The initial meeting with a patient provides the opportunity to ask why therapy is being sought. This question begins the collaborative process of goal and agenda setting. Often, patients with schizophrenia cannot give a reason for coming to therapy. They may have been coerced by parents, professionals, or the legal system to attend therapy sessions. This coercion might then become the presenting problem (David Fowler, personal communication, April 23, 2004): "My parents want me to come to therapy, and I don't see why I need to."

Sometimes the initial question can reflect the apparent mood of the patient. If the patient looks irritated, the therapist can say, "You look upset. Is there anything bothering you right now?" This approach can provide empathy as well as lead to the chief concern. It is not necessary, however, to start with the presenting problem, since some patients may prefer starting with less emotional topics first. On the other hand, there may be a need, before any complete assessment is done, to address emergencies (e.g., serious suicidality, violence, psychotic breaks) if they occur from the start.

There may be more than one reason for seeking therapy. A problem list can be developed and then items prioritized based on (1) importance to the patient, (2) feasibility of being resolved in therapy, and (3) dependence of one problem's solution on the prior elucidation of other problems (Morrison, Renton, et al., 2004).

Next examined is the background of the present situation that led to seeking (or being coerced to seek) therapy. Fowler et al. (1995) suggest starting with 5–15 minutes of unstructured conversation, allowing the patient to express current concerns while the therapist uses empathic statements and summaries, but mainly listens. The patient may actually appreciate that someone is listening to the background story instead of just pushing treatment without trying to learn about him or her as a person first.

The interview then proceeds with a detailed examination of what led up to the presenting problem. This includes events, emotions, thoughts, and behaviors that occurred just prior to the onset of the chief concern, as well as historical events that appear to the patient to have led to the current problem. The therapist and patient need to decide collaboratively how much detail to pursue about past events at this point and how much to return to later as part of the standard interview. For instance, a patient had the delusion that men at his church thought he was trying to have an affair with their wives. The therapist could choose to pursue questions about his relationship history at this point to clarify possible sources of this belief (e.g., a lack of intimate relationships, a prior actual affair) or wait to ask those questions during the personal history part of the interview. Kingdon and Turkington (1994, 2005) state that one advantage of going through a detailed discourse of all possible events leading up to the current situation is that the patient can then see how the current problem developed and how past events and stressors can have an impact on the formation of contemporary beliefs and symptoms.

Appendix C provides a fairly comprehensive list of topics for the initial evaluation, useful for psychiatrists, nurses, psychologists, social workers, counselors, and case workers. Some items were derived from other reviews of assessment (Fowler et al., 1995; Kingdon & Turkington, 1994, 2005; Morrison, Renton, et al., 2004). Again, not all of the issues need to be examined in the initial session(s), as some are better approached as rapport is established. However, sometimes it is easier to provide information about delicate topics during a dry, clinical interview by an unknown therapist than to do so later when emotions may be higher, and inhibitions, such as not wanting to disappoint a likable therapist, might develop. The possibility of some symptoms getting worse in the short term after disclosure of personal information can be discussed and handled with emphasis on the long-term benefits of addressing ongoing problems. Using an individualized approach that incorporates collaboration with the patient is a good rule of thumb for determining how extensive an interview to conduct.

In ending the initial session, it is useful to explain the purpose, theory, and mechanics of cognitive therapy. Some therapists prefer not to give a formal explanation of this approach, but rather to provide information in context, as therapy progresses. Before the initial session is over, it is important to assess the safety of the patient by making sure to ask questions regarding current suicidality and violence. In addition, determine if coping strategies and social supports are in place or if some easy coping strategies need to be provided during the initial session (Morrison, Renton, et al., 2004).

DIAGNOSTIC INTERVIEWS AND RATING SCALES

Although used mainly in research settings, the diagnostic interviews and rating scales presented here and elsewhere in this book can be useful in the clinical settings either in their original form or with modifications. The lengthy diagnostic interview can be performed before formal therapy begins, while the typically shorter rating scales can be used at each session to monitor progress or setbacks in symptomatology (Sajatovic & Ramirez, 2003). Kingdon and Turkington (1994, 2005) claim that rating scales can interfere with rapport and introduce too mechanistic an atmosphere. Therefore, they recommend using them only after the therapeutic relationship is established. Others use rating scales from the beginning to determine the baseline symptomatology. However, there is the possibility, as stated above, that the patient will not be completely forthcoming at this early stage due to lack of established trust, shame, misunderstanding of the questions, and so forth.

Diagnostic Interviews

Present State Examination, 9th Edition (PSE-9)

This 140-item semistructured interview was developed by Wing, Cooper, and Sartorius (1974) for use by the World Health Organization in its International Pilot Study of Schizophrenia. It takes about 90–120 minutes to administer, is meant to be conducted by a trained interviewer, and has excellent interrater reliability and good validity. Only the patient's responses are used in the assessment (i.e., no other sources such as family are used), and symptoms are assessed in terms of those during the month prior to the interview. A strength of this assessment is that a large amount of psychopathological information is obtained. Items include information about health worries, tension, autonomic anxiety, thinking, depressed mood, sociality, appetite, libido, sleep, retardation, irritability, expansive mood, speech, obsessions, depersonalization, perceptual disorders, thought reading, hallucinations, delusions, sensorium, memory, insight, drug abuse, affect, and mood.

Schedule for Affective Disorders and Schizophrenia (SADS)

Endicott and Spitzer (1978) developed this semistructured interview as a means to distinguish mood disorders from schizophrenia. It takes about 60 minutes to administer, is meant to be conducted by a trained interviewer, and has high interrater reliability. It consists of open-ended questions. Part I concerns the week before the interview and the worse week in the past year. Part II addresses past history and treatment history.

Schedules for Clinical Assessment in Neuropsychiatry (SCAN)

Wing et al. (1990) developed this semistructured interview as part of a project with the World Health Organization and the National Institute of Mental Health in their Joint Project on Diagnoses and Classification of Mental Disorders, Alcohol, and Related Problems. It is a variation on the PSE, but is a more comprehensive assessment, allowing sources outside of the patient and assessing the present state, the present episode, or the presence of the symptoms in one's lifetime. It takes 90–120 minutes to administer, is meant to be conducted by a clinician, and has an intraclass correlation coefficient of .67 and an overall reliability of lifetime diagnosis of .60.

Structured Clinical Interview for Axis I DSM-IV Disorders (SCID)

This structured interview (First et al., 1995) takes 60–90 minutes to administer, is meant to be conducted by a trained interviewer, and has a test–retest reliability above .60. It includes a screening section before proceeding to appropriate modules for each class of diagnosis.

Rating Scales

Brief Psychiatric Rating Scale (BPRS)

This 18-item, 7-point rating scale, developed by Overall and Gorham (1962), takes 15–30 minutes for the interview and has reliability correlation coefficients of .56–.87 (depending on the version). Strengths of this assessment include the fact that it is brief, easily administered, widely used, and well researched (Lukoff, Nuechterlein, & Ventura, 1986). Its limitations include its somewhat ambiguous criteria for various levels of severity and potential overlap between some items. Items include major psychotic and nonpsychotic symptoms, with some symptoms based on observations by the interviewer and others by subjective report. The symptom range covered in this instrument includes emotional withdrawal, conceptual disorganization, tension, mannerisms and posturing, motor retardation, uncooperativeness, blunted affect, excitement, disorientation, somatic concern, anxiety, guilt feelings, grandiosity, depressive mood, hostility, suspiciousness, hallucinatory behavior, and unusual thought content.

Comprehensive Psychopathological Rating Scale (CPRS)

This 65-item (not including a global rating and assumed reliability rating), 4-point (but allowing for half-steps) rating scale was developed by an interdisciplinary task group (Asberg, Montgomery, Perris, Schalling, & Sedvall, 1978) and meant to be used to measure changes in psychopathology over time. It takes 45–60 minutes to administer, is meant to be conducted via a clinical interview, and has an interrater reliability of .78. Strengths of this assessment include the sensitivity of the items to change and the clear descriptions of the items. Disadvantages include its relatively long administration time for a rating scale. Items include 40 verbal reports (11 related directly to psychosis) and 25 observation (5 related directly to psychosis).

Manchester Scale

This 8-item, 5-point rating scale was developed by Krawiecka, Goldberg, and Vaughan (1977), takes 10–15 minutes to administer, and is meant to be conducted via a standardized clinical interview, by someone who knows the patient well, to monitor changes in clinical status for psychosis. It has an interrater reliability of .65–.87. Strengths of this assessment include its brevity, clear guidelines, and ease of administration. Disadvantages include a lack of sensitivity for some severity ratings and the exclusion of mania. Items include depression, anxiety, flattened or incongruous affect, psychomotor retardation, coherently expressed delusions, hallucinations, incoherence or irrelevance of speech, and poverty of speech or mutism.

Positive and Negative Syndrome Scale for Schizophrenia (PANSS)

This 30-item, 7-point rating scale (Kay et al., 1987; Kay, Opler, & Lindenmayer, 1988), adapted from the BPRS, takes 30–40 minutes to administer and is meant to be conducted by an experienced interviewer using a semistructured clinical interview (the Structured Clinical Interview for the PANSS [SCI-PANSS]) to assess symptoms typically from the past week. It has high internal reliability, homogeneity among items (.73–.83 for each scale), good split-half reliability for the General Psychopathology Scale (.80), and discriminant and convergent validity of dimensional assessment with respect to other measures (e.g., clinical, psychometric). There are three subscales with the following items—positive, negative, and general psychopathology:

- Positive—delusions, conceptual disorganization, hallucinatory behavior, excitement, grandiosity, suspiciousness, and hostility.
- Negative—blunted affect, emotional withdrawal, poor rapport, passive/apathetic social withdrawal, difficulty in abstract thinking, lack of spontaneity and flow of conversation, and stereotyped thinking
- General psychopathology—somatic concern, anxiety, guilt feelings, tension, mannerisms and posturing, depression, motor retardation, uncooperativeness, unusual thought content, disorientation, poor attention, lack of judgment and insight, disturbance of volition, poor impulse control, preoccupation, and active social avoidance.

Scale for the Assessment of Negative Symptoms (SANS)

This 25-item, 6-point rating scale, developed by Andreasen (1984b, 1989), takes 15–20 minutes to administer and is meant to be conducted by a trained rater or clinician via a standardized clinical interview to measure both baseline and change. It has internal consistency (Cronbach's alpha—.67–.90 for five subscales) and correlates well with negative symptom items on the PANSS and BPRS. Symptom classes include alogia, affective flattening, avolition-apathy, anhedonia-asociality, and attention. All but the last item, plus inappropriate affect, are used in a subscale designated as Negative Symptoms. This scale's strengths include its relative ease of administration and well-researched reliability.

Scale for the Assessment of Positive Symptoms (SAPS)

This 34-item, 6-point rating scale (Andreasen, 1984c) takes 15–20 minutes to administer and is meant to be conducted by a trained rater or clinician via a standardized clinical interview to measure both baseline and change. It has less reliability data than the SANS, generally good interrater reliability, and weighted kappas for most items from 0.7–1.00. Symptom classes include hallucinations, delusions, bizarre behavior, and formal thought disorder. The former two comprise a psychoticism score and the latter two, plus inappropriate affect from the SANS, comprise a Disorganization subscale.

Psychotic Symptoms Rating Scale (PSYRATS)

This 11-item, 5-point scale (Haddock, McCarron, Tarrier, & Faragher, 1999) measures various dimensions of hallucinations (AH subscale—five items) and delusions (DS subscale—six items). It has excellent interrater reliability with both subscales having unbiased estimates above 0.9 except for the disruption items and the control item of the AH subscale.

Beliefs about Voices Questionnaire—Revised (BAVQ-R)

This 35-item, 4-point scale (Chadwick & Birchwood, 1995) measures people's beliefs about their voices and their emotional and behavioral responses to them. There are five subscales: three related to beliefs (malevolence—six items; benevolence—six items; omnipotence—six items), one measuring resistance (with five items of emotion and four of behavior), and one measuring engagement (with four items of emotion and four items of behavior). The mean Cronbach's alpha for the five subscales was .86 (range .74–.88).

Peters Delusions Inventory

This 21-item scale (Peters et al., 1999) measures a number of dimensions of delusions and has a Cronbach's alpha coefficient of .82, item-to-whole correlations of .35–.60, and test–retest reliability coefficients of .78–.81 for the various subscales. The inventory shows the best discriminant power in the dimensions of preoccupation, conviction, and distress.

Interpretation of Voices Inventory

This 26-item, 4-point self-report scale (Morrison, Wells, & Nothard, 2000) lists beliefs people have about their voices. The beliefs are divided into categories of malevolence, positive aspects, and loss of control.

Other Measures

There are numerous other rating scales, structured interviews, and tests to measure such areas as insight, mood, general functioning, schemas/attitudes, and neurocognitive functioning. These scales can assist clinicians in determining baseline functioning and degree of improvement in people engaging in cognitive therapy. A few of these measuring instruments are referenced here:

- *Insight into illness.* Insight and Treatment Attitude Questionnaire (McEvoy et al., 1989), David Insight Scale (David, 1990; David, Buchanan, Reed, & Almeida, 1992), Personal Beliefs about Illness Questionnaire (Birchwood, Mason, MacMillan, & Healy, 1993).
- *Cognitive insight.* Beck Cognitive Insight Scale (Beck et al., 2004)
- *Mood.* Beck Depression Inventory (Beck, Ward, Mendleson, Mock, & Erbaugh, 1961; Beck, Steer, & Brown, 1996), Beck Anxiety Inventory (Beck & Steer, 1990), Novaco Anger Scale (Novaco, 1994), State–Trait Anxiety Inventory (Spielberger, Gorusch, Lushene, Vagg, & Jacobs, 1983).
- *General functioning.* Strauss–Carpenter Level of Functioning Scale (Strauss & Carpenter, 1972), Quality of Life Scale (Heinrichs, Hanlon, & Carpenter, 1984).
- *Schemas/attitudes.* Dysfunctional Attitudes Scale (Weissman & Beck, 1978), Young Schema Questionnaire (Young & Brown, 1994), Personal Style Inventory (Robins et al., 1994), Meta-Cognitions Questionnaire (Cartwright-Hatton & Wells, 1997).
- *Cognition tests.* Cognitive Estimations Test (Shallice & Evans, 1978), Probabilistic Reasoning Task (Huq, Garety, & Hemsley, 1988), Schizophrenia Cognition Rating Scale (Keefe, Poe, Walker, Kang, & Harvey, 2006).

ASSESSMENT IN THERAPY SESSIONS

Assessment occurs during every moment of every therapy session. Facial expressions, words used, responses or lack of responses, everything that a patient does or does not do in session as well as reports of how the prior week went are all potentially useful signs of how the patient is doing and how therapy is progressing (or not progressing). No rating scales or diagnostic interviews can replace the art of being aware of interactions with a patient at each session and what they mean clinically as well as personally for the given individual.

Elaboration over Assumption

As new situations occur in the patient's life during the course of therapy, there is the need for assessment of reactions to each pertinent situation. Even though patterns of reactions are likely to emerge, each new situation must be assessed initially independently of previous ones to avoid a bias that may block the therapist from seeing variations in the reactions, including subtle signs of improvement and change. There is a tendency in humans to listen to what another person is saying while at the same time, adding one's own thoughts (based on expectations, biases, and assumptions) into the story without even realizing it. If a friend asks us to go to a mall on a rainy day, we might assume it is an indoor mall and not bring an umbrella. The word *mall* conjures up the image of an indoor structure with controlled climate. Likewise, when a patient tells the story of hearing neighbors through the walls, making plots to attack, it would be useful to know (and not assume) whether the patient lives in an apartment rather than a house, and if the latter, how close the nearest neighbor is. This information could help determine whether there is misinterpretation of actual sounds of people talking versus hallucinations with delusional interpretations. In other words, assessment of each presented problem or situation is best achieved by putting together a detailed picture of the event and the patient's reactions based on what is *said* rather than what one assumes. We tend to fill in missing parts of a story with what is familiar or makes sense to us. A therapist must learn to recognize and resist this habit and instead plead ignorance and go ahead and ask for elaboration.

As an example, Ruth reported to her therapist that a staff member from her residential program had sexually assaulted her. The therapist asked where this event had happened. Ruth replied that it had occurred when she was in the bathtub at her mother's house (where the patient lives on the weekends). The therapist asked what the patient saw or heard. The patient replied that she did not see or hear anything; she just felt like she was being violated by that person. Having learned throughout therapy of "reconsidering" her beliefs, she then stated, "I think I may have just been feeling like this happened. There is no evidence that it really did happen."

In the above example, the therapist asked for more information before making any conclusion about what actually had happened. The statement by the patient that she was at her mother's house, away from the residential program, could lead the therapist to believe that this was a delusion. However, the therapist does not stop there. The further question of what the patient saw or heard helped lead to the patient's admission that the assault was imagined. Had the therapist not asked about this, the question could still remain of whether the staff member had actually assaulted the patient at her home (maybe after dropping her off to an empty house and returning later). The questions need to be asked in an unbiased, nonjudgmental manner, especially in this example where, had there been an actual assault, the patient might have retracted her accusation, due to embarrassment or shame, if she sensed a lack of belief on the part of the therapist. Sometimes collaborative information from family members and others is needed to clarify the picture. This same patient told of relationships with a number of famous people, including having as an uncle someone who was a well-known politician. Her mother confirmed that there was a close connection with the latter, to the extent of calling him an uncle, but there were no real associations with the other famous people.

Cognitive Assessment of Psychotic Events

When initially presented with a situation by the patient, the therapist can conduct a thorough assessment for that event using the cognitive model. The details comprising the cognitive assessment of the various symptoms of schizophrenia are presented in chapters dealing with each symptom. Here we present an overview, using an instrument, the Cognitive Assessment of Psychosis Inventory (CAPI; see Appendix D), as a guide to facilitate the interview. The CAPI focuses on three types of symptoms: hallucinations, delusions, and bizarre behavior. First, the patient describes the eliciting event(s) in detail. Next, the therapist asks questions about the nature of the symptom in terms of type, intensity, frequency, and content. The patient then identifies automatic thoughts about the event and/or the symptom and describes his or her emotional and behavioral reactions to the event. The therapist should watch for, and explain, any compensatory strategies (e.g., avoidance, substance use, thought stopping) the patient uses. Some of these strategies (e.g., relapsing on illicit drugs) can be viewed as new events themselves, worthy of further cognitive assessment.

A similar approach to assessing significant events is to examine the components of the five systems model (Greenberger & Padesky, 1995). This model has been applied specifically to psychosis by Morrison, Renton, et al. (2004). The *five systems* refer to cognitive, behavioral, affective, physiological, and environmental domains. Cognitive components include negative automatic thoughts and images and the cognitive distortions associated with them, appraisals of automatic thoughts, and attentional priorities (i.e., which thoughts are most noticed by the patient). Behavioral components include safety behaviors—most notably, avoidance—and any actions that precede, accompany, or follow the event. The affective and physiological components are the emotions and bodily reactions that precede, accompany, or follow the event. The environmental component includes triggers and mediators of the reactions.

The CAPI contains additional items of inquiry, such as insight into the symptoms in terms of a disorder model. Lastly, historical antecedents and core beliefs—possible progenitors of the symptoms—may emerge, not necessarily for each analysis of each event, but more likely at some time after several situations have been investigated. Historical antecedents may include early upbringing, traumatic events, and genetic and perinatal predispositions. Core beliefs include general, long-held views about the cognitive triad of self, others (the world), and the future.

In this assessment inventory, hallucinations are considered to be events. The automatic thoughts, beliefs, and assumptions about the hallucinations are explored, including beliefs about their origin. Hallucinations can also represent automatic thoughts. To determine this, patients can be asked if they themselves agree with what the voices tell them. If so, the voices can be considered automatic thoughts at that time, but the question may need to be asked again at other times, even if the content of the voices does not change. For instance, a voice may tell the patient that therapy is harmful. The patient might believe this at first, but not later, despite the persistence of the voice.

This inventory considers delusions as beliefs. In this case, it is useful to examine events just prior to the occurrence of the delusional beliefs in an effort to determine what situations activate them. However, the eliciting events may not be time-locked with the delusional belief, especially in the case of long-held delusions. Thinking one is a member of the CIA could go back to seeing a movie about it some years ago. Nonetheless, it can be useful to check if certain events trigger the current recalling of that belief.

Bizarre behavior is a behavioral reaction, according to this inventory, and examination of potential beliefs that lead to the behavior can be telling. Wearing an aluminum hat can be secondary to the belief that aliens are trying to read one's thoughts and that aluminum will block their efforts. In these circumstances, the focus may shift from the behavior itself to the beliefs driving the behavior, as the behavior may be a logical consequence of illogical beliefs.

The therapist can determine core beliefs by (1) direct questioning of a patient, (2) the downward arrow technique (a series of questions aimed at ascertaining the personal meaning underlying automatic thoughts), or (3) identifying a pattern of automatic thoughts with respect to various situations. Appendix E presents possible core beliefs for various types of delusions, organized by the cognitive triad. Some delusions have apparent core beliefs that may belie hidden, truer core beliefs. For instance, grandiose delusions give the appearance of a core belief about oneself as "I am special," while further examination can reveal a core belief of "I am inadequate" that is compensated by the manifest positive core belief. Paranoid delusions can seem to be guided by a core belief that "I am vulnerable," hiding the deeper core belief that "I am special" (and therefore worthy of being followed). This in turn may hide an underlying core belief of "I am defective," again leading to the compensatory belief of being important enough to be followed. The core beliefs listed are potential beliefs that can serve as a guide in questioning patients for their actual beliefs.

As a final aid to assessment during the course of therapy, we present, in Appendices F and G, lists of cognitive distortions potentially found in the form of delusions. Appendix F includes cognitive distortions commonly found in the context of other psychiatric diagnoses, and Appendix G presents those more specific to psychotic conditions, including schizophrenia. These distortions are organized into five groups: categorization/generalization, selection bias, attributions of responsibility, arbitrary inference, and assumption.

As with the process of therapy itself, accurate assessment depends on viewing the patient as an individual. One of the most striking aspects, when first encountering someone with schizophrenia, is how much of an individual he or she is compared with the stereotype portrayed in movies and books as well as newspaper accounts. Even textbooks of psychiatry and psychology paint a picture of disorder, whereas the actual person has personality that can come in as many forms as in those without schizophrenia. All of the above is a guide. A true evaluation requires getting to know the person sitting in front of you.

SUMMARY AND CLINICAL APPLICATION

The enormous number of scales, structured interviews, and tests can be overwhelming for the typical therapist. Researchers struggle to select which measures are essential for a given study and which must be abandoned so as not to fatigue the subject as well as the research assistants and students. Clinicians face the same dilemma of completeness versus efficiency. The extensive presentation here of multiple forms of measurement is not meant to create some feeling of obligation on the part of the therapist, but rather to allow choices in determining what works best for a given patient, therapist, and stage of progress in therapy as well as other possible salient factors. The sections on assessment in the chapters pertaining to individual symptom groups focus on the essential items in terms of conducting cognitive therapy. The sections on cognitive conceptualization in those chapters explain how to bring together the various bits of information into a formulation for the individual patient.

CHAPTER 8

Engagement and Fostering
the Therapeutic Relationship

A number of clinical research teams conducting cognitive therapy for schizophrenia have arrived at similar conclusions about the ideal nature, timing, and process of sessions. There is widespread agreement that conducting cognitive therapy with individuals suffering from delusions, voices, prominent negative symptoms, significant thought disorder and communication difficulties, limited insight, and potentially overlapping comorbid conditions, does not differ markedly from cognitive therapy with individuals suffering from anxiety, depression, and a host of other psychiatric conditions. Rather, the basic assumptions and treatment intervention strategies, with some minor variation, flow directly from the cognitive therapy treatments of depression (Beck et al., 1979) and anxiety (Beck et al., 1985). However, there are some important considerations that require attention before embarking on therapy with this population. The remainder of this book considers the details of engagement, assessment, formulation, and intervention strategies for the main targets of treatment. This chapter focuses on general aspects of fostering the therapeutic relationship and reducing barriers to engagement. We suggest strategies to enhance the therapeutic alliance even in the presence of potentially significant barriers.

BUILDING THERAPEUTIC RAPPORT

The sine qua non of conducting cognitive therapy effectively is creating a therapeutic climate of mutual respect and trust. The presence of a strong therapeutic relationship is absolutely pivotal when working with individuals who may be exquisitely sensitive to having their beliefs questioned and examined. In contrast to referrals for cognitive therapy for anxiety and depression, who are often aware of, and insightful about, their difficulties and seeking treatment, patients referred for treatment of the symptoms of schizophrenia may not know themselves why they are scheduled to see the therapist, and they may have no insight into their specific difficulties around delusions, voices, or negative symptoms. Furthermore, they may have no interest in therapy, or worse, feel coerced and/or trapped into attending, with the accompanying predictable feelings of resentment and hostility.

With each of these possibilities, it is imperative that the therapeutic relationship be based on warmth and concern; the patient's perception of being supported may determine whether he or she attends the early sessions of treatment. In subsequent stages of therapy, a solid therapeutic relationship will allow the exploration and testing of strongly held and emotionally charged beliefs. Finally, in the latter stages of treatment, where the work typically focuses on painful longstanding core beliefs and associated experiences, a warm and caring relationship will be instrumental in providing an alternative basis to beliefs regarding interpersonal vulnerability and rejection. So, first and foremost, the success of cognitive therapy for schizophrenia is contingent on the continuity of a warm, respectful, trusting, safe, and accepting therapeutic relationship.

To facilitate the therapeutic relationship and early engagement in therapy, the first several sessions are usually open and exploratory, without a fixed agenda on clinical issues. The therapist aims to be person-focused, making emotional contact with the patient and avoiding formal assessment procedures and any kind of active techniques to change appraisals or beliefs. As developed by Kingdon and Turkington (1994), the early phase of treatment focuses on "befriending" the patient; that is, trying to connect with the patient in the way one would with a colleague or a new neighbor. Topics for discussion are ideally neutral in affective tone, but also engaging, as they reflect the patient's personal interests, such as seasonal holidays, upcoming events, or hobbies and the like. While all sessions are scheduled with some degree of flexibility, the early sessions, particularly, can be adjusted (shorter or longer) to facilitate the therapeutic relationship. For instance, the patient who appears somewhat uncomfortable with the inter-personal demands of one-on-one conversation may benefit from the thera-pist's attempts to instill a spirit of lightness by keeping the sessions short in duration, chit-chatty, and spattered with appropriate humor.

Alternatively, for the patient with significant cognitive interference and lengthy perseveration, a slowly paced session with frequent breaks and limited topics may be ideal. In short, in the early sessions the therapist is especially careful to notice the mood states of the patient and to exercise emotional attunement by adjusting the content, pacing, and duration of the session to "fit" the patient's apparent style. In general, the guiding prin-ciples and strategies of collaborative empiricism (Beck et al., 1979) serve as the basis for the early sessions in the treatment of psychosis.

Key components of collaborative empiricism are expressed in attitudes of equality, teamwork, shared responsibility for change, unconditional pos-itive regard, and nonjudgmentalism. The spirit and approach of collabora-tive empiricism may be harder to maintain when the patient is extremely paranoid, expressing more bizarre delusional beliefs, incoherent due to substantive thought disorder, or exceedingly reticent due to overarching negative symptoms. The key is for the therapist to maintain a stance of flexibility and patience, and recognize that although it may be difficult to understand some aspects of the person's presentation, many other aspects will be readily understandable, and understanding improves with time and persistence. It is also helpful to remember that the therapist's persistence in the face of confusion and incomprehensibility may aid in instilling hope in the patient.

SUITABILITY FOR COGNITIVE THERAPY

Patients treated in cognitive therapy trial studies have been typically selected for inclusion if they are experiencing distressing positive symptoms. In our own work, we have maintained considerably broader inclusion criteria for determining patient suitability for cognitive therapy. Patients seeking, or at least open to receiving, help for their negative symptoms, comorbid anxi-ety, depression, or substance-related symptoms, as well as general stress management, could be considered for cognitive therapy. Beyond this focus of treatment are a number of other nonspecific suitability factors that may make some patients more suitable for treatment than others. Patients who have a greater awareness of their thoughts and can readily understand the associations between thoughts, feelings, and behaviors may be more likely to embrace and work within the cognitive model. Patients who are willing to take some responsibility for their own improvement and to make an effort to complete in-session therapeutic tasks that are difficult, such as exposures or the reduction of safety behaviors and between-session homework tasks, would seem to be ideally suited. However, it should be noted that currently, we have little understanding of who is likely to benefit from cognitive therapy. As such, it is our outlook that any patient who is willing to attend sessions regularly and attempt to learn and benefit from cognitive therapy is a possible candidate for this treatment for psychosis. Rather than patient factors being seen as a priori limitations and the basis for exclusion from treatment, we view these factors as barriers only to engagement, which can be addressed and diminished or removed in the process of cognitive therapy.

BUILDING MOTIVATION

Cognitive therapy, irrespective of the specific treatment focus, works best when the therapist and patient are engaged in the effort, share responsibility for progress, and are motivated to work toward mutually generated goals. However, clients with schizophrenia, particularly those in the chronic phase of the illness, often have been struggling with a protracted range of symptoms and problems and are demotivated and demoralized. In addition, many patients have had numerous trials of medications and met with various therapists, only to experience modest benefits or sometimes none at all. Further, some patients have been left with the understanding that their illness is entirely biological in nature, with little hope of exerting direct influence through nonmedical interventions. For many, the success of cognitive therapy will be contingent on overcoming some degree of hopelessness and demoralization.

The first step in this process is the development of good rapport through the demonstration of respect, openness, and appropriate concern. The therapist also builds motivation through the communication of the cognitive rationale, where anticipated improvements in patients' distress levels can occur as they begin to better understand the sources of their distress and the thinking and behavioral patterns that get activated around important life events. Motivation for treatment is also enhanced through the therapist's willingness to be helpful in any way possible, beyond the familiar symptom targets. For instance, helping with housing forms or meeting with family members to advocate for the patient would demonstrate the therapist's flexibility and goodwill. There are several specific therapist and patient factors that may represent barriers to engagement and motivation; these are addressed in turn.

THERAPIST BARRIERS

A starting point in the conceptualization and treatment of the symptoms of schizophrenia is that they rest on a continuum. However, this outlook may be new to many junior and senior therapists alike and may require some shift in perspective. Before starting cognitive therapy, the therapist needs to become aware of his or her own beliefs, appraisals, and expectations as they relate to working with someone with a schizophrenia-spectrum diagnosis. Can a person's delusions and voices be understood, or will they remain incomprehensible? Can the symptoms of psychosis be understood as variants of normal behavior? Can patients expect to improve with cognitive therapy—and retain benefits after therapy has been discontinued? If schizophrenia is a biological disease state, how can a talking therapy have an impact on it? The way in which the therapist thinks about these questions will inevitably affect the therapeutic process. Therapists need to be aware of their own beliefs and potential prejudices and to have a context (most often, supervision) in which to talk about beliefs that might act as barriers to engagement and the therapeutic process across treatment. In general, the goal of therapy is to see the person's world from his or her point of view, understanding what it must be like to hold his or her beliefs and grapple with the emotional and behavioral consequences that such beliefs generate.

Cognitive therapy for schizophrenia can often be a slow process. Therapists who have experience in treating people with mood and anxiety disorders may find that the pace is slower, that patients require more frequent capsule summaries of material just covered, and overall, that they may have to adjust their expectations to reflect more modest and focused goals, although this is by no means always the case.

PATIENT BARRIERS

Suspiciousness/Paranoia

It is essential to establish a high degree of trust before any direct questioning of beliefs or evidence taken in support of delusional beliefs is undertaken.

This is especially true for patients who have a high degree of suspiciousness and who are experiencing paranoia. As suggested, early sessions are aimed at communicating warmth, concern, and nonjudgmental acceptance. As the work transitions into more active questioning and cognitive restructuring, the therapist treads carefully, paying close attention to shifts in mood states reflecting annoyance, frustration, hostility, and the like. The therapist may need to back off and refocus on relational aspects that build trust and safety, often involving a discussion of more neutral topics. In short, the framework is to focus on building trust and to avoid direct challenging or argument around beliefs, however tempting this may be at times.

Another important goal in working with the highly suspicious patient is to avoid becoming part of the perceived conspiracy or unwittingly providing additional support or "colluding" with the persecutory belief. If the patient suspects the therapist of persecution, all efforts to proceed forward to questioning and testing the delusional belief should be temporarily suspended as the therapist again directs efforts to reestablish trust and safety. This effort may focus on openly communicating openly his or her caring for the patient and a desire to help the patient with his or her difficulties. Additionally, the therapist should avoid providing any direct support for, or acceptance of, the delusional belief as true. Rather, the therapist is careful to convey that he or she is not sure whether or not the belief is true, but that the goal is learn more about the circumstances of the belief and to work together to find ways of helping the patient feel better about the problem.

Negative Symptoms

We presented a cognitive-behavioral model of negative symptoms in Chapter 5, detailing how negative symptoms are not simply due to underlying biological deficits but rather represent a more complex interplay between appraisals, expectancies, and beliefs as well as characteristic cognitive and behavioral coping strategies. We also outlined a framework for the assessment and treatment of negative symptoms, based on the cognitive-behavioral conceptualization of these symptoms described in Chapter 5. Specifically, a cognitive set characterized by low expectancies for pleasure, success, acceptance, together with a perception of limited resources, are pivotal to the production of negative symptoms—and these will likely be expressed in relation to cognitive therapy. When patients experience apathy, low motivation, and lack of energy in their day-to-day lives, it is likely that the treatment in cognitive therapy will be approached in a similar way. For instance, based on limited success in past treatments, the patient may expect to benefit little from engaging in yet another treatment. Similarly, a patient may be reluctant to disclose the full nature of his or her thoughts, beliefs, feelings, and experiences out of fear of being judged as "crazy" or "weird," and the like. Moreover, some patients may be reluctant to engage in treatment because they anticipate failing to live up to personally derived expectations.

Moreover, and as reviewed in Chapter 5, the types of dysfunctional beliefs that have been found to correlate with the presence of negative symptoms may also have an impact on therapeutic engagement. For instance, patients with prominent negative symptoms tend to endorse such beliefs as "Taking even a small risk is foolish because the loss is likely to be a disaster"; "If I do not do something well, there is little point in doing it at all"; and "problems will go away if you do not do anything." Therapeutic engagement can be enhanced by identifying and addressing these beliefs from the early stages in therapy. Importantly, low engagement and limited effort to pursue cognitive therapy can provide important material to address in session, with the therapist targeting negative appraisals about engaging more fully in treatment.

Thought Disorder

Therapists may find it particularly challenging to engage with patients who are less comprehensible and demonstrate significant tangentiality in their thoughts and communication. As discussed in Chapter 6, strategies to heighten the focus of discussion can be applied. First, therapists can listen carefully for threads of meaning and provide frequent summaries in attempts to refocus the patient. Second, if the patient is speaking extremely quickly, and it is difficult to get a word in edgewise, the therapist can listen carefully for when the patient takes a breath and interject short questions. Third, as reviewed in Chapter 6, research demonstrates that patients become particularly more tangential and incomprehensible when discussing topics that are emotionally salient. Therapists should listen very carefully for any change in the rate of speech to better understand the topics that are of emotional significance to the patient. Socratic questioning focused on these "hot" themes will serve to keep the patient focused. Fourth, as a related strategy, therapists can steer away from hot topics to reduce arousal and improve comprehension, if it is determined that remaining focused on the hot themes is proving too difficult. Finally, it is important to note that many patients with thought disorder report benefits from just feeling *lis-*

tened to. Careful listening, with displays of empathy and acceptance, can itself produce direct improvements (Sensky et al., 2000).

Cognitive Rigidity

One of the principal aims of cognitive therapy for psychosis is to lessen the distress associated with delusional beliefs by reducing the conviction and increasing the flexibility associated with such beliefs. Some patients have greater flexibility in their beliefs before embarking on treatment, and clinical experience would suggest that these patients may be comparatively better at identifying and testing alternative explanations for their experiences than patients with greater rigidity. Previous research has suggested that delusions are more likely to change across time naturalistically if patients believe that they could be possibly mistaken about these beliefs (Brett-Jones, Garety, & Hemsley, 1987). Other research has shown that there is considerable interdependency between delusional conviction and belief flexibility, with greater inflexibility being related to greater delusional conviction (Garety et al., 2005). However, it is important to note that many more patients appear to derive some benefit from cognitive therapy than appear to have flexibility in their beliefs prior to treatment. For instance, approximately 50% of delusional patients reject the possibility of being mistaken about their beliefs prior to receiving cognitive therapy (Garety et al., 1997, 2005). And although the possibility of being mistaken about delusional beliefs has been found to predict eventual outcome to cognitive therapy (Garety et al., 1997), it should be remembered that there are multiple therapeutic outcomes of which the reduction of delusional conviction is one. For instance, a parallel goal is to improve social and functional outcomes, irrespective of the degree of delusional conviction, as is discussed in Chapter 9. There we highlight how a patient can continue to maintain 100% delusional conviction but still make changes to the way he or she acts on the belief to improve the quality of life. As illustrated, a patient with a longstanding paranoid belief that his colleagues were out to kill him, was able to return to work and remain employed, despite no change in his delusional beliefs, with the help of the therapist, on-site medical staff, and selective friends and family.

Additional goals of cognitive therapy include the improvement of negative symptoms, reduced stress, improved coping, reduced anxiety and depression, improved interpersonal skills, and so on. In other words, although belief inflexibility can make it more difficult to shift the patient to less distressing beliefs, this stance need not prevent progress in other domains of the person's life.

PROCESS OF THERAPY

General Structure of Therapy

A generic template of the treatment intervention in cognitive therapy can be seen in Table 8.1. Similar to cognitive therapy for depression and anxiety, cognitive therapy for psychosis is active, appropriately structured, time-limited (between 6–9 months, on average), and typically delivered in an individual format—although cognitive therapy can be also delivered in group format for homogeneous symptom groups, such as patients who hear voices. As seen in Table 8.2, individual cognitive therapy sessions involve checking on the patient's mood over the previous week and identifying any irregularities in medication use. The therapist aims to maintain continuity between sessions by reviewing the important areas addressed in the previous session and by checking for updates over the past week. The therapist then sets a structured agenda that includes a mutually prioritized focus for the session (typically a problem from the problem list developed during the assessment phase). After implementing in-session cognitive and behavioral strategies, the therapist assigns homework to focus the patient on monitoring and then testing their beliefs with behavioral experiments. Although the format of cognitive therapy for schizophrenia is similar to that of other cognitive therapy interventions, sessions may be shorter in duration (15–45 minutes), include breaks, have more focused and limited homework tasks, and offer greater flexibility in terms of session-to-session goals. Agitated and/or confused patients may attend multiple short visits rather than one comparatively long session. Certain elements of the cognitive therapy session require additional comment, such as setting the agenda, checking on mood, pacing, and setting and reviewing homework.

Structuring and Pacing the Therapy Session

Setting the Agenda

In the treatment of anxiety or depression, the cognitive therapist would typically bridge the previous session to the current one and establish a series of specific goals to work through in a session. In the cognitive therapy of schizophrenia, it can be more difficult to establish formal goals for,

TABLE 8.1. Cognitive Therapy for Schizophrenia

- Establishment of the therapeutic alliance
  - Acceptance, support, collaboration

- Development and prioritization of problem list
  - Symptoms (e.g., delusions, hallucinations)
  - Life goals (e.g., work, relationships, housing, education)

- Psychoeducation and normalization of symptoms of psychosis
  - Discussion of the role of stress on the production and persistence of symptoms
  - Discussion of biopsychosocial aspects of the illness
  - Reducing stigma through education

- Development of a cognitive conceptualization
  - Identifying links between thoughts, feelings and behaviors
  - Identifying underlying themes in symptoms and problems
  - Sharing formulation and cognitive focus with patient

- Implementation of cognitive and behavioral techniques to treat positive and negative symptoms
  - Socratic questioning (i.e., Columbo technique)
  - Testing/reframing beliefs
    - Weighing the evidence
    - Considering alternative explanations
    - Engaging in behavioral experiments
  - Hierarchy of fears/suspicions
    - Engaging in imaginal exposures
    - Engaging in *in vivo* exposure tasks
    - Reducing safety behaviors
  - Eliciting self-beliefs (e.g., weak–strong, worthy–worthless)

- Implementation of cognitive and behavioral strategies to treat comorbid depression and anxiety.
  - Adapt standard cognitive therapy strategies for anxiety/depression
  - Test/reframe appraisals/beliefs related to anxiety (e.g., danger and vulnerability) and depression (e.g., worthlessness and hopelessness).
  - Engage in exposure exercises and create activity schedules
  - Engage in behavioral experiments
  - Engage in relaxation/exercise/breathing retraining

- Provision of relapse prevention strategies
  - Identifying high-risk situations
  - Providing skills training
  - Establishing step-by-step action plan to deal with setbacks

Note. Adapted from Rector and Beck (2002). Copyright 2002 by the Canadian Psychiatric Association. Adapted by permission.

SCHIZOPHRENIA

TABLE 8.2. Typical Session of Cognitive Therapy (25–50 Minutes)

- Elicit update on mood since last session.
  - Complete mood ratings.
  - Check on medication adherence.
  - Update on use of other services and progress.
- Provide bridge from last session.
  - Summarize previous session and important issues addressed.
  - Identify possible agenda items for focus in the session.
- Set structured agenda.
  - Psychosis symptom focus (e.g., cognitive strategies for delusions)
  - Comorbid symptom focus (e.g., developing hierarchy for social anxiety triggers)
  - Nonsymptom problem focus (e.g., coping with housing crisis)
  - Relapse prevention (e.g., developing list of resources)
- Provide summary and homework plan.
- Provide summary and elicit patient's feedback on session.
- Provide overview of treatment plan until next session (e.g., schedule of day service visits; meetings with case manager; medication repeats).

Note. Adapted from Rector and Beck (2002). Copyright 2002 by the Canadian Psychiatric Association. Adapted by permission.

say, the reduction of a delusional belief or the targeting of a delusional interpretation of a voice. Whereas the agenda can be set and prioritized explicitly with some patients, other patients will require a more flexible and implicit structuring of the session. That is, the standard format of setting a quick, prioritized list of agenda items, with preset time allotments for each topic, is not appropriate for some patients. For instance, a therapist may have decided that the principal goal of the upcoming session should be to continue where they left off in the previous week, examining evidence pertaining to a central delusional belief. However, if the patient expresses upset, agitation, or disinterest, the therapist should adjust the focus to better understand and work with these current feelings, even if it takes the entire session. This modification should not be construed as a limitation: If the overarching goal in cognitive therapy is to help patients recognize that their thoughts, appraisals, and beliefs contribute to their emotional and behavioral reactions in relation to their life experiences, then any session that permits an opportunity to build upon the understanding and strategies of the cognitive model will serve this goal.

Mood Check

The therapist conducts a mood check at the start of each session in the standard way, although, again, he or she is likely to devote greater time to addressing any concerns that have come up over the week. The therapist is also attentive to other aspects of care that might impact on the client's mood states, such as medication adherence and attendance at other key services over the previous week. The mood check can take longer in the cognitive therapy of psychosis, as part of the monitoring may involve socializing and educating the patient about the nature of moods and factors that cause their fluctuation. Further, if the patient is able to spontaneously link mood changes to his or her experience of psychotic symptoms, then the therapist can use this opportunity to sharpen the agenda for the session, returning to the aspect of the client's life that is an important source of distress.

Pacing

The therapist also displays flexibility in the pacing of the session. Particularly with patients who have prominent negative symptoms, cognitive therapy can be a relatively slow process. The therapist needs to attend to the patient's speed of processing thoughts and feelings and adjust his or her own speed accordingly. Although some sessions will require considerable patience on behalf of the therapist, appropriate slowing down will serve to enhance the alliance. For instance, many patients with negative symptoms feel as if they are being forced to increase their activity level by family and carers. Patients experience considerable pressure around these demands, which only serves to perpetuate their disengagement, and they may experience the therapist as similarly controlling and demanding. The therapist who effectively demonstrates patience and pacing is communicating acceptance and empathy for the patient. In contrast, the patient who is extremely talkative and easily distracted, and makes it difficult to get a word in edgewise, may just require greater space to continue with his or her fast pace. However, as noted in the earlier section, the therapist will need to interject questions and clarifying summaries to keep the session focused and moving toward some clinical goal. In summary, the pacing of the session is flexible and is always geared toward reducing distress and enhancing the therapeutic relationship.

Setting and Reviewing Homework

There is considerable variability in the quantity and quality of homework in the cognitive therapy treatment of schizophrenia, as there is the treatment of nonpsychotic disorders (Helbig & Fehm, 2004). Common factors that interfere with homework compliance in patients with schizophrenia include low motivation, trouble taking initiative, and lack of energy. In a survey of psychologists' use of homework with patients with schizophrenia, Deane, Glaser, Oades, and Kazantzis (2005) found that the top five barriers to homework completion were little motivation, ineffective decision making, social withdrawal, distractibility, and difficulty initiating activities. In a study that focused on patients' experience and perspective of homework tasks in cognitive therapy (Dunn, Morrison, & Bentall, 2002), factors cited as affecting homework compliance also included low motivation, putting off the assignment, and lack of effort. However, cognitive therapy can contribute to the reduction of negative symptoms by helping patients learn to identify and reduce the triggers for their activation and/or develop strategies for the alleviation following onset. Common strategies include the use of activity schedules, graded task assignments, assertiveness training, and thought records to target negative expectancies. Much of the progress in reducing negative symptoms is achieved through the successful completion of homework tasks between sessions (see Chapter 11).

The basic tenet that between-session activities facilitate consolidation and generalization of skills practiced in sessions is important to the fundamental goals of cognitive therapy for schizophrenia: normalizing and reducing stigma-associated symptoms, helping patients to identify and reframe delusional beliefs, questioning the content and the secondary delusional beliefs pertaining to voices, reducing negative expectancies regarding social and emotional engagement, and improving functional outcomes.

Strategies to improve homework compliance would be aimed at both the *assignment stage* and *review stage*. With respect to the former, set small and manageable goals and probe for expectancies around anticipated success with the homework. Work with distorted appraisals and beliefs around the task and arrive at a perspective that makes homework a "no-lose" proposition wherein the task is to *try* rather than to succeed itself (Tompkins, 2004). At the review stage, it is important to make sure that, first, *all* homework is actually reviewed. All efforts to complete homework are generously rewarded with praise and support. Further, cognitive distortions need to be addressed carefully during the review stage, given that many patients tend to minimize their efforts, accomplishments, and pleasure taken in tasks (Rector et al., 2005). Finally, since it is important for patients not to experience performance pressure around their treatment, the therapist also must be flexible and never make them feel pressured about homework assignments.

There are also more disorder-specific factors that may reduce homework compliance: namely, the cognitive impairments of poor attention, few, if any, organization strategies, and poor memory (e.g., Nuechterlein & Dawson, 1984). A study by Dunn and colleagues (2002) found that problems with cognitive functioning and poor insight can make it difficult for patients to accurately recall, execute, and then remember the outcomes of homework assignments. To improve compliance in the face of these real limitations, therapists can aim to (1) provide a very clear set of instructions for homework completion, with check-in efforts to make sure that the patient understands the assignment; (2) provide the patient with written or audiotaped summaries of homework instructions; (3) outline when and where the task will be completed; (4) provide reminder cues (e.g., sticky notes) to be posted in the patient's residence; (5) limit requirement of extensive written summaries of homework; and (6) where feasible, include caregivers in the homework equation (Rector, 2007).

SUMMARY

The foundation for effective cognitive therapy of schizophrenia is the development of a mutually respectful, trusting, and nonjudgmental therapeutic relationship. Rather than being a static variable, the therapeutic relationship requires attention and fostering in each and every session. The barriers to engagement reflect those commonly seen in the cognitive therapy of other disorders. However, in this chapter we have noted a number of disorder-specific barriers that can be identified and reduced. More generally, we have discussed possible modifications to agenda setting, session pacing, and homework setting and reviewing that can enhance the relationship and foster engagement.

CHAPTER 9

Cognitive Assessment
and Therapy of Delusions

Despite the obvious rigidity of delusional beliefs, there are now a broad range of cognitive therapy strategies that have been shown to help patients reduce distorted delusional interpretations and accompanying distress. In this chapter we describe the evidence-based assessment and treatment of delusions. As outlined in Chapter 3, the cognitive foundation for the later development of delusional beliefs in adulthood typically occurs in the adolescent period. The actual delusional content of the beliefs is commonly an extension of beliefs held prior to the onset of the delusion. Once initiated, cognitive distortions, categorical thinking, emotion- and somatic-based reasoning, and information-processing biases such as "jumping to conclusions," and failing to reality-test serve to further consolidate the delusional beliefs and prevent opportunities for disconfirmation (Garety, Hemsley, & Wessely, 1991). In addition, the behavioral responses prompted by the delusional beliefs, such as avoidance, withdrawal, and other safety behaviors, contribute significantly to the distress and the maintenance of the delusions.

The cognitive therapy of delusions is based on this specific cognitive formulation and focuses initially on understanding (1) antecedent factors in the development of the belief(s), (2) perceived evidence in support of the beliefs, (3) current online misinterpretations of day-to-day events that contribute to new sources of perceived evidence, and (4) momentary distress. Treatment also addresses the underlying nondelusional cognitive schemas that make the patient vulnerable to relapse and the recurrence of delusional beliefs. Moreover, treatment aims to reduce maladaptive behavioral responses such as withdrawal, avoidance, reassurance seeking, and other safety behaviors. Collectively, treatment strategies aim to reduce delusional rigidity, preoccupation, and distress while permitting the patient to achieve better functioning.

Prior to intervening with delusional beliefs, it is important to complete a comprehensive assessment, identifying when the belief(s) emerged, the critical evidence seen as supporting the delusional beliefs, and evidence that was previously considered supportive but has been relinquished. The current impact of the delusion(s) on patients' functioning can be formally assessed with standardized measures and by conducting a functional assessment. As in cognitive therapy for other emotional difficulties, the therapist aims to assess developmental contributions, including early life experiences and distal vulnerabilities, that occurred prior to the onset of the delusion(s). Because delusional beliefs are hypothesized to emerge from central nondelusional self-beliefs, we outline next how the development of a case conceptualization can reduce the stigma of having unusual beliefs, promote insight, and facilitate changes in belief. An overview of the treatment approach for delusions can be seen in Table 9.1.

ASSESSMENT

Assessment of Symptoms/Cognitions

The assessment of delusions occurs during early therapy sessions, with the therapist practicing nondirective, guided discovery to elicit information about current problems. Some patients have discussed cognitive therapy with their referring clinician and arrive at the first session willing and ready to address their most difficult problems, including delusions. However, many patients present without a clear understanding of why they have been referred and/or with very distressing delusions and minimal insight. It is not customary to start by discussing the delusions unless the patient prompts this focus. Because the therapeutic relationship is central to the success of treating delusions, the therapist should defer direct intervention with the delusions until he or she has conducted a thorough assessment and established a strong therapeutic alliance (Rector et al., 2002). The therapist begins the assessment phase by listening to the patient describe his

TABLE 9.1. Cognitive Assessment and Therapy for Delusions

Assessment

- Assessment of symptoms/cognitions
  - Elaborating on delusional focus
  - Assessing cognitive distortions
  - Examining emotional and behavioral responses to delusional interpretations
  - Ascertaining key evidence taken to support delusions
  - Assessing cognitive schemas underlying delusional beliefs and interpretations

- Conducting a functional assessment
  - Identifying delusional triggers
  - Assessing specific delusional appraisals
  - Assessing emotional and behavioral responses to delusional appraisals

- Developing the case conceptualization
  - Synthesizing distal and proximal factors that contributed to the development and the current persistence of delusions:
    - Predisposing factors
    - Precipitating factors
    - Perpetuating factors
    - Protective factors

Treatment

- Providing psychoeducation and normalization
  - Sharing the cognitive conceptualization of current difficulties
  - Normalizing delusional beliefs

- Socializing the patient to the cognitive model
  - Developing awareness of interaction between thoughts, feelings, and behaviors as they pertain to delusional interpretations
  - Testing and correcting delusional interpretations

- Applying cognitive and behavioral approaches
  - Strategies for questioning evidence in support of delusional beliefs
  - Building alternative beliefs
  - Targeting nondelusional core beliefs
  - Consolidating alternative beliefs
  - Using behavioral experiments

or her circumstances, ongoing difficulties, and symptom problems, and by identifying areas that appear to elicit the most distress and the patient's appraisals. The therapist aims to impart a nonjudgmental tone of openness, acceptance, and curiosity about what the patient is experiencing. As noted in Chapter 8, the principal goal during the first several sessions of therapy is to build rapport and trust with the patient and to identify areas of distress and disturbance (Kingdon & Turkington, 1994).

The therapist also introduces the patient to the cognitive model, highlighting the relationship between thoughts, feelings, and behaviors in response to experiences and perceived problems, both external and internal. For example, a patient presented for treatment with a 3-year delusional belief of persecution, but in the first several sessions of treatment, he was most interested in discussing his housing problems. He was currently living in a shared residence and was frequently bothered by loud music and uninvited visitors. The therapist used this focus as an opportunity to understand better what aspects of these experiences were problematic for him and to begin to identify his appraisals, beliefs, and behavioral responses to these problems. The therapist communicated empathy and warmth and validated the "frustration" that the patient felt during these times as well as the "upset" that others' "disrespect" for him provoked. This topic also provided an early opportunity for the patient and therapist to collaborate in problem solving: developing a few new options to try out at home to reduce the noise (e.g., use earplugs, request that the TV to be turned down before he gets too angry) and the visitors (e.g., developed a visitor schedule for the kitchen area). As trust builds, the therapist can begin to transition toward a greater focus on the delusional beliefs. For instance, with this patient the therapist was able to return to the theme of being "disrespected" by others as an entry into the more pronounced delusional beliefs.

Elaborating on Delusional Focus

There are a number of inroads to discussing delusional beliefs. Some patients want to discuss their delusional beliefs from the start, whereas others are reluctant. In our experience, we have found it most effective to allow patients to discuss their life problems broadly and to allow the delusional beliefs to emerge during open-ended discussion. If the patient has multiple delusional beliefs, it is likely that he or she will gravitate toward discussing the belief that is most distressing. However, if there are multiple beliefs and the therapist is in the position to choose where to focus, it is best to start with the more peripheral as opposed to highly charged delusional beliefs. For instance, a patient participating in cognitive therapy had the belief that periods of time were "stolen" from her as well as a Capgras delusion that her mother and father were imposters (American Psychiatric Association, 2000). The former belief was less threatening to her than was the latter, so treatment focused on this belief first.

While more formal questions pertaining to the content, duration, and distress associated with delusions may have been addressed with psychiatric interview protocols that provide the opportunity to rate the presence, severity, distress, and impact on quality of life, the early sessions of therapy focus on a more in-depth assessment of past and present delusional beliefs, particularly if they have been identified as a primary goal on the problem-list. The aim is to collect sufficient information to understand when the delusions first emerged, the extent to which they became elaborated based on negative life experiences, and pre-onset preoccupations and/or fears.

In some instances, it is easiest to start by discussing the most immediate delusional beliefs and then work backward in time to establish information that has been taken to support them. In other cases, it may be easier to start with a discussion of events preceding onset and then focus on the period when the problems first began. Notwithstanding the particular starting point, it is important to collect as much information as possible to complete the cognitive conceptualization. General questions can be asked; for example, "When did you first begin to have difficulties?" or "You mentioned that you were in the hospital in (date). What sorts of problems were you having at the time?" Depending on the openness of the patient, more specific questions will typically elicit more detailed information about the delusional beliefs; for instance, "When was it that you first came to realize that you were capable of bringing the world to an end?" The therapist proceeds cautiously when seeking to identify periods that the patient finds too difficult to recall specific memories. When this occurs, it is best to return to asking more general questions about things that were going on around the time of the heightened emotional distress.

It is also important to understand the contextual features related to the development of delusional beliefs. Delusions develop slowly over time for many patients, and critical incidents that were related to the themes of the delusions are very hard to identify. Here, questions can focus on "What was happening at that time in your life when you first started feeling [scared, confused, angry, etc.]?" Or, "Did something happen that really convinced you that [e.g., you had the power to bring the world to an end?"] Some patients, as in the following example, can recall vivid life events that represent proximal triggers to the emergence of their delusions:

THERAPIST: Mary, when did you first start noticing that things were changing for you?

PATIENT: I lost all peace of mind on the day of the first anniversary of 9/11.

THERAPIST: Can you tell me more about why you lost peace of mind during that time?

PATIENT: I saw the wave.

THERAPIST: What was the wave that you saw Mary?

PATIENT: I had been day trading on my computer for 3 days straight without an hour of sleep, and I began to see patterns in the trades that reflected the perfect wave.

THERAPIST: And what was the importance of the perfect wave?

PATIENT: I felt terrified; I knew it was a sign that everything was going to collapse.

THERAPIST: Do you mean that you had discovered a clue that the stock market was going to crash?

PATIENT: No, it was much bigger than that; it was a message to me that the world was coming to an end.

THERAPIST: I see, so the pattern in the trading, the perfect wave, was a sign to you to prepare for the end of the world? Did you have a sense of who was communicating this sign to you?

PATIENT: The devil had been tempting me for days. He had been sending messages, but I was able to ignore them. Everywhere I looked, there were signs—the computer flashing, the dog barking, on the radio, feeling hot and cold. . . .

THERAPIST: So the perfect wave seemed like the final big sign, even though there had been many smaller signs over those few days. . . . Is that right?

PATIENT: There was a battle going on between good and evil, and the devil was letting me know that evil was going to win and that the world would end. I turned on the TV and the devil was on the screen laughing at me—it was awful.

Mary was readily able to identify the acute activation of her religious-paranoid delusion approximately 3 years earlier. Additional information was sought around the nature of her beliefs regarding why there was a battle between good and evil, as well as what the particular signs were (e.g., dogs barking signified that the evil force was in the home).

Once the particular period of onset is identified, the therapist moves backward in time to collect more information—important beliefs, attitudes, fears, etc.—about the premorbid phase, as well as other life events of significance. The therapist also traces the delusional belief forward in time, collecting information since it first developed and that is seen as providing evidence of its basis.

Cognitive Distortions

The therapist assesses the presence, range, and frequency of general cognitive distortions relevant to the misinterpretation of ongoing events and of specific hot situations that lead to misinterpretation and putative support for the delusional beliefs. Such cognitive distortions as all-or-none thinking, selective abstraction, and catastrophization are as important to the misinterpretation of situations as they are in the experience of other emotional difficulties. Further, as outlined in Chapter 3, certain cognitive distortions are more characteristic of delusional interpretations, in particular. Therapists aim to identify the particular interpretations that reflect internalizing, externalizing, and egocentric cognitive distortions. Although much of therapy is aimed at identifying, questioning, and seeking to reduce the cognitive distortions that fuel overestimations of the perceived probability that a delusional interpretation is correct, it is also important for the therapist to address the cognitive distortions relating to the perceived *consequences* of the delusions. With a patient who has generalized anxiety, for example, it might be routine to identify the consequences by asking something like "And what would be the worst thing if you did, in fact, lose your job?" In the case of a delusional patient who believes he or she is being persecuted by the Hells Angels biker gang, the therapist would not ask the related "And so what is the worst thing about being persecuted by the Hells Angels?", because the therapist would appear to be colluding with the original delusional interpretation and implying that he or she does indeed believe that the patient is being persecuted by the Hells Angels. Rather, the alternative strategy is to elicit the perceived negative consequences by proposing the inverse notion, "If, by chance, you found out that the Hells Angels were *not* after you, how would that change things for you?" The answer could lead to the identification of current negative consequences that could be improved—for example, "Then I could leave my house and walk the dog, go to the mall, eat take-out food again, and enjoy my life outside of the house"— and that could then become the focus of treatment.

A patient with a 20-year history of paranoid delusions believed that members of her department were conspiring to have her removed from her job. In moments when her delusional interpretations were triggered, she believed them 100%, the consequences included two passive and one more serious suicide attempt since the onset of her psychosis. In treatment, she was able to identify and reduce her delusional interpretations in work-related situations by becoming aware of cognitive distortions pertaining to jumping to conclusions, all-or-nothing thinking, and so on. In addition, the therapist was able to focus on the perceived consequences of the delusions by drawing out the catastrophic consequences with the downward arrow technique. The patient feared that her colleagues disrespected her and that they were collecting information about her and working together with the head of the department to have her removed. At one level, she was concerned about being "disgraced." However, the more fearful consequence was that she would lose her office if she were removed from her department. And if she lost her office, she would have nowhere to go and no one to see. And if she became isolated, she would become depressed and eventually "crazy." And if she became "crazy," she would kill herself. The therapist's approach was not to focus on decatastrophizing the actual moment-by-moment delusional interpretations (e.g., "And so what is the worst thing about your colleagues not respecting your work?"). Rather, the therapist worked with the catastrophic consequences of (1) losing her office, (2) having nowhere to go and no one to see, (3) becoming isolated and depressed, (4) going crazy, and (5) killing herself. At each step, the therapist tries to find alternative perspectives and coping approaches. The perceived consequences for this patient were independent of the apparent "truth-value" of her beliefs. The therapist was able to weaken the perceived catastrophic consequences by shifting them away from the delusion by simply confirming that she would have all of the same fears if her department closed due to budget cutbacks.

As such, the therapist approached the perceived consequences as follows. The therapist discussed with the patient what she could do if she lost her office (e.g., renting another office on campus, establishing a desk at the college library). Together, they listed social connections she had outside of work (the patient had friends whom she saw at least monthly, she sat in a regular spot in the coffee shop with her newspaper everyday and people would say hello, she routinely went to the library, and she was considering volunteering). To decatasophize this perceived consequence, the therapist introduced relapse prevention strategies (identifying triggers, developing an action plan, identifying times when she was down but did not attempt suicide, identifying times when she was down but the delusional intensity did not become intensified, and drawing attention to the alternative evidence that she had coped well with some of these experiences and without a suicide attempt for 5 years). The therapist also discussed the availability of new resources the patient had not had in the past but that she now had— namely, a team of caring and supportive mental health professionals. With time, the patient was able to reduce delusional interpretations following situational triggers by catching distortions (jumping to conclusions) and considering alternative explanations. She was able to approach her work without believing that her "life was on the line" everyday.

Emotional and Behavioral Responses to Delusional Interpretations

Assessment also examines the specific emotional (e.g., fear) and behavioral consequences (e.g., avoidance, safety behaviors) created by the activation of the delusion. The various strategies that patients employ to cope with the fear, embarrassment, anger, sadness, etc., that the delusional beliefs create often serve to prevent corrective feedback. Just as patients with anxiety avoid situations that trigger fear, patients with delusions avoid hot situations that are likely to provoke their fears. Those with persecutory fears avoid situations where they expect to be demeaned or attacked, whereas patients with religious delusions may escape from situations that they perceive to be immoral: for example, engaging in a conversation that includes explicit reference to sexual intercourse. Patients with delusions also engage in subtle avoidances or strategies akin to those observed in patients with anxiety disorders. For instance, a patient refused to remove a headband because he believed that it was responsible for holding his mind together. Mary, described earlier, engaged in repetitive and excessive checking behavior of stock trends via the Internet to the point where she could not remember what she was actually seeing when she checked.

The collection of information regarding the delusional beliefs is woven into the process of engagement with an emphasis on gentle questioning and paying close attention to, and balancing the focus on, areas that seem to elicit greater and lesser emotion. Patients are often referred to a cognitive therapist with the explicit aim of helping them address their delusional beliefs. The therapist may know before starting the assessment phase what the patient's hot spots are—topics that, when broached, run the risk of eliciting agitation and other negative affect in the session. In general, regardless of how much is known about the patient before starting treatment, it is important for the therapist not to push too hard for details pertaining to the delusional beliefs and to be prepared to back off and consider other areas of focus, depending on overt as well as covert signs of agitation, distress, etc., in the interview. The particular content of the delusional beliefs may correspond to likely emotional states experienced in the session. For instance, the paranoid patient may be at comparatively greater risk of becoming agitated, annoyed, and defensive, whereas the patient with religious delusions may experience increased sadness and guilt during questioning. An early understanding of the meaning associated with the delusional beliefs will alert the therapist to likely hot spots that might occur during early sessions.

It is important for the therapist to avoid using labels such as *delusions* or *symptoms of schizophrenia* when discussing the patient's beliefs. A more normalizing alternative is to refer to delusional beliefs as simply *beliefs* or *ideas*, and the like. As detailed by others (Chadwick et al., 1996; Kingdon & Turkington, 2005; Nelson, 2005), the assessment proceeds by attempting to enter the perspective of the patient. Taking the other's perspective leads to a natural curiosity about the patient's experience. However, it may be the case that certain patients are harder to empathize with, due to the unusual or bizarre nature of their beliefs or other aspects of their presentation. The problem of feeling empathy toward the patient who continuously presents a bizarre, potentially offensive (e.g., anti-Semitic) or otherwise wholly inaccurate belief has been aptly titled the "fading empathy effect" and requires special effort on the part of the therapist to overcome (Nelson, 2005). The goal is to remain focused on what it must feel like for the patient to hold these beliefs and experience the emotional and behavioral repercussions of such beliefs.

Ascertaining Key Evidence Taken to Support Delusions

As the assessment process unfolds, the therapist identifies the full range of current delusional beliefs as well as previous delusional beliefs that are no longer held. The therapist also aims to understand the interrelationship between beliefs. For each belief, the therapist identifies when it originated, what the contextual features at the time it originated, and the immediate impact that it has on the patient's life. Also, events and experiences that are taken as evidence in support of the delusional beliefs are assessed. It is likewise important for the therapist to obtain conviction ratings for each belief and the extent to which each piece of evidence is seen to either directly or indirectly support the delusion. Some patients are able to clearly articulate the nature of their beliefs and the distinct critical situations that were seen to provide confirmation of their delusional ideas, whereas others are less able to do this. If the patient demonstrates difficulties in recalling information or seems to have difficulty discussing the delusions, it is important to proceed with caution.

It is similarly not helpful to collude with the patient's delusional beliefs to reduce momentary distress. When the patient asks the therapist directly as to the whether or not his or her beliefs are correct, he or she is usually seeking to be understood more than attempting to be "right" (Chadwick et al., 1996, p. 54). As the therapist ascertains the current and historical basis of the delusional beliefs, assessment transitions to the day-to-day delusional misinterpretations of events.

Assessing Beliefs Underlying Delusional Beliefs and Interpretations

In addition to assessing the conviction and pervasiveness of the delusional beliefs and the delusional negative automatic thoughts, it is essential for the therapist to identify the underlying self- and other beliefs that give rise to the themes of the delusional beliefs. The seemingly bizarre content of delusions can become more comprehensible when understood within the interpersonal context of a person's life. Delusions appear to be based on an organization of dysfunctional cognitive schemas that are gradually formed over time, starting in adolescence or even earlier in some cases.

The understanding of the patient's dysfunctional attitudes and beliefs provide direct clues to the formation and content of the delusions. For instance, we have found that grandiose delusions may develop as a compensation for an underlying sense of loneliness, unworthiness, or powerlessness. Many of the patients with grandiose delusions have experienced prior life crises characterized by a sense of failure or worthlessness and subsequently began to think of themselves as being famous, divine, or all-powerful. As noted (see Chapter 3), the proximal antecedents of a paranoid delusion, on the other hand, may include the fear of retaliation for having done something that offended another person or group (Beck & Rector, 2002).

The core beliefs underlying delusions can be assessed directly during the clinical assessment phase, using the downward arrow method, which can reveal the continuous extension of core belief themes embedded in the delusional beliefs, or, alternatively, show how the delusional belief represents a defensive reaction to an apparent degraded self-concept, as revealed in the following excerpt:

> THERAPIST: Susan, can you imagine for a moment that you are not the Poet Laureate. If this were, by chance, true—how would you feel?
>
> PATIENT: I would feel empty. . . . I wouldn't have lived up to the family name.
>
> THERAPIST: OK, and if that was, by chance, true, would that say anything about you?

PATIENT: That I will not get a stamp of approval.

THERAPIST: And, what would it say about you if you did not get others' approval?

PATIENT: That I'm worthless.

As discussed later in this chapter, treatment of delusional beliefs also entails the direct targeting of nondelusional core beliefs, so it is important during the assessment phase to collect information and formulate the nature of the patient's core beliefs. In previous research we found that elevated interpersonal (i.e., sociotropic) concerns, as assessed by the Dysfunctional Attitude Scale (DAS), tend to be especially associated with increased suspiciousness and paranoid delusions (Rector, 2004). We recommend that the clinical assessment be supplemented with the administration of the DAS (or a related measure) to further identify the role of dysfunctional attitudes and beliefs in the development and persistence of the delusional beliefs.

Conducting a Functional Assessment

The functional assessment permits closer examination of what situations trigger distinct delusional interpretations and the factors that are central to the maintenance of, and ongoing distress caused by, the delusional beliefs, such as cognitive distortions, attentional vigilance, and behavioral responses focusing on avoidance and withdrawal, or confrontational behaviors. It should also be noted that although possibly less common than avoidance and safety behaviors, a significant number of patients also engage in reassurance-seeking behaviors and neutralizing strategies. For instance, a patient who had delusions of thought withdrawal believed that other people could "steal" his ability to enjoy pleasure. When he passed a stranger on the street and it occurred to him that the person may be attempting to "steal away" his pleasure, he neutralized the likelihood of this occurrence by stating that he "loved music and movies." By announcing his pleasures to the person first, he believed that he could prevent him or her from withdrawing his pleasure.

Identifying Delusional Triggers

Delusional beliefs often vary in intensity and distress, depending on the presence or absence of distinct triggers. For instance, the paranoid patient may be consistently apprehensive and mistrusting of others, although only specific contexts (e.g., certain people, large crowds, work versus home) trigger full-fledged delusional interpretations and attendant distress. During the assessment phase of cognitive therapy, the therapist elicits situations that were recently interpreted as supportive of the delusional belief. It is often easiest to focus on triggers in the past week, although sometimes patients are better able to discuss a very emotionally salient event from the recent past. As in the functional assessment of other problems, the aim is to identify the situational triggers for experienced emotional distress (e.g., sadness, anger, anxiety). If the patient finds it difficult to identify distinct situations that lead to delusional interpretations, then it may be better in the early sessions to focus on educating the patient about different emotions by having him or her monitor moods on a daily basis. The focus is on understanding the patient's appraisals of events and experiences. In the cognitive therapy of the emotional disorders, the aim would be to identify negative automatic thoughts; similarly, in the assessment of delusions, the therapist aims to identify delusional automatic thoughts, misinterpretations, and distortions of current experiences due to the presence of delusional beliefs. It is helpful to complete a dysfunctional record in session regarding a particular situational antecedent for the activation of the delusion (i.e., collecting information about the nature of the situation, the moods experienced, and the [delusional] automatic thoughts). It is not customary to name delusional beliefs or delusional interpretations as such. Rather, the delusional automatic thoughts can be referred to simply as "thoughts about the situation" or "interpretations of the situation" and recorded in the usual way.

The functional assessment provides an opportunity to collect detailed information about the idiosyncratic aspects of the situational triggers, delusional interpretations, emotional and behavioral responses, and functional impairments created by the delusions.

Developing the Case Conceptualization

Completing a cognitive conceptualization provides the framework for understanding how past and present factors contribute to the development and persistence of the patient's delusion(s). Since the organization of dysfunctional cognitive schemas takes root early in life (i.e., in adolescence or perhaps earlier), it is important to assess distal life experiences during this time that were instrumental in shaping the person's cognitive organization. The case conceptualization should lead to initial hypotheses about the role of distal environmental factors that contribute to activation of the delusion, the content embedded within the delusions, as well as the characteristic situations, events, and experiences (internal and external) that are likely to be personally important.

Take, for example, the conceptualization of a patient's religious, grandiose, and persecutory delusions. As detailed elsewhere (Rector, 2007), Elizabeth was a 35-year-old single female living on her own in a large city. Ten years earlier, she had experienced her first psychotic episode, in which she heard delusional voices that focused on religious, grandiose, and persecutory themes. Elizabeth's past psychiatric troubles included ongoing positive symptoms of psychosis and two major depressive episodes. Before being referred, she had received case management that involved weekly meetings with a clinical nurse specialist and options for specialized day treatment services, which she attended irregularly.

Elizabeth had experienced considerable exposure to religious themes growing up because both of her parents were dedicated Catholics. Yet, from an early age, she had demonstrated some resistance to her religion. For instance, in an early session Elizabeth recalled "pretending" to pray as a child, while, in fact, she was intentionally thinking blasphemous thoughts, including "praying to the devil" as a form of rebellion. She also explained that in her mid-20s she had experienced a period of more extreme religious rebellion, during which she was quite promiscuous, and this period led her to feel great shame later in life. She became preoccupied with the thought that she had "sinned" and would go to "Hell" for her behavior.

Closer to the onset of her psychosis, she confessed her period of promiscuity to her boyfriend, which resulted in his calling her a "slut" and breaking off the relationship. She experienced an intense downward spiral of rumination about events from the past and began to see herself as "bad" and "evil." Soon thereafter this, Elizabeth heard a voice that called her a "slut," which she perceived to be that of her boyfriend. She also heard a voice that said "I know the real you," which she interpreted to be the devil intercepting her prayers. She began to believe that she was "possessed" and that she was a "fallen angel" destined to do harm to other people. She was hospitalized following an appearance at a crowded venue where she had urged everyone around her to "save themselves." At the time of the first meeting, she stated that she believed that she was a "fallen angel" (belief rating: 100%) and that the "devil was using me to harm others" (belief rating: 80%).

The religious structure of the delusions took shape within the environment in which Elizabeth was raised. Following from previous formulations of grandiose beliefs (Beck & Rector, 2002, 2005), the therapist hypothesized that the grandiose nature of her delusional system functioned to compensate for her perception of herself as bad, worthless, and powerless.

The assessment phase provides the opportunity to consolidate the therapeutic relationship and to collect different sources of information to complete an initial case conceptualization, with an understanding of when the delusional belief(s) emerged, past evidence taken in support of the delusional belief(s), the nonpsychotic beliefs and core beliefs underlying the delusional belief(s), and the current sources of misinterpretation that perpetuate situational distress and contribute to intensification of the delusional belief(s).

It is also helpful to have an understanding of the broader factors that impact on vulnerability to, and maintenance of, the psychosis, including *predisposing factors* (e.g., family history of schizophrenia, prolonged home-lessness, schizotypal beliefs), *precipitating factors* (e.g., traumatic event, interpersonal rejection, achievement failures), and *perpetuating factors* (e.g., high expressed emotion in home environment, isolation). Finally, in addition to detailing aspects of vulnerability and maintenance, it is important to note the strengths or *protective factors* that can be harnessed in therapy (e.g., presence of positive relationships, skills and interests) (Kingdon & Turkington, 2005).

The final aspect of the assessment phase is to agree upon the specific prioritized goals of treatment. Patients present with varying degrees of insight about their delusional beliefs. Before starting to directly target delusional beliefs for change in therapy, it is essential that patients (1) recognize that their delusional interpretations contribute to distress and/or impairment in their lives, or at least that the theme of the delusions is pertinent to their current life difficulties, and (2) are open to exploring possibilities of feeling better, or learning to cope better with the beliefs. In instances where the delusional themes focus on persecution or religious themes, the associated distress is clear, at least to the therapist. However, as outlined in Chapter 3, grandiose delusions may serve to protect vulnerable self-esteem and may promote a sense of well-being (Beck & Rector, 2002). In cognitive therapy, the goal is not to reduce grandiose beliefs directly but to reveal the underlying negative core beliefs for which the grandiose belief is serving as a protection.

TREATMENT

The cognitive therapy treatment of delusions is focused on reducing the conviction, pervasiveness, and distress associated with beliefs that are presently leading to personal suffering and functional impairments. With patients who have multiple delusional beliefs with varying levels of distress, it is customary to begin with less highly charged beliefs before focusing on those that are more central and firmly held. However, in many cases the assessment phase has clarified the range of important delusional beliefs, and it may be the case that the patient is clearly wishing to focus on a particular delusional belief that, in fact, may be the most central in the pathology. The risk in evaluating a belief in which the patient has a high degree of conviction is that any attempts to chip away at its stronghold may be experienced as threatening and lead to psychological reactance (Brehm, 1962). This, in turn, may have the paradoxical effect of enhancing, rather than diminishing, the patient's conviction in the belief. The aim, therefore, is to work with the *evidence* for the delusional belief rather than confronting it head-on. Irrespective of whether the belief is central or peripheral, primary or secondary, the initial goal is to work with evidence that is more peripheral as opposed to central, providing the opportunity to instill a questioning mode with beliefs that are less emotionally charged in the first instance.

While the principal aim is to weaken the delusional beliefs by creating alternative perspectives on the events and experiences that have been taken to support the beliefs, there are several other aspects of delusional beliefs that the therapist must address. As articulated within the cognitive approach, delusional beliefs appear to incorporate the themes of nonpsychotic beliefs. Nonpsychotic beliefs may reflect particular sociocultural themes related to acceptance of supernatural, technological, or religious beliefs. For instance, a study conducted by Cox and Cowling (1989) shows that a significant percentage of the community believe in ghosts (25%), superstitions (25%), and the devil (23%). It is has been our experience that patients who develop religious delusions about being possessed, or punished by the devil, have had longstanding and predelusional beliefs about the existence of such phenomena as possession and the devil within their particular religious beliefs. As another example, the patient who believes that his thoughts are being broadcast via a radar chip in his brain is likely to have underlying nonpsychotic beliefs about the functional aspects of technology (e.g., computers, digital equipment, solar disks) that provide the basis for the delusional belief.

In addition to questioning the evidence in support of the delusional beliefs, a frequent treatment goal is the successful targeting of these underlying nondelusional beliefs. Therapists, however, need to be cautious when tackling underlying sociocultural–religious beliefs that are held by the patient's sociocultural–religious affiliative groups, because doing so could adversely affect their identity or role in these groups if changed.

Elizabeth's case clarifies this point. She maintained the delusional belief that her prayers were intercepted by the devil and transformed into death wishes for people in the world. Part of this delusion was a belief that these misguided prayers had led to natural disasters, tragedies, and illnesses throughout the world. The goal of treatment was not to question the existence of the devil, but rather the extent to which, within her religious faith, it was possible for the devil to intercept prayers between Elizabeth and her God, as well as whether it was possible for the devil to misuse "good prayers." Her delusional beliefs revolving around being responsible for world suffering were contingent on a nondelusional understanding of the role of the devil in religious scripture during prayer. In this treatment, the therapist and Elizabeth worked together with a senior and understanding leader of her religious faith to clarify that within the tenets of Catholicism, prayers to God cannot be intercepted by the devil.

As elaborated in Chapter 3, the themes of nondelusional beliefs are embedded within a patient's delusions and underlying dysfunctional beliefs and attitudes. Treatment aims to modify these beliefs either in tandem with the delusional beliefs or in a focused fashion following inroads with the delusions. In some instances, negative core beliefs and dysfunctional beliefs may be elicited first because it is clear that the entire delusional system is resting on a negative self-view, and any improvements will successfully weaken the delusional belief and lead to its outright collapse. For example, Elizabeth heard a voice calling her a "slut" and believed that this taunting was a fair punishment for her promiscuous behavior. The aim at the beginning of therapy was to target the guilt and shame associated with underlying beliefs about being "bad" and "irresponsible" for having been promiscuous in her mid-20s.

Finally, cognitive therapy aims to further reduce delusional conviction and distress by targeting the cognitive misinterpretations of newly emerging events and situations to prevent the accrual of further evidence in support of the delusional beliefs and to reduce situational distress caused by such interpretations.

Psychoeducation and Normalizing

The first goal of intervening and reducing distress associated with delusional beliefs is to share a cognitive conceptualization of the patient's current difficulties. By highlighting the importance of situational and personal factors in the development and persistence of the delusion, the patient develops a broader understanding of the factors relevant not only to reducing current distress but also reducing the probability of relapse. The sharing of the cognitive conceptualization is also the first step in normalizing the experience of delusions. It is not necessary to share all aspects of the case conceptualization with the patient. Rather, only aspects that are relevant to helping the patient understand his or her difficulties within a diathesis–stress perspective need to be shared. The majority of patients arrive for treatment with an internalized view of their experiences as being "weird," "crazy," "scary," "nuts," etc., and a diagnosis of schizophrenia as representing "insanity," "danger," and "a burden to society." An important goal is to humanize or normalize these experiences by showing their continuity with ordinary experiences. As outlined by Kingdon and Turkington (1994, 2005), the approach is to clarify the role of stress in eliciting such experiences as voices and delusional beliefs. For instance, certain circumstances may lead to the natural evolution of psychotic symptoms, including sensory and sleep deprivation, traumatic situations such as intense physical and sexual abuse, and organic states such as delirium, alcohol and illicit-drug intoxication and withdrawal, and periods of bereavement.

Another aspect of the normalizing approach is to highlight for patients how their experiences face on a continuum of experiences reported by the broader community (Kingdon & Turkington, 1991, 2005). The majority of people report having had the experience of hearing a doorbell ring when they are waiting for someone to ring the doorbell, or have "heard" a group of people speaking about them when, in fact, they were not, or have thought that a loved one has had an accident because he or she failed to arrive home on time. While briefer in duration and prompting less distress than experienced by people with persistent delusions, such experiences of misperceiving a situation and feeling distress as a result occur for everyone.

We will use Elizabeth's case again as an example. Elizabeth was aware that she needed help with her difficulties, and she was extremely compliant with her treatment. In accordance with a case conceptualization perspective and the goals of normalizing psychosis (Kingdon & Turkington, 1994), the therapeutic aim was to achieve an acceptable explanation for all of her symptoms. Even though Elizabeth's delusions and hallucinations caused her great distress, a range of benefits was afforded to her within this belief system. For instance, feeling responsible for the world allowed her to feel powerful instead of powerless. The belief that she was a fallen angel made her feel special instead of insignificant. It was essential to determine what Elizabeth would feel if these beliefs were successfully modified. The principal goal was to explore Elizabeth's understanding of her symptoms, the evidence that seemed to support her beliefs about being a fallen angel and controlled by the devil, and the agency of the voices she heard, so as to arrive at a shared understanding of her problems that would (1) normalize some of these experiences, (2) reduce self-blame, while (3) not necessarily removing some of the perceived benefits of the delusional system that bolstered self-esteem.

One aim of the normalizing approach was to validate her perceived importance of God, the devil, Heaven, Hell, punishment, sin, etc., as key articles of her faith shared by millions of people. The therapist also offered a normalizing perspective on Elizabeth's distress around her experiences during the onset of symptoms (e.g., she believed that her behavior warranted punishment). Finally, Elizabeth and her therapist shared a normalizing perspective around her reasonable attempts to understand the agency of the voices that she heard.

Socializing the Patient to the Cognitive Model

The next phase of therapy socializes the patient to the cognitive model by developing an awareness of the interrelationship between his or her thoughts, feelings, and behaviors, facilitated by the completion of a standard dysfunctional thought record in session and as part of homework. Through guided discovery, the therapist begins to help the patient identify cognitive biases and distortions. Just as cognitive distortions, such as the depressed person's tendency to overgeneralize or the anxious person's tendency to catastrophize, have been shown to perpetuate negative moods, cognitive biases serve to maintain the delusional patient's sense of personal threat. As detailed in Chapter 3, delusional thinking demonstrates several common cognitive biases, including an *egocentric bias* by which patients become locked into a construal of information as self-relevant when it is not; an *externalizing bias* in which internal sensations or symptoms are attributed to external agents; and an *intentionalizing bias* in which patients attribute malevolent and hostile intentions to other people's behavior (Beck & Rector, 2002). Further, the establishment of an early questioning mode through guided discovery lays the foundation for more direct exploration of cognitive distortions, faulty appraisals, and dysfunctional beliefs associated with the positive and negative symptoms. The thoughts and images that patients experience prior to escaping from the hot situation are similar to those reported by patients with social anxiety problems, particularly agoraphobia. For instance, when Elizabeth became anxious in group situations, she would begin to think: "If I stay, I'm going to lose control," "If I lose control, then others will take advantage of me," or "If they see me this way, then they will think I'm crazy and try to have me hospitalized." These thoughts would trigger her impulse to run out of the room.

As another example, consider this patient who had held a paranoid delusional belief for 5 years that she was being persecuted for cheating on a scholastic exam.

THERAPIST: Can you tell me more about that situation in the past week when you started feeling scared?

PATIENT: I was sitting in my dentist's office waiting for my appointment. There were different magazines and books to choose from, and I picked one up and started to read an article about someone who had cheated on his income tax and got caught (*pause*). I was so upset.

THERAPIST: So you felt upset? What were you thinking about when you were reading the story?

PATIENT: I don't know, I started feeling like a failure.

THERAPIST: Jane, what was it about the story that made you start to think of yourself as a failure?

PATIENT: I don't know . . . I got to thinking about (*long pause*) when I cheated in school (*long pause*), I feel so guilty. . . . Then I started to think that my dentist had left the reading out to let me know that he knows that I'm a cheat and that he's going to report me.

THERAPIST: How were you feeling in that moment?

PATIENT: Terrified. I couldn't stand it and left.

THERAPIST: If 100% is the most terrified you've felt and 0% is not feeling terrified in the least, how terrified do you think you were in that moment?

PATIENT: Near the top, 90%.

The situational trigger and attendant thoughts, moods, and behaviors are readily apparent. Another patient who believed that he was being persecuted by the police for a crime that he did not commit was engaging in delusional interpretations nearly every hour of the day. Common triggers included passing police cars, policemen on the streets, identification of unmarked police cars, the nightly news involving arrest reports, and so on. As one example, he awoke one night to find noise and three unfamiliar cars on the street. His automatic thought was "They're organizing an arrest." His emotional response was fear (80%). Questioning the delusional interpretation led to evidence that was seen to support the initial interpretation: It is unusual for cars to be out front at 1 A.M., and the cars seem to have positioned themselves to prevent escape from his cul de sac. However, the patient was also able to stand back and evaluate evidence that did not support his interpretations, recognizing that neither car was a police car, the drivers were young and in T-shirts, a young woman whom he recognized as his neighbor was speaking to the men in the car and laughing, suggesting that they knew each other, and with further thought recognized that he had seen one of the cars before dropping off this woman. The consideration of this evidence led to the alternative conclusion, "Nothing happened, just young people arriving home late," and his fear declined to 0%.

Elizabeth similarly began to make progress in identifying, testing, and correcting her delusional interpretations. For instance, when a member of her church became sick, her automatic thought—"I caused this to happen"—emanated from the delusional belief that her prayers were being intercepted by the devil and converted into death wishes. The evidence in support of the interpretation was stated as the belief itself: "The devil is intercepting my prayers—many people have been harmed in the past." However, Elizabeth was able to consider other, nonsupportive evidence, including the fact that the person had had three previous strokes, was 88 years old, and was very sick even before she knew him. Her alternative conclusion was that "he is sick but it's not my fault."

Cognitive and Behavioral Approaches

Initially, the therapist deals with interpretations and explanations that are peripheral to more central and highly charged beliefs. Take, for example, a patient with an elaborate paranoid delusional system that includes the local phone company because of an earlier disagreement over an unpaid bill. The patient describes the following events in the past week that are seen to support persecution by the phone company: The phone rang and then stopped before she could pick it up; she could hear faint interference on the line during several phone calls; there was a telephone cable truck in front of the house 2 days earlier; and someone "pretended" to call with the wrong number. The therapist proceeds to assess the range of automatic thoughts (delusional inferences) in response to each of these events along with a belief conviction rating. The patient is least convinced of the importance of the truck incident. The therapist chooses to begin guided discovery through Socratic questioning on this information:

"What was it about the truck's presence that led you to believe that it was there for you?"

"Did anything else happen that day that led you to doubt this, by chance?"

"Has anything else happened in the past couple of days that led you to doubt this?"

"Are there any other possible explanations why the truck may have been on your street that day?"

By questioning the inference, the patient considers a range of alternative evidence: "Well, the truck driver did go in and out of the neighbor's house—he was carrying equipment . . . he seemed pretty busy," "The neighbors did just move in . . . they might need a new line," and "He didn't take notice of me when I came outside—I guess if he was following me, he'd try to hide." The therapist helps to elicit an alternative balanced explanation for the event, and the patient concedes, "Maybe he was just installing new cable." With repeated practice in generating alternative explanations for the range of evidence in session and then, increasingly, as part of assigned homework, the patient begins to see his or her interpretations and inferences as hypotheses to be tested rather than as statements of fact (Watts, Powell, & Austin, 1997).

Other cognitive approaches routinely employed to instill a questioning perspective include the survey method (e.g., "Can you ask your three good friends whether they ever get static [wrong numbers, hang-ups, etc.] on their phone line?" and pie charts (e.g., "Let's summarize all the different possible reasons why the phone would ring and then stop ringing before you could pick it up"). Through the downward arrow technique, the therapist also aims to uncover the underlying core beliefs (e.g., "worthless" and "vulnerable") and assumptions (e.g., "If I'm not watchful 100% time, then I'm likely to be taken advantage of,"), which give rise to the misinterpretations of others' intentions and behaviors.

In Elizabeth's treatment, one goal was to create new explanations for her beliefs about being a fallen angel. She cited a variety of experiences as evidence for her beliefs: "I sinned so badly in the past" (referring to promiscuity); "My prayers are intercepted by the devil"; and "I have been to Hell" to mention but a few. Elizabeth's reasons for believing her primary delusions (that she is a fallen angel and that she is controlled by the devil) reflect *secondary delusional beliefs* about having special powers and the devil intercepting her prayers and *misappraisals of experiences* (e.g., going to Hell). Elizabeth completed belief ratings on the items she listed as evidence supporting her beliefs, and the item "I have been to Hell" was targeted first for cognitive restructuring because it was the weakest and most peripheral evidence cited. As detailed, it appeared that Elizabeth had experienced a panic attack and misinterpreted the normal symptoms of autonomic arousal, such as feeling hot and flushed, sweating, and tightening, as signs that she was in Hell (belief before: 80%). The clinician provided an alternative perspective, sharing with her the new information that these feelings were normal when people felt scared or anxious, and providing psychoeducation about the nature of the fight-or-flight response.

Elizabeth completed dysfunctional thought records both in session and as homework for new situations that triggered delusional beliefs as they emerged, to practice finding alternative evidence for her beliefs. By the end of this phase of treatment, Elizabeth's belief rating about being a fallen angel had dropped to 20%, with a worsening occurring on days when she felt more distressed. She also became better at using thought records in the moment to reduce catastrophizing and delusional cycles.

Behavioral Experiments

In addition to verbal strategies, the cognitive therapist aims to change delusional thinking by setting up behavioral experiments to test the accuracy of different interpretations. For instance, one of our patients had a 9-year paranoid delusional belief that once a group reached critical mass (which he defined as 20 or more members), it was likely to become violent and attack him. Whenever he saw large groups of people, he would quickly escape to a quiet and safe place. The treatment approach included having the patient focus on his hypothesis about groups of 20 or greater and observing their behavior. Initially, this meant watching groups on television and in the movies, progressing to the observation of large group behavior from a safe distance (e.g., 100 yards from a large gathering watching a varsity sport). Consideration of this evidence in relation to the delusional belief "Large groups have it out for me" provided enough change to permit the patient to begin to enter (with the aid of therapist) situations where large groups gathered.

Another of our patients was experiencing longstanding delusions of reference and believed that when people spat on the ground, they were actually spitting to communicate a message to her that she was "not welcome there." After a number of sessions of considering alternative explanations for this behavior, she was willing to test two hypotheses: People were either truly spitting to communicate a message to her, or people sometimes spat and this was not meant to communicate a specific message to her. Her behavioral experiment was to go to the busy downtown street where she experienced this delusion often and to observe the frequency of this behavior, first away from the sidewalk and then once again while walking on the sidewalk. She and the therapist reviewed the data generated by the behavioral experiment (i.e., the frequency of the behavior was the same when she was present or absent from the sidewalk), and the patient was able to accommodate this information and shift her interpretation of the behavior.

Targeting Nondelusional Core Beliefs

To consolidate progress and reduce risk of relapse, it is important to address the underlying beliefs and assumptions that are conceptualized as conferring vulnerability to symptom development. For instance, in the treatment of Elizabeth a critical unknown was, Why would Elizabeth intentionally pray for people to be harmed or to die in the first place? Despite considerable reduction in her delusional beliefs about being a fallen angel and controlled by the devil, it was a challenge to find an alternative perspective on it being acceptable to intentionally pray and wish for people to die. This question puzzled Elizabeth as much as the clinician.

By probing and monitoring triggers for her prayers, her therapist ascertained that Elizabeth only prayed for people to be harmed when she felt *powerless*. For instance, with exploration, Elizabeth was able to see that in the past, when she was pulled over and "harassed" by a police officer, she had prayed that harm would come to him for making her feel worthless. Or in another example, she prayed for a man at her church to become ill because she really wanted to have his position in the church and given the respect he seemed to receive from others. In an example from the prior week, she wished for something bad to happen to her nephew, because she felt that her sister had achieved everything that she never could. The therapist shared this formulation with Elizabeth—that praying for others to be harmed was not a sign of evil but rather a sign of feeling vulnerable and powerless. Elizabeth fully accepted this formulation and also agreed it accounted for the times when she had prayed to the devil as a child. The treatment progressed by working on her core beliefs pertaining to vulnerability and powerlessness. Strategies included the use of core belief records, developing more task-oriented coping skills, and behavioral experiments.

Consolidation of Alternative Beliefs

As outlined, the reduction of delusional beliefs occurs at different levels of intervention, often conducted concurrently: questioning, testing, and creating alternative perspectives on the evidence taken in support of the beliefs; identifying the link between underlying core beliefs and their role in the maintenance of the delusional beliefs and moment-by-moment delusional interpretations; and similarly, identifying delusional interpretations that are fueled by cognitive distortions and biases that contribute to further confirmation of the beliefs and failures to disconfirm the beliefs. These are all strategies that can help reduce the belief in, and the distress resulting from, delusional beliefs. As the therapist makes inroads to creating more flexibility in patients' beliefs and interpretations, attention shifts to building alternative beliefs to replace previous delusional beliefs. Indeed, even prior to intervening with delusions, therapists must begin to identify likely alternative beliefs that will be reasonable substitutes for the previous delusional beliefs.

It has been our experience that the development of alternative beliefs is less necessary in the treatment of paranoid delusions. Rather, progress in reducing the perception of interpersonal threat and providing acceptable alternative explanations for the evidence previously taken in support of paranoid interpretations are sufficient. However, if the patient has believed that he or she is an important religious figure, entertainer, or some other grandiose identity, the chipping away at these beliefs may also pose a threat to self-esteem, because these beliefs are likely protecting vulnerable self-esteem. Nelson (2005) has discussed, in considerable detail, the extent to which the therapist needs to decide early in treatment whether he or she is going to aim for a full or only a partial reduction of the delusional belief because some aspects of the belief may contribute to positive self-esteem, are important aspects of the person's sociocultural–religious identify, or appear to have little bearing on the maintenance of the belief. For example, that the full reduction of a delusional belief pertaining to being persecuted by the FBI would be expected to lead to comparatively better outcomes for the person. However, if the patient believed that he or she had special talents or abilities that made the FBI interested in him or her in the first place, then the therapist would likely not reduced these beliefs, given their function in maintaining a positive sense of self for the person.

Reducing the Aversive Consequences Associated with the Delusional Beliefs

For some patients, creating a "kink in the chain" of their delusional beliefs remains insurmountable. Yet, it is still possible to substantially reduce the distress and interference of the belief system if the consequences emanating from the belief are reduced. For patients with whom cognitive and behavioral strategies have led to more modest belief change, an alternative approach can help them examine the advantages and disadvantages of acting on the delusional beliefs. The goal is to increase patients' repertoire of coping responses to the presence of delusional interpretations, with an emphasis on improving functional outcomes in spite of persistent delusions (Cather et al., 2005). Take, for example, a patient who developed the delusional belief that workers in his employment setting were conspiring to murder and dispose of him because he had had an intimate relationship with a woman believed to be involved with one of his coworkers. Each day began with the expectation of being murdered at the end of the shift. Despite the absence of any indirect or direct threats from his coworkers prior to or during this period, the belief remained fixed, pervasive, and extremely distressing. Following a 10-day period of acute distress, he was subsequently hospitalized and remained in lengthy residential treatment with only limited improvement. He was subsequently referred to a cognitive therapist to work on the delusional belief with the aim of aiding his return to work. He had enjoyed his work immensely and was recognized as performing consistently well before the onset of his delusional system. He felt his work was the best part of his life and wanted desperately to return but, at the same time, felt unable to, for fear of his life. In the initial assessment phase, attempts to test his responses to hypothetical alternatives, in order to gauge flexibility in the belief system, led to unequivocal rejection of all hypothetical alternatives.

Further, early work at identifying and testing alternative explanations for his delusional belief about his coworkers also led to rejection of viable alternative explanations. However, the patient was able to acknowledge that if he were to return to work and there was no harm done to him in the first month, he would then have to conclude that his coworkers would not harm him. With this proviso, treatment shifted from attempts to reduce his delusional belief about being harmed to preparations to manage fear and a graduated return to work. The clinician worked with the employer to prepare documents regarding the company's interest in supporting his return to work, its ability to ensure his safety at all times by providing a mentor and maintaining zero-tolerance of harassment and/or violence on the premises, and his right to carry a cell phone to call his clinician if he was feeling threatened at any point. The patient was able to believe the information provided by the employer and felt prepared to try to return to work particularly because the mentor was his lone trusted friend at work with whom he had maintained contact. He and the employer developed additional safety precautions to have the mentor present with him at all times in the early phase of returning to work and then to gradually reduce the mentor's presence. The remaining aspects of treatment focused on helping the patient understand and cope with anxiety and fear as well as the development of a step-by-step action plan for getting through the day. Consistent with John's Nash goal of becoming "a person of delusionally influenced thinking but of relatively moderate behavior," the patient was able to return, and remain at, work despite his delusional belief (Nash, 2002, p. 10).

SUMMARY

As outlined in this chapter, the cognitive therapy of delusions focuses on understanding the antecedent factors in the development of the belief(s), considering the evidence that has accrued over time in perceived support of the beliefs, and examining the day-to-day misinterpretations of experiences and events that contribute to new sources of evidence and momentary distress. Once the patient can question sources of evidence and develop and test alternative explanations, treatment addresses the underlying nondelusional cognitive schemas that are seen to confer vulnerability for relapse and recurrence of delusional beliefs. As outlined, a number of strategies are also aimed at reducing maladaptive behavioral responses such as withdrawal, avoidance, and other safety behaviors that prevent opportunities to disconfirm delusional beliefs as well as the underlying negative self-beliefs. In some instances, achieving reduction in delusional intensity and rigidity is more difficult, and the goal shifts to focusing on improved social and occupational outcomes in spite of the presence of the delusional beliefs.

CHAPTER 10

Cognitive Assessment and Therapy of Auditory Hallucinations

Patients report a range of auditory phenomena, including nonverbal material such as music, buzzing, tapping, and the like, although cognitive therapy is specifically aimed at helping patients with the distress that is created by the experience of hearing voices. Although the cognitive therapy approach focuses on auditory hallucinations, strategies can be modified easily to address hallucinatory phenomena in other modalities.

In this chapter, we outline strategies for the cognitive treatment of voices. The approach is based on the cognitive conceptualization outlined in Chapter 4. As detailed, cognitive expectancies, appraisals, beliefs, and assumptions are pivotal to the development, persistence, and distressing nature of the voices. The cognitive model conceptualizes voices as externalized automatic thoughts. As such, voice content is essentially stream-of-consciousness thoughts that "pop up" to be experienced as externally derived voices. The patient develops a range of nondelusional (e.g., "I will be hospitalized") and delusional beliefs about the origins, meaning, and power of the voices that, in turn, contribute directly to the distress experienced. Further, behavioral responses to voice activity are also important: Patterns of avoidance and/or safety behaviors can either exacerbate or attenuate the distress associated with voices. Although the ultimate elimination of voice activity may not be an achievable goal for patients, the principal goal of cognitive therapy is to reduce the patient's experience of distress around the voices and improve his or her quality of life. Distress resulting from the experience of voices can be reduced by four inter-related treatment targets: (1) reducing the distress associated with content of the voices, (2) reducing the distress associated with the nondelusional beliefs about the voices, (3) reducing the distress associated with the delusional beliefs about the voices, and (4) reducing the distress associated with the underlying self-evaluative beliefs associated with the voices. As such, the general approach to treating the beliefs about voices parallels the approach to treating delusional beliefs, as outlined in Chapter 9.

Prior to the introduction of cognitive strategies, a thorough assessment establishes the frequency, duration, intensity, and variability of the voices. What situations or circumstances are likely to trigger the voices? Are there circumstances in which the patient can expect *not* to experience voices and/ or to retreat in an effort to attenuate them? Stressful situations are likely to trigger voices. For instance, patients report hearing voices more frequently when there are interpersonal difficulties, daily hassles, and negative life events (e.g., financial strain, housing crises). Internal cues can also trigger voices, particularly emotional upset. As part of the early assessment phase, patients learn to monitor the relationship between situational triggers, mood states, and the activation of voices using a modified thought record. However, even prior to conducting a detailed functional assessment of voice activity, the therapist should consider obtaining formal ratings of the severity and interference caused by voices.

Patients may be reluctant to engage in frank and open discussion about their voices, perhaps out of fear that their discussion will make them worse or result in some of form of punishment, control, or manipulation from the voices. In addition to the steps outlined in Chapter 8 toward facilitating engagement, it is important to approach the assessment and treatment of voices sensitively with guided discovery. However, the extent to which therapists can nudge patients toward a discussion of their voices is likely to determine the degree of both indirect and direct benefits. The indirect and implicit benefits include the therapist's communication of empathy and respect for this aspect of patients' inner experience, the empowerment of the patient that may follow the mere discussion of voices, and the strengthening of the therapeutic alliance through the therapist's establishment of a safe and collaborative environment for their discussion. An overview of the treatment approach for voices can be seen in Table 10.1.

TABLE 10.1. Cognitive Assessment and Therapy for Auditory Hallucinations

Assessment

- Assessment of symptoms/cognitions
  - Physical properties of voices
  - Frequency and severity of voices
  - Beliefs about voices

- Conducting a functional assessment
  - Monitoring voices
  - Identifying voice triggers
  - Assessing emotional and behavioral responses to voices
  - Identifying historical antecedents of voice development and beliefs/appraisals across time

- Developing the case conceptualization
  - Identifying cognitive factors that contribute to the specific content of the voices and the beliefs about the agency, meaning, purpose, and consequences of the voices

Treatment

- Providing psychoeducation and normalization
  - Educating the patient on the stress–vulnerability model of voice development

- Socializing the patient to the cognitive model
  - Developing awareness of the role of appraisals and beliefs in the production of distress around the voices

- Implementing cognitive and behavioral approaches
  - Implementing behavioral strategies
  - Targeting of voice content
  - Targeting delusional beliefs about voices
  - Targeting underlying self-evaluative beliefs associated with voices
  - Targeting safety behaviors

ASSESSMENT

Assessment of Symptoms/Cognitions

The broad range of clinician-administered instruments described in Chapter 7, which assess for the presence and severity of the symptoms of schizophrenia, typically do not provide an opportunity for the detailed assessment of voices, in particular. The Psychotic Symptom Rating Scale (PSYRATS; Haddock et al., 1999), however, is a reliable and valid measure of voices (and delusions) that covers questions pertaining to the physical properties, the degree of distress created, and beliefs about the voices, and appears to offer the most detailed of assessments among currently available measures. Given that it is a relatively brief measure, we strongly encourage its administration to gauge hallucinatory severity and to gauge progress throughout the course of therapy. As such, the therapist is encouraged to administer the

PSYRATS, which offers a greater sensitivity to any changes in voices that occur in the course of cognitive therapy.

There is also a self-report measure, the Topography of Voices Rating Scale (Hustig & Hafner, 1990), that therapists can easily incorporate into the initial assessment package as well as the functional assessment, given that it measures aspects such as frequency, loudness, clarity, distress, and distractibility of the voices over the preceding few days.

In addition to the use of standardized clinician-administered and self-report measures, the therapist also conducts an open-ended assessment of the physical characteristics of the voices, using probing questions such as the ones outlined in Table 10.2.

Assessment of Beliefs of Voices

An explicit component of the cognitive approach to treating voices is the identification and reduction of faulty beliefs about the voices. An excellent measure to assess the patient's beliefs about the meaning and purpose of the voices is the Beliefs about Voices Questionnaire—Revised (BAVQ-R), which includes items such as "My voice is punishing me for something I have done," "My voice is evil," and "My voice wants to harm me." The scale has been shown to have acceptable reliability and is sensitive to treatment effects with cognitive therapy (Chadwick et al., 1996).

Given that the aim of cognitive therapy is not to necessarily reduce the frequency of voice activity, but rather the patient's negative beliefs and appraisals pertaining to the voices, the BAVQ-R becomes an important outcome measure to assess progress. The therapist begins to collect information about the precise nature of voice appraisals and beliefs by asking the type of probing questions outlined in Table 10.2.

Conducting a Functional Assessment

In addition to the administration of validated clinician-based and self-report measures, the cognitive therapist attempts to get *verbatim* accounts of what the voices say. Typically, patients report hearing critical one-word utterances, such as "Jerk," "Loser," or similar two-word utterances, "You're worthless," "Go on" and the like. At other times, they may be questions. A patient started each day with the voices, question "Are you sure you are who you say you are?" Voices might offer a running commentary on the patient's activities or deliver commands instructing the patient to per-

**TABLE 10.2. Assessment of Voices
in the Clinical Interview**

Assessment probes for physical characteristics

"Do you hear voices that others cannot hear?"
    "Can you tell me about that?"
"What does the voice say?"
"Is there more than one voice?"
"Do you recognize the voice?"
"When do you hear the voice?"
"How loud is the voice?"
"How do you feel when you hear the voice?"
    (If the patient responds with only negative feelings)
        "Does the voice ever make you feel happy?"
    (If the patient responds with only positive feelings)
        "Does the voice ever make you feel distressed?"
"What do you do when you hear the voice?"
"Overall, how does the voice affect your life?"

Assessment probes for appraisals/beliefs about voices

"Why do you think others can't hear your voices?"
"How do you feel about hearing voices?"
"Do the voices seem very powerful?"
"What is the purpose of the voices?"
"Do the voices make you feel exposed or vulnerable?"
"Can the voice harm you in any way?"
"Does the voice ever instruct you to do things that you
do not want to do?"

form certain activities, ranging from the mundane, such as "Pick up those clothes" to more dangerous and potentially violent edicts. As part of the functional assessment, patients are requested to monitor their voice content between sessions. Although patients may find this task to be cumbersome, it has been our experience that they are more open to keeping weekly logs of voice activity if the sheets are simple and require minimal writing, as in the monitoring sheet outlined in Figure 10.1.

As shown, patients record what they were doing when the voices started. It is often the case that patients are unaware of the specific triggers that activate their voices. Triggers for voices often include situations or contexts that are personally threatening to the patient. As previously mentioned, frequent triggers include isolation, large groups, interpersonal stress and conflict, performance pressures, as well as drug and alcohol use. Voices are frequently triggered by a range of internal cues as well, including negative emotional states, paranoia, fatigue, and loneliness, as well as spe-

Date: _____

In the first blank column, note what you were doing at the time the voice spoke. In the second column, note the content of the voice that you heard. In the third column, record how loud the voice was (0–10). In the fourth column, rate the amount of distress you felt (0–10). In the fifth column, note what you were feeling at that moment. In the last column, record the way that you coped with the voice.

Time	What were you doing?	What did the voices say?	How loud was the voice? (0–10)	How distressed were you? (0–10)	How were you feeling at that moment?	What did you do to cope?
8–9 A.M.						
9–10 A.M.						
11–12 P.M.						
12–1 P.M.						
1–2 P.M.						
2–3 P.M.						
3–4 P.M.						
4–5 P.M.						

FIGURE 10.1. Form for monitoring voice activity.

cific internal states that are associated with delusional beliefs. For example, a patient with encapsulated religious delusions regarding themes of sinful sex would experience the trigger of voice activity in response to emerging sexual arousal.

When monitoring the frequency and duration of voices, it is also important to identify whether there are specific situational factors that relate to the reduction of voice activity. It is common for voice activity to emerge during periods of isolation but for voices to stop once the person engages in conversation. Identifying the full range of possible offset factors is a prelude to teaching the patient to apply offset strategies in treatment.

Finally, the therapist assesses the patient's emotional and behavioral reactions to the voices. Frequent repetition of criticisms, insults, commands, and other attacking comments often lead to feelings of sadness, despair, anger, and helplessness. Patients' behavioral responses may include their shouting back at the voices and/or escaping situations to terminate the voices. Although patients first respond to their voices with surprise and puzzlement, over time they tend to establish an interpersonal relationship with them (Benjamin, 1989). Beliefs about the voices may determine the emotional reaction and behavioral responses. For instance, if the patient sees the voices as benevolent, they are frequently followed by positive emotions and the patient engages with them, whereas if they are malevolent, the patient is likely to experience a range of negative emotions and cope by resisting the voices (Birchwood & Chadwick, 1997).

As the therapist begins to collect *in vivo* information from the functional assessment, the aim is to examine when the voices occur/do not occur; specific triggers such as fatigue, isolation, stress, or an emotionally salient memory; the patient's awareness of the voice triggers; and/or the varied emotional responses that are experienced. Patients have a myriad of responses to voices, including yelling back and arguing (as noted above) to the other extreme of active listening and engaging in efforts to cooperate with the voices. Chadwick et al. (1996) have suggested that most behaviors in response to voices can be categorized as either resistant or engagement behaviors. Indifference is a very atypical response to the presence of voices. Romme and Escher (1994) have described how over time, the typical patient establishes a stabilization phase characterized by a less disabling relationship with the voices.

The therapist also aims to elicit all of the beliefs the patient has about his or her voices. For instance, what agents (e.g., God, the devil, dead relatives) are purportedly talking to the patient? Beliefs about the voices can range from bizarre delusions to the ordinary, and the sources of the voices may seem to belong to known, unknown, or deceased persons or to super-natural entities or machinery. A significant number of patients have posi-tive interpretations of their voices and experience positive emotions when they occur. Receiving direct communication from God, Jesus, or a knight of the Round Table sets the person apart from others and is accompanied by feelings of excitement and power. The therapist aims to elicit how the patient would feel if the voices were not present as a way of unmasking the underlying feelings of loneliness and inadequacy for which these voices may be providing compensatory protection. The therapist strives to identify all beliefs and record the evidence that the patient contends supports these beliefs. It is important to recognize that voice content and beliefs about the voices may be at odds with one another. In previous research, upwards of two-thirds of patients still believed that their voices were malevolent even though the content was benign. For instance, a patient perceived a voice that said "Time to start the day" as ridiculing and chastising him for not working. During the assessment phase, as attention moves from monitoring physical characteristics of the voices to more detailed discussion of apprais-als and beliefs, the therapist can introduce a second monitoring sheet for homework, such as the type outlined in Figure 10.2, which provides an opportunity for the patient to list appraisals/beliefs associated with the voices.

Situation	Voice	Appraisal of voice	Mood	Behavior
Quietly watching television	"You're not who you think you are."	"I'm hollow—not a real person." "I'm losing my mind."	Fear Hopelessness	Mentally ruminate to discover the "real me"
Riding the bus	"You're a goof."	"My brother continuing to punish me."	Angry Frustrated	Scream "shut up"
Alone reading	"They're OK, you're OK."	"Doctor is providing reassurance."	Relief Pleasant mood	Continue reading
Walking to doctor's appointment	"You bitch."	"Being judged for asserting myself—being kept in place."	Fear Anger Resentment	Retreat and isolate
Knitting quietly	"You're useless and weak."	"Being shamed for a character flaw."	Discouraged Helpless	Give up

FIGURE 10.2. Monitoring appraisals/beliefs associated with voices.

Historical Antecedents of Voice Development and Beliefs/Appraisals across Time

Just as in the assessment of delusions, the therapist aims to identify the distal and proximal life circumstances surrounding the initial onset of the voices: That is, what events occurred just prior to their onset and how does the specific voice content and the patient's beliefs about the voices reflect his or her prehallucinatory fears, concerns, interests, preoccupations, fantasies, and so on. To better understand the patient's idiosyncratic triggers, the therapist assesses the pattern of voice activity across time, noting periods of heightened activity and any periods in which voices are in remission. The therapist also notes changes in the beliefs about voices over time.

Developing the Case Conceptualization

As introduced in Chapter 9, the development of the case conceptualization sheds light on the role of early life experiences, beliefs, and precipitating factors in the onset of Elizabeth's voices. She suffered guilt and remorse for defying her parents and God. Core beliefs included being "bad" and "evil," among other pejorative attributes. Precipitating events included the one-night stand, subsequent promiscuity, and shame around "pretending to be good" with her new boyfriend. The proximal precipitating event was the breakup with her boyfriend. The religious structure of the delusions seems to be predicated on religious beliefs that she had held throughout her life. The content of the voices would appear to reflect her own "hot" negative automatic thoughts that transitioned from first person, "I'm a slut" to second person, "You're a slut" (Beck & Rector, 2003). This conceptualization is outlined in Figure 10.3.

TREATMENT

Psychoeducation and Normalization

As discussed broadly by Kingdon and Turkington (1991), patients vary in the degree to which they want an explanation for the occurrence of their voices. Some patients explain the voices as a function of having schizophrenia. As part of the early psychoeducation process, patients are socialized to the stress–vulnerability view of psychosis and hallucinatory activity, in particular. As such, explanations to enhance understanding of the role of vul-

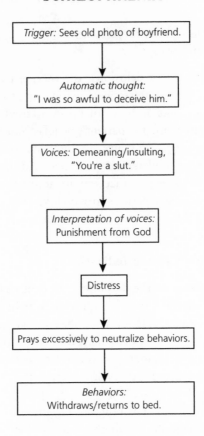

FIGURE 10.3. Conceptualization of the vicious cycle pertaining to voices.

nerability factors can draw on a number of critical biological (e.g., genetics) psychological (e.g., developmental experiences), and social (e.g., isolation and marginalization) variables that make sense to the patient in terms of comprehension and experience. The role of traumatic events, aversive interpersonal events, loss, and life challenges (e.g., moving out and attending university) are potentially important triggers to be discussed in relation to the initial onset of voices. Some key points that can be shared with patients in a clear and simple manner include:

- Five percent of the population reports hearing voices at some point in life.
- Studies with college students show upward of 30–40% reporting voices.

- Torture and solitary confinement can produce voices.
- Loss of a loved one can lead to hallucinations during the process of bereavement.
- People experiencing distress and emotional upset can hear voices (voices are noted in patients with psychotic depression, bipolar disorder, and posttraumatic stress disorder [PTSD]).

The provision of psychoeducation with a "normalizing" rationale also initiates the accumulation of evidence to fuel alternative explanations of the voices, which will be the key component of their successful treatment.

Beyond predisposition factors, part of the psychoeducation process is helping patients identify the situational precipitants of their voices. The patient's particular triggers for voices will become clearer during the assessment process and the completion of self-monitoring forms between sessions, but during the psychoeducation phase, typical triggers can be discussed. This may also present the opportunity for the patient to discuss such familiar triggers as:

- Alcohol and drug use (e.g., LSD, cocaine)
- Alcohol withdrawal
- Sleep deprivation
- Anxiety
- Sadness
- Suspiciousness
- Fatigue
- Interpersonal conflict
- Contexts with loud and monotonous background noise
- Watching television

Knowing the psychological factors that contribute to the persistence of voices can help the patient as part of the psychoeducation process. For instance, the therapist can explain the role of expectancies (e.g., hearing the phone ring while waiting for a call), and mistaking one's own thoughts for others (e.g., externalizing bias), both as a way of reducing the apparent stigma associated with voices and as a starting point to socializing the patient to the cognitive model. The therapist can also discuss the role of common cognitive distortions in skewing experience (e.g., jumping to the conclusion that chest pain after dinner is the sign of a heart attack). If deemed appropriate, it can also be valuable for the clinician to share one of his or her own experiences of distortion to get across the idea that we all have "odd" experiences from time to time. Additionally, as outlined by Nelson (2005), it can be helpful to discuss how firmly held beliefs can still be wrong by discussing commonly held childhood beliefs about Santa Claus and the tooth fairy. Part of the discussion should highlight the extent to which changing these believes is normal once we come to recognize them as wrong.

Patients anticipate being seen as "crazy" or judged in some negative way for experiencing voices. Romme and Escher (1994) first developed the Hearing Voices Network in Holland, and these networks now exist in numerous countries. Many people who hear voices report that connections with the network instill hope and reduce stigma, and so patients are encouraged to seek out these links. Further, written materials on the nature of hearing voices can be provided. Overall, one of the core aims of the psychoeducation process is to establish the universality of the problems the patient is experiencing and to enhance dignity and respect.

Socializing the Patient to the Cognitive Model

In our clinical experience, patients often find it easier to understand how the role of appraisals and beliefs contribute to their experience with voices if they have developed an understanding of the role of appraisals and beliefs in their day-to-day lives around their general experiences. Early in the assessment phase and psychoeducation, the therapist aims to socialize the patient to understanding how thoughts, feelings, and behaviors connect around life experiences. Most patients present to sessions with a range of problems, and the therapist can begin to use a dysfunctional thought record approach in session to not only teach the cognitive model but attempt to alleviate distress through cognitive restructuring. This serves as a "hook" to the cognitive model before getting to the more rigid and affectively laden beliefs about the voices.

During this phase, the therapist teaches the patient how to identify distortions, consider alternative evidence to arrive at more balanced conclusions, and consider the advantages and disadvantages of holding certain beliefs. A standard list of cognitive distortions can be used to introduce the patient to the role of cognitive distortions. Importantly, the approach is collaborative and nonchallenging and attempts to move the patient into a questioning mode. The precise timing of targeting the voices will, of course, depend on their position on the patient's problem-list. The benefits of this approach include socializing the patient to the questioning mode, using a structured approach in the session, using self-monitoring forms for homework, and developing an early skill set around identifying and testing the role of appraisals before getting to potentially more threatening and delusional interpretations. In some instances, it is easy to transition from teaching the cognitive model around a recently problematic situation to the cognitive model of voices, as shown in the case below.

Cognitive and Behavioral Approaches

Introducing Simple Behavioral Strategies

A simple starting point to help the patient cope with voices is to build on an already-existing repertoire of coping strategies (Tarrier, 1992). Most patients will already have developed their own strategies to cope with the voices and will report varying degrees of success with these strategies. For instance, many patients describe isolating themselves when they hear voices, whereas some others will use various types of audio equipment (e.g., earplugs, radios, Walkmans, Discmans, and iPods). In addition to refining and practicing coping strategies already available to the patient to enhance his or her more regular and effective use, the therapist can introduce additional behavioral strategies that have shown promise. For instance, if the patient has not already tried to use a Walkman or earplugs, this can be an easy place to start. While potentially providing only short-term relief, many patients experience immediate reductions in the frequency and/or volume of the voices with earplugs, and some even report longer-term effects—perhaps due to an enhanced sense of control over the voices. It is recommended that patients try the earplug in either ear and identify which ear appears to produce the greatest effects. If at home or in a place where it would not be dangerous to do so, patients can also wear earplugs in both ears. Further, the vast majority of patients report benefits in the use of a Walkman; patients can be instructed to adjust the volume to match the threshold of the voices.

In addition, most patients report using distraction techniques naturally as an effective tool to increase control over voices. Basically, any activity that diverts attention away from the voices, such as watching television, listening to music, making conversation, reading, or playing a (video) game, can be potentially effective. Further, more effortful activities, including playing sports, working out, or simply going for a walk, can also reduce voice activity.

Because most patients experience voices during states of anxious arousal, behaviors that reduce arousal—such as taking a bath, reading quietly, or applying relaxation strategies—may lead to an attenuation of voice activity. There is also considerable support for the use of speech or subvocal activity to reduce voices (Carter, Mackinnon, & Copolov, 1996). Humming, for example, can be very helpful. Patients can be asked to begin humming once the voices have been activated or to try to speak to themselves (or sing quietly) at a low level to avoid embarrassment.

Another behavioral strategy (Nelson, 2005) is to introduce "voice time," a period of time during which the patient can intentionally produce and focus on voice activity but then agree to not pay attention at other times of the day if, by chance, the voices are further activated. This strategy is akin to assigning "worry time" to patients who engage in excessive worrying. Establishment of a parameter that determines when to focus, or not to focus, on internal cognitive operations enhances perceived control over them. During voice time the patient should be asked to focus on the physical characteristics of the voice(s), location of the voices, and their specific content.

The voices may be too distressing for some patients to focus on fully during voice time. A strategy to ensure a safe approach is to teach the Subjective units of Distress Scale (SUDS) ratings, from 0–100, and establish an agreed-upon limit at which the focusing approach will be terminated. For example, if the anxiety generated reaches beyond a comfortable level (e.g., 70%), the patient should discontinue the exercise. However, as is the case when this strategy is used with other emotional difficulties, just the request to self-monitor voices with a detached attitude can lead to reduced frequency and distress. A final step to be considered during voice time is for the patient to monitor the relationship between their thoughts and the content of the voices, by having the patient keep one thought record for negative automatic thoughts and a separate thought record for the verbatim account of what the voice(s) say.

Finally, because some patients experience the onset of their voices in contexts that provide too much stimulation (e.g., loud, noisy malls), another behavioral coping strategy that has been shown to work is to have patients take steps to remove themselves from the straining context.

Overview of Appraisals and Beliefs to Be Targeted in Cognitive Therapy

As seen in Table 10.3, four primary cognitive domains should be considered when treating voices: (1) targeting the content of the voices, (2) targeting the nondelusional beliefs about the voices, (3) targeting the delusional

TABLE 10.3. Taxonomy of Voice-Related Cognitions

	Voice-related cognitions	Nonpsychotic equivalent
Voice content	• "You're not who you think you are."	Stream-of-consciousness thoughts
	• "You're worthless."	Negative automatic thoughts
Nondelusional beliefs	• Belief of losing control	Negative automatic thoughts
	• Belief that one will be hospitalized	Underlying assumptions
Delusional beliefs	• The voice is Satan's, and is punishment for sexual thoughts. The voice comes from dead grandfather.	No delusional beliefs, only interpersonal beliefs related to perceived • Origin of voices • Meaning of voices • Power of voices
Self-evaluative beliefs underlying voices	• Think of self as bad, worthless, and evil	Core beliefs • Autonomy • Sociotropy

beliefs about the voices, and (4) targeting the underlying self-evaluative beliefs associated with the voices. It is also important to target for reduction the avoidance and safety behaviors pertaining to each of these cognitive domains.

Targeting of Voice Content

Irrespective of the beliefs about the voices, many patients are extremely distressed by the content of the voices, which is frequently demeaning, insulting, shaming, and critical. The content of the voices can reflect worries and concerns, important life events, or memories from the past. The content of voices can be delusional (e.g., "You are the devil's son") or nondelusional (e.g., "You're a fool"). The goal is to discredit and reduce the impact of the voices. The strategy may not lead to the termination of the voices, but it can help the patient feel less distressed, upset, angry, and fearful of the voices. In many cases, the frequency of the voices also decreases following targeted cognitive interventions.

Basically, the approach is to question the accuracy of the voice content, just as a negative automatic thoughts would be questioned, tested, and corrected through Socratic dialogue. Because the content of the voice is frequently taken as further evidence for the beliefs held about the voices (e.g., "I know it's God because he's the only one that knows I doubt him"), targeting the perceived accuracy of the voice content can also serve to question the accuracy of the beliefs about the voices (e.g., "Would a Chinese warlord from the 15th century really speak English?"). Again, if the patient has been socialized to the cognitive model and has already been using a dysfunctional thought record as part of his or her homework, this transition can be handled seamlessly.

However, a modified thought record will be required, as shown in Figure 10.4. To use this record, patients write down what the voices say verbatim and then examine the evidence for and against the accuracy of the statement. As in standard cognitive therapy practice, patients report the extent to which they believe the content of the voices before and after evidence gathering and generating alternative explanations. Like the cognitive content in other psychiatric disorders, the voice content typically reflects themes that are important to the patient in some way—a worry, belief, memory, or important idea or topic. In the case example in Figure 10.4, the trigger for the patient's voice was her perception that she was underperforming at a task. Initial self-critical thoughts would transition into critical voices. As suggested, the therapist begins by helping the patient iden-

Situation	Voice content	Mood	Evidence for	Evidence against	Alternative or balanced thoughts	Rate mood
Making a doll and stitching comes undone	Thoughts: "I can't do anything right; I'm a wimp." Voices: "You can't do anything right"; "you're a loser"; "you're worthless."	Sadness: 70%	The craftsmanship is poor. The belly isn't big enough. "I made so many mistakes." "I planned it for a long time."	"It was my first attempt." "I made the pattern myself." "It may look better later." "It is recognizable." "I tend to want things to look perfect the first time." "I can plan changes."	"It's my first attempt and I'll keep trying."	Sadness: 0%

FIGURE 10.4. Modified dysfunctional thought record for voices.

tify cognitive distortions in the voices' statements, "You can't do anything right," reflecting extreme black-and-white thinking, and "Loser," reflecting the labeling distortion. Next, the therapist asked, "What evidence do you have that supports the truth of the statements made by the voices?" With repeated practice, the patient became adept at identifying cognitive distortions in the voices' comments and generating alternative perspectives on the perceived truthfulness or accuracy of the voices' comments.

It is not infrequent that the voice content reflects some action about which the patient feels shame from the past. For instance, one patient not only heard a scolding voice stating "Slut," she also misheard people's coughs, sneezes, and throat clearings as stating "Slut." Despite years of experiencing this voice content, she continued to be hurt and saddened each time it occurred. The voice content reflected a belief that she maintained about herself that she was a "slut" for having been promiscuous during a troubled period in her late teens. In her late 20s she had become a born-again Christian and felt increasingly "disgusted" with herself for having engaged in such "sinning." To lessen the distress associated with this voice content, her therapist knew they must change the belief that she maintained about herself that she was a "slut that would go to Hell." In beginning cognitive therapy with her, the therapist considered two strategies: (1) provide psychoeducation and normalization of teenage sexuality and engaging in "acting-out" behaviors following personally traumatic events, and/or (2) engage a nonjudgmental minister to communicate a message of forgiveness and acceptance. It was decided that efforts to build an alternative perspective on her past behavior would be best accomplished if they were consistent with her currently held religious beliefs. Her previous discussions had indicated that her minister was kind and moderate and frequently attempted to assuage her tendency to be self-critical and feel excessive guilt. In preparing for her meeting with the minister, the question was posed: "What question would you like to ask the minister to learn more about how you would be seen by your church and faith?" The patient responded, "Is my past promiscuity a sign of evil and will I go to Hell?" The response that she received from the minister was very comforting and indicated that since she had atoned for her sins, she would not be punished. Although this feedback led her to feel less fear in relation to her religious beliefs, she still had difficulty extending self-acceptance. Here, the therapist focused on different aspects of teenage life and the natural aspects of sexual curiosity. The therapist also focused on the particular events occurring in her life during this time (e.g., troubled home life, academic failure, negative peer influence) that can impact on decisions and personal vulnerability.

Some patients believe that their voices can be heard by others and experience embarrassment and shame when they are occurring. As outlined by Kingdon and Turkington (2005), patients can conduct a survey to see if trusted others can hear their voices when they occur, or alternatively, if the patient is prone to experiencing voices during a clinical session, an audiotape recording of the session can be used to provide alternative evidence that others cannot hear the voices.

Dealing with Threats and Commands

The content of the voices can be threatening—saying, for example, that they (the voices) will physically harm the patient if he or she does not act in a specified way or that they will make the patient harm him- or herself. The therapist's first step is to obtain verbatim accounts of whatever imperatives or threats the voices are actually making; the second step is to evaluate whether or not the patient sees any past events as supporting the power of the voices to make real-life aversive events occur; third is to begin to evaluate the evidence supporting the perceived consequences of disobeying the commands; fourth, to highlight the advantages of not obeying the voices and the disadvantages of complying. It is important to recognize that most commands will be embedded in delusional beliefs about the power and origins of the voices. In this way, reducing threatening voice content may require immediate attention to the delusional beliefs surrounding the voices, particularly the perceived power of the voices. Some patients may feel too threatened to question the accuracy of the voices because they believe that the voices are all powerful and will punish them. For these patients, it is probably better to start by targeting the beliefs about the voices as opposed to the actual voice content.

After identifying what the voices are requesting the patient to do, the therapist also obtains information as to how the patient is currently coping with these commands—in other words, what strategies has the patient developed to successfully resist carrying out the commands? The next step is to evaluate the evidence that the patient takes as supporting the voices' power to cause physical events in the world. For instance, one patient believed that her voices were responsible for the deaths of six members of her church organization. As such, the patient believed that there was considerable past support for her fear of disobeying, and this perceived support served to consolidate the fear of disobeying voices presently. The voices would threaten to "kill" additional members of the church if she chose to disobey their commands. Questioning revealed that six church members had indeed died over an 18-month period. However, as the patient considered the evidence for these deaths, she discovered that, in each case, there was an alternative explanation—the person had died of disease, accident, or natural causes.

Finally, it is important that the therapist help the patient identify the full range of disadvantages to obeying the threats for themselves (e.g., remorse, hospitalization, possible legal consequences) and others (e.g., harmed and made to suffer) as well as to question any perceived advantages (e.g., reduced distress, peace of mind). In addition to harnessing a cognitive shift so that the patient can keep the disadvantages of obeying in clear sight during the threatening voices, it is also important that the patient have in hand a behavioral coping plan that includes some alternative behavior to pursue, such as calling someone, watching television, and so forth. The patient should be asked to monitor all "successes," wherein he or she did not act on the voices' instructions, as a means of developing self-efficacy around noncompliance. Once the full evidence has been collected to question the accuracy of the voices, it should be recorded for easy access as a "coping card," so that the patient can refer to it the next time the voices are activated, and he is feeling distressed.

Targeting Nondelusional Beliefs about Voices

It is common for patients to maintain nondelusional as well as delusional beliefs about the voices. Therapists should encourage patients to speak about all of their voice-related beliefs, past and present. In getting started, patients can be asked: "What did you think about the voices when they first started?" or "What do you think about your voices now?" While the therapist may have gleaned some of the patient's beliefs about the voices following the administration of the BAVQ, the therapist should ask more specific questions about the perceived agency ("Can you recognize the voice—do you know who it is?"), purpose ("What explanations have you generated to explain why you're hearing the voices?"), danger ("Do you have any fear associated with hearing the voices?"), and consequences of the voices ("Do you worry about your life being affected if you continue to hear the voices?"). The extent to which patients appraise the voice activity as a sign of impending danger, distraction, or interference is directly associated with the level of distress experienced following their activation (Baker & Morrison, 1998).

Frequently, nondelusional beliefs about the voices focus on the implications of hearing the voices as, for example, an indication of "going crazy," "losing control," "relapse," and "likely hospitalization." One of our patients believed that the initiation of voice activity was a sign that she was going to lose her mind and be hospitalized. At the time of her first onset 7 years earlier, the experience of frequent and distressing voices did lead to her hospitalization and a lengthy inpatient stay. Since onset, she continued to experience persistent voices on a periodic basis, and although certainly distressing, had never led to a significant sustained worsening or hospitalization. The approach was to help her identify and examine her fears about the voices directly by considering the evidence. Despite the possibility that increased voice activity could precipitate more significant worsening, this had never been the case over the past 7 years. Following the examination of the evidence, the therapist and patient reviewed the cognitive distortions of jumping to conclusions, catastrophizing, and emotional reasoning. Finally, the therapist provided empathy and support for the pain and fear associated with the first hospitalization. Subsequently, this patient carried a coping card and whenever the voices started, she used it to deescalate the fear cycle of losing control and requiring hospitalization. Paradoxically, the reduction of acute fear about the dangers associated with the voices led to an attenuation of the voices, providing her with greater control over them.

Targeting Delusional Beliefs about Voices

Although some patients have no beliefs or explanations for their voices, the vast majority of patients have developed beliefs about the voices as an attempt to make sense of them and reduce attendant anxiety. As reviewed in Chapter 3, the importance of delusional beliefs about voices has been demonstrated insofar as the experience of hallucinations alone does not lead to psychosis, but the development of delusions about the voices, particularly their special significance, predicts the development of psychosis (Van Os & Krabbendam, 2002). Chadwick and colleagues (1996) have suggested that the delusional beliefs about the voices may have a greater impact on the experienced emotions and behavioral reactions than the content of the hallucinations. Patients often identify the voice content as support for the perceived delusional beliefs about the voices, which in turn, intensify the importance of the voices. If the patient has already been working on changing his or her interpretations of the voice content, the related beliefs about the voices may be less rigid and impenetrable. Further, as noted, although sometimes it is necessary to start with either the voice content or the delusional beliefs about the voices, it is often the case that these aspects are targeted simultaneously in treatment.

Delusional beliefs pertaining to the voices are often reflected in the perceived origins of the voice, agency of the voice (e.g., God, the devil, dead relatives), and the perceived power and control of the voice (Chadwick et al., 1996). The distress caused by voices is not just what is said, but their perceived origin. For instance, a patient hearing a voice announce "You're the devil's child" is more likely to be distressed if it is perceived to be coming from the devil than a disliked acquaintance. As such, generating alternative explanations for the origins of the voices can lead to significant reductions in distress. However, in cases where the perceived origins of the voices create positive well-being for the patient—for instance, believing that the pleasant voices emanate from God, or a deceased loved one, or an old friend—the therapist may choose not to target delusional beliefs about the origins of voices in light of these benefits. However, one approach is to ask how the patient would feel if the voices were not present, as a way of uncovering the underlying feelings of loneliness and powerlessness from which these voices may be providing compensatory protection.

A common origin of voices is the experience of past trauma: Just as traumatic events lead many to relive their experiences in graphic flashbacks and intrusions, 50% of the themes in the voice content and beliefs pertain to the patient's past experience with trauma (Hardy et al., 2005). Following the normalization of the patient's explanation for the voice, one way of creating alternative evidence to undermine the apparent vividness of the voice is to discuss the role of extreme psychological distress and traumatic intrusions and memories. Following efforts to understand the patient's explanation for his or her voices, and attempts to normalize the experience of voices, the therapist begins to employ gentle questioning to elicit alternative perspectives on the beliefs. First, the therapist directly asks whether the patient has ever considered alternative explanations for his or her voices. Next, through Socratic questioning of the evidence, the therapist attempts to raise doubt and puzzlement around the purported agent, to help the patient arrive at the conclusion that although the belief is understandable, it is nevertheless mistaken, and alternative explanations are more valid.

Establishing behavioral experiments to test out delusional and nondelusional interpretations is especially helpful in creating alternative, less distressing interpretations. For instance, a patient believed that his neighbours were conspiring to have him removed from his apartment and that he heard them speaking to him on a daily basis (Rector & Beck, 2002; Rector, 2004). As the neighbors arrived home from work and walked up the stairs, the creaking sounds of the stairs would activate the patient's voices. When asked in session how he knew it was his neighbors' voices, he alluded to the perceived likeness and vividness of the voices: "They sound exactly like my neighbors." To generate alternative explanations, the therapist asked: "Are there other possible explanations? Has it ever been the case that you heard the creaking stairs and did not hear the voices? Have you ever heard the creaking stairs and then voices that you thought were your neighbors, but then looked outside to find that it wasn't your neighbors passing? If you found this on occasion or even repeatedly, would that change your view about the origin of the voices?"

As outlined in Chapter 4, beliefs pertaining to the omnipotence, omniscience, and uncontrollability of the voices are especially important and can be alleviated by a number of cognitive and behavioral strategies. Beliefs pertaining to uncontrollability can be addressed by demonstrating to patients that they can initiate, diminish, or terminate the voices (Chadwick et al., 1996). For instance, based on knowledge gleaned from the functional analysis of the patient's voices, the therapist can present the patient with the cues that activate the voices, such as discussing an emotionally salient topic, and then direct the patient to engage in an activity known to terminate the voices, such discussing the patient's hobbies or leaving the office for a walk. This strategy then produces alternative evidence that weakens the belief that the voices are uncontrollable. In a similar way, setting up experiments to demonstrate that the patient can ignore the voices' commands and that anticipated consequences do not occur, tackles the omnipotence and omniscience beliefs.

Targeting Underlying Self-Evaluative Beliefs Associated with Voices

As outlined in Chapter 4, a fundamental assumption of the cognitive model of voices is that schemas, once activated by congruent events, lead to negative automatic thoughts, self-evaluations, self-commands, self-criticisms, and prohibitions, as they would in, say, depression, but become perceptualized in the form of hallucinations in people suffering from psychosis. In addition to targeting the voice content and the nondelusional and delusional beliefs about the voices, it is important that the therapist identify the underlying core beliefs that shape the themes of the voice content and the beliefs about the voices. For instance, the degree of belief around the perceived powerfulness and controlling nature of the voices often seems to parallel the patient's own degree of perceived powerlessness and vulnerability. It is not uncommon to quickly ascertain core belief content from what the voices say, as in the case above, where the patient heard voices attesting to her "worthlessness" and being a "loser." As outlined in the treatment of delusions in Chapter 9, standard strategies for identifying, testing, and creating alternative core beliefs that underlie the beliefs about voices can be employed, such as the use of core belief records and conducting behavioral experiments to develop configurational support for new, alternative core beliefs.

Targeting Safety Behaviors

As outlined in Chapter 4, patients who hear voices also engage in behaviors intended to mitigate the activation of voices, to neutralize the perceived negative consequences of hearing the voices, and/or to appease the perceived agent of the voices—all commonly referred to as safety behaviors (Morrison, 2001). Unfortunately, the effort spent on avoiding and neutralizing leads to reduced engagement in activities and socializing, leaving the person more isolated, which, in turn, can trigger an increase in voice activity. This vicious cycle then perpetuates the hallucinations and does not permit the patient to test out alternative and more adaptive ways of coping with the voices. It also precludes having experiences that would lead to evidence disconfirming some of the beliefs about the voices. As in the treatment of panic disorder, social phobia, and other anxiety disorders, the therapist identifies the full range of safety behaviors that the patient is currently using to either prevent activation or continuation of the voices. Similarly, the therapist identifies the specific safety behaviors that the patient engages in to neutralize the (delusional) beliefs about the voices, then orders these safety behaviors in a hierarchy based on the perceived anxiety that would ensue if the behavior were eliminated. Next, the therapist aims to help the patient develop more functional coping strategies so that the safety behaviors can be systematically reduced. As in the treatment of anxiety and phobic conditions, a graded hierarchy is most effective when the patient first drops safety behaviors that lead to relatively mild-to-moderate anxiety before proceeding to eliminate safety behaviors that lead to high levels of anxiety. Because avoidance and safety behaviors are inextricably bound to the cognitive appraisals and beliefs pertaining to the voices, their reduction should occur in tandem with the cognitive restructuring exercises. For instance, if targeting the content of the voices is the focus, then the therapist would also address avoidance and safety behaviors pertaining to the content of voices. Similarly, the targeting of avoidance and safety behaviors pertaining to the beliefs about the voices would occur at the time when these beliefs are being targeted for change.

SUMMARY

The distress and interference associated with the experience of auditory hallucinations can be significantly reduced through a number of effective cognitive-behavioral strategies. Beyond the use of distraction methods, cognitive therapy approaches focus on reducing the distress associated with voice activity by helping the patient question, and ultimately develop a critical attitude toward what the voices actually say by identifying cognitive distortions and other inaccuracies in their statements. The approach also focuses on the perceived fear and danger associated with hearing voices and the delusional beliefs that have formed regarding the perceived origins, meaning, and power of the voices. The treatment of voices includes attention to the underlying core beliefs of the person that so often reflect themes of helplessness, powerlessness, worthlessness, and the like, and that shape the content, beliefs, and specific reactions to the voices. Finally, we have outlined the importance of tackling avoidance and safety behaviors.

CHAPTER 11

Cognitive Assessment and Therapy
of Negative Symptoms

Historically, the characteristic features of negative symptoms such as low motivation, diminished energy, restrictions in emotional and verbal expressiveness, and social disengagement have been construed as "deficits" that are not amenable to change with psychological interventions. Yet, we know that the negative symptoms wax and wane for the vast majority of patients who experience them. Internal (e.g., hearing voices) and external (e.g., hospitalization) triggers have been associated with their onset, and internal (e.g., reduced hopelessness) and external (e.g., acquisition of a part-time job) events have been observed in relation to their reduction. These observations suggest that psychological treatments can contribute to the reduction of negative symptoms by helping patients learn to identify and reduce the triggers for their activation and/or develop strategies for the alleviation following onset. We presented a cognitive-behavioral model of negative symptoms in Chapter 5, detailing how negative symptoms are not simply due to underlying biological deficits but rather represent a more complex interplay between appraisals, expectancies, and beliefs as well as characteristic cognitive and behavioral coping strategies. In this chapter, a detailed framework for the assessment and treatment of negative symptoms is outlined based on the cognitive-behavioral conceptualization of these symptoms described in Chapter 5.

Alpert and colleagues (Alpert, Shaw, Pouget, & Lim, 2002) found that, in contrast to the presumed "bottom-up" or part-to-whole ratings, clinicians' ratings of negative symptoms were derived from an undifferentiated global impression. This lack of differentiation may reflect patients' clinical presentation, which in some cases, may include the presence of all negative symptoms in a syndromal fashion. For other patients, only selective symptoms meet actual clinical threshold. In a recently completed clinical trial study by one of us, patients completed the PANSS interview prior to treatment initiation and were found to have considerable variability in their negative symptom presentation; the average patient presented with between three to four clinically significant negative symptoms (Rector, Seeman, & Segal, 2003). A careful assessment of the negative symptoms includes diagnostic considerations, a complete functional analysis, an evaluation of symptom-related cognitive appraisals and beliefs, an understanding of the course of the symptoms with attention to distal and proximal factors involved in their precipitation, and their explicit formulation within the cognitive case conceptualization. An overview of the treatment approach for negative symptoms can be seen in Table 11.1.

ASSESSMENT

Assessment of Symptoms/Cognitions

Often negative symptoms emerge as the secondary consequence to medication side effects, hallucinations and delusions, anxiety and mood disorders, and environmental understimulation (American Psychiatric Association, 2000, p. 301).

Medication Side Effects

Since all neuroleptic medications have sedating effects, some patients may appear flat, unresponsive, and lacking in motivation as a secondary consequence of their medications. Particularly for patients at the time of first onset, it can be difficult to negotiate the balance between achieving a sufficient dose of medication to reduce the positive symptoms such as delusions and hallucinations, but not lead to oversedation and the predictable effects of lethargy, apathy, and low motivation. The well-described neuroleptic-induced deficit syndrome has been found to be difficult to distinguish from negative symptoms that are not medication-induced. Neuroleptically induced negative symptoms may be most apparent (and identifiable) when

TABLE 11.1. Cognitive Assessment and Therapy for Negative Symptoms

Assessment

- Assessment of symptoms/cognitions
  - Medication side effects
  - Environmental overstimulation/understimulation
  - Negative symptoms secondary to mood or anxiety disorder
  - Negative symptoms as secondary to positive symptoms
  - Diagnostic assessment

- Conducting a functional assessment
  - Assessment of beliefs and appraisals associated with negative symptoms
  - Assessment of continuity and discontinuity of symptoms across time

- Developing the case conceptualization
  - Focus on dysfunctional performance beliefs and negative appraisals in the development and persistence of negative symptoms

Treatment

- Providing psychoeducation and normalization
  - Sharing a stress–vulnerability conceptualization of negative symptoms
  - Formulating patient's negative symptoms as response to threat and stress

- Socializing the patient to the cognitive model
  - Developing awareness of interaction between thoughts, feelings, and behaviors

- Implementing cognitive and behavioral approaches
  - Targeting secondary negative symptoms
  - Targeting primary negative symptoms
  - Targeting low expectancies for pleasure
  - Targeting low expectancies for success
  - Targeting the impact of stigma
  - Targeting perception of low resources

the patient's negative symptoms emerge or worsen just following the introduction or change in medications, or alternatively, when the patient's medications are tapered and the negative symptoms appear to be improving.

Overstimulation/Understimulation (Institutionalization)

Some patients resort to withdrawal and isolation as a way of coping with an overstimulating environment. In the living environment, the hustle and bustle of morning preparations or evening chatter with phones ringing, television blaring, and, in group homes, frequent entrances and exits from rooms, may lead to a sense of "stimulus overload." Further, disengagement may serve a protective function in homes where there is frequent quarreling, conflict, and high-expressed emotion. In contrast, "shutting down" in response to environmental understimulation, including institutionalization, has been described for decades (e.g., Strauss, Rakfeldt, Harding, & Lieberman, 1989). Therapists should consider the extent to which there is environmental impoverishment and its association with apathy, affective flattening, and reduced motivation.

Negative Symptoms Secondary to Mood or Anxiety Disorder

As noted in Chapter 5, the high rates of depression and anxiety comorbidity in schizophrenia may lead to a clinical picture that, in some respects, mirrors the symptom presentation of selective negative symptoms; for instance, depression can result in apathy, affective flattening, reduced motivation, and social withdrawal. Further, the behavioral avoidance germane to the anxiety disorders may be associated with secondary negative symptoms. For instance, the patient experiencing significant panic symptoms may avoid taking transit to appointments, using elevators, or leaving the home altogether, in fear of experiencing a panic attack. The patient with secondary social phobia may have difficulties with eye contact, self-disclosure, and the interpersonal intimacy that is required in most treatment milieus. As such, the active avoidance and safety behaviors used to cope with anxious arousal may be misconstrued as lack of energy or emotional disengagement.

Negative Symptoms as Secondary to Positive Symptoms

Negative symptoms that are present in relation to acute positive symptoms often reflect compensatory strategies that serve as a form of protection from personal and/or social threat. A patient with an encapsulated paranoid delusion spent the entire day in bed to prevent activation of the dreaded fear sensations that accompany the perception of being monitored by government officials, were he to leave his house. Another patient presented himself as "cold" as possible in fear that if he were to express his happiness, others would attempt to "steal" away these feelings. Social interactions (Chadwick & Birchwood, 1994) frequently trigger voice activity, and so many patients withdraw and isolate themselves to reduce the fear and confusion that often accompanies this experience. Other patients avoid specific situations wherein they anticipate that their voices will be triggered. For instance, one patient avoided malls out of fear of experiencing a voice commanding her to steal, whereas another patient avoided taking the subway because the screeching sounds activated a high-pitched critical voice. In addition to the use of withdrawal and isolation as a protection from social threat, other patients may engage in similar disengagement in order to spend more time with their voices (Chadwick & Birchwood, 1994).

Diagnostic Assessment

There are a number of reliable and valid clinician-administered rating instruments to determine the presence, severity, and degree of interference of negative symptoms. These measures were outlined in Chapter 5. Clinician-administered interviews to assess negative symptoms, for example, the SANS or PANSS, include dimensional ratings pertaining the comparative absence of affective expression, speech, motivation, and other symptoms comprising the negative symptom dimension. The clinical rating of negative symptoms can be done quickly and efficiently, and the clinician should obtain objective clinical ratings prior to treatment for several reasons. First, the best way of knowing whether your treatment has had a successful impact on negative symptoms will be to gauge changes from pre- to posttreatment on objective, behavioral indicators, the kind provided in standardized negative symptom ratings. Second, since few patients highlight their negative symptoms as central to their difficulties, it is important that the clinician be explicitly directed to judging the clinical significance of these symptoms with the aim of adding them to the problem-list, if so indicated. Third, patients may report a range of problems that are reflective of negative symptoms but may be missed if a formal rating were not conducted, because the language used by the patient typically does not reflect the actual symptom description. For instance, patients often state that they do not really like to talk about their problems, but they rarely spontaneously report being bothered by their tendency to provide brief and laconic replies to posed questions (alogia).

Conducting a Functional Assessment

In addition to collecting standardized ratings of negative symptoms, a complete assessment includes gaining an understanding of the unique cognitive, behavioral, and situational features associated with their activation and persistence. The starting point of the functional analysis is to determine the patient's level of understanding and insight into the presence and triggers of their negative symptoms. Questions such as "What do you like to do?", "What don't you like to do?", and "Are there times when you find it hard to express yourself in words?" help to elicit the idiographic triggers for the person's symptoms. A range of possible probes with which to identify situational factors can be seen in Table 11.2.

Some patients indicate that they have felt less energetic since their medications were changed, or that their voices are "stronger" and they would rather be left alone. In our clinical experience common proximal environmental triggers for negative symptoms include situations that are perceived as personally threatening, such as social interactions, performance evaluations, relationship conflicts, appointments with professionals, situations that demand significant effort, and the considerable disruption introduced

---

TABLE 11.2. Functional Assessment Probes for DSM-IV Negative Symptoms

Affective flattening

"What things interest you?"
" Are there times when you're interested in things, but it's hard to show it?"
"Are there situations in which you try to hold back showing your feelings?"
"Have there been times before that you were feeling quite positive inside, but others commented on how down you seemed? How did that make you feel?"
"Does the way you express your feelings ever cause difficulties in your life?"
"Have other people ever commented on it?"

Alogia

"Are there situations in which you find it hard to express what you mean?"
"If yes, any idea what makes this difficult?"
"Are there situations in which you just prefer to be quiet and say little?"
"Are there certain topics that you'd rather not discuss?"
"How do you feel when those topics come up? What do you do?"
"What about the opposite—what things do you like to talk about?"
"Are there times when you feel it's really important to get your words exactly right?"

Avolition

"What kinds of things do you like to do?"
"Are there some things that you feel pressured to do but don't really want to do?"
"Are there things that you would like to do but find it hard to get motivated to do them?"
"What are your current goals?"
"Are there things that sometimes get in the way of your reaching your goals?"

Anhedonia

"What things do you derive pleasure from?"
"Are there times when it's hard to feel pleasure? Are there specific situations/times when this is most likely to occur?"
"Were there things that you enjoyed in the past but find hard to enjoy now?"
"Is the ability to experience pleasure important to you? If you find yourself not enjoying things the way you expect to, how do you react? What do you feel?"

---

by hospitalizations. Unlike the situational triggers that often appear contiguous with the expression of anxiety and depression, in many instances, negative symptoms are activated by actual or perceived negative events that occurred days, weeks, months, or even years earlier.

For some patients, particularly those in the chronic phase of the disorder, their negative symptoms may seem to be less and less connected to specific situational triggers. They may also seem less bothered because they have created a "safety zone" characterized by avoidance and withdrawal from triggering situations. They may have little insight into their behavior and/or feelings. As previously described, some patients with negative symptoms simply seem locked into a negative "mode" characterized by chronic disengagement with little interest or responsiveness to others around them. Importantly, the functional assessment also provides the opportunity to assess the full range of activities in which the patient engages and to determine important missing activities and goals. Cognitive therapy, in part, focuses on helping patients who have a range of activities continue to maintain these goals in the face of setbacks, perceived failures, and other negative appraisals that can activate downward spirals of emotional and social withdrawal. For other patients, who demonstrate more significant impairment in motivation and goal pursuit, the cognitive therapy is used to help them reestablish meaningful life goals, either by harnessing old goals that were perceived to be lost, or by creating new goals that can be pursued and maintained over time. To gauge the patient's current range of activities, interests, and goals, the self-monitoring of activities can be accomplished with a standard activity schedule. The activity schedule provides online information about the frequency of events, interpersonal contacts, "lost time," and other aspects of a person's day-to-day life.

Assessment of Beliefs and Appraisals Related to Negative Symptoms

We have previously (Chapter 5) outlined the core negative expectancy appraisals identified with the initiation and persistence of negative symptoms. It is important to assess for the presence of negative cognitive appraisals as part of the *in vivo* assessment of activity schedules and in the spontaneous comments made by patients in therapy. Therapists can obtain information about the negative appraisals related to the experience of negative symptoms by directly inquiring about their presence: "How do you think you came across today in the day treatment group?" or "When you began to consider [starting a job retraining program], what went through your mind?" or "Last week you had dinner with your parents, how did that go? Was there any point at which you began to feel uncomfortable?" Some patients are less readily able to identify and communicate the nature of their thoughts and appraisals related to different situations. Questions pertaining to negative appraisals can result in brief and closed-ended replies such as "don't know," and the like. It is important for the therapist not to push on the exploration of these thoughts during the early phase of assessment, if the patient has difficulty identifying thoughts and appraisals, appears to be easily confused, or simply is not interested in talking about his or her thoughts. In our clinical experience, emphasis on behavioral change via the implementation of graded task assignments and mastery and pleasure activities, and the like, will increasingly bring symptom-related cognitive appraisals and beliefs to the "surface" for evaluation and discussion in treatment.

Dysfunctional attitudes and beliefs related to themes of autonomy and sociotropy have been found to be associated with different symptom presentations in schizophrenia, especially negative symptoms (Rector, 2004; Rector et al., 2005). Because dysfunctional autonomous/performance-related beliefs have been found to be most associated with negative symptoms, the administration of scales that assess these beliefs, such as the DAS (Weissman & Beck, 1978), can provide valuable information for the cognitive conceptualization of these symptoms.

Assessment of Continuity and Discontinuity of Symptoms across Time

Since most patients experience a waxing and waning of their negative symptoms across the course of the illness, it is important to map out the pattern of negative symptoms across time to better understand the distal and proximal factors related to their expression and to better understand how negative symptoms connect to the patient's broader life narrative. Inevitably, the tracing of negative symptoms usually leads back to the premorbid phase prior to first onset of the disorder. Whereas negative symptoms were often thought to emerge during the chronic phase of the disorder, recent research has pointed to the emergence of emotional and social withdrawal as the characteristic feature of the premorbid phase (Lencz et al., 2004; Miller et al., 2002). As in the assessment of past depressive episodes, we have found it helpful to chart the time course of negative symptoms from the premorbid phase to the time of assessment, as seen in Figure 11.1.

Because it is difficult for most patients to describe problems related to affective flattening, poverty of speech, and lack of drive and interest in daily

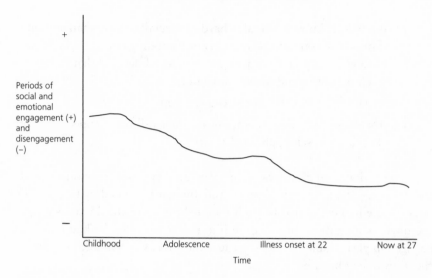

FIGURE 11.1. Mapping out timeline for periods of engagement and disengagement.

activities, we have found it useful to map out periods when the patient felt connected to important goals, and periods when he or she let go of those goals. Take, for instance, the assessment of Jim, who described a 25-year history of psychosis, with the development of negative symptoms occurring only following his relinquishment of goals in the past several years:

THERAPIST: You've told me that there are many things that you used to like to do.

PATIENT: I used to go to judo. I had a part-time job, I used to play pool, and I'd spend time with my guitar. I was pretty well occupied. Yeah, I could do all of those things when I was OK.

THERAPIST: Even though you have had difficulties for some years now, it seems that you used to do all of these things until just a few years ago.

PATIENT: Well, I thought the only way to beat this schizophrenia was to keep busy and power my way through it. Well, that wouldn't work, of course, but that's what I thought. And so I kept going to the gym, took karate, and cycled.

THERAPIST: And when did things change for you?

PATIENT: You know it's really hard. Especially, with schizophrenia, you know you got no emotions or no feelings that you know and you just . . . you . . . it just got hard and I decided that I might as well pack it in and live out my fate.

THERAPIST: How do you feel as you say that?

PATIENT: Just a little bit down, but not really. I just, I expect as much because I'm schizophrenic, right?

The resignation to "pack it in" was an important proximal trigger for the onset of apathy, withdrawal, and anergia presented by this patient. Whereas he had continued to push forward for 22 of the 25 years despite the obvious limitations imposed on him by the disorder, he had remained engaged in pleasurable activities because the effort still had meaning within the *narrative* of his life.

Developing the Case Conceptualization

The cognitive conceptualization provides the framework for understanding how past and present factors contribute to the development and persistence of the person's current problems. While the diagnostic and functional assessment provides important information about which negative symptoms are present and the possible cognitive and behavioral factors related to the patient's expression, it is also important to assess the role of early learning experiences, critical incidents, the timing and nature of formation of dysfunctional beliefs and assumptions, and the coping behaviors developed over time to cope with stressors and the illness, in particular. The case conceptualization should lead to (1) initial hypotheses about the role of distal environmental factors that contribute to a vulnerability for avoidance and disengagement (e.g., bullying, rejection, few friends, early academic failures, reduced opportunity for social skills development, turbulent and demanding family environment.) as well as (2) the consolidation of negative attitudes toward social affiliation, and (3) negative dysfunctional performance beliefs.

It is also important to carefully assess the early emergence of negative symptoms during the premorbid phase and/or during the first onset of psychosis. Consider these questions:

Was there an increasing pattern of emotional and social withdrawal prior to the development of positive symptoms, or did negative symptoms mostly emerge subsequent to the development of other aspects of the disorder, including delusions and hallucinations?

In the early emergence of the disorder, to what extent were goals interrupted—was there loss of work or ruined relationships, for example?

What is the patient's account of how he or she reacted to the start of the illness?

Since the onset of the disorder, have some negative symptoms showed a stable course?

When do exacerbations occur? That is, what specific symptoms seem to intensify in response to which specific stressors (including the absence of stress and challenge)?

How does the person's view of him- or herself, others, and the world shape the specific responses that may either intensify or attenuate negative symptoms?

Finally, the case conceptualization should steer the therapist toward formulating the problem list for therapy and the place of negative symptoms within the problem list.

Initially, cognitive therapy for the symptoms of psychosis aimed to select patients for treatment who reported experiencing distress pertaining to their positive symptoms, specifically delusions and voices. However, these patients typically present with a broad range of clinical problems, many of which bear greatest affinity to the negative symptoms, especially problems of being socially isolated, lonely, aimless; thinking that life is meaningless; and feeling stigmatized, pressured by others, hopeless. Few patients present for treatment with the aim of reducing poverty of speech or affective flattening, per se, but if these symptoms are conceptualized as part of a broader pattern of emotional disengagement with their cognitive counterparts, then it is not especially important to have any one symptom as the target.

As such, the treatment of negative symptoms can proceed in a number of different ways. First, the therapeutic goal may be to reduce the negative symptoms indirectly by reducing the factors that lead to their secondary activation. For example, treatment may begin by reducing the negative symptoms (e.g., social withdrawal, emotional disengagement) that emerge as coping responses to the presence of delusions and voices. Second, negative symptoms can be targeted directly on the problem list. For instance, a patient with mild-to-moderate religious delusions preferred to work on goals pertaining to her social isolation and lack of "meaning" in life. Her prioritized treatment goals were to (1) spend more time with her nieces, (2) attend church weekly, (3) spend more time with two selected friends from the past, (4) engage in entertaining activities, and (5) shop with her mother weekly. Finally, we would assert that any treatment goals that directly or indirectly lead to enhanced self-efficacy, greater pleasure in life, reduced stigma, and a perception of greater psychological resourcefulness has the potential to attenuate negative symptom functioning.

Summary

Careful diagnostic and functional assessment of negative symptoms directs the clinician to explicitly consider their importance in the treatment plan. A core goal of the assessment phase is to identify the nature and role of stressful life events, dysfunctional beliefs and assumptions, and negative expectancy appraisals in the production and persistence of negative symptoms. These symptoms may require specific interventions, such as scheduling pleasurable events and mastering the ability to rate different levels of pleasure as a way to reduce affective flattening and lack of interest in social activities. The general approach to treatment, however, will involve efforts to improve drive and motivation by helping the patient generate meaningful and realistic short- and long-term goals and consolidate cognitive and behavioral strategies to overcome the barriers that characteristically lead to the derailment of those goals over time.

TREATMENT

Following the careful assessment and formulation of the psychological factors involved in the development, persistence, and periodic exacerbations of the negative symptoms, and the understanding of these symptoms within the case conceptualization, treatment of these symptoms can begin. Many of the general cognitive therapy strategies are outlined in Chapter 8; the remainder of this chapter focuses on particular approaches for the reduction of negative symptoms. In general, we find that focusing on *concrete goals* (e.g., work, school, independence) identified by the patient facilitates motivation and engagement and provides a means for dealing with negative symptoms as they emerge as barriers to the overarching goals. For example, a patient who wanted to return to school complained of severe concentration problems. He believed that he could not read. The therapist introduced graded task assignments to improve his reading and disprove the belief.

Homework assignments initially featured very small written snippets on interesting topics, but ultimately worked up to full chapters drawn from college textbooks. Along the way, the therapist created quizzes to assess concentration and retention. The patient's performance on these quizzes provided counterevidence to his negative expectations regarding reading. In the following sections, we outline step-by-step strategies with which to target negative symptoms and increase concrete goal achievement.

Further, in treating negative symptoms, we highlight the need to adjust the outlined interventions in accordance with the patient's level of neurocognitive impairment. Patients with impairment in neurocognitive tasks of attention, memory, and abstraction require special adjustments to therapy in order to produce efficacious results. To ensure that these patients grasp the concepts being discussed, we advise the use of multiple modalities of learning. Thus, writing important concepts on a whiteboard (visual) as well as saying them (auditory) helps to reinforce the points being made. Additionally, writing out as much of the results of each session in the form of summaries, coping cards, and handouts can help the patient remember to do his or her homework and apply the principles between sessions. We also advise suspending Socratic questioning with cognitively impaired patients to promote progress. Therapists should speak in direct, declarative sentences (i.e., "Tell me what was upsetting during the past week" rather than asking "What was upsetting during the past week?") designed to hold the patient's attention and not significantly tap memory. Distilling key points made during the session and the use of repetition will maximize the chances of retention. We also recommend the use of external study aids such as therapy folders and palm pilots. For example, a Palmtop program was used to assess one patient's current activity (including indices of pleasure and mastery) and reminded her of activities she identified in session whenever she reported that she was doing nothing or being inactive. It also reminded her of lessons learned in therapy (e.g., coping statements). Bringing the family into session is another means to reinforce the general approach, facilitate the patient's compliance with homework assignments, and reduce conflict and misunderstandings. With this proviso, we now outline the key strategies for targeting negative symptoms.

Psychoeducation and Normalization

The first step in addressing negative symptoms in treatment is to help normalize these symptoms for patients. Many patients have come to perceive their difficulties with motivation as indicative of laziness, weakness, and part of the inevitable outcome of having schizophrenia. One of us (A.T.B.) first described the importance of providing patients with an explanation for their symptoms, and this normalizing approach has been extended to help patients experiencing psychotic symptoms, especially positive symptoms (Kingdon & Turkington, 1991). Just as the therapist can explain positive symptoms on a continuum with normal experiences (i.e., normalize them) within a stress–vulnerability model, negative symptoms can be framed as a response to past and present internal and external stressors. The following points can help patients understand their negative symptoms:

- Everyone has problems staying motivated at times; this may be especially hard to do when we are under stress and experiencing a range of problems that makes us feel vulnerable (*link to original development of negative symptoms*).
- Too much stress can lead to an automatic "shutting down" as a way of protecting ourselves from feeling overwhelmed; this response can actually be quite adaptive (*link to particular expression of negative symptoms*).
- If we continue to experience many life challenges and have feelings of being overwhelmed, our "thermostat" can become reset at lower levels of motivation and activity (*link to current symptoms as sign of new baseline compared to before the illness started*).
- Overall, some people may have a greater tendency for their "thermostat" to reset under periods of stress (*link to patient's behavioral disposition prior to the onset of illness*).

The aim of the normalizing approach is to convey to patients the usually new idea that their problems are familiar to most people at some time in their lives, but for a variety of reasons they (patients) have experienced these problems for a longer period of time. It is important to provide a multidimensional view of the development and maintenance of negative symptoms, including biological (e.g., automatic resetting of the thermostat) and psychological (e.g., reducing activity to prevent being overwhelmed) explanations. Additional points that can be discussed include the problems of approaching goals under pressure, with links to areas in their life where they perceive themselves to be under pressure. Kingdon and Turkington (1998) use the analogy of requiring a period of recovery or "convalescence" to heal from the effects of a serious illness. During the convalescent period, both patient and carers need to be patient and not try to "push" the patient out of the negative symptoms (Kingdon & Turkington, 1998).

Socializing the Patient to the Cognitive Model

Importantly, improving motivation in cognitive therapy focuses on helping the patient generate meaningful goals and then to stay engaged with these goals. The cognitive therapy goal is *not* to simply engage the person in more activities for the sake of it. Rather, one of the early aims of therapy is to socialize the patient to the cognitive, emotional, and behavioral aspects of their problem with an example from their own life. For instance:

THERAPIST: Welcome back. I thought we might start by setting out a rough plan of what we can do today. What would you like to talk about?

PATIENT: I don't know, not much.

THERAPIST: When we first met, you mentioned that you might like to go for more walks.

PATIENT: Yeah, I wanted to go for a walk on Friday and Monday afternoons, but was content to sleep instead. The afternoons are the hardest time for me.

THERAPIST: Well, how about if we start our session talking about the afternoons?

PATIENT: OK. Usually, I get up at noon, have a sandwich, and then just ride the bus until 5 P.M.—things just don't go smoothly during this time.

THERAPIST: What is it about riding the bus in the afternoons that doesn't make it go smoothly?

PATIENT: I just run out of things to do, and it's boring. I just wish I could do better. I feel that I can't do anything like I used to.

THERAPIST: When you say this to yourself, how do you feel?

PATIENT: Just wiped out.

THERAPIST: Does this outlook affect your behavior too?

PATIENT: Yeah, it's like I don't expect much, so I don't try much.

THERAPIST: You mentioned that the afternoons don't go smoothly. Are things different in the morning?

PATIENT: In the morning, I've got a plan. I wake up, have a coffee, speak to my dad and sometimes my brother, and go to walk a dog for a family friend.

THERAPIST: How do you feel during these times?

PATIENT: I feel all right, it's good.

THERAPIST: Maybe I could take a few minutes to summarize some of the important things that you have said so far. You identified the afternoons as a time that does not run as smoothly as you'd like it too—a time when you would like to be less bored. It seems that right now when you think to yourself "I can't do anything like I used to," it makes you feel hopeless and sometimes stops you from trying to do new things in the afternoon. But in the morning, it seems that you start off with a different outlook, that there are worthwhile things to do, and you end up doing things that make the mornings run smoothly. This is a good example of what we are going to focus on in our treatment—how our thoughts and feelings can influence our behaviors—what we decide to do or not to do.

The therapist then explained the cognitive model, demonstrating the interconnections between thoughts, feelings, and behaviors and how they lead to different outcomes from the mornings to the afternoons.

For patients whose negative symptoms are secondary to delusions and hallucinations, socialization to the cognitive model for negative symptoms may be introduced as a component of the cognitive model for these positive symptoms. Here, avoidance and withdrawal behaviors are explained as resulting from perceived threats, whether internal or external, that beliefs or voices will be triggered, and the associated feelings of fear and anxiety. Similar to the cognitive conceptualization of avoidance and safety behaviors in the anxiety disorders, escape and avoidance behaviors are framed as adaptive short-term solutions for reducing distress and possibly real exacerbation of distressing positive symptoms. However, part of treatment is devoted to gradually reducing these safety behaviors. A way of getting patients interested in the therapy process is to build hope that they will be increasingly able to participate in situations that attract them in a more comfortable way.

Cognitive and Behavioral Approaches

Treating Secondary Negative Symptoms

As previously noted, we have found that negative symptoms that are secondary to delusions and delusional beliefs about the voices (e.g., regarding agency, control, meaning) are either *coping strategies* intended to reduce the threat associated with having these symptoms, or they are *behaviors* that have meaning within the delusional system. Similar to the role of avoidance and withdrawal behaviors in the anxiety disorders, patients often begin by avoiding situations that have recently led to the triggering of their fears/ voices. Depending on other factors, such as the prominence of current stressors, the breadth and rigidity of the delusional beliefs, and availability of social support, an increasing number of situations have the potential to elicit fear and avoidance. A steady downward spiral ensues wherein patients fear that making an effort may trigger frightening symptoms. Patients may also fear that making an effort may trigger symptoms that will lead to a full relapse and possible hospitalization. Initial situation-specific avoidance can increase to limited activities and social contact. In turn, this isolation can create fertile ground for rumination and/or more active voices, leading to further distress, withdrawal, and reduced motivation, thus becoming a vicious cycle. As in the treatment of anxiety and depression, an important aim of treatment is to help patients learn strategies to resist getting "stuck" in the downward spirals.

Irrespective of the particular content of the delusions, patients report escaping or avoiding situations where they anticipate having fear-related (delusional) thoughts. For some, these situations may extend to nearly all interpersonal contexts and result in minimal contact with even family members and health care workers. Similarly, patients who hear voices report a wide range of behavioral avoidance and safety behaviors to reduce (1) their activation, (2) their persistence, or (3) the distressing delusional beliefs about the voices. When negative symptoms are actually coping strategies to deal with positive symptoms, they can be tackled in conjunction with the cognitive-behavioral approach for positive symptoms.

The treatment of negative symptoms that are secondary to delusions and voices is analogous to the treatment of panic disorder. Patients with panic disorder are typically exposed to *in vivo* situations to overcome avoidance and safety behaviors after they have made progress in conceptualizing their panic attacks within the cognitive framework and developed at least some preliminary skills to deal with elevated distress in difficult situations. Similarly, patients with secondary negative symptoms who are experiencing threatening delusions and hallucinations can make the most out of their exposure exercises after they have made progress in identifying, testing, and creating alternative interpretations of their delusions and voices outside of hot situations. Then the reduction of secondary negative symptoms can proceed with the development of a graded hierarchy listing situations that are feared and avoided. As in the treatment of anxiety disorders, exposure to situations proceeds from least to most distressing. The main goal is for the patient to gradually reduce emotional, social, and behavioral avoidance strategies. There are several important stages in conducting exposures:

1. Conduct a review of progress that the patient has made in questioning delusional interpretations and building alternative perspectives before exposure work starts.
2. Establish training in anxiety ratings (SUDS) well before exposures start, with an established "safety net" whereby the patient can exit exposures if his or her fear exceeds a personally defined upper limit of acceptable anxiety level.
3. Review experience and feedback from the exposure task within a thought record approach to address progress as well as concerns that may have been raised by the situation.

When the negative symptoms result from delusional beliefs, they are ideally addressed within the overall cognitive-behavioral treatment of the delusions. As suggested, patients' delusional belief systems will undoubtedly affect their behavior and, in many cases, lead directly to the expression of certain negative symptoms. One patient was virtually mute (i.e., expressing extreme alogia) out of fear that speaking about his personal interests would lead to their withdrawal by evil forces. Another patient presented to weekly sessions silent and expressionless, gripped by the belief that she was responsible for numerous deaths through cognitive processes akin to thought–action fusion. Her delusional belief, "I've killed numerous innocent people" was followed by the belief "I don't deserve a moment of happiness on this earth," which contributed to her affective flattening and lack of interest in daily activities. Many patients with command hallucinations fear that making an effort on days when they are tired or feeling vulnerable will lead to commands that will be too hard to resist. The main aim of treatment is to reduce these behaviors by targeting the delusional beliefs that lead to their activation.

Treating Primary Negative Symptoms

Whereas the treatment of secondary negative symptoms focuses on limiting the extent of disengagement due to the presence of threatening thoughts and experiences associated with the positive symptoms, the treatment of negative symptoms that are not secondary to positive symptoms typically requires strategies to harness motivation and emotional reengagement with meaningful life goals. In the treatment of depression, a motivating factor for patients is that they can ordinarily expect to return to previous levels of functioning once they have successfully reduced biased thinking and behavioral inertia. This optimism may not be warranted in the treatment of negative symptoms, especially for patients who have been in the chronic phase of the disorder for many years. Here the goal is not to expect to restore previous levels of social and occupational functioning but rather to establish new, meaningful goals within the context of the patient's current life situation. Greater scheduling of mastery and pleasure events, more socializing, and pursuit of meaningful tasks is important. However, the central feature of the cognitive approach to negative symptoms is the attempt to enhance behavioral activation toward changing the negative expectancies and performance beliefs that represent the more enduring vulnerability for chronic disengagement.

Targeting Low Expectancies for Pleasure

Patients with prominent negative symptoms typically report that they find little enjoyment in their lives and, in turn, expect to receive minimal enjoyment when presented with the opportunity to participate in activities. As discussed in Chapter 5, patients often think to themselves "What's the point? It's not fun like it used to be," or "It's boring," or "It's too much of a hassle," and so on, when prompted with the opportunity to do something that might be fun. This negative expectancy toward the possibility of pleasure leads patients to miss pleasurable events and opportunities and affirms the self-fulfilling prophecy that "nothing" in life is enjoyable. Since we know from clinical experience and experimental research (Gard et al., 2003) that these patients, once engaged in activities, derive pleasure in the same way that others do, the major treatment goal is to create a list of idiosyncratically defined pleasurable activities, increase the scheduling of these activities day to day, and to chip away at the negative expectancy for pleasure so that it does not become a barrier to participation. The steps in the treatment approach follow this sequence: (1) Identify cognitive distortions in low pleasure expectancies; (2) work with disconfirming evidence pertaining to low expectancies; (3) schedule meaningful activity; (4) record "online" pleasure ratings *in vivo*; (5) use feedback to shift low expectations.

Many patients state that "nothing" is enjoyable like it used to be and so is not worth the effort. This all-or-nothing view can crystallize to the point where some patients assert that there is *absolutely nothing* that can bring them enjoyment. An initial aim of therapy is to overcome this all-or-nothing view by establishing a continuum perspective on pleasure. Take the following example of all-or-none thinking: A patient with enduring negative symptoms reported on his enjoyment of watching a televized football game the night before. The therapist asked: "How much enjoyment did you experience last night during the game—say, from 0 being none at all to 100 being extremely enjoyable?" The patient reported the complete absence of any pleasure (0%) and added that it always used to be 100%. The therapist then asked: "I'm wondering if you sometimes sort of expect that you'll get nothing out of things when you wish you could get everything out of things. Is there a possibility for a middle ground?" The patient replied "No, it's just that I can't find any if there is. If there was a middle ground, then I'd be OK . . . I could try to do things."

By frequently asking about the level of enjoyment derived from different activities, the therapist can move patients toward seeing shades of gray in their experienced pleasure. Patients are also asked to monitor their activities and make pleasure ratings (along with mastery ratings, which are described in the next section) on a continuous measure to further consolidate the view that at least some activities bring (some degree of) pleasure and are worth pursuing. In addition to all-or-nothing thinking, patients focus their attention on the negative aspects of the situation when prompted to participate, and this serves to heighten expected displeasure. Therapists aim to identify patients' mental filtering (selective attention) toward the negative details of the situation to help them see the full range of possibilities.

Some patients are readily able to acknowledge a range of activities that brings varying degrees of pleasure to them when they are asked to discuss things that interest them or when the activities of their past week are reviewed. In this way, the therapist accumulates considerable evidence with which to work to disconfirm the belief that nothing is enjoyable and therefore not worth the effort.

For instance, a patient who had attended a dance class on a Tuesday and rated it to be moderately enjoyable stated in the morning of Thursday that she did not want to go again that afternoon because it was not going to be fun. Here it was relatively easy for the therapist to use the evidence from the Tuesday dance class ratings to help the patient see that attending the class had brought considerable fun just 2 days earlier and that Tuesday morning was better when she was engaged in the task than in the afternoon when she resorted to the familiar routine of watching television.

With some patients it may be comparatively more difficult to generate alternative evidence pertaining to low expectancies for pleasure. They do not see any recent activities as enjoyable and may report the near absence of enjoyment in the recent past. This stance may reflect either the comparative absence of scheduled activities or the minimization of enjoyment in pleasure derived from the activities. First, the therapist sees if there is any disconfirming evidence to harness from the self-monitoring forms or any of his or her observations of the patient in recent activities that could be used to create an alternative perspective. Second, the therapist can shift focus to activities and interests that were seen to be pleasurable in the past. In what activities did the person engage in the past that he or she is not currently attempting? What, in particular, was it about those past activities that made them pleasurable? Therapists assess the full range of activities that was once experienced as pleasurable and attempt to identify a simple activity that could be successfully scheduled at the present time. Take the example of a patient who used to swim for his high school swim team but has not swum for the past 10 years. A new community swimming pool had just been built, and as he passed it the week before, he thought to himself "I'd like to swim—but what's the point?" Otherwise, his days were spent awaking at noon and watching television throughout the afternoon.

THERAPIST: You mentioned that you once liked swimming very much.

PATIENT: That was before.

THERAPIST: What was it about swimming that you liked?

PATIENT: I used to get up and be at the pool at 7 A.M. every morning. I was in the water before anybody else—I really liked it, and I was good at it too.

THERAPIST: Did you have a favorite swimming stroke?

PATIENT: No, not really, I did everything.

THERAPIST: When you passed the new pool last week, did you think that you might like to swim again sometime?

PATIENT: For a second I did, but what's the point. It won't be like it used to be.

THERAPIST: Of the different things we've discussed, it seems as if swimming might be the activity that you miss the most. But when you think about how pleasurable it was in the past in contrast to what you expect now, it just doesn't seem worth it?

PATIENT: Yeah.

THERAPIST: Now, the one thing that strikes me is that it's been almost 10 years since you were last in a swimming pool. Is it possible that it may not be just like it was then but that there could be at least a little enjoyment, somewhat more than zero?

PATIENT: Maybe.

THERAPIST: You're right, maybe it will, maybe it won't. Would you be willing to test out whether swimming might be still somewhat enjoyable for you?

PATIENT: You mean, like go to the new pool and try it out?

THERAPIST: Yeah, what do you think?

PATIENT: I can't get up early like I used to.

THERAPIST: How about if you planned to swim in the afternoon at a time that was good for you?

PATIENT: But I'd miss my game show [on television].

THERAPIST: How about if we scheduled it for after the game show so that you didn't miss it?

PATIENT: All right.

THERAPIST: If through this experiment we found that swimming could still bring you some enjoyment, would that matter to you?

PATIENT: I might be able to pass the time a little better.

The therapist then scheduled the swimming class on the activity schedule and the patient was requested to rate the enjoyment of swimming from 0 to 10. It is important to not only schedule the activity but also to address any barriers that might get in the way of its completion. In the preceding example, it is clear that if the therapist did not proceed to schedule the swimming activity with the patient, then the patient would have seen the morning wakening or the missed game show as a reason not to swim. This patient attended the swimming pool that week but left without getting into his swimming trunks because he thought "It's not going to fit, and I'll look stupid." This barrier was addressed in the next session, and it was decided that he would get a new pair of trunks and attend the following week, which he was able to do. In discussing the first time in the pool, he reflected on "how it didn't feel as good as it used to," but in review in his pleasure ratings, he was able to see that his time at the pool, rated as "3," was still higher than his typical afternoon periods when he was doing nothing. The scheduling of swimming at the community center became a weekly event to which he increasingly looked forward and from which he was able to derive more pleasure than at first.

As therapists begin to make headway in scheduling pleasurable activities and obtaining pleasure ratings, the frequency of pleasure activities can be increased. It may be that scheduling one pleasurable event a day becomes a reasonable goal for some patients, especially at the beginning. The goal is to continue to build momentum by increasing the scheduling of pleasurable activities and for more activities to be perceived by patients as providing some pleasure. This momentum not only leads to increased activity but additional evidence to be used toward shifting the patient away from a low and rigid expectancy for lack of pleasure. It is important to have patients monitor pleasurable activities "online" during their experiences so that their subjective accounts of pleasure can be used to offset any minimization of pleasure that may occur out of the situation. Just the day before the scheduled session with his therapist, one patient had been seen laughing and fooling around during a "food fight" in the kitchen of the day treatment program. At the start of the next therapy session, the therapist was asked: "How was your day yesterday, anything pleasurable?" to which the patient responded "Nothing." The therapist added, "I just happened to be passing the kitchen and saw you immersed in a pretty intense food fight . . . you seemed to be having a pretty good time?" The patient then responded "Oh, yeah, that was fun." The therapist was able to use this example of the ways in which pleasurable activities are either minimized or ignored, feeding the belief that "nothing" is enjoyable—which contributes, in turn, to apathy and low motivation.

Targeting Low Expectancies for Success

Contributing to the pattern of withdrawal and low motivation are patients' expectations that if they push themselves to meet goals, they are likely to fail or to achieve some substandard level of performance. The relinquishing of goals becomes a strategy for self-protection against feelings of inadequacy, shame, and humiliation. Because the treatment goals are focused on harnessing intrinsic motivation, one of the early goals of treatment is to reduce some of the external pressure that patients feel coming from family, friends, health care professionals, work settings, and so on. The first step in this process is to help patients identify areas in which they feel pressured to perform beyond what they feel they can handle. This phase in therapy may involve working with the perceived sources of pressure. For instance, family-based cognitive therapy for helping patients' family members establish and maintain realistic expectations around motivation and not construe negative symptoms as signs of laziness has been nicely illustrated in clinical case material (Pelton, 2002). There is also some preliminary evidence to support the benefits of reducing familial demands toward reducing negative symptoms.

Once external pressures are reduced, treatment focuses on helping patients establish and pursue realistic and meaningful goals. This phase involves helping patients identify possible long-term goals that are worth striving for, as well as shorter, week-to-week goals as steps toward the long-term goals. Some patients overshoot their estimates of what they can achieve, setting up the likelihood of reaffirming their belief in their failure and their subsequent withdrawal, whereas other patients have relinquished goals altogether. The determination of what constitutes a "realistic" goal for the patient will be shaped by past history, current functioning, personal resources, skills, supports, and perhaps a multitude of other factors considered on a case-by-case basis. Notwithstanding the specific nature of the identified goals, the therapist's aim is to (1) socialize the patient to the importance of setting goals, (2) break down broader goals into small, manageable steps, (3) structure and schedule the steps to be completed, (4) deal with barriers to engagement, and (5) negotiate setbacks.

Similar to the cognitive distortions involved in minimizing expected pleasure, patients often pass on opportunities to gain mastery because they expect to fail, seeing themselves as "useless" and "incompetent." On the one hand, past goal interruptions due to the illness need to be acknowledged, validated, and normalized (as described previously). On the other hand, the black-and-white view of task outcomes can be addressed by helping patients see their performance along a continuum as opposed to fixating on static and all-or-none categorizations. The tendency to minimize successes can be reduced by having patients monitor activities throughout the week on an activity schedule with applied mastery ratings on a continuous scale (as described by Beck et al., 1979). Other cognitive distortions that fuel negative expectancies for success, such as overgeneralization, mental filtering, and disqualifying the positive can be similarly addressed as patients report on weekly updates.

For patients who are currently engaged in goal-related pursuits, the activity schedule provides an inroad to identifying and reducing cognitive distortions around performance. As cognitive distortions are addressed in therapy, patients can complete dysfunctional thought records in conjunction with scheduled goal activities in the ordinary way. For patients who have either no goals and/or few activities during the week, the first aim is to identify a personally relevant goal and then to explore the goal with the patient, giving attention to cognitive distortions that emerge around its consideration. For example, a 23-year-old patient with a 5-year history of schizophrenia regularly attended outpatient doctor appointments but had virtually no other activities listed. Through discussions with his therapist, it was established that he might like to do some volunteer work at a local store. He had volunteered at a local grocery store 3 years earlier, but that store had now closed. In discussing this further, he stated, "I'm afraid that I'll make mistakes," "It could cost the store business," and "I'm not able to do a good job anymore." Initially, the therapist focused on the probability and consequences around his making mistakes, the likelihood that most people have some tolerance for mistakes, and the fact that we all learn from our mistakes. The therapist also discussed the probability and consequences of the store losing business on his account and steps that he and the owner could take to reduce this possibility (checking in each day for feedback around his performance). Finally, the contention that he was "not able to do a good job anymore" was questioned, and alternative evidence was generated around past performances, including the fact that he had been frequently commended for his volunteer performance in a store 3 years earlier, and that this same grocery store had once called him back to volunteer again before it subsequently went out of business. As the therapist attempted to reduce his negative expectancies around success, the patient further admitted that even if he could do the volunteer work, he would not know where to start.

Here the therapist helped the patient identify the different steps that would be involved in finding a volunteer position, including (1) developing a list of grocery stores in his area, (2) getting the phone numbers of these different stores from the Yellow Pages, (3) prioritizing the grocery stores that he could contact, (4) developing his introduction statement, (5) scheduling when the calls could be made, and (6) following through with the schedule as part of the graded task assignment. Given the lack of guarantee that he would find a volunteer position this way, the therapist also helped the patient recognize other volunteer possibilities based on personal interests (e.g., pet grooming).

Finally, while the initial work focuses on helping the patient learn to identify and question his or her negative expectancies for success as a means of enhancing engagement, successful treatment requires some attention to the deeper dysfunctional attitudes and beliefs the person holds in regard to performance. As outlined in Chapter 5, patients with prominent negative symptoms are more likely to endorse such dysfunctional beliefs as "If I fail partly, it is as bad as being a complete failure," or "Taking even a small risk is foolish, because the loss is likely to be a disaster," or "If a person asks for help, it is a sign of weakness." Similar to the cognitive treatment of other psychiatric disorders, these beliefs can and should be addressed with standard cognitive restructuring and core belief therapeutic approaches (e.g., J. S. Beck, 1995).

Targeting the Impact of Stigma

The personal anguish and shame surrounding the diagnosis of schizophrenia, forced hospitalizations, and antipsychotic medications should never be underestimated. The demoralization due to the stigma of schizophrenia contributes to the development and persistence of emotional and social disengagement, as we discussed in Chapter 5. Because schizophrenia is frequently (mis)represented in the broader culture as reflecting "craziness," "dangerousness and violence," and a "hopeless psychiatric condition," patients unfortunately have considerable evidence to support their perceptions that others view them as "different" and "unwanted."

Although it may be difficult to fully reduce the experience of stigma, there are a number of strategies that therapists can use to reduce this problem. First, stigma can be reduced by normalizing the symptoms of psychosis, as described previously in this chapter and by Kingdon and Turkington (1991, 2002). In addition, the dysfunctional beliefs that patients hold about themselves and others have often emerged in response to adverse life experiences and circumstances, and these beliefs can, in many instances, be understood (normalized) as sequelae of these experiences. For instance, the patient who was bullied through grade school because he was seen to be "slow," experienced repeated academic failures in high school leading to his dropping out in grade 11, and was subsequently fired from every job he ever had due to poor performance, developed the not-unexpected self-belief that "People probably think less of me if I make a mistake." Just as the traumatized patient requires support for exaggerated beliefs that others are "malevolent" and the world is "dangerous," the beliefs of patients with negative symptoms need to be understood and supported in light of difficult circumstances.

Another strategy for reducing stigma and enhancing self-esteem is to help patients make personal connections with other patients who have had similar experiences. Although not all patients have access to the Internet, there are now numerous links to peer support groups for patients with psychosis throughout the world. In addition to addressing the "real-world" problems of living with a stigmatizing illness, cognitive therapy aims to help patients identify and reduce exaggerated negative expectancies pertaining to stigma. Patients anticipate being left out, rejected, and ridiculed for "being weird" in social situations. Part of the therapeutic aim is to identify high-risk situations where the experience of stigma may be more likely. However, in situations where stigma seems to be less likely, the patient's expectations to be rejected are identified and addressed through cognitive restructuring exercises. Take the following example of a patient considering going to a local pool hall to play billiards:

PATIENT: My friend plays pool all the time and what's interesting is he's a schizophrenic . . . I don't bother trying, I just continue where I am.

THERAPIST: Is there something that makes it hard to try?

PATIENT: A lot of times, I expect I can't play anymore because I've got schizophrenia. You get all screwed up, and I don't want people to see it.

THERAPIST: How do you think your friend does it?

PATIENT: Boy, he just keeps barreling through it.

THERAPIST: Do people seem to respond to him in a different way when he plays pool?

PATIENT: No, you can't tell he's a schizophrenic just by looking at him.

THERAPIST: Is this somehow different for you?

PATIENT: Well, no, you can't really tell that anyone has schizophrenia unless you get inside their head.

THERAPIST: That's an interesting point—if you were playing pool, would you have the option to not let people into your thoughts, just focusing on playing and enjoying the game instead?

PATIENT: But if I'm not on the ball, maybe they'll tell that I've got a few cards missing.

THERAPIST: How does your buddy stay on the ball when he's playing?

PATIENT: He just plays his game.

THERAPIST: How about if you were to focus just on playing your game?

PATIENT: Yeah, I could focus on playing, I guess, but even if I made a shot, I'd still come across as lifeless.

THERAPIST: Are you referring to your facial expressions?

PATIENT: Yeah, facial expressions. I don't react to anything, and I think they can see that, and they'll wonder what's wrong with the guy. There is nothing I can do, I feel hopeless.

THERAPIST: When your buddy makes a shot, does he show a lot of life each time?

PATIENT: Sometimes he does, sometimes he doesn't.

THERAPIST: When he doesn't react, what do you think?

PATIENT: I think he's focused on his game.

THERAPIST: Do others seem to notice?

PATIENT: Not really, not that I can tell.

THERAPIST: Is it possible that others might not notice your reactions or assume that you're just focused on your game if you're not always so expressive around your shots?

PATIENT: Yeah, it's a possibility.

THERAPIST: Well, how would you feel if we tested out how others react when you play pool sometime this week?

PATIENT: OK.

The patient went to the pool hall the next day with his friend. His account of the afternoon focused on how poorly he played, but the therapist focused on the accomplishment of *making an effort* as the real success of the day. While the patient seemed initially to forget that he had expected to be rejected and stigmatized at the pool hall, with prompting he was able to acknowledge that "No one seemed to give a damn if I was there or not."

In addition to targeting the negative expectancy appraisals regarding stigma in order to reduce barriers to engagement, cognitive therapy helps patients learn to conduct behavioral experiments to test out their beliefs and to develop a coping plan for dealing with situations in which stigma is actually (or perceived to be) experienced.

Targeting Perception of Low Resources

The experimental literature supports an important connection between reduced cognitive processing resources and the presence and severity of negative symptoms in schizophrenia. Patients exhibit a range of difficulties pertaining to attention, memory, and skills associated with planning and organization (Nuechterlein & Dawson, 1984), all of which undoubtedly contribute to limitations in effortful and fluid day-to-day task accomplishment. However, the simple linear view that reduced cognitive processing leads to worse negative symptom functioning is challenged by the finding that negative symptoms fluctuate over time, only a minority of patients appear to have structural changes and/or functional processing limitations, and the preliminary evidence that negative symptoms respond to cognitive-behavioral therapy (see Chapter 5). Similarly, a behavioral account for negative symptoms could be postulated whereby, as a result of limited cognitive resources, exposure to demanding situations and tasks could lead to an immediate escape or withdrawal response (the former representing a classical conditioned response and the latter being enhanced through negative reinforcement). However, we propose that patients' subjective appraisal that they lack the requisite personal resources and coping skills to face challenges undermines initiation of initiating of goal-directed activity and persistence in the face of demanding tasks. The goal in therapy, then, is to break this self-perpetuating cycle of perceived limited resources, reduced effort, withdrawal, perceived resourcelessness, and so on.

As before, the use of the graded task assignment can help patients more realistically assess what resources are required to complete a task, once the goal has broken down into more manageable parts. It is important for the therapist to ascertain what the patient perceives is required to complete the task and to determine whether he or she expects to be able to engage with and complete the task. Patients frequently state, "I'm too tired," "It's not worth the work," "It's too hard," and the like. Therapists are attentive to cognitive distortions in these expectancy appraisals, aiming to help patients identify and correct all-or-none thinking and minimization of resources.

As before, it is helpful for the therapist to introduce a continuum perspective so that the patient can overcome the tendency to see things as categorically burdensome. The continuum perspective could be introduced through the metaphor of a gasoline tank ranging from near–empty, to a quarter full, all the way to full. The patient identifies activities that are easy to do on a full tank, still relatively easy but somewhat harder at three-quarters full, and so on, down to tasks, activities, situations, etc., that are perceived as overwhelming. The first benefit of the continuum approach is that a range of activities can be identified as "doable" even under a higher stress load. Second, with this continuum approach, patients develop the ability to reduce the initial negative automatic response of choosing not to make an effort, because some activities have been idiosyncratically labeled as "doable." Third, the approach identifies more difficult demands that initially seem out of reach to be brought into reach through graded task assignments, role playing, and problem-solving strategies.

This approach allows for a collaborative determination of which activities may be legitimately beyond reach versus those that can be typically achieved. Patients arrive at a more nuanced understanding of their personal abilities so that they can more realistically assess when to "push" because they can reach their goal and when to "accept" because it may be temporarily beyond reach. One common additional problem is that patients worry about experiencing "stimulus overload" if they try exposing themselves to activities that require sustained effort or to complex social activities that include heightened interpersonal demands. The therapist can address this fear by having patients identify and rank situations according to how "challenging" they seem and to conduct graduated exposure exercises.

Another concern of patients is one of expectations: If they make an effort and accomplish more on a given day, then others will begin to request more of them to a level beyond comfort. Similarly, patients fear that making an effort and accomplishing something well will lead to a greater failure the next time they have to do something similar. These beliefs contribute further to apathy and lack of goal directedness. Therapists aim to elicit and work on these fears as they pertain to scheduled activities. As suggested earlier, efforts here may require coordination with family members and caregivers not to communicate increased expectations during early periods of behavioral change.

SUMMARY

We have outlined a cognitive approach to the treatment of negative symptoms that highlights strategies to limit patterns of disengagement following internal and external triggers of stress as well as strategies to rebuild patients' enthusiasm and resources to reengage in pursuits left behind. It has been our clinical experience that therapists feel most helpless and hopeless when attempting to discuss and change their patients' apparent behavioral inertia. However, framing these symptoms in cognitive-behavioral terms provides a road map for how patients can overcome the pattern of passivity and withdrawal in their day-to-day lives.

CHAPTER 12

Cognitive Assessment and Therapy of Formal Thought Disorder

As mentioned in Chapter 6, formal thought disorder is probably the symptom of schizophrenia least explored in the field of cognitive therapy for schizophrenia. As such, treatment of this type of positive symptom receives little attention. In fact, many studies in this area exclude those potential subjects who exhibit significant formal thought disorder due to its interference with the very process of therapy, which involves verbal communication. Even when allowing as subjects those who demonstrate formal thought disorder, no studies to date have reported the effects of cognitive therapy on formal thought disorder itself. In short, despite being found anecdotally to be useful, techniques employed specifically for formal thought disorder have not been systematically tested for their effectiveness. Outcome studies that include a focus on formal thought disorder are needed to elevate the status of knowledge about the usefulness of cognitive therapy for formal thought disorder to that of the other symptoms of schizophrenia.

Despite the lack of formal experimentation in this domain, it is useful to learn of the current status of assessment and treatment of formal thought disorder, as is outlined in this chapter. Formal thought disorder can be as disabling as the other symptoms of schizophrenia, limiting social interactions, scholastic achievement, and job placement. Furthermore, formal thought disorder can impede the use of cognitive therapy for the other symptoms of schizophrenia as well as for any depression, anxiety, or anger problems. Addressing formal thought disorder can open the door to treatment of these other symptoms.

Based on the cognitive formulation of formal thought disorder established in Chapter 6, stressful situations are seen as eliciting a disruption in the organization of thought that is most evident in the production of speech. Formal thought disorder is seen as a physiological response to stress similar to stuttering but at an earlier stage of speech production than motoric output. This outlook is based on the observations of the varying severity of formal thought disorder, with increases in severity related to the presence of stressful situations. Given this formulation, treatment centers on examining dysfunctional automatic thoughts, attitudes, assumptions, beliefs, and schemas in a manner similar to the treatments for emotional disorders such as depression, anxiety, and anger.

There are a few modifications particular to formal thought disorder, however. A necessary additional ingredient in working with a person who has a formal thought disorder is the use of a battery of techniques aimed at reducing the formal thought disorder directly so that cognitive therapy may proceed sufficiently unhampered by the communication barriers presented by this symptom. As well, extra effort needs to be made in determining what meaning, if any, might be camouflaged in the verbal content of disordered speech. It is easy for important information to be lost in the crowd of apparently senseless utterances. Finally, there may be themes in the automatic thoughts, similar to the case of negative symptoms, related to low expectations of success, but perhaps more specific to success (or lack thereof) in social interaction, particularly communication.

As with other symptoms of schizophrenia, as well as with symptoms of mood disorders, treatment also centers on cognitive, emotional, and behavioral reactions to the symptom itself. Since a person with formal thought disorder often has poor insight, there might be a lack of distress associated with this symptom itself. However, the social distancing and functional limitations created by formal thought disorder might produce a secondary distress that can be addressed using standard cognitive-behavioral therapy techniques.

Whereas treatment of most symptoms of schizophrenia (and other psychological conditions) depends on first conducting a detailed assessment, preliminary treatment of formal thought disorder is often necessary as a first step before detailed assessment, which relies on meaningful communication, can proceed. The assessment of the presence, nature, and severity of formal thought disorder can be made to some extent by direct observation using standardized assessment measures. Assessment of situational triggers of onset and worsening or reduction of symptoms might also be made from observations in session and discussion with family members or agency staff. Developmental history of the symptoms as well as their effects on functioning can also be procured from family or staff members. However, assessment of the cognitive components of automatic thoughts, beliefs, expectancies, appraisals, and assumptions, and of associated mood states, hinges on sufficient reduction in the formal thought disorder to allow for adequate communication. The complete assessment of formal thought disorder ultimately includes all these components as well as a cognitive case conceptualization explaining their interactions. An overview of the treatment approach for formal thought disorder can be seen in Table 12.1.

ASSESSMENT

Assessment of Symptoms/Cognitions

Formal assessment of the nature and severity of formal thought disorder can be made with a limited number of standardized rating scales. Some instruments have formal thought disorder as a single item on a general schizophrenia rating scale (e.g., PANSS, BPRS). Two that delineate the subtypes of formal thought disorder are Andreasens's Thought, Language, and Communication (TLC) scale (Andreasen, 1979) and the subsequent widely used Scale for the Assessment of Positive Symptoms (SAPS; Andreasen, 1984c). The SAPS is sufficient for determining the severity of the various types of formal thought disorder, as outlined in Chapter 6. Here are examples for each of the categories of formal thought disorder:

- Derailment (or loose associations): "I went to buy some food. Loose lips sink ships."
- Tangentiality: Therapist: "How are you feeling today?" Patient: "There's nothing in the bucket."
- Loss of goal (or drifting): "I want to talk about going back to school. I went to school when I was young. I have a younger brother. He lives in Oregon."
- Incoherence (or word salad): "Little does he know . . . no life . . . a little bit more . . . fast pace . . . lifeboat."
- Illogicality: "I should be able to get a job easily since many people work long hours."
- Neologisms: "I felt a little dizziwhelmed."

TABLE 12.1. Cognitive Assessment and Therapy for Formal Thought Disorder

Assessment

- Assessing symptoms/cognitions
  - Assessing frequency and severity of formal thought disorder using open-ended questions
  - Observing antecedents in session of occurrence or worsening of formal thought disorder
  - Assessing cognitive distortions related to occurrence of formal thought disorder if the patient is aware of its occurrence
  - Assessing cognitive distortions related to stressful situations

- Conducting a functional assessment
  - Identifying triggers of occurrence or worsening of formal thought disorder
  - Assessing emotional and behavioral responses to occurrence and consequences of formal thought disorder
  - Assessing beliefs and appraisals associated with formal thought disorder, including those related to socialization stress
  - Identifying historical antecedents of formal thought disorder and of potentially related conditions, such as socialization stress
  - Assessing motivating factors for formal thought disorder

- Developing the case conceptualization
  - Synthesizing distal and proximal factors that contributed to the development and the present occurrences of formal thought disorder:
    - Predisposing factors
    - Precipitating factors
    - Perpetuating factors
    - Protective factors
  - Assessing core beliefs in terms of the cognitive triad

Treatment

- Providing psychoeducation and normalization
  - Assessing and developing awareness of symptom occurrences
  - Educating the patient about the stress–vulnerability model
  - Normalizing formal thought disorder

- Socializing the patient to the cognitive model
  - Developing awareness of the interaction between events, thoughts, feelings, and behaviors as they pertain to formal thought disorder

- Implementing cognitive and behavioral approaches
  - Using communication-clarification techniques in session
  - Addressing the handling of stressful situations, including consequences of exhibiting formal thought disorder
  - Targeting core beliefs associated with socialization stress
  - Deciphering, confirming, and addressing relevant material contained within formal thought disorder communication

- Word approximations: "I need to gather time to clean my room."
- Blocking: "I took a walk in the park . . . (*long pause*) . . . someone was walking a dog."
- Poverty of content of speech: "My goal is to do things that I want to do in my life so that I can accomplish them and know that I did them while I was alive and having goals."
- Concreteness: "I can have a goal if I play hockey."
- Perseveration: "She's tall for her age. [pause] She's tall for her age."
- Clanging: "That looks nice, spice, twice, lice, mice."
- Echolalia: Therapist: "How long have you lived there?" Patient: " . . . have you lived there?"

Currently, there is no scale for formal thought disorder that is parallel to the Psychotic Symptom Rating Scales for hallucinations and delusions (PSYRATS; Haddock et al., 1999). Such a scale would separate out different aspects of severity, such as duration, frequency, severity (in terms of comprehensibility of speech), distress, and functional impact. However, these categories can be assessed directly by therapists without a formal assessment tool. An untested sample rating scale (Thought Disorder Rating Scale; THORATS) is available in Appendix H.

Assessment of formal thought disorder, with or without rating scales, depends on listening to the patient carefully. Sometimes a therapist will think that a word or two has been missed while listening to a patient when, in fact, it is formal thought disorder on the patient's part and not a lapse in attention on the therapist's part. To detect formal thought disorder, it is necessary to allow for lengthy responses with an open-ended question such as "Can you tell me a bit about yourself?" early in the initial interview, rather than rattling off a series of short-answer questions.

Since patients often have poor insight into the presence of formal thought disorder, it is difficult to assess, by direct questioning, various aspects of the factors involved in producing occurrences or exacerbations of it. Precipitants of other symptoms of schizophrenia are more readily obtained. Patients can more easily report when they hear voices or when odd beliefs come to mind, and what was happening at the time. With formal thought disorder, the therapist needs to rely on close observation of the context in which formal thought disorder presents or is changed in severity in session. This context can include who is present (e.g., family members), what topics are being discussed, the affect of the patient, and recent situations (e.g., starting a job).

Direct discussion of formal thought disorder would require education of the patient regarding what formal thought disorder is and how it manifests in him or her. Many sessions of building rapport may have to precede this discussion. As with other symptoms, the starting point is the patient's expressed issues. Connections between these issues or problems and formal thought disorder can be made by the therapist in a gradual manner. The presenting problems may be consequences or causes of the formal thought disorder. It may be difficult to assess the cognitions preceding and following the occurrence of formal thought disorder, since such an assessment would require the patient's awareness of when these symptoms are occurring. Further complicating the picture is the likelihood that the cognitions associated with formal thought disorder are disordered themselves. Until a patient has a clear understanding of the nature of formal thought disorder, assessment of the cognitions related to formal thought disorder will depend on observations by the therapist of antecedents to the in-session instances of symptom onset or variability.

An alternative approach, once the therapist notices the connection between symptoms and stressful situations, is to talk with the patient in terms of stress. In other words, focus on assessment of anxiety and use this as a guide. Ask the patient what situations seem to bring on stress, what thoughts are associated with these situations, how he or she notices stress, and even whether stress makes it harder to communicate or think clearly.

Conducting a Functional Assessment

As with the other symptoms of schizophrenia, a comprehensive functional assessment includes a developmental history and information about cognitive distortions, eliciting and preventing events, common triggers and safeguards, dysfunctional attitudes, interpretations, core beliefs, schemas, and cognitive, emotional, and behavioral responses to the symptoms and their social and functional consequences. The level of insight into each of these components is another ingredient of the functional assessment.

This assessment is derived partly from taking a detailed history from the patient and, if permitted, from family and agency staff members. Other information emanates from ongoing session interviews. The therapist may need to ask about known situations rather than asking for examples of emotional situations. For example, a therapist may know that a patient stays with parents on the weekends and therefore ask at each session how the weekend went, was it comfortable or stressful, what thoughts came to mind, and so forth.

As in depression and anxiety disorders, specific types of automatic thoughts and distorted beliefs may lead to the occurrence of formal thought disorder symptoms. Defeatist attitudes regarding social performance and speech performance are likely candidates. Preliminary research by some of us supports this idea: Patients with elevated thought disorder tend to express heightened concern regarding the possibility of being rejected by others. Further, rejection sensitivity moderates the relationship between cognitive impairment (attention, working memory, and executive function) and thought disorder, a finding that is independent of hallucinations, delusions, negative symptoms, depression, and anxiety (Grant & Beck, 2008d). We propose that negative appraisals about acceptance instigate communication anomalies in individuals with a pre-existing diathesis for imperfect speech production. While this research is in its infancy, we believe that the understanding of formal thought disorder will be greatly advanced by studies exploring associated beliefs and expectations.

According to Kingdon and Turkington (2005), garbled communication can result from various psychological/motivational contributions. Assessment of these motivating factors can uncover potential avenues for treatment. These reasons include diversion from uncomfortable topics, avoidance of direct interactions with others, desire to challenge or tease others, and grandiosity in the sense of having a "hyperintelligent language."

Developing the Case Conceptualization

The case conceptualization brings together the various past and present factors, gathered in the functional assessment, to formulate a story of how they influence(d) the onset and maintenance of the patient's formal thought disorder symptoms.

As with the other symptoms of schizophrenia, historical antecedents of the formal thought disorder can be helpful in formulating the case conceptualization. Genetic factors certainly play an important role, but the therapist should also try to identify life events both distal and proximal to the initial onset of formal thought disorder, if that period of onset can be pinpointed. If not, it is still useful to recognize what events precede initiation, exacerbation, or remission of these symptoms. As with other symptoms, the factors that affect vulnerability to formal thought disorder can be categorized as predisposing (e.g., family history of schizophrenia, obstetrical complications), precipitating (e.g., real or imagined interpersonal rejection, such as the birth of a younger sibling), perpetuating (e.g., social isolation, being teased), and protective (e.g., good social support from family, personal interests).

Since it is difficult to know with certainty what factors specifically led to the onset and maintenance of the symptoms, it is best to collect general information about premorbid events regardless of a definitive connection to the symptoms. These include early learning experiences and traumatic events (including such incidents as frequent changes of residents, family financial stresses, death of a loved one, being held back in school). The onset of formal thought disorder might not have occurred abruptly, so any changes in speech patterns should be assessed (e.g., stuttering, making up words, talking gibberish to oneself, rhyming words under one's breath). If further research confirms that formal thought disorder is related to social aversion, then early signs of shyness and social isolation should also be examined. After the onset of symptoms, coping behaviors tend to develop to manage the symptoms as well as their consequences. Some coping behaviors, such as social isolation, may also function as perpetuating factors as well as early signs of symptom formation. Similarly, the negative consequences of symptoms often add to their perpetuation. The timing and sequence of the various factors and symptoms can give clues as to what led to what, but be aware of the multiple roles (as precipitant, consequence, and early sign) of any factor.

Although assessing the factors prior to, and soon after, onset of the symptoms depends on recall by the patient and family and therefore tends to be sketchy, assessment of current specific stressors leading to variations in symptom severity relies additionally on the skills of the therapist to notice changes in severity and link these to current situations and to the patient's cognitions. Cognitions can include attitudes about the cognitive triad of self, others (the world), and the future.

The case conceptualization should produce a problem and goal list that includes formal thought disorder and its consequences, even if the patient is not yet ready to recognize its occurrence. After all, case conceptualizations help guide the therapist in conducting therapy even before the time is right for its presentation to the patient.

TREATMENT

Treatment begins with rapport building and assessment. Coping strategies to reduce stress quickly may be needed to allow therapy to proceed. When appropriate, psychoeducation (including normalization) is introduced to reduce stigma and improve understanding of symptoms. Introduction to the cognitive model might happen in one session, when the patient is ready, or it might be gradually incorporated across a number of sessions until all the pieces of the model have been demonstrated by examples and can be then described as a whole unit to the patient. Specific cognitive and behavioral approaches are introduced, as needed. In the case of formal thought disorder, behavioral approaches are often needed to bring about the sufficiently clear communication upon which the other stages (psychoeducation, normalization, and socialization to the cognitive model) depend. Therefore, the order presented here is not necessarily the order of stages of therapy for every patient; stages need to be adjusted to the particular symptoms and individual patient.

Psychoeducation and Normalizing

As with the other symptoms of schizophrenia, educating the patient about the nature and causes of these symptoms can help demystify them and reduce the stigma associated with them. However, the patient's lack of insight about schizophrenia makes this process difficult and delicate. With formal thought disorder, it is even more difficult due to the lack of insight that there is anything wrong at all. This lack of insight seems to generally exceed that associated with other symptoms of schizophrenia. Patients can recognize voices as being a problem. Delusions are typically not recognized as delusions, but the subject matter of the belief is seen as pertinent. Patients may not directly recognize negative symptoms, but they can see the immediate effects of avolition and asociality (no job, no relationship). With formal thought disorder (as well as affective flattening and alogia), the patient is usually not even aware of the symptom, let alone able to identify the symptom as a problem, or further, as part of a condition.

Psychoeducation begins, then, with assessing the patient's degree of insight into the occurrence of the symptoms. Given the strong probability of poor insight, the therapist first will need to illustrate the consequences of the symptoms. The patient may be aware that others do not understand his or her speech or avoid him or her. With time and the establishment of rapport, the therapist can begin to point out occasions in session when symptoms occur. Sometimes it is necessary for a patient to hear a tape of the disordered speech to be able to notice the problem. Care needs to be taken in educating a patient about what is likely an ignored problem. Awareness could lead to embarrassment, anxiety, depression, or anger. Some patients can be rid of formal thought disorder without ever having been aware of its presence. Therefore, the therapist needs to weigh the consequences of improving insight. As in other aspects of cognitive therapy, an individualized approach is best. If insight is an appropriate goal, or if it occurs spontaneously, the therapist should be prepared for emotional reactions. Educating the patient about how insight can lead to improvement can provide hope in the face of previously hidden difficulties.

Once awareness of the presence of symptoms is achieved, psychoeducation focuses on explanations for the symptoms. Again, it is an individualized endeavor in that some patients do not want, nor would they benefit from, an explanation. Some already have an explanation, and it is therefore useful to begin by assessing the patient's own current understanding of the causes of his or her symptoms. Some patients associate symptoms with schizophrenia. The therapist needs to explore what *schizophrenia* means to the patient, since for some it could be just a phrase learned without any depth of meaning. The therapist can proceed, if appropriate, to provide education about schizophrenia.

Regardless of whether the patient is informed about schizophrenia, the therapist can present the stress–vulnerability model in general terms. Vulnerability derives from various biological, psychological, and social causes that are understood by different patients to different degrees. The effect of stress on this vulnerability is demonstrated both in terms of initial onset and early development of the symptoms (predisposing factors) as well as current occurrences (precipitating factors). The most influential demonstrations of the connection between stress and symptom occurrence are those that happen in session. As samples accumulate, formulation of the case conceptualization evolves. Eventually, the therapist presents the individualized conceptualization to the patient, either as a whole or in parts, depending on readiness. Typical triggers, expectancies, and cognitive distortions are discussed. Any particular emotional state associated with symptom onset can be identified and examined in terms of cognitive progenitors. As connections are made between situations, cognitions, emotions, and formal thought disorder symptoms, the stigma associated with the symptoms and their consequences can be reduced as the patient gains an understanding of this process.

If a patient is aware of symptoms and views them as stigmatizing, learning about the connection between the symptoms and stress can normalize the symptoms. The therapist can draw comparisons to the way other people respond to stress, including tremors, stuttering, sweating, avoidance, nail biting, hyperventilating, and so on. In addition to reducing the stigma through normalization, presentation of the stress–symptom formulation can provide hope by revealing a means of experiencing symptom reduction: namely, by reducing stress.

The therapist proceeds to normalize formal thought disorder by providing examples of how these symptoms can arise in almost everyone. Nearly all of us have experienced a slip of tongue even without being under stress. Poets and writers use literary license to create compositions that could easily be viewed as formal thought disorder. The therapist can bring in examples of the books of Lewis Carroll, James Joyce, and John Lennon.

Certain conditions can create disorganized thought and speech. These include:

- Intoxicating drugs, such as alcohol and certain medications
- Drifting into or just coming out of sleep
- Sleep deprivation
- Public speaking (or other stressful situations)
- Having much to say in too short a period of time
- Illness, such as a viral infection
- Medical conditions such as thyroid disorders

Both psychoeducation and normalizing help to destigmatize the condition of formal thought disorder and provide hope by suggesting that it can be corrected and managed.

Socializing the Patient to the Cognitive Model

Demonstrating connections between stressful situations and the onset or worsening of symptoms of formal thought disorder (or their consequences, if insight is still lacking) is often the beginning of socializing the patient to the cognitive model. The cognitive components are added next in an effort to illustrate how situations are deemed stressful because of the attitudes, appraisals, interpretations, assumptions, and beliefs about them. The cognitive model takes shape as repeated episodes of events leading to cognitions, cognitions resulting in emotions, and emotions producing symptoms of formal thought disorder, are discussed in session. If able, the patient can enhance this knowledge by producing dysfunctional thought records as part of homework. Otherwise, this process takes place in session. Again, the best examples tend to be those happening in sessions when the patient can more easily recall automatic thoughts, emotions, and reactions in the form of symptoms of formal thought disorder. It may be difficult for a patient to even notice instances of formal thought disorder without the feedback from the therapist or family members.

It could be more productive to start with incidences of stress reactions regardless of whether the stress produces formal thought disorder symptoms or not. A patient's awareness of feeling stress can be used as a guide to show how stress reactions stem from automatic thoughts about situations. The patient can be socialized to the cognitive model in this general way, and his or her formal thought disorder may improve merely as a result of learning how to reduce emotional reactions to situations by evaluating cognitive appraisals of these situations. In other words, rather than focusing on the formal thought disorder, the therapist can work with the patient on cognitive models of stress reactions in general and observe whether symptoms of formal thought disorder improve as part of a general reduction in the stress response. The situations chosen should include those presented as problems by the patient, especially those relating to any goals for therapy. In this way, therapy starts with the stated goals of the patient, leads to the situations that frustrate these goals, proceeds to cognitive approaches to addressing the situations, and culminates in improvement of formal thought disorder by way of stress reduction.

In addition to learning the relationship between events, automatic thoughts, emotions, and behaviors, the patient learns how to recognize cognitive distortions and consider alternative perspectives. As ever, the approach is one of collaboration with the use of guided discovery based on a temperate questioning mode.

Behavioral and Cognitive Approaches

Manuals describing methods for applying cognitive therapy to the treatment of schizophrenia have been sparse in their handling of specific techniques for formal thought disorder. Nonetheless, the few techniques described in the literature can help previously unaware patients learn how their manner of speech is hard for others to understand and how they can improve their communication. If a patient is aware of having symptoms of formal thought disorder, the therapist can inquire whether the patient uses compensatory strategies already. These can be reinforced and incorporated into standard approaches.

Behavioral Approaches

Role playing can help patients, when taking the position of the recipient, understand how their communication is not comprehended by others (Kingdon & Turkington, 1994). This method has some support from studies showing that patients are able to explain previously expressed thought-disordered discourse (Harrow & Prosen, 1978), including providing meanings of neologisms (Foudraine, 1974), and to improve communication after listening to audiotapes of prior conversation (Satel & Sledge, 1989).

A similar, more immediate technique is that of questioning patients directly when units of speech are not understood (Nelson, 1997, 2005). Other methods include (1) the five-sentence rule, in which therapist and patient limit speech to five sentences at a time so that disorganization has less chance of worsening with length of conversation; (2) taking 2-minute relaxation breaks using deep breathing or switching to a neutral topic when emotionally laden material elicits thought disorder symptoms; and (3) asking about communication difficulties with others (Pinninti, Stolar, & Temple, 2005).

Nelson (2005) suggests conducting cognitive therapy in the earlier part of the session, then using listening with nonverbal expressions of interest and empathy when thought disorder worsens later in the session, as expected. Patients have reported to Nelson that the listening mode was helpful.

Kingdon and Turkington (2005) suggest interjecting short "guess" questions when some items seem important or are close to being understood, but allowing moments of just listening is recommended if the patient appears irritated by the questioning. They also describe how to probe thought linkage by asking the patient how one statement leads to a disconnected second statement.

Throughout the therapy sessions, the therapist has to repeatedly refocus the patient on the immediate topic. This is a way of fortifying the attentional skill. For example:

THERAPIST: What important things have happened since I saw you last?

PATIENT: My son is graduating from high school today—I—I got high on High Street, Street . . . street-cleaner . . .

THERAPIST: (*interrupting patient*) You say your son is graduating from high school. How do you feel about it?

PATIENT: I feel sad. I should be there, but my wife—midwife, baby, Baby Ruth, home run—

THERAPIST: (*refocusing patient*) Can you tell me more about how you feel regarding your son?

By repeatedly refocusing the patient, the therapist is able to get him to talk about his sadness from not attending the graduation ceremony. The expression and sharing of feelings helps to defuse the arousal and at the same time gives the patient practice in refocusing.

Since many people with thought disorder are unaware of their communication difficulties, pointing out instances of disorganized speech in session can facilitate greater recognition of this problem. In addition, the therapist's frankly pointing out when the patient's speech is not coherent erases the possibility that thought disorder persists, in part, due to listeners' acting as if they understand. Motivation for change can be enhanced by illustrating how communication problems can interfere with interpersonal relationships. With the patient's consent, encouraging family members to also mention to the patient occurrences of thought disorder can extend the awareness gained in sessions to the patient's daily life.

Cognitive Approaches

Given that people with schizophrenia exhibit more thought-disordered speech when discussing personal, emotion-laden items (Docherty, Evans, Sledge, Seibyl, & Krystal, 1994; Docherty, Hall, & Gordinier, 1998; Haddock, Wolfenden, Lowens, Tarrier, & Bentall, 1995), we suggest that another useful strategy for reducing thought disorder symptoms is to utilize therapeutic methods aimed at emotion regulation (Morrison, 2004) and stress reduction. In other words, standard cognitive therapy for managing depressive, anxiety, and anger difficulties (modified for use in those with schizophrenia) as well as for ameliorating the emotional effects of hallucinations and delusions indirectly help to improve organization of speech. (Behavioral techniques for reducing stress are also useful in this respect.)

As an example, the patient who showed an increase in thought disorder during sessions in which his mother was present got still worse when his mother made suggestions about his life, such as whether he was ready to drive again or move into his own apartment. Being in his 40s, the patient had automatic thoughts (expressed in a previous private session) of "My mother should not be telling me what to do," and "It's none of her business;

she's just trying to control me." When his mother explained that she gets involved because he has needed her assistance when he gets into trouble, he became less disorganized but still disgruntled. I further explained that the goal is to allow him to regain his greater independence but to proceed at a pace that prevents repetition of his moving forward too quickly and then getting worse again. He was able to proceed with the family session and individual sessions focused in part on his anger management.

Standard cognitive therapy in the treatment of formal thought disorder examines situations that elicit or intensify the symptoms via automatic thoughts, assumptions, and emotional and behavioral responses. These situations can be routine events that are perceived as stressful, events that most people would view as stressful, or events that are consequences of exhibiting thought disorder (such as people staring). Using guided discovery, the therapist explores the patient's cognitive distortions and alternative perspectives, noting and conceptualizing patterns of automatic thoughts in terms of core beliefs about self, others (the world), and the future. If appropriate, the therapist devises behavioral experiments to challenge beliefs.

Our cognitive conceptualization of formal thought disorder suggests an additional approach of eliciting and examining automatic thoughts associated with the presence of thought disorder. To reiterate, disparaging automatic thoughts contribute to socialization stress and worsening of thought disorder (e.g., "I might say the wrong thing" or "I'm not understood"). As rapport develops in the course of therapy, and as the patient learns that the therapist is honest and interested enough to acknowledge when he or she does not understand the patient, the patient may more easily identify automatic thoughts and core beliefs specifically associated with occurrences of thought disorder.

It is best to use reflective listening for those passages that are clearly understood so that the patient gets positive feedback for precise communication (and correction can be made if those passages are not understood correctly). Focus can then be made on the incoherent items. More general questions ("What do you mean by . . . ?") can be followed, if necessary, by suggested meanings based on the context and tone of the item in question. The therapist can ignore clearly divergent, irrelevant material (e.g., clanging) for the most part, but should take care not to "throw out the baby with the bath water" by mistaking emotionally relevant material for impertinent minutiae.

As examples of how to search for emotionally relevant material in thought-disordered communication, the samples of types of thought disorder given above are explored here for possible pertinent material or, at least, for some hidden connections:

- "I went to buy some food. Loose lips sink ships." (derailment/loose associations)
  > The patient grabbed some loose change before leaving for the store. *Loose* was then associated with a known proverb.
- THERAPIST: How are you feeling today?
  PATIENT: There's nothing in the bucket. (tangentiality)
  > The patient feels empty.
- "I want to talk about going back to school. I went to school when I was young. I have a younger brother. He lives in Oregon." (loss of goal/drifting)
  > The patient goes from one idea to another. The associated ideas seem less relevant than the initial statement, so refocusing to that would be best.
- "Little does he know . . . no life . . . a little bit more . . . . fast pace . . . lifeboat." (incoherence/word salad)
  > The patient may be thinking "I have no life" and that "life has a fast pace." The therapist needs to explore these possibilities.
- "I should be able to get a job easily since many people work long hours." (illogicality)
  > The patient may think that since other people are working hard, there must be plenty of work to go around. The therapist can explore this possible line of thinking and help the patient get a clearer picture of job availability.
- "I felt a little dizziwhelmed." (neologism)
  > The patient is overwhelmed with dizziness or overwhelmed by things such that a dizzy feeling follows.
- "I need to gather time to clean my room." (word approximation)
  > The patient needs to make time to clean the room.
- "I took a walk in the park . . . (*long pause*) someone was walking a dog." (blocking)
  > The pause could be due to the patient's not having much to say or avoidance of thoughts that came up when taking this walk.
- "My goal is to do things that I want to do in my life so that I can accomplish them and know that I did them while I was alive and having goals." (poverty of content of speech)

> The patient has no specific goals but wants to be able to accomplish something. The therapist can help the patient explore possible goals.

- "I can have a goal if I play hockey." (concreteness)
  > The patient wanted to talk about personal goals but got caught in the concrete meaning of the word. Using a series of concrete questions, the therapist can see if the patient means personal goals.
- "She's tall for her age. (*pause*) She's tall for her age." (perseveration)
  > The patient may be repeating information that has some personal meaning, or he or she may be intimidated by the height, for instance.
- "That looks nice, spice, twice, lice, mice." (clanging)
  > There is probably no meaning past the first of the rhyming words. At times, a later rhyming word might have some significance.
- THERAPIST: How long have you lived there?
  PATIENT: . . . have you lived there? (echolalia)
  > Again, there is probably no real meaning. If only certain sentences or phrases are echoed, those might have more significance.

Since the use of cognitive therapy for the treatment of schizophrenia has not yet focused on formal thought disorder, much work remains to be done to test the usefulness of these focused approaches. Improving the flow of speech can enable many people with schizophrenia and thought disorder to then engage in the approaches for hallucinations, delusions, and negative symptoms (as well as for depression, anxiety, and anger) that previously would have been hampered by the thought disorder itself. There is a Catch-22, however, of needing to address these symptoms to be able to reduce thought disorder, and needing to reduce thought disorder to be able to address these symptoms. The therapist needs to take a stepwise, leap-frog approach of moving forward on one part to facilitate progress on the other parts and oscillating between efforts on the various symptoms. Attending to the therapeutic alliance by using empathic statements and reflective listening as well as starting with agenda items having less emotional strength go a long way in helping to minimize stress while initiating the therapeutic process.

SUMMARY

Cognitive therapy can be useful in the treatment of formal thought disorder. Increasing a patient's awareness of its occurrence can decrease its frequency and severity. Examining and correcting automatic thoughts that are precipitants to the stress leading to thought disorder can do the same, perhaps in a more enduring manner, as previously tense situations are evaluated better. In other words, the same principles behind the use of cognitive therapy for depression, anxiety, anger, and other conditions can be applied as well to formal thought disorder.

CHAPTER 13

Cognitive Therapy
and Pharmacotherapy

The use of cognitive therapy (as well as other psychosocial interventions) in the treatment of schizophrenia does not eliminate the current need for using medication to ameliorate the symptoms of this condition. Cognitive therapy is meant both to supplement the use of medication in lessening the impact and severity of these symptoms and to address the psychological meaning behind psychotic symptoms in order to recognize (in a manner often missing in straightforward medication management) the human face associated with the experiences of hallucinations, delusions, thought disorder, and the negative syndrome.

Some have argued that medication is not needed in the treatment of schizophrenia when sufficient psychotherapy is provided. Although this may be true for certain other forms of psychosis, it is not likely to be the case for schizophrenia. The *personal preference* of a practitioner to avoid the use of medication is not a good reason for denying medication treatment to those who could benefit from this form of care and who may experience detrimental consequences if denied it. The use of cognitive and other forms of therapy may lessen the amount of medication needed but not eliminate that need completely. Future advances in our understanding of schizophrenia may produce medication-free treatment protocols, but that is not the situation currently.

On the other extreme of the biopsychosocial spectrum is the belief that the ability of neurophysiology-altering substances (i.e., psychotropic medications) to produce changes in cognition, emotions, and behavior in those with schizophrenia means that the etiology is wholly based in neurophysiology. The usefulness of antipsychotic medications that increase serotonin or decrease dopamine does not, *quid pro quo*, mean that schizophrenia is due to imbalances in these chemicals. By analogy, the usefulness of a pain medication after incorrectly lifting a heavy load does not imply that the etiology of the pain is a deficit in opioid neurotransmitters. Psychological stressors (acute traumatic events and/or years of lower-level stressful situations) as well as psychological reactions to those stressors may produce psychiatric conditions, including schizophrenia, that are then treatable by altering brain chemistry. These stressors and the reactions to them either alter neurotransmitter levels or they have some effect that is then partially reversed by chemically altering the levels of certain neurotransmitters. In the back pain example, pain is produced by the lifting, mediated by pain neurotransmitters (substance P), and relieved by increasing the opioid neurotransmitter effect by providing exogenous opioids. Again, the pain is not due to an opioid insufficiency, just as psychosis may be due to something besides purely a dopamine excess. Certainly, the ability of medications that alter certain neurotransmitters to alleviate psychotic symptoms has helped to guide research into the etiology and development of schizophrenia as well as to partially ease the burden of this condition. However, our premise is that biological *and* psychological factors contribute to both the etiology and the treatment of schizophrenia.

This chapter includes a presentation of the primary medications used in the treatment of psychosis, a discussion of how cognitive therapy can mimic the effects of pharmacotherapy, and an examination of how to integrate cognitive therapy and medication management.

PHARMACOTHERAPY

The Introduction of Neuroleptics

As with many other classes of psychotropic medications, the antipsychotic medications were discovered serendipitously. In 1952, Henri Laborit, a French physician, using chlorpromazine (brand name Thorazine) as a sedative for minor surgery, observed how it caused patients to have less interest in their environment. This finding led to its use in psychiatric patients and ultimately to a revolution in the treatment of schizophrenia. Psychiatric institutions ("insane asylums") were now able to start releasing their occupants to the communities as chlorpromazine, and the multitude of similar medications that soon followed, reduced the severity of their patients' psychoses.

These antipsychotic medications have been variably called neuroleptics (based on their effects on motor functions) and major tranquilizers (as opposed to the minor tranquilizers, such as the benzodiazepines, including clonazepam [Klonopin], alprazolam [Xanax], and diazepam [Valium]). With the advent in the 1980s of the use of a newer type of antipsychotic medication, members of this older group were then renamed first-generation, typical, classical, or conventional antipsychotics to distinguish them from the newer second- and third-generation, or atypical, antipsychotics.

In the mid-1970s, Seeman, Chau-Wong, Tedesco, and Wong (1975) discovered that the first-generation antipsychotics had their effect by blocking dopamine receptors, in particular the D_2 subtype; hence the term *dopamine antagonist antipsychotics* (DAAs). It is this property and the usefulness of these medications in the treatment of schizophrenia that led to the dopamine theory of schizophrenia. As stated above, treatment does not imply etiology. However, the discovery that first-generation antipsychotics block D_2 receptors led to the extensive search for how dopamine transmission may be related to the symptoms of schizophrenia. It was logical to suppose that if blocking the transmission of dopamine from one nerve cell to the other helps alleviate psychosis, excess dopamine transmission must be the primary psychophysiological cause of schizophrenia. However, this hypothesis is still not confirmed. What is known with some certainty is that the antipsychotics work via postsynaptic D_2 receptor blockage.

Although the rapid sedative effects of many of these antipsychotics are useful in managing the acute agitation often seen in psychiatric emergency rooms and inpatient units, it is the dopamine blockade and the reactive up-regulation (increased number of receptors in reaction to the blockage) of postsynaptic D_2 receptors occurring 3–6 weeks later that account for the delayed antipsychotic effects. Positive emission tomography shows that 65–70% occupancy in D_2 receptors is needed to achieve clinically significant results (Nasrallah & Smeltzer, 2002).

DAAs are divided into a number of subclasses based on their chemical structures (listed in Table 13.1). These medications have half-lives ranging from 16 to 45 hours. A half-life is the time it takes for half of the medication to be eliminated from the body. This elimination is usually by way of demethylation or hydroxylation in the liver and excretion by the kidney or gastrointestinal tract. Some DAAs (haloperidol and fluphenazine) have

TABLE 13.1. Dopamine Antagonist Antipsychotic Medications

Class/subclass	Generic name	Brand name(s)
Phenothiazines		
Aliphatic	Chlorpromazine	Thorazine
	Triflupromazine	Vesprin
	Promazine	Sparine
Piperazine	Trifluoperazine	Stelazine
	Fluphenazine	Prolixin, Permitil
	Perphenazine	Trilafon
	Prochlorperazine	Compazine
	Acetophenazine	Tindal
	Butaperazine	Repoise
	Carphenazine	Proketazine
Piperidine	Thioridizine	Mellaril
	Mesoridizine	Serentil
	Piperacetazine	Quide
Butyrophenones	Haloperidol	Haldol
	Droperidol	Inapsine
Thioxanthines	Thiothixene	Navane
	Chlorprothixene	Taractan
Dibenzoxazepine	Loxapine	Loxitane
Dihydroindolone	Molindone	Moban, Lidone
Diphenylbutylpiperidine	Pimozide	Orap

depot injection formulations with a decanoate attachment allowing for a half-life of 2–6 weeks, thus requiring only biweekly or monthly injections. DAAs are highly protein-bound, meaning that they attach strongly to proteins, such as albumin, found in the bloodstream. They are also lipophilic, meaning that they bind to fats (lipids). Therefore, they have high concentrations in the brain.

Although DAA medications have reduced the suffering of many individuals and their families, they do have a number of limitations and adverse effects. For one, they do not help every individual who has schizophrenia. Although in most cases, if one medication is not effective, another may be so, there are individuals whose psychotic symptoms are not significantly affected by any medication. Secondly, DAAs usually treat only the positive symptoms (hallucinations, delusions, and thought disorder), not the negative symptoms (excepting those aspects stemming from reactions to the presence of positive symptoms) or cognitive deficits. Finally, as with all medications, there are a host of potential side effects. These include the chronically debilitating tardive dyskinesia (a late-occurring involuntary movement disorder) and the potentially fatal neuroleptic malignant syndrome (consisting, in part, of hyperthermia and severe rigidity). To begin to comprehend these limitations, it is helpful to understand the physiology involved in the actions of these medications.

The Pharmacodynamics of DAAs

The benefits and side effects of DAAs can be described in terms of the neurotransmitter systems they affect (Nasrallah & Smeltzer, 2002; Stahl, 1999; Wilkaitis, Mulvihill, & Nasrallah, 2004). In addition to dopamine, other involved neurotransmitter systems are the muscarinic subtype of the cholinergic system, the α_1-adrenergic system, and the histaminergic-1 (H_1) system.

The dopamine system has five neurotransmitter subtypes (D_1–D_5) and four major pathways in the brain. The mesolimbic and mesocortical tracts start in the ventral tegmental area (VTA) in the midbrain and travel to the nucleus accumbens (part of the limbic system) and cortex, respectively. It is believed that the positive symptoms of hallucinations, delusions, and thought disorder are due to overactivity of dopamine in the mesolimbic system and that the negative symptoms are due to decreased dopamine activity in the mesocortical system. The nigrostriatal tract originates in the substantia nigra, projects to the basal ganglia, and is involved in movement control. Degeneration in this system can lead to Parkinson's disease. The tuberoinfundibular tract connects the hypothalamus to the anterior pituitary gland to inhibit the release of prolactin, an enzyme that promotes milk production.

Although the dopamine blockade of the mesocortical projection (in addition to the mesolimbic one) aids in alleviating positive psychotic symptoms, it can also worsen the patient's negative symptoms (decreased motivation, speech, and emotional expression). Reducing dopamine transmission by blocking at least 80% of the available postsynaptic receptors in the nigrostriatal tract can lead to the extrapyramidal system (EPS) side effects, including parkinsonian-like symptoms of intention tremors (tremors during initiated movements), shuffling gait, and masked facies (an expressionless face). Additional side effects include acute dystonia (spasms or sustained muscle contractions), akathisia (motor restlessness), akinesia (lack of movement), and, as noted, tardive dyskinesia (TD), a severely debilitating condition characterized by involuntary choreoathetoid (dance-like or writhing) movements. TD is believed to be due to up-regulation of postsynaptic D_2 receptors, can occur years after initiating treatment with DAAs, and is unrelated to dose.

The dopaminergic neurons in the nigrostriatal pathway inhibit acetylcholine neurons in the striatum. Therefore, when antipsychotics block dopamine, acetylcholine release is increased, leading to the EPS side effects. Thus, anticholinergic agents (that block acetylcholine transmission) can help to offset this increase in acetylcholine release. However, this can lead to anticholinergic side effects, already present due to the anticholinergic activity of DAAs themselves.

The dopamine blockage in the tuberoinfundibular tract disinhibits the release of prolactin, leading to hyperprolactinemia, which can result in galactorrhea (lactation unrelated to pregnancy), decreased sexual desire/function, gynecomastia (male breast enlargement), infertility, and amenorrhea (lack of menstruation).

Another severe side effect that may become life-threatening is neuroleptic malignant syndrome (NMS). Believed to be caused by dopamine effects on the hypothalamic temperature regulation system, NMS involves severe body stiffness and excessive body temperature. Relief from NMS requires emergency room treatment.

In addition to side effects caused by unintended dopamine blockades, there are adverse effects due to antagonistic effects of DAAs on other neurotransmitters. Among these is the muscarinic (M_1) subtype of the cholinergic system, leading to possible side effects of dry mouth, blurred vision, constipation, urinary retention, sedation, and slowed cognition.

Two other neurotransmitters blocked are the alpha-adrenergic (a_1) and histaminergic (H_1) systems, leading, in the former case, to sedation and orthostatic hypotension (decreased blood pressure when rising from lying to sitting to standing, often producing dizziness) and in the latter case, to sedation and weight gain.

Beneficial effects and side effects of DAAs can be grouped according to levels of potency. Haloperidol, trifluoperazine, thiothixene, and fluphenazine are considered high-potency DAAs; chlorpromazine, mesoridazine, and thioridazine are considered low-potency; and most of the other antipsychotics lie somewhere in between these two. Since high potency is due to higher affinity for D_2 receptors, medications with high potency also carry with them the detrimental effects of dopamine blockage, namely the increased possibility of EPS side effects, TD, and NMS. They also exhibit prominent α_1-adrenergic side effects. On the other hand, the side effects associated with the H_1 and M_1 neurotransmitters are less severe when using high-potency DAAs. Low-potency antipsychotics have the opposite profile—less EPS side effects, TD, NMS, and α_1-adrenergic side effects and more histaminergic and muscarinic side effects.

The Advent and Advantages of Second-Generation Antipsychotics

With the reintroduction of clozapine (Clozaril), a dibenzodiazepine, in the late 1980s after an initial withdrawal from use in 1975 due to the potentially fatal side effect of agranulocytosis (severe reduction of a type of white blood cell), a new era of antipsychotic medication use began. Second-generation antipsychotics (listed in Table 13.2) have the advantages of producing less EPS and TD side effects, reduced hyperprolactinemia, and improved treatment of negative symptoms as well as cognitive and affective problems (Daniel, Copeland, & Tamminga, 2004; Goff, 2004; Lieberman, 2004b; Marder & Wirshing, 2004; Nasrallah & Smeltzer, 2002; Schulz, Olson, & Kotlyar, 2004; Stahl, 1999). It is believed that these improvements over DAAs is due to less D_2 binding (low affinity) and the addition of serotonergic ($5\text{-}HT_{2A}$) binding. In fact, second-generation antipsychotics may be termed serotonin–dopamine antagonist antipsychotics (SDAAs).

Clozapine, the first SDAA, is still considered to be the most effective. In addition to being effective in treating the positive and negative symptoms while producing less EPS and TD side effects, it has also been seen to reduce violence (including suicide) and aggression (Stahl, 1999) and improve already existing TD. Improvement with clozapine continues over years of treatment. Its use has mainly been limited by the 0.5–2% occur-

TABLE 13.2. Serotonin–Dopamine Antagonist Antipsychotic Medications

Generic name	Brand name	D 1	D 2	D 3	D 4	5-HT 1A	5-HT 1B	5-HT 1D	5-HT 2A	5-HT 2B	5-HT 2C	5-HT 3	5-HT 5	5-HT 6	5-HT 7	M 1	H 1	α 1	α 2	SRI	NRI
Clozapine	Clozaril	✓	✓	✓	✓	✓*			✓		✓	✓	✓	✓	✓	✓	✓	✓	✓		
Risperidone	Risperdal		✓						✓						✓			✓	✓		
Olanzapine	Zyprexa	✓	✓	✓	✓				✓		✓	✓		✓		✓	✓	✓			
Quetiapine	Seroquel	✓		✓*					✓		✓		✓	✓	✓		✓	✓			✓
Ziprasidone	Geodon		✓	✓		✓		✓	✓		✓				✓			✓		✓	✓
Loxapine	Loxitane	✓	✓		✓							✓	✓	✓	✓		✓	✓			
Paliperidone	Invega	✓	✓	✓					✓		✓				✓			✓	✓		
Asenapine	Saphris	✓	✓	✓	✓	✓	✓		✓	✓	✓	✓	✓	✓			✓	✓	✓		
Iloperidone	Fanapt	✓	✓	✓					✓		✓			✓	✓		✓	✓	✓		
Lurasidone	Latuda		✓						✓				✓		✓						

Based on information from Neuroscience Education Institute (2010).

Note. D, dopaminergic; 5-HT, serotonergic (5-hydroxytryptamine); M, muscarinic; H, histaminic; α, alpha-adrenergic (norepinephrine); SRI, serotonin reuptake inhibition; NRI, norepinephrine reuptake inhibition; *partial agonist.

rence of agranulocytosis, requiring blood tests of complete blood counts weekly for 6 months, then semimonthly, and eventually monthly. There are also risks for seizures, weight gain, sedation, sialorrhea (excessive drooling), diabetes mellitus (DM), and dyslipidemia (increased cholesterol and/ or triglycerides). Currently, clozapine is used for those patients who have not improved enough with other SDAAs (Practice Guideline for the Treatment of Patients with Schizophrenia, 2004).

The improvement in the lives of those taking clozapine led to a search for other medications that could do the same but without the risk of agranulocytosis. Other SDAAs now used in the United States include risperidone (Risperdal), olanzapine (Zyprexa), quetiapine (Seroquel), ziprasidone (Geodon), paliperidone (Invega), asenapine (Saphris), iloperidone (Fanapt), and lurasidone (Latuda). An older antipsychotic with similar neurotransmitter properties is loxapine (Loxitane).

Risperdone was the first SDAA introduced that did not require frequent blood tests. In 2004, the Food and Drug Administration recommended that all patients taking SDAAs take periodic blood tests for blood glucose, cholesterol, and other lipids due to the risk of DM and hypercholesterolemia (although the risk with risperidone is not as great as with clozapine and olanzapine). Initially, the dosage of risperidone was recommended to be quickly titrated to 6 milligrams (mg) a day, but this has since been altered with the finding that lower doses are effective and that at doses higher than 6 mg a day, EPS side-effect occurrence is similar to that of haloperidol. Risperidone also has a relatively greater risk of causing hyperprolactinemia compared to the other SDAAs. However, there is less weight gain than with clozapine.

Olanzapine followed risperidone with an advantage of being more highly sedating than risperidone (but less so than clozapine), thus helping with insomnia and aggression. There are only mild EPS side effects even at higher doses (above 15 mg), occasional akathisia (physical and psychological restlessness), and some transient hyperprolactinemia, but the most significant concern is the fairly common and noticeable weight gain as well as DM and hypercholesterolemia.

Quetiapine also can be helpful with aggression and cognitive deficits as well as mood, including depression and anxiety. In treating the negative symptoms it is useful only if compared to placebo but not if compared to haloperidol. It can be sedating and cause some weight gain. It may cause DM and dyslipidemia. An initial concern that it might cause cataracts (an effect discovered in a study involving beagles) is still a matter of debate (Shahzad et al., 2002).

Ziprasidone has an advantage of not being associated with DM or hypercholesterolemia, and being less likely to cause weight gain. There may be occasional akathisia, transient hyperprolatinemia, and a slightly prolonged QT interval (a measure involving the heart rhythm). This medication may help depression and anxiety, but there can be dizziness (at higher doses) and sedation (although twice-daily dosing is not uncommon, despite these potential side effects). Ziprasidone should be taken with food to increase its bioavailability.

Loxapine can cause some EPS, TD, and hyperprolactinemia side effects. It does produce less negative symptoms than the DAAs. It helps reduce some symptoms when added to clozapine (Stahl, 1999). Although introduced with many of the other DAAs, in the late 1990s it was discovered to be an SDAA, especially at lower doses. It produces the least amount of weight gain and may actually cause weight loss. In addition, it might help reduce depression.

Paliperidone is an active metabolite of risperidone, but with less EPS and sedation, possibly due to its being taken once daily. It can cause weight gain, DM, and prolactinemia.

Asenapine might be helpful in managing depression possibly due to its blocking 5-HT_{2C} and α_2. It must be taken sublingually and kept from being washed out by avoiding food or drink for 10 minutes. A common side effect is hypoesthesia (a decreased sensitivity to sensory stimuli, particularly touch).

Iloperidone may cause orthostasis and must be titrated slowly in patients at risk for orthostasis. Weight gain is comparable to that with risperidone.

Lurasidone is the newest antipsychotic medication. It can be started at its therapeutic dose since there is minimal effects on M_1 and H_1 receptors. It may also have a lower probability of side effects of EPS, akathisia, weight gain, DM, and dyslipidemia. Its blockage of 5-HT_{1A} and 5-HT_7 receptors may explain its possible antidepressant and cognition-enhancement effects.

The Pharmacodynamics of SDAAs

Serotonergic neurons project from the median raphe nuclei in the brainstem to many areas of the brain and spinal cord, including the prefrontal cortex, basal ganglia, limbic cortex, and hypothalamus. Serotonin is involved in depression, obsessive–compulsive disorder, pain suppression, memory, anxiety, appetite, sexual behavior, and sleep. Serotonin receptors include subtypes 1A, 1B, 1D (presynaptic), 2A, 2B, 2C, 3, 4, 5, 6, and 7.

In the striatum (part of the basal ganglia) and pituitary gland, serotonergic neurons inhibit the release of dopamine (targeted for D_2 receptors) by attaching to 5-HT_{2A} receptors on the axon terminals of the dopaminergic neurons. Serotonin antagonistic (blocking) actions of SDAAs prevent the inhibition of dopamine neurons by serotonin (a process known as *disinhibition*) and therefore counteract the dopamine antagonistic actions of these antipsychotics, thus preventing the EPS and hyperprolactinemia side effects more typically present with the more specific DAAs. An analogy would be a moving car (dopamine) with a foot about to press the brake pedal (serotonin) and someone (SDAA medications) holding that foot back. The disinhibition of dopamine release counteracts the blockade of dopamine at the dopamine receptors. An analogy to this would be increasing the number of goalies (dopamine antagonists) guarding a soccer goal (dopamine receptor) but also preventing (inhibiting) the referee (serotonin) from limiting the number of soccer balls (dopamine) players can shoot at the goal at one time.

Disinhibition of dopamine release by a blockade of inhibitory serotonin may also play a role in the mesocortical dopaminergic tract, resulting in a reversal of the dopamine deficit (or serotonin excess) in the cortex that may be responsible for the presence of negative symptoms.

In addition to the disinhibition of dopamine neurons via blockade of serotonergic presynaptic inhibition, there is another mechanism whereby some SDAAs, particularly clozapine and quetiapine, may prevent the adverse effects of purely blocking D_2 receptors. *Rapid dissociation* is a process in which the D_2 antagonism is short-lived, thereby limiting the effects of the blockade and reducing EPS, TD, negative symptoms, and hyperprolactinemia side effects. Presumably, the beneficial effects of reducing positive symptoms require only that D_2 receptors are blocked for short periods at a time. Clozapine and quetiapine take advantage of this property with their rapid dissociative actions (Kapur & Seeman, 2001).

As with DAAs, SDAAs affect multiple transmitter systems, leading to additional beneficial effects in some cases and to side effects (which can be beneficial for some patients in certain situations, e.g., sedation, when insomnia is a problem) in other cases. The comprehensive receptor profile of these antipsychotics include dopamine $(D_1–D_4)$, serotonin $(5\text{-HT}_{1A}, 5\text{-HT}_{1B}, 5\text{-HT}_{1D}, 5\text{-HT}_{2A-C}, 5\text{-HT}_3, 5\text{-HT}_5, 5\text{-HT}_6, 5\text{-HT}_7)$, norepinephrine $(\alpha_1, \alpha_{2A-C})$, muscarine (M_1), histamine (H_1), as well as serotonin and norepinephrine reuptake inhibition (SRI, NRI, respectively). The specific receptors affected by each SDAA are listed in Table 13.2. Although the effects of blockage in many of these receptors remains unclear, we do know (in addition to what has already been explained for dopamine and serotonin receptor blockage) that blockage of α_1-adrenergic receptors causes drowsiness, dizziness, and decreased blood pressure; of muscarinic receptors causes constipation, blurred vision, dry mouth, and drowsiness; of histaminergic receptors causes weight gain and drowsiness; and of serotonin and norepinephrine reuptake, possibly contributing to antidepressant and antianxiety effects.

Third Generation Antipsychotics and Their Pharmacodynamics

In 2002, a new type of antipsychotic medication, a dopamine partial agonist called aripiprazole (Abilify) was released for public use (Lieberman, 2004a). This medication is currently in a class by itself, although others may follow. The mechanism of action is generally that of stabilizing dopamine release so that it is increased in areas of the brain where its release is too low, decreased in areas where its release is too high, and maintained in areas where its release is sufficient. Its precise mechanism of action is unknown, but it may be that D_2 postsynaptic receptors are blocked but also stimulated to a sufficient degree. This is analogous to using shades to block out sunlight from a photography darkroom, but using lights of sufficient brightness to be able to see what one is doing. Without the shades, there might be too much light from outside, if it is daytime. Without the darkroom lights, the light blockage would be too much.

Another possible mechanism is that aripiprazole produces a balance between blockage of presynaptic D_2 receptors (that act as a thermostat-like inhibitor of dopamine release) and postsynaptic D_2 receptors. The presynaptic D_2 receptors on the dopaminergic neuron axon terminals are normally less sensitive to dopamine than are the postsynaptic D_2 receptors, so they do not cause inhibition of dopamine release until the release is too high (as with a thermostat turning off heat production at a preset temperature).

Aripiprazole has similar advantages to the SDAAs in that there is reduced EPS, TD, negative symptoms, and hyperprolactinemia side effects. There may also be advantages of reducing cognitive and mood problems. It can have activating properties in some people, but this can vary with dosing. As with ziprasidone, there is less concern regarding weight gain, DM, and dyslipidemia.

COGNITIVE THERAPY AS IT RELATES TO PHARMACOTHERAPY

Cognitive Therapy as Pharmacotherapy

The concept of the brain as a bidirectional transducer was introduced in the neurobiology chapter. The brain can transform psychological events (e.g., long-term conditions or acute traumatic situations) into physiological changes (e.g., synapse formation, synapse strengthening, cell death) as well as translating physiological alterations (e.g., use of medications, street drugs, toxins, electroconvulsive therapy) into psychological changes (e.g., thoughts, emotions, behavior). In fact, any stimulus input (e.g., conversation, a sunset, the temperature) causes physiological alterations of at least a short-term, if not a longer-term nature, and these physiological alterations can lead to other physiological alterations leading to psychological alterations in our thoughts, emotions, and behavior. There is no reason not to hypothesize that the waves of psychological stimuli provided by psychotherapy that lead to changes in thoughts, emotions, and behavior would also involve physiological changes in the brain. A few brain imaging studies have already demonstrated physiological changes of brain metabolism in certain brain regions following the use of cognitive therapy for depression and anxiety disorders (Linden, 2006; Roffman, Marci, Glick, Dougherty, & Rauch, 2005). These findings show that psychotherapy, specifically cognitive therapy, can be considered metaphorically as a form of pharmacotherapy or chemotherapy. Even if the physiological changes are not long-lasting following the termination of therapy, this would not be much different from the effects of medication, which typically require ongoing usage to maintain physiological (and psychological) effects. In fact, it is more likely that cognitive therapy would result in longer-lasting physiological changes, reflecting the acquisition of new skills in evaluating situations differently from one's habitual mode of interpretation.

To date, there have not been any brain imaging studies of the effects of cognitive therapy in the treatment of schizophrenia; however preliminary work is being done by D. Silbersweig and colleagues (personal communication, May 26, 2006), and other studies are likely to emerge in the next decade. There are a number of ways in which cognitive therapy may be predicted to lead to physiological brain changes. These include synaptic formation in neural pathways representing new thinking habits of how to interpret environmental stimuli, less frequent firing of neural pathways representing acute stress responses, and less accumulation of long-term brain responses to stress.

In the 1970s, Diamond et al. (Diamond, Rosenzweig, Bennett, Lindner, & Lyon, 1972) discovered that rats that were allowed to play in enriched environments showed growth in the cerebral cortex compared to those that were kept in more restricted environments during early development. This plasticity was later found to be due to dendritic growth and branching and synaptic development. What was once thought to be an early developmental process was later discovered to continue into adulthood. Although the long-held belief that the total number of neurons does not increase with age has been challenged by more recent findings (e.g., Eriksson, Perfilieva, Björk-Eriksson, et al., 1998), much of our learning is likely to rely on new synapses, representing connections between previously unassociated ideas, or on the strengthening of already-existing, but not often used, synapses. Therapy can be viewed as the learning of cognitive processes (e.g., examining the evidence for one's beliefs) via instruction and/or modeling. The patient then learns, through repetitive exercises, to use these habits of thoughts without reliance on the therapist. At that point, the neural connections for these new ways of thinking are more solidified in the patient's brain.

Our current methods of brain imaging may not be sensitive enough to detect these new synapses or new neural pathways, let alone the strengthening of existing synapses and pathways. There would need to be substantial changes in specific areas of the brain to produce the mass effect detectable by current methods of brain imaging. One measurement device, electroencephalography (in the form of event-related potentials), may be sensitive enough to detect such changes because it has the temporal resolution to note subtle differences in the way information is processed. However, this technique cannot pinpoint the locations in the brain where the differences in activity are occurring.

The area most likely to be affected by cognitive therapy (or psychotherapy, in general) is the frontal cortex, which is responsible for executive functions such as planning and decision making. However, these changes may not be as simple as increases or decreases in metabolic activity, as measured by current brain imaging methods. There may be some rewiring that leaves unchanged the total metabolic activity requirement. In addition to potential changes in the frontal cortex reflecting new ways of thinking, there may be changes in other brain regions secondary to the frontal cortical alterations. As a patient learns to examine the evidence for his or her beliefs, the convictions for delusions and beliefs about voices may lessen, and the stress related to those beliefs may diminish as the convictions diminish; doubting that others are poisoning his or her food may lessen the anxiety occurring while eating. There may be a decrease in activities of the amygdala, cingulate cortex, and other limbic areas as well as the phasic state of the dopamine system. This dampening of the stress response systems may further reduce the strength and frequency of psychotic symptoms by halting the vicious cycle of stimulus to stress to psychosis to increased stress, and so on. Even cognitive therapy directed at nonpsychotic stressors (e.g., anxiety about finding a job or meeting a new person; depression due to isolation) may help reduce stress and lessen the effects of the phasic response of the dopamine system, thus producing a psychologically based partial blockade of dopamine.

The long-term effects of continued cognitive therapy may be to lessen the damage produced by long-term sequelae of stress, namely, cortisol-induced hippocampal cell damage, particularly if treatment is started in the prodromal phase before much of the damage may already have been done.

Interactions of Cognitive Therapy and Medication Management

Since cognitive therapy alone cannot treat the symptoms of schizophrenia, and since medication management by itself may miss the human aspect of treatment in that the psychological meanings of symptoms may be ignored (and medication compliance may be sacrificed), there is a need to integrate these two approaches to the treatment of schizophrenia. These approaches may intersect in a number of ways. There may be psychiatrists who practice therapy as well as prescribe medication, there may be agencies with psychiatrists managing the medications and therapists providing group and/or individual psychotherapy, and there may be psychiatrists managing the medications for patients who separately see therapists for cognitive therapy. Each of these arrangements requires some coordination of these two treatment modalities. In addition, other psychosocial services, such as case management, structured housing, and day programs, as well as family involvement, come into play.

When a psychiatrist also provides cognitive therapy for patients with schizophrenia, there is the advantage of having, in one person, the means of determining how to specifically combine the two types of treatment based on consistent data (i.e., what the psychiatrist observes or is told by the patient). However, there are still factors to consider when providing dual treatment.

How much to provide of each modality is one consideration. When a patient currently on medication and in weekly cognitive therapy sessions decompensates as a result of losing a job, is it wiser to quickly increase the dose of the current antipsychotic, change medication, explore what led to the reaction regarding the job loss, or determine how the job was lost and a new one might soon be acquired? The psychiatrist may have a bias to first use cognitive therapy to see if the patient might recover as the issue is addressed in therapy. Successful recovery without changing medications could bolster the psychiatrist's pride in having a more direct impact on the patient's health than by writing out a prescription. However, there may be pressure from the family or the patient to not wait to see if the next few therapy sessions help, but instead to intervene pharmacologically. Delaying medication changes runs the risk of extending the psychosis and producing more stress, leading to worsened psychosis. On the other hand, increased doses or changed medications can be hard to reverse even after the acute episode has subsided. Months or years of increased cost and increased side effect potentials may be the price of not having first attempted to correct the situation psychotherapeutically. Even if both treatments are changed together, the psychiatrist will need to decide, once there is recovery from the episode, when it would be appropriate to reduce the medication to the earlier dose.

Having a separate psychiatrist and therapist complicates this issue in that each clinician may have different opinions as to what changes should occur in treating exacerbations. Although each may claim that his or her approach is more effective and should be the focus when decompensation occurs or even at initiation of treatment, the opposite also occurs, with each believing that the other is not doing enough to help and that he or she has done as much as possible with the single approach. The patient may get caught in the middle and even end up being the means of communication between the two clinicians.

Another source of confusion in split treatment occurs when the patient communicates different things to each clinician. This discrepancy may occur because (1) delusions or thought disorder cloud the communication with one or both of the clinicians, (2) a better rapport exists with one of them, the two clinicians ask different questions, the patient forgets, or other reasons. Add in communications with the family and outside agencies and there is the potential for multiple discrepancies as to what has been communicated.

One partial solution is for clinicians to communicate directly with each other rather than rely on the patient or family. Optimally, this could be done periodically in the presence of the patient and possibly the family and agency representatives. In this way, the key figures are hearing the same message (even if interpretations differ) and discrepancies can be addressed directly. Convenience dictates that much of the communication between clinicians will occur with them alone, but occasional team meetings would be helpful.

Communication between the psychiatrist and the therapist should include examination of the symptoms, psychological underpinnings of the symptoms, goals of the patient (as well as family and agencies), and treatment strategies of the two clinicians. They should jointly assess what has worked best and under what conditions so as to guide future treatment decisions. Knowing more about what is going on psychologically with the patient can help the psychiatrist see the human side of the patient's symptoms, improve the patient's insight and medication compliance, and open up a dialogue between the patient and psychiatrist, including discussing what schizophrenia is and how medications contribute to the treatment. Knowing more about what is going on medicinally with the patient can help the therapist understand what cognitive changes may be due to beneficial effects of the medication and what side effects may be interfering with therapy.

Using Cognitive Therapy during Medication Sessions

The principles of cognitive therapy in the treatment of schizophrenia may be applied by psychiatrists even when providing medication management only. In the United States, psychiatrists engaged in medication management typically have 15-minute sessions every 1–3 months. Although this brief period of time barely allows for proper assessment of the condition, adjustment of medication, and explanation of treatment to the patient, there are ways to incorporate cognitive therapy techniques into a medication management practice in ways that can increase the efficiency of this treatment (Pinninti, Stolar, & Temple, 2005).

As part of medication management, cognitive therapy can enhance treatment in a number of ways: It can (1) facilitate communication between the patient and psychiatrist, (2) improve the patient's insight, (3) improve medication compliance, and (4) lessen the severity of psychotic symptoms. Cognitive therapy has been recommended as a form of treatment, especially for treatment-resistant patients, in the Practice Guideline developed by the Work Group on Schizophrenia of the American Psychiatric Association (Practice Guideline for the Treatment of Patients with Schizophrenia, 2004).

One of the principles of cognitive therapy for the treatment of schizophrenia is that the patient's hallucinations and delusions may reflect, and/or be based on, automatic thoughts; that is, they may reflect the patient's ideas. In some instances, they may be ways in which a patient communicates needs and desires—but only if the communication is interpreted as such.

For example, an elderly woman living in a community residential rehabilitation housing unit and diagnosed with schizophrenia was seen monthly for delusions. She had been taking the same antipsychotic medication for years. She seemed oblivious to her condition and had blunted affect as well as other negative symptoms, and a recurring delusion that neighbors were breaking into the building at night and stealing her unborn child from her uterus. The patient never seemed to be very distressed by this delusion, and her condition was managed with medication. At one point, after months of hearing this delusion, the psychiatrist decided to ask for details. He asked the woman why she thought that her neighbors were stealing her fetus, and what evidence she had that this had happened. She replied that she would wake up and discover that "my water had broken." The psychiatrist determined from this explanation that the patient had been having episodes of enuresis that she had not reported to the staff. The exploration of the evidence for the delusion led to proper handling of the urinary incontinence that had gone unreported for so long. Later, the patient had to be treated for heart problems. The only manner in which she could describe her chest pain was by reporting a delusion in which she was being stabbed in the back but that the knife went through to her chest on the left side.

Sometimes patients communicate their needs through the use of delusions. By recognizing that most delusions are interpretations of actual events or feelings, psychiatrists can learn to utilize the delusions as openings to explore what the patient is thinking. It may take only a few short questions to uncover important pieces of information.

A middle-aged woman diagnosed with schizophrenia presented for her first visit to a psychiatrist after transferring to an unfamiliar community mental health center. She reported voices telling her that the center meant her harm by giving her medication. The psychiatrist asked her if she believed what the voices were telling her. She admitted that she was concerned that medications would make her "like a zombie," as she had seen happen to others at community mental health centers. The psychiatrist educated her about the newer antipsychotic medications and their decreased possibility of causing side effects leading to a "zombie" state. The psychiatrist also informed her of the ability to change medications if she were to develop side effects as well as her right to refuse medications at any time. She agreed to start an SDAA medication at a low dose. After a few months, she found relief from her paranoid delusions and continued her medication (with a few, brief exceptions) from then on. She reported that she came to realize how important it had been to continue the medication, especially after noticing a recurrence of the delusions when she did not faithfully take the medication. Never since the initial discussion with the psychiatrist about medication did she report any voices telling her that the agency was trying to harm her with medication.

It is worthwhile to explore the content of voices, partly by asking patients whether, and to what extent, they believe what the voices say. In this case, discussion of the voices revealed the patient's medication concerns and headed off what could have been an extensive compliance issue. The patient likely felt listened to by the psychiatrist, who used the content of the voices as a conduit to the thoughts and feelings of the patient.

One goal of using cognitive therapy in the treatment of schizophrenia is to improve insight. Part of this goal can be accomplished by educating the patient about schizophrenia as a psychiatric illness. Although this education can be achieved more thoroughly and in a gradual, deliberate manner with weekly therapy, psychiatrists can contribute to this endeavor by providing information about schizophrenia and the purpose of antipsychotic medication. Care must be taken first to determine how the patient views psychotic symptoms and schizophrenia in order to then develop a plan for working with him or her in a collaborative manner to construct alternative models of how the symptoms and illness may be conceptualized. The psychiatrist can contribute to this collaboration by maintaining contact with the therapist and adding to the patient's knowledge of how the brain works and how medications can affect brain processes. Some patients are relieved to know that their voices and delusions are not their own fault and do not signal real dangers but are part of a medical illness. This knowledge (sometimes kept from them for years, possibly due to the belief that they would not understand the concept) can lessen the distress associated with voices and delusions—and then reduce the intensity of the symptoms as a result of the diminished distress. Other patients respond negatively to information about schizophrenia by assuming that the label means there is something inherently wrong with them. They may feel distressed and depressed to discover that they are, in their own words, "crazy" or "insane," that they may have wasted years living in the midst of their beliefs, and that comforting beliefs and hallucinations are no longer true. Therefore, it is best to coordinate psychoeducational plans with the therapist. If the patient is not seeing a therapist, the psychiatrist should carefully assess his or her ability to absorb information about schizophrenia as an illness before providing much information about it.

Insight into the illness can enhance medication compliance as the patient comes to realize the purpose and importance of the medication. Even if insight into illness is not achieved, cognitive therapy techniques can be applied to facilitate medication compliance by having the patient examine the evidence of how things have improved since starting a certain medication and/or how things may have worsened at times when medication was not taken. The clinician can also address poor medication compliance by inquiring about the automatic thoughts that the patient associates with taking medications. There may be erroneous beliefs about side effects, the need for daily usage, or the need for continuous usage. Simply reinstructing the patient to take the medication regularly misses the basic tenet of cognitive therapy: Examine the thoughts that guide behavior.

Finally, psychiatrists can contribute to the diminution of psychotic symptoms themselves through the brief use of cognitive therapy techniques during 15-minute medication sessions. For instance, a patient with the delusion that people parking outside his apartment building were going to invade his apartment was asked to record, in two columns, when the belief came true and when it did not. A month later, he returned to his medication management session with the two columns, the latter with many ticks and the former with none. The patient concluded that his belief that his apartment was going to be invaded had no basis, as his monitoring exercise demonstrated.

Other cognitive therapy techniques can be easily utilized during the brief medication management session (see Pinninti et al., 2005). Although complete, hour-long, weekly sessions are preferred in the use of cognitive therapy for the treatment of schizophrenia, the current emphasis on pharmacological treatment for this condition, as provided by psychiatrists during 15-minute monthly to trimonthly visits, creates the need for psychiatrists to provide whatever brief aspects of psychotherapeutic assistance to patients that they are able to do. Cognitive therapy allows for such a concise, yet useful, intervention during medication management sessions.

SUMMARY

Cognitive therapy for schizophrenia depends most often on patients being on antipsychotic medication. A general knowledge on the part of therapists of how these medications work and what side effects they may cause can facilitate successful communication between the therapist and the psychiatrist. Likewise, if psychiatrists learn some basic cognitive techniques and actually discuss and use them with their patients, a better understanding of the work of the therapist will follow. Good coordination between the two modes of treatment aids in furthering the progress of the patient.

CHAPTER 14

An Integrative Cognitive Model
of Schizophrenia

Despite many years of investigation and countless scientific articles, the construct of schizophrenia is still cloaked in mystery. Is it a single disease or a conglomerate of several different diseases? What is the etiology? Is there a common pathway, or are there multiple pathways to the full expression of the disorder? It has been well established that no set of biological or psychological abnormalities is found exclusively in schizophrenia (specificity) or encompasses all cases (sensitivity). Notwithstanding this fact, there are enough commonalities among the clinical features, neuroendocrine abnormalities, and psychological aberrations to warrant the formulation of a tentative model of the developmental pathways to the disorder or disorders.

The clinical presentation of schizophrenia includes four separate sets of symptoms or behaviors: delusions, hallucinations, thinking/discourse disorder, and negative symptoms (John, Khanna, Thennarasu, & Reddy, 2003). Although factor analyses have consistently demonstrated that the first two sets load on a common factor, often named "reality distortion," it is difficult to discern meaningful connections between the sets of symptoms. Further, the relation of these symptoms to one another as well as to the broader cognitive dysfunction, such as attenuated reality testing and neurocognitive impairments, is not clear. We attempt to address the following questions in this chapter: What processes can account for the diverse and apparently unconnected symptomatology and its relation to structural and neurophysiological abnormalities? Is there a common denominator underlying the cognitive dysfunction and symptoms? What pathways lead to the development of the disorder? We explore these questions in terms of the interaction of inadequate cerebral functioning; aversive life experiences; and excessive psychophysiological reactions and their relation to the cognitive, affective, and behavioral abnormalities characteristic of schizophrenia.

Only recently have writers attempted to integrate neurophysiological findings with a cognitive model of schizophrenia (Bentall et al., in press; Broome et al., 2007a; Broome et al., 2005; Garety, Bebbington, Fowler, Freeman, & Kuipers, 2007). In this chapter we attempt to incorporate the relevant neurocognitive findings into our integrative model. Although experimental findings are presently insufficient to provide validation of the proposed model of schizophrenia, a theoretical formulation offers a framework for understanding the phenomenology of schizophrenia, suggests avenues for future research, and provides some clues regarding how cognitive therapy of schizophrenia may help to ameliorate the symptoms of this disorder. The emphasis of this chapter consequently emphasizes the development, symptomatology, and therapy of schizophrenia from a cognitive as well as a neurophysiological perspective. Where available, supportive empirical findings are presented.

SUMMARY OF THE INTEGRATIVE MODEL

Previous studies have shown that specific regions of the brain and specific functions (e.g., short-term memory and executive functioning) play a central role particularly in the formation of negative symptoms and disorganization of thinking (Heydebrand et al., 2004; Kerns & Berenbaum, 2003); these findings, however, do not account for delusions, hallucinations, and loss of insight into the illness. We take the view that a broader perspective on schizophrenia may be more illuminating than an exclusive focus on specific functional domains or brain regions. Although tests of attention, memory, executive functioning, and flexibility are useful indicators of neurocognitive deficits, they do not directly measure the disruption in the total integrative functions of the brain. Based on the analogy of impaired cardiac function, the broader concepts of cognitive "insufficiency," "decompensation," and "failure" can be applied to the complex interaction of the predisposing neurobiological, environmental, cognitive, and behavioral factors in the development of schizophrenia. Implicit in these constructs is the notion that the combination of two factors—namely, *excessive cognitive load* (imposed by hypersalient beliefs) and *marginal cognitive resources* (resulting from a deficiency across many domains of cerebral function)—interfere with the adaptive evaluation and integration of internal as well as external experiences. As shown in Figure 14.1, the decompensation of the shaky cognitive functions leads to the development of the specific symptoms of schizophrenia.

The breakdown is foreshadowed by hyperreactivity to stress, subtle cognitive impairments, and tendencies to withdraw from other individuals. As stressors accumulate, the resulting neuroendocrine cascade has a toxic impact on brain functions, leading, for example, to excessive activation of certain brain regions by dopamine and probably other neurotransmitters. This hyperactivation imposes a significant load on the limited cognitive resources. Thus, progressive depletion of marginal cognitive resources

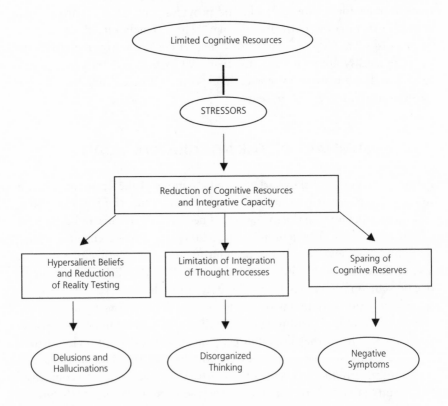

FIGURE 14.1. A modified diathesis–stress model: Diminished cognitive resources facilitate emergence of symptoms of schizophrenia.

sets the trajectory from cognitive insufficiency to cognitive decompensation and, in severe cases, to cognitive failure. This course is manifested clinically by the emergence of delusional beliefs and hallucinations, on the one hand, and a diminished capacity to evaluate them realistically, on the other. Although the progression of the disorder is characterized by an attenuation of cognitive resources, patients retain sufficient cognitive reserve to carry out less demanding operations of everyday life. The reserve is insufficient, however, for more complex, effortful operations involved in reality-testing hypersalient beliefs and misinterpretations. Negative symptoms may be due, in part, to reduced resources for planning and carrying out activities; they may also serve as a means of protecting the cognitive reserve. The conservation system is represented in negative expectancies, diminished motivation, and social avoidance, as well as a generalized reduction in constructive activity (for a discussion of cognitive reserve in other conditions, see Stern, 2002.)

Cognitive biases play a significant role in the progression from constitutional vulnerability to the prodromal state to overt psychosis. The resultant cognitive distortions lead to extreme appraisals of aversive life situations and to the consequent formation of pathogenic schemas (incorporating distorted beliefs and representations). The dysfunctional cognitive schemas become hypersalient and "hijack" the information-processing system, which further biases the person's interpretations of experiences. These erroneous interpretations conform to the content of the beliefs incorporated within the cognitive schemas. The hyperactivation of the schemas (associated with neurochemical dysregulation) leads to uncontrolled aberrant thinking, which is unchecked because of deficient cognitive resources. The hypersalient beliefs and ideation associated with activation of the dopaminergic and probably other neurotransmitter (e.g., glutamatergic) systems are represented in the form of delusions and hallucinations; the longstanding defeatist attitudes and negative expectancies (associated with dopamine deficiency in the prefrontal cortex) are instrumental in the production of negative symptoms.

PREDISPOSITION TO,
AND DEVELOPMENT OF, SCHIZOPHRENIA

Predisposition

The diathesis–stress model (Zubin & Spring, 1977) has guided studies of the development of schizophrenia for several decades. A large literature attests to the diathesis in schizophrenia. Various combinations of contributing factors establish the constitutional vulnerability. These include genetic, prenatal and postnatal adversities, psychosocial stressors, and neurodevelopmental and neuroendocrine problems in adolescence and early adulthood (Walker, Kestler, Bollini, & Hochman, 2004). Damage to the hippocampus has been singled out not only as a contributor to vulnerability but also as a factor in the precipitation and maintenance of psychosis (Walker et al.). Loss of gray matter due to pruning (McGlashan & Hoffman, 2000) and dysregulation of neurotransmitter systems (Walker & Diforio, 1997) also appear to play a role in the predisposition to, and maintenance of, psychosis. Studies have documented the impact of disturbances in the activity of neural circuitry on components of perception, cognition, and behavior (Jarskog & Robbins, 2006). These disturbances are manifested by measurable cognitive impairments of executive function and working memory as well as by the formation of symptoms of schizophrenia. The cumulative effect of these impairments and other as yet unidentified impairments evidently contributes to a reduction in the available pool of cognitive resources (Nuechterlein & Dawson, 1984).

Although the prevalence of schizophrenia has been estimated at approximately 1% in the general population, higher prevalences of isolated psychotic symptoms (5% prevalence) or more broadly defined psychotic experiences (15% prevalence) have been identified (Cougnard et al., 2007). Prospective studies (e.g., Owens & Johnstone, 2006; Cougnard et al.) have provided evidence for an interactive developmental model of psychosis. Further, psychological trauma in general has been associated with the development of psychosis (Spauwen, Krabbendam, Lieb, Wittchen, & van Os, 2006). Cougnard et al. found that the nonclinical expressions of sporadic psychotic experiences interacted with specific environmental risk factors for psychosis (cannabis use, childhood trauma, and urbanicity) to cause abnormal persistence of psychotic symptoms in participants and eventually the need for treatment. The environmental risk factors acted additively in producing clinical psychosis. These impairments and symptoms evidently exist in a subclinical form in individuals vulnerable to the development of the disorder but make their more florid appearance only in a relatively small proportion of cases, especially those exposed to traumatic experiences.

Several lines of evidence support the continuity hypothesis. Epidemiological studies, for example, show a continuum between subclinical signs and symptoms in high-risk individuals and full-blown symptoms of those with the disorder. Other studies show that certain traits, such as neuroticism and the attribution of voices to external forces, predispose an individual to psychosis (Escher, Romme, Buiks, Delespaul, & van Os, 2002a). Further, there is evidence that the accumulation of minor stressful conditions may precipitate the disorder or exacerbate symptoms during a quiescent period.

One way of determining the diathesis for psychosis generally, and schizophrenia specifically, is to investigate whether there are phenotypic and genotypic characteristics of this disorder in individuals with subclinical symptoms (as in schizotypal disorder) and in the relatives of these individuals as well as patients. A review by Myin-Germeys, Krabbendam, and van Os (2003) presents compelling evidence of a continuity among subclinical *psychotic symptoms* in the general population with symptoms in clinically diagnosed patients with psychosis (also see Lincoln, 2007; Schürhoff et al., 2003). These authors also present evidence of an *etiological* continuity between individuals in the general population and patients with psychosis as well as similarities between *schizotypy* and *psychosis*. The same clinical dimensions (positive, negative, and disorganized symptoms) characterize both schizotypy and psychosis. Further, *psychosocial factors* such as child abuse and poor adaptation to increased level of urbanicity are associated with both syndromes. *Cannabis use* is associated with both schizotypy and psychosis. Schizotypal individuals using cannabis show attentional disinhibition similar to that seen in patients with the positive dimension of psychosis.

Neuroticism, characterized as exaggerated stress reactivity, anxiety proneness, depressive symptoms, and autonomic lability, is also a risk factor for psychosis in adult life. Patients with psychosis and their first-degree relatives are characterized by increased levels of neuroticism. Moreover, neuroticism appears to contribute to the risk of developing psychosis-like symptoms. *Genetic studies* also seem to support a continuity hypothesis. Studies of twins as well as familial clustering of psychopathology have shown significant genetic and familial transmission of the typical negative symptom dimension and of the disorganization dimension. Further, positive symptoms in patients with nonaffective psychosis are correlated with positive schizotypy in their relatives, and negative symptoms are predictive of negative schizotypy in their relatives. *Neurodevelopmental* and neuropsychological characteristics of patients with schizophrenia are also found in individuals with schizotypy as well as in the first- and second-degree relatives of patients (Schürhoff et al., 2003). Various *physiological abnormalities,* such as increased skin conductance and early sensory gating deficits, are found in both full-blown schizophrenia and schizotypy. Finally, negative symptoms in high-risk individuals and schizophrenic patients show the same kind of defeatist attitudes (see Chapter 5).

In summary, there is a broad continuum in the predisposition to schizophrenia in untreated individuals and patients' relatives in the community as well as in patients diagnosed with schizophrenia involving: psychotic-like symptoms; etiological, environmental, and demographic factors; neuroticism; dysfunctional attitudes; genetics; neurocognitive impairment; and psychophysiological aberrations.

Stressors and Neuroendocrine Hyperreactivity

The relation of stress to psychosis has been studied by a number of investigators. The general finding has indicated that the course of psychosis is influenced less by relatively rare major life events and more by the accumulation of much more prevalent smaller events that occur in daily life (Malla & Norman, 1992). The same may be true of stressors leading to the first psychotic episode. Monroe (1983) reported that minor daily events have an impact on psychological symptoms in general. Malla, Cortese, Shaw, and Ginsberg (1990) reported the association between minor life events and relapse rates in schizophrenia, and Norman and Malla (1991) showed the relationship between minor life events and subjective stress in these patients. Further, Myin-Germeys, van Os, Schwartz, Stone, and Delespaul (2001) reported changes in mood in patients with psychosis as well as their first-degree relatives following minor stress.

A series of articles supports the notion that individuals at high risk for psychosis manifest a hyperreactivity to stress (Myin-Germeys, Delespaul, & Van Os, 2005; Walker, McMillan, & Mittal, 2007). This hyperreactivity evidently persists through the prodromal phase into the fully active psychotic period and may contribute to relapses. The empirical evidence for the physiological overreaction to stress in psychosis has considerable support in the literature (e.g., Corcoran et al., 2003; Walker & Diforio, 1997). Schizotypal individuals, for example, show thinking problems analogous to those found in schizophrenia and similarly overreact physiologically to stress (Walker, Baum, & Diforio, 1998). Further, appraisals of social threat are correlated with excessive cortisol release (Dickerson & Kemeny, 2004).

A relevant study by Myin-Germeys et al. (2005) used the experience sampling method to study the association between minor life events and psychotic symptoms. The investigators found that the occurrence of minor stressors is clearly associated with the intensity of psychotic experiences in two groups with a higher-than-average level of liability to psychosis: patients with a diagnosis of psychosis in a state of remission and first-degree relatives of patients with a diagnosis of psychotic disorders. Because the results were based on cross-sectional analyses of the data, it was not possible to establish a causal relationship. However, a plausible interpretation is that minor stressors cause an increase in the intensity of psychotic symptoms. The authors propose that the sensitization in relationship to environmental stress could be interpreted in light of the *dopamine sensitization* hypothesis of psychotic symptoms. They point to the hyperresponsiveness of dopamine neurons to environmental stimuli, in which even exposure to moderate levels of stress are associated with excessive dopamine.

Corcoran et al. (2003) summarize findings in support of a hypothesis proposed by Walker and Diforio (1997) that the HPA axis constitutes an endocrine-neural-system risk factor in the initiation and course of schizophrenic psychosis. An increase in cortisol levels (presumably due to the impact of stress on the HPA axis) has been associated with the onset of psychosis. Also, there is a correlation between average age of onset of psychotic disorders and a rise in cortisol levels during adolescence and young adulthood, lending circumstantial evidence to the theory of Walker and Diforio (1997) regarding the relation of stress to cortisol and psychosis. Walker et al. (2007) list accumulating evidence that the HPA–hippocampal system is dysregulated in patients with schizophrenia and other psychotic disorders and that this is due to environmental factors, at least in part. They base their thesis partly on findings from discordant monozygotic twins. Importantly, they report that HPA–hippocampal impairment *precedes* the onset of the clinical disorder. Moreover, the volume of the hippocampus is reduced and cortisol is elevated in young first-episode patients who have never been treated. Finally, hippocampal volume continues to decrease as the disorder becomes more chronic (Velakoulis et al., 2006.)

This pattern of findings is consistent with the thesis that stress-induced disturbance in the HPA–hippocampal system can influence the expression of psychosis in vulnerable individuals. Chronic stress downregulation of the HPA axis, which fails to moderate cortisol secretion, leads to cell death in the hippocampus. Walker et al. (2007) further show that dopamine activity is increased by the release of cortisol and that this may account for the apparent exacerbations of psychotic symptoms during stress exposure. Additional evidence supports Walker and Diforio's (1997) theory. For example, a rise in cortisol levels occurs *prior* to psychotic relapse. Also, baseline cortisol levels correlate with symptom severity at follow-up

(Walker, 2002). Evidently, stress as indexed by cortisol levels is a precursor to, and not a consequence of, psychosis.

In summary, based on a large number of studies (for summaries, see Broome et al., 2007b; Garety et al., 2007), it is possible to formulate a plausible neurophysiological pathway to psychosis. The reduction in hippocampal volume as a result of any combination of prenatal and postnatal environmental events (Walker et al., 2004) predisposes the individual to excessive stress-related cortisol release. Hypercortisolism can further reduce hippocampal volume. Since the hippocampus controls the mesolimbic dopamine system, damage leads to dopamine sensitization. The hyperreactivity of the dopaminergic system is a crucial factor in the precipitation of psychosis. This progression is abetted by corticolimbic circuitry dysfunction, which results in reduced braking of dopamine activity by the prefrontal lobes. The idea that stress, elevated cortisol, and hippocampal damage are related has also been applied to a theory of the etiology of schizophrenia as a consequence of childhood trauma/PTSD (Read, van Os, Morrison, & Ross, 2005).

THE ROLE OF APPRAISAL IN STRESS REACTIONS

Much of the work in the biological responses to stress in psychosis-prone individuals postulates a direct sequence from *diathesis* to *stimulating event* to *neuroendocrine response*. The literature, however, suggests that the stress response is mediated by the appraisal of the event; that is, an event becomes a stressor by virtue of the meaning attached to it (Pretzer & Beck, 2007; Lazarus, 1966).

Dickerson and Kemeny (2004) elaborate on how cognitive appraisals affect physiology by activating specific cognitive processes and their central nervous system underpinnings. The thalamus and frontal lobes (e.g., prefrontal cortex) first integrate and appraise the significance or meaning of the potential stressor. Appraisals of threat and uncontrollability, for example, can lead to the generation of emotional responses via extensive connections from the prefrontal cortex to the limbic system. The limbic structures (e.g., the amygdala and hippocampus), which connect to the hypothalamus, serve as a primary pathway for activating the HPA axis. The HPA axis is activated by the hypothalamic release of corticotropin releasing hormone (CRH), which stimulates the anterior pituitary to release adrenocorticotropin hormone (ACTH). This hormone, in turn, triggers the adrenal cortex to secrete cortisol into the bloodstream. Dickerson and Kemeny (2004) conclude, on the basis of an extensive meta-analysis, that the experimental conditions that most consistently activate the HPA axis (evaluation and uncontrollability) are relevant to appraisals of threat. These experimental findings are congruent with the report by Horan et al. (2005) that the appraisal of uncontrollability of life events was the most stressful for patients with schizophrenia. Figure 14.2 illustrates the pathway of dysfunctional appraisals of life events to neurophysiological changes to toxic impact on cerebral functions.

Individuals who are susceptible to psychosis appraise certain innocuous situations in an idiosyncratic way and presumably feel more threatened and stressed than the average person. Freeman, Garety, Bebbington, et al. (2005), for example, reported that individuals who received high scores on a paranoia scale were prone to interpret computer characters (avatars) in a virtual reality scene as hostile and conspiratorial toward them. In this study, the tendency to attach a personal meaning with paranoid overtones to scenes that were objectively neutral demonstrates the individual's self-focus and paranoid bias, which converts an innocuous scene into a stressful experience. A later study by Valmaggia et al. (2007) obtained similar results with a group of high-risk individuals.

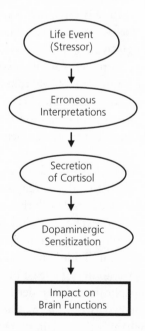

FIGURE 14.2. From stressors to disturbance.

TRANSITION INTO PSYCHOSIS

There are obviously many pathways that may lead to schizophrenia. Very often, the earliest subjective changes involve perceptual changes, which can include changes in the experience of the self and/or the world (Klosterkotter, 1992). Typically, vulnerable individuals also experience *neurocognitive dysfunction* prior to the onset of psychotic symptoms (Walker, 2002). At-risk individuals, as well as patients, show a number of specific impairments demonstrated in neurocognitive tests: attentional problems, impaired working memory, and defective executive function (Walker et al., 1998; Nuechterlein & Dawson, 1984). These indices of cognitive insufficiency impede these individuals' academic and social adjustment and, when combined with hypersensitivity to stress, create relevant conditions for the development of schizophrenia. This cognitive dysfunction appears to affect their psychological functioning and socialization, as manifested by decreased motivation and socialization (Cornblatt, Lencz, & Kane, 2001). Evidently, the combination of these neurocognitive, psychological, and social difficulties interferes with the development of age-relevant social skills (see Broome et al., 2005) and social and academic performance. These problems produce negative attitudes about the self and others, leading to social anxiety and depression. At some point, these individuals either voluntarily withdraw from social interactions or experience social isolation from others.

The importance of cognitive impairment in accounting for both laboratory and clinical findings in patients with paranoid delusions is demonstrated by the findings of Bentall et al. (2008) that tests of current neurocognitive impairment are associated with anticipation of threat and paranoid beliefs. The prominence of threat anticipation is represented symptomatically by excessive anxiety and the progressive sense of social and academic defeat, by depression.

Studies have shown that anxiety and depression frequently precede the development of psychosis. Escher et al. (2002a) found that the combination of anxiety and depression is associated with the development of minor psychotic symptoms during the prepsychotic period, and Cannon, Caspi, et al. (2002) found that preschizophrenic children experience excessive depression and social anxiety. As the individual moves closer to the experience of psychosis, there is a high probability of a least one frank episode of depression in the year prior to hospitalization (an der Heiden & Häfner, 2000).

A crucial factor in the progression to psychosis is the development of dysfunctional cognitive schemas that facilitate the onset of aberrant experiences such as hallucinations and delusions. Stressful conditions lead to dysfunctional beliefs (e.g., "I'm inferior," "People are against me") and, consequently, dysfunctional cognitive appraisals of specific experiences and maladaptive behaviors (e.g., social withdrawal). These problems evoke more aversive experiences that, in turn, consolidate the dysfunctional beliefs and behaviors. The social-aversion attitudes may lead to suspiciousness and odd ideas about other people—characteristic of schizotypal disorder. The repeated dysfunctional appraisals resulting from cognitive biases increase the amount of psychophysiological stress. Ultimately, the combination of stressors activating dysfunctional attitudes and the resultant impact on the HPA axis and dysregulation of the dopaminergic system drives the progression to a psychotic state.

Defeatist attitudes regarding performance lead to the loss of motivation, reduced interests, and sadness characteristic of depression, or may be integrated into the personality structure and manifested as schizoid personality disorder. A study by Perivoliotis et al. (2008), for example, showed that high-risk individuals with defeatist attitudes about performance were prone to showing diminished motivation. These premorbid characteristics crystallize into the typical negative symptoms of schizophrenia.

How do persecutory and anomalous beliefs and, ultimately, delusions develop from dysfunctional representations such as those characteristic of depression and anxiety? Previous research has shown that depression-prone individuals have negative core beliefs about themselves incorporated in cognitive schemas (Beck, 1967). Patients at high risk for schizophrenia appear to have similar negative core beliefs about themselves. Barrowclough et al. (2003), for example, has found that patients with schizophrenia show low self-esteem, which correlates with the positive symptoms. Unlike "pure" depression, however, schizophrenia embodies negative core beliefs about others as well as about the self (Smith et al., 2006). The precise content of the delusions is related to the nature of the self-representations (e.g., vulnerable, powerless, or strong) and representations of others (e.g., malicious, intrusive, or controlling). Delusions of persecution, for example, appear to stem from beliefs of personal vulnerability and strong beliefs regarding malicious intent in others. Delusions of influence (anomalous or control delusions) appear to be based on representations of the self as powerless and others as powerful. The same disparity in power appears to be intrinsic to the belief system in cases of auditory hallucinations.

The contents of these persecutory and anomalous delusions have themes in common with those of anxiety, depression, and schizophrenia. The impact of the two concepts of threat (anxiety) and social defeat (depression) on the developing belief system leads to representations of others as threatening, rejecting, or dominating, and of the self as vulnerable and helpless. These two conceptual components (threat and defeat) of the belief system become consolidated as aversive experiences (e.g., teasing, abuse, bullying, manipulation) accumulate. Taken as a whole, the clinical findings suggest that when the intellectual functioning is impaired, this sequence of events occurs: Individuals are prone to retain the fundamental attribution error (Heider, 1958; Gilbert, 1991), which automatically attributes life experiences to external causes. Unlike normal individuals, who dismiss erroneous external attributions automatically, delusion-prone individuals have great difficulty in evaluating the attributions as thoughts rather than an accurate representation of external reality. Because many of these attributional errors are concerned with threat, excessive memories of threat are more likely to be incorporated into the recollective system (Bentall et al., 2008). Moreover, memories of threat are coupled with expectations of future threat (Bentall et al.). This fixation on threat has pathological consequences.

Memories and anticipation of threat lead directly to suspiciousness and anxiety (Freeman, 2007) as well as setting up biased interpretations of innocuous situations as threatening (Bentall et al., 2008). Vulnerable individuals become hypervigilant toward potential social threats and look for signs of malevolent intentions, expressed as suspiciousness. Concerns that others may want to harm or control them lead to an accumulation of "evidence" that purportedly supports this notion. The more they misread others' innocent behavior, the stronger the belief becomes that others have specifically targeted them and wish to diminish or hurt them in some way. Concomitant positive attitudes toward others, such as trust, tend to diminish. Eventually, the representations of the self as victim and others as victimizers harden into delusions of persecution or influence. The paranoid mode co-opts the information-processing system to the point that random, irrelevant, and insignificant events are interpreted as personally meaningful. As more events are interpreted in this way, the boundaries of the delusions spread out, so that an increasing number of situations is perceived as directed against the patient. Eventually, this egocentric focus becomes so pronounced that almost any stimulus—noises in the next room, passing vehicles, or television news reporters—convey messages directed to the patient. Similarly, the interpretations of subjective experiences—aches and pains, buzzing in the ear, and anomalous experiences—may be ascribed to the workings of external entities.

Expectations about others' intrusive intentions (as well as patients' self-image of powerlessness and permeability of mind) play a central role in the formation of delusions due to their profound impact on the information processing. Initially, these beliefs make the individual suspicious of others' motives: "Are they putting me down? Do they want to control me?" As a result of their suspiciousness, patients tend to misinterpret others' behavior as unfriendly, and their beliefs about other people's negative intentions harden. The common denominator of delusions of control or influence and pathogenic hallucinations is their perception of the self as permeable or manipulated by powerful external entities (voices or delusional agents).

The distorted information processing imposes the kind of biases demonstrated in investigations of depression, anxiety, and other disorders: attentional biases toward events congruent with the pathogenic beliefs, selective extraction of these events, distortion and exaggeration of their meaning, and exclusion of alternative explanations. These processes combine to bolster the delusional belief (confirmation bias). The content of the distorted interpretation and conclusion, of course, reflects the content of the delusional beliefs. In time, the belief not only becomes fixed but is extended to a widening array of internal and external events in a process akin to stimulus generalization.

When the first episode of schizophrenia occurs, the schemas incorporating these negative beliefs become hypersalient. They dominate the information processing, thus producing highly distorted interpretations of others' behavior. These distortions further feed back into and reinforce the core schemas. As these schemas become hyperactive, their incorporated beliefs become more extreme, unchecked by the normal reality testing that operates in nonpsychotic disorders. This escalation in the content of beliefs may progress, in a typical case, from "People do not care about me" to "They are unfriendly" to "They want to harass me."

In summary, the hijacking of the information-processing by the delusional beliefs leads to the biases that have been largely demonstrated: self-referential, causal, attentional focus, external, attributional, and confirmation biases. Similar processes may be identified in other types of paranormal and delusional thinking.

THE RELATION OF DELUSIONS AND DEPRESSION TO HALLUCINATIONS

One of the most challenging questions for investigators is the high degree of association between hallucinations and delusions (Lincoln, 2007; Peralta, de Leon, & Cuesta, 1992). This is puzzling at first because hallucinations are experienced in the sensory or perceptual domain, whereas delusions involve cognitive and conceptual mechanisms. This association is observed not only in patients with schizophrenia but in nonclinical populations as well (Stefanis et al., 2002; Lincoln, 2007). Hallucinations at age 11, for example, which occur in about 8% of children, are likely to progress to delusional thinking by age 26 if initial appraisals of the voices assign their origin outside of the person, as unfriendly, or as the voices of parents (Escher et al., 2002a). Similarly, Krabbendam and Aleman (2003) found that delusions appear to mediate hallucinations and schizophrenia. In our own work with outpatients with schizophrenia, 30 out of 34 hallucinatory patients also had delusions, whereas only two patients had delusions alone.

The sequence of hallucinations, followed at a later date by depression, constitutes a robust risk factor for psychosis (Krabbendam et al., 2005). As suggested by Krabbendam and colleagues, the sense of entrapment by a powerful other leads to a feeling of powerlessness. The belief in one's own powerlessness is an important feature of depression and is also reflected in the patient's feeling of impotence in coping with the omnipotent voices. Thus, the attribution of the hallucinatory experience to an overpowering entity leads to the crucial delusions in hallucinations, namely that they are externally generated and uncontrollable (see also Birchwood & Chadwick, 1997).

The common thread that runs through the content of hallucinations and delusions is that patients are the object of external forces beyond their control. The pathogenic beliefs about the power of voices are analogous to the delusions of being controlled, intruded upon, and persecuted. Hallucinating patients attribute omnipotence and omniscience to the voices. In her sample of patients with a lifetime history of schizophrenia, Lincoln (2007) found that hallucination proneness correlated most highly with delusions of control, delusions of being influenced, and beliefs about thought reading, insertion, echo, and broadcast. Similarly, Kimhy et al. (2005) found that delusions of control correlated with hallucinations but that delusions of self-significance and persecution did not.

There appears to be a special pathway to hallucinations in those individuals who eventually transition into psychosis. These individuals have a particularly high incidence of childhood trauma (Fowler, 2007). Why the proneness to both hallucinations and delusions? Sometimes patients have delusions without hallucinations but rarely do verbal hallucinations exist in schizophrenia without delusional beliefs about them. (In fact, the existence of delusional beliefs about the voices contributes to the labeling of hallucinations as a psychotic symptom.) Delusions and hallucinations in schizophrenia have in common an interpersonal orientation—the patient is focused on receiving (actually, interpreting) messages from the outside as disparaging, persecuting, intrusive, and so forth. In delusions, these interpretations are based on patients' observations of others' behavior (e.g., their gestures, facial expressions, direction of gaze, or speech have specific and significant meaning). Their delusional world is just as real as their perceptual world. Their sensitivity to the interpersonal content is reflected in their representations of others talking to them (hallucinations), about them (ideas of reference), and influencing them (delusions of control, interference, persecution). In auditory hallucinations, the communication takes a verbal form, which suggests that the same mechanism that lowers patients' threshold for persecutory (external) interpretations lowers the threshold for voices.

Traumatic childhood events are sometimes represented in hallucinations. The traumatic experience, perhaps woven into other aversive interpersonal events in childhood, implants an image of the self as helpless and of others as all-powerful. Not only abuse during childhood but also the experience of depression seems to facilitate the persistence of hallucinations (Escher et al., 2002b). It is possible to discern the same characteristics of the voices in depression as in the childhood trauma. The voice content is directed at disparaging the patient, and the voices themselves are all-powerful. Thus, the underlying schema centers on the patient's total subordination to others. The voices often encapsulate the actual traumatic events by reproducing the voices of both the victimizer and the victim, as illustrated in the case below.

A 25-year-old man with schizophrenia heard two sets of voices that would talk to him and also about him, generally making derogatory comments about him such as "fag," "wimp," or "queer." One voice was that of a 12-year-old boy and the other, a 6-year-old boy. Prior to the onset of psychosis, the patient had undergone two hospitalizations for depression. On questioning, the patient revealed that when he was 6, he was sexually assaulted by a 12-year-old. Interestingly, he did not see the connection between this experience and the voices. As a result of the childhood trauma, the patient had an image of himself as helpless and others as more powerful. This image caused the patient to feel vulnerable and self-conscious in the presence of others. He interpreted his experiences through the template (or schema) of social subordination. He tended to exaggerate negative experiences and interpret what might be an accidental or incidental event as something directed against him. Eventually, this hyperreactivity to the stressors of everyday life, as well as more intense stressors (including actual putdowns), led to hospitalizations for depression and later for delusions and hallucinations. The content of the voices incorporated the early childhood image and reproduced the meaning he attached to the experience, namely that he was not only weak but also contemptible (a "queer"). Read, Perry, Moskowitz, and Connolly (2001) have proposed that as a result of the stress, increased cortisol, and (mainly) hippocampal damage that results from trauma, aspects of trauma-related memories can remain unintegrated or decontextualized. For example, an adult with schizophrenia (with a history of childhood trauma) may experience a hostile voice that is actually a remembered fragment of an abuse experience. But, because the memory trace is decontextualized (i.e., disconnected from other aspects/memories of the experience), the person experiences simply a hostile voice, which can easily be assumed to be an external hostile voice.

The prototype for delusional explanations of voices—namely, the preemptive externalizing bias—apparently exists prior to hearing voices. When patients hear a voice for the first time, they generally look around to ascertain its origin (they may check with other people and discover that they don't hear the voice). Instead of considering that the auditory hallucinations may be a mental phenomenon, these individuals latch onto the belief that they are externally caused (because this explanatory bias has already been formed). Patients' external explanation for the phenomenon seems to stem from early representations of the self as the passive object of external influence from the powerful other. This conception leads patients to a unique mode of causal explanations: Internal experiences are caused by external forces or entities. Patients apply this explanatory mode to account for a variety of paranormal experiences besides hallucinations: thought capture, mind reading, thought insertion, and so forth. In fact, the whole gamut of what is labeled interference, control, or persecutory delusions can be understood in terms of the self and other representations, which direct information processing to external causes. It is interesting that patients may attribute far more power to the voices themselves than to the supposed agent. A man felt totally subordinate to the hallucinated voice of his brother but did not feel as powerless when his brother spoke to him in reality.

Although the evidence is sparse, there are suggestions from the clinical data that the prepsychotic individuals already have ideas that others are controlling and observing them, and they are prone to regard themselves as the target of other's "intentional" intrusions. This conception is reflected in their attributions regarding hallucinations and intrusive thoughts as well as delusions.

The tendency to make external attributions, of course, is a characteristic of the general population. Heider (1958) first described this phenomenon, and it has been described at length by Gilbert (1991). Psychosis-prone individuals, presumably because of aversive life experiences, are likely to overinvest in these attributions and because of cognitive impairment, are less able to evaluate and dismiss them. As shown in Figure 14.3, the sequence of negative representations and the consequent biased information processing leads to the formation of delusions and hallucinations.

THEORETICAL CONSIDERATIONS AND CONCLUSIONS

The causal bases of the limited cognitive insight and disorganized thinking of schizophrenia appear to be a direct consequence of neural system dysfunctions. The concept of the interaction of limited cognitive capacity (due to neural deficits) with stress helps to explain symptom expression but also patients' difficulties in evaluating and correcting unrealistic ideas. Although the focus on defective localized, specialized functions of the brain has dominated the research on these higher brain functions in schizophrenia in recent years, Phillips and Silverstein (2003) point out that these locally specialized functions must be complemented by processes that coordinate them, and they propose that impairment of these coordinating

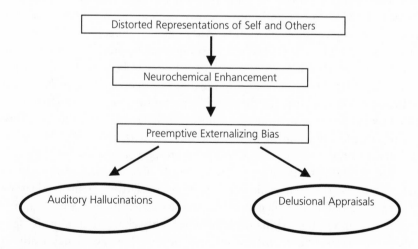

FIGURE 14.3. Pathway from dysfunctional representations to psychotic symptoms.

processes may be central to schizophrenia. They suggest that this important class of cognitive functions can be implemented by mechanisms such as long-range connections within and between cortical regions that activate synaptic channels and synchronize the oscillatory neural activity in the brain. The intellectual capabilities that these mechanisms provide have been shown to be impaired in schizophrenia.

This formulation by Phillips and Silverstein (2003) suggests a broader conception of the problems in high-level cognitive processing in schizophrenia, viewing them not simply as a consequence of domain-specific deficits but also as an impairment of the integrative functions of the brain. Diminished integration may be represented at an anatomical level as an excessive pruning, during adolescence, of synaptic connections (McGlashan & Hoffman, 2000) or as hypofunction of NMDA (modulatory) receptors (Olney & Farber, 1995). Studies of unaffected relatives of patients with schizophrenia also suggest that psychosis-prone individuals are genetically endowed with limited cognitive competencies (Gur et al., 2007), perhaps the consequence of smaller brain volume, especially in the hippocampus (Boos et al., 2007). The impairment not only reduces the resources for coping with stress and aligning erroneous appraisals with reality but also increases the sensitivity to aversive life experiences, leading to dysfunctional beliefs and behaviors.

Taking the global view regarding impairment of the total integrative function of the brain can shed some light on how schizophrenia develops. Given the limitations on the cognitive capacity of the brain, external stressors increase the cognitive load and divert resources to buffer the excessive impact of the stressors and consequently deplete the resources available for maintaining cognitive flexibility. Although certain cognitive functions, such as vocabulary and procedural learning, may be preserved, the relative impairment of complex, resource-demanding psychological functions—such as self-reflectiveness, self-monitoring, perspective shifting based on changes in context, correction of misinterpretations, and responsiveness to corrective feedback from others—removes the barrier (i.e., adequate reality testing) to the development of dysfunctional beliefs (especially delusions) and impedes the development of complex interpersonal skills.

Patients with schizophrenia are generally able to successfully utilize their cognitive skills in evaluating their own relatively neutral ideas or the erroneous ideas of other people, but they generally lack the cognitive capacity to apply those skills to their own highly charged appraisals, specifically those associated with delusional beliefs. This deficiency leads to the clinical concepts of "impaired insight" and "deficits in reality testing." The impaired capacity to recognize delusional ideas as unrealistic (cognitive insight) and therefore as symptoms of an underlying disorder (clinical insight), provides one index for the diagnosis of schizophrenia.

This combination of cognitive insufficiency and the resultant stressful conditions provides a path for the progression from the prodromal state to the cognitive decompensation manifest in the symptomatology of schizophrenia: The hyperactivation of dysfunctional schemas, combined with reduced reality testing, is manifested in delusions and hallucinations, the resource sparing in the negative symptoms, and the collapse of organized semantic structure in formal thought disorder. The loss of context or set described in thought-disordered patients (Chapman & Chapman, 1973a) and hallucinators (Badcock, Waters, & Maybery, 2007) may be attributed, in part, to the relative paucity of resources available for short-term memory, for adhering to rules of coherent communication, and for inhibiting intrusion of inappropriate ideas. The profound disengagement manifested by alogia, affective flattening, and anergia (the negative syndrome) may be viewed as a result of resource sparing. Resource sparing is also evident in the predilection for making easy but erroneous associations to verbal prompts (Chapman & Chapman).

A similar weakening of cognitive inhibition appears in the thinking disorder, characterized by derailment, loss of referents, and so forth, especially when the patient is experiencing external stress or is discussing an emotionally salient subject. Disorganization can also be seen as resulting from a rapid switching between network states. That is, the lack of integrative ability in the brain leads to the formation of transient, relatively random network states (Wright & Kydd, 1986; Gordon, Williams, Haig, Wright, & Meares, 2001). In this view, disorganization is the core dysfunction in schizophrenia, and other symptoms represent compensations to this core deficit. For example, Gordon et al. found that the Reality Distortion factor was associated with increased gamma activity (i.e., overprocessing), and the formation of stable but aberrant cortical networks (i.e., "parasitic foci"; Hoffman & McGlashan, 1993) that can lead to hallucinations or delusions in response to target stimuli; the Psychomotor Poverty factor is associated with a process of compensatory "shutting down," characterized by decreased response to target stimuli (i.e., underprocessing); but the Disorganization factor was correlated with decreased response to *nontarget* stimuli. These findings suggest that disorganization represents the most profound failure of integration. Disorganization is not compensated for by consistent over- or underprocessing, and the rapid and transient nature of the network states that are formed is thought to produce "hebephrenic" symptoms such as thought disorder, unusual movements, and so forth.

In our formulation, the depletion of cognitive resources associated with schizophrenia prevents the individual from being able to accurately evaluate the nature of positive symptoms caused by aberrant but stable network states, or the defeatist beliefs associated with the shutting down seen in negative symptoms.

There is experimental support for our clinical formulation, as research has demonstrated that under cognitive load, the cognitive functioning of patients with schizophrenia deteriorates (Nuechterlein & Dawson, 1984; Melinder & Barch, 2003). Defective pupillary responses (lack of dilation; Granholm, Morris, Sarkin, Asarnow, & Jeste, 1997) and antisaccadic reactions (Curtis, Calkins, Grove, Feil, & Iacono, 2001) are postulated as indirect evidence of attenuated cognitive resources. A more specific index of the integrative capacity of the brain is the ability to detect erroneous thinking and to reframe its responses. The Beck Cognitive Insight Scale indirectly tests the impairment of the higher-level functions in schizophrenia (Beck & Warman, 2004). The high degree of certainty in one's unrealistic interpretations and lack of self-reflectiveness are indicative of the limited cognitive resources. The process of distancing oneself from strongly held beliefs, evaluating them, and applying rules of evidence and logic places a substantial demand on cognitive resources. These processes require the integration of a number of complex functions represented in different regions of the brain. The attenuation of resources in schizophrenia and reduced integrative functioning hinder the processing necessary for reality testing of hypersalient delusional beliefs. Reduction in executive function represents a marker of a reduced ability to test the reality of beliefs. A way to study the route from impaired executive function to delusions is to examine the relationship of cognitive insight to executive function and delusions. The index of overconfidence ("self-certainty") in the reality of unusual experiences and capacity to view them in perspective ("self-reflectiveness"), as measured by the Beck Cognitive Insight Scale (Beck & Warman 2004), has been useful in demonstrating a link between executive function and delusions. Specifically, self-certainty correlates with both forms of pathology and is a mediator between them (Grant & Beck, 2008a). We also found a moderate correlation between impaired executive function and impaired self-reflectiveness.

Other studies (e.g., Beck et al., 2004) found a correlation between executive function and delusions in an inpatient sample but not in the outpatient group. Further, self-certainty correlates significantly with both thought disorder and hallucinations (Grant & Beck, 2008a). These findings show that either the hypersalience of delusional beliefs swamps flimsy reality testing or that attenuated reality testing allows beliefs to attain enhanced degrees of conviction. Negative symptoms, on the other hand, appear to be based on the defeatist attitudes generated by negative experiences resulting from the deleterious impact of cognitive impairment on social and academic performance (Grant & Beck, in press).

Cognitive insufficiency obviously varies over time and is frequently improved, or compensated for, by pharmacotherapy, which reduces the cognitive load produced by delusions and hallucinations. Individuals predisposed to schizophrenia often attempt to compensate for their deficits; for example, they protect themselves from stressful situations through social isolation (e.g., Lencz et al., 2004). Nonetheless, stressful situations or neurotoxic substances such as cannabinoids can directly or indirectly diminish accessible cognitive resources and lead to cognitive decompensation and the recurrence of symptoms.

Integrating the research findings of schizotypal individuals, those at ultra-high risk for schizophrenia, the families of schizotypal individuals, and patients with schizophrenia can provide an outline of the pathways (or "hits") leading to at least one subtype of schizophrenia. The pathway represented in the research on patients and their families suggests an innate predisposition to develop positive and negative schizotypy. Findings of subtle cognitive impairment and subclinical disorganization in family members as well as individuals with overt schizotypy suggest that these clinical features have a genetic basis. The attraction of paranormal ideas (e.g., mind reading, intrusive thoughts) for the relatives of patients with schizophrenia is represented in patients who not only believe in the paranormal phenomena but actually experience them. This schizotypal subtype is best characterized in terms of Schneiderian first-rank symptoms (Schneider, 1959).

The other pathway is the gradual reduction of cognitive resources due to maturational changes (e.g., pruning of connections in adolescence), the impact of childhood and adolescent stress (Read et al., 2001), and the resultant "neurochemical cascade" (Corcoran et al., 2003). The first pathway can account for the strange ideas and withdrawal and the second for difficulties in reality testing them.

Recent studies of adjunctive cognitive therapy in the treatment of schizophrenia indicate that it is possible to ameliorate the major symptoms by activating patients' "higher cognitive functions," such as distancing from dysfunctional interpretations, evaluating the evidence, and exploring alternative explanations—all of which are essential components of "cognitive insight" (Beck & Warman, 2004). Granholm et al. (2005), for example, found that cognitive insight improved in patients receiving cognitive therapy but not in those receiving "treatment as usual." The same kind of introspective techniques are also helpful in identifying and modifying the underlying dysfunctional beliefs. The efficacy of cognitive therapy in improving higher-level functions is of special interest because it appears to be inconsistent with the notion that the pathogenic beliefs are fixed because of their neural basis. We propose that cognitive therapy taps into patients' cognitive reserve (Stern, 2002) by activating alternate brain structures or networks that are not ordinarily engaged. Landa (2006) and D. A. Silbersweig (personal communication, May 26, 2006) have preliminary evidence that cognitive therapy reduces the reactivity of the amygdala in patients with chronic paranoid schizophrenia.

In summary, schizophrenia may be viewed as an outcome of the cycling interaction of reduced processing capacity, weakened neural integrative capacity, stressful environmental events, and resultant dysfunctional beliefs and interpretations. Although cognitive therapy may not affect the basic neurophysiological diathesis (vulnerability) involved in schizophrenia, it can modify the resultant dysfunctional beliefs, thereby protecting against stress, its associated physiological cascade of toxic effects, and exacerbations of the neurocognitive deficits. Psychotherapeutic as well as pharmacological treatments can dampen down the hyperactive cognitive schemas and thus free up resources for further reality testing (cognitive compensation). The observation that patients can be trained to modify the faulty beliefs that contribute to and aggravate delusions, hallucinations, and negative symptoms suggests that the therapy is able to reduce the cognitive load imposed by the delusional symptoms and consequently make available cognitive resources for further dealing with the various symptoms. Cognitive therapy can also reduce arousal level and thus indirectly free up cognitive resources.

Many of the theoretical propositions in this volume are readily testable. Some headway has already been made in identifying certain core beliefs associated with the persecutory delusions (Fowler et al., 2006), hallucinations, and negative symptoms (Grant & Beck, in press). A study could, for example, examine the continuity of core beliefs during the prodromal phase and after the transition into psychosis. Another study could investigate the relation of the content of patients' automatic thoughts to hallucinations. Finally, brain imaging studies could compare the changes in a combination of cognitive therapy and pharmacotherapy with cognitive therapy or pharmacotherapy alone.

The interplay between attenuated resources, weakened integrative capacity, dysfunctional attitudes and appraisals, and salient life events in the development and maintenance of the major symptom domains in schizophrenia can be further evaluated. If cognitive therapy can free up latent resources, the functioning of additional resources should be apparent in improvement both on tests assessing cognitive capacity and on measures of integrative ability, such as those involving context processing or fMRI indices of functional connectivity (Foucher et al., 2005; Zhou et al., 2007b; Liang et al., 2006). Altogether, the combination of neuropathological and psychological research as well as clinical observations of patients with schizophrenia should not only further the understanding of this puzzling disorder but provide new and more effective avenues of treatment.

Appendices

Beck Cognitive Insight Scale (BCIS)

Name: _____ Today's date: ___/___/___

     Last   *First*   *Middle Initial*   *Mo.* *Day* *Year*

Gender: M F Ethnicity: White Black Hispanic Other Age (years): _____

Below is a list of sentences about how people think and feel. Please read each sentence in the list carefully. Indicate how much you agree with each statement by placing an X in the corresponding space in the column next to each statement.

	Do not agree at all	Agree slightly	Agree a lot	Agree completely
1. At times, I have misunderstood other people's attitudes toward me.^{SR}				
2. My interpretations of my experiences are definitely right.^{SC}				
3. Other people can understand the cause of my unusual experiences better than I can.^{SR}				
4. I have jumped to conclusions too fast.^{SR}				
5. Some of my experiences that have seemed very real may have been due to my imagination.^{SR}				
6. Some of the ideas I was certain were true turned out to be false.^{SR}				
7. If something feels right, it means that it is right.^{SC}				
8. Even though I feel strongly that I am right, I could be wrong.^{SR}				
9. I know better than anyone else what my problems are.^{SC}				
10. When people disagree with me, they are generally wrong.^{SC}				
11. I cannot trust other people's opinion about my experiences.^{SC}				
12. If somebody points out that my beliefs are wrong, I am willing to consider it.^{SR}				
13. I can trust my own judgment at all times.^{SC}				
14. There is often more than one possible explanation for why people act the way they do.^{SR}				
15. My unusual experiences may be due to my being extremely upset or stressed.^{SR}				

SC = Self-Certainty subscale; SR = Self-Reflectiveness.

Scoring and Interpretation of the Beck Cognitive Insight Scale (BCIS)

The BCIS comprises two subscales: Self-Reflectiveness and Self-Certainty. The total score for each scale is the sum of the item scores that comprise it (see below). The BCIS composite index is calculated as Self-Reflectiveness minus Self-Certainty. Poorer cognitive insight is indexed by *lower* scores on the Self-Reflectiveness subscale, *higher* Self-Certainty scores, and *lower* BCIS composite index scores.

Step 1. Score every item on the BCIS from "0" to "3" according to the following rule:
- "Do Not Agree at All" = 0
- "Agree Slightly" = 1
- "Agree a Lot" = 2
- "Agree Completely" = 3

Step 2. Calculate Self-Reflectiveness subscale: Sum items 1, 3, 4, 5, 6, 8, 12, 14, and 15.

Step 3. Calculate Self-Certainty subscale: Sum items 2, 7, 9, 10, 11, and 13.

Step 4. Calculate BCIS composite index: Calculate Self-Reflectiveness *minus* Self-Certainty.

Suggested Outline for Initial Psychological/Psychiatric Evaluation

Examination Data
    date(s) of examination
    name of interviewer
    site of interview
    source of referral
    reason for referral

Current General Patient Information
    name
    date of birth/age
    race
    gender
    marital status; duration of current status
    children: number
    occupation/financial support/grade in school (if student)
    telephone numbers; degree of confidentiality available for messages at each number
    home address
    work address
    housing situation (e.g., house, apartment, rooming house, parents' house)
    occupants of dwelling
    social contacts: frequency, duration, closeness

Chief Concerns

History of Chief Concerns
    symptoms: type, frequency, duration, severity, distress, consequences, beliefs
    content/meaning of symptoms
    interaction/co-occurrence of symptoms
    eliciting situations/triggers/mediators
    reaction/coping strategies
    current other stressors/events of prior week
    onset of first occurrence: time, events, initial reaction
        beliefs formed in first episode and development/reinforcement
        premorbid beliefs

Review of Symptoms (current and past):
    hallucinations (all modalities); delusions (all classes); depressive episodes; manic episodes; panic attacks; phobias; obsessions; compulsions; intrusions/avoidance of traumatic memories; eating problems; sexual concerns; suicidality: thoughts, plans, attempts; violence: recurrent thoughts, plans, attempts; attentional problems; other emotional concerns

(continued)

Health Habits
  illicit substance use (current and past)
    type, onset, last use, frequency/amount (current and at time of maximum use), reasons for use, effects (including effects on symptoms), need for higher doses, withdrawal effects, attempts to discontinue, legal and social effects (including parental and marital relationships)
  nicotine use: amount
  caffeine use: amount, latest use in a typical day
  diet (e.g., regular, junk food, diabetic, vegan/vegetarian, weight reduction)
  exercise: frequency
  sleep: total hours, pattern
  safety (e.g., seat belts, sunblock, smoke detectors)

Physical Health
  height/weight
  allergies to medications
  illnesses, injuries, surgeries, and limitations (present and past)
  physical review of systems (present and past)
    seizures; loss of consciousness; major head injury; hypertension; diabetes; stroke; hypercholesterolemia; cancer; HIV; history of chemical exposure; and neurological, cardiac, pulmonary, gastrointestinal, hepatic, renal, thyroid, or hormonal problems

Current Treatment
  current medications
    name, purpose, dose, frequency, duration (at current dose and total usage), side effects, effectiveness
  current therapy, programs, groups, self-help books, coping strategies

Psychiatric/Psychotherapeutic Treatment History (emphasis on first and most recent treatments)
  date (onset, completion)
  circumstances at onset (including thoughts, emotions, behaviors, substance use)
  circumstances of obtaining treatment (e.g., voluntary, involuntary, coercion)
  name of treatment personnel or institution (psychiatrist, therapist, hospital, day program)
  diagnoses
  treatment type (e.g., medications, ECT, therapy)
  effectiveness

Family Psychiatric History
  relation to patient (including side of family)
  condition (diagnosis; if unavailable: symptoms)
  basis for diagnosis (e.g., professional, suspected by patient)
  treatments (therapy, hospitalizations, medications)

(continued)

Personal/Social History
    parents: age, ethnic background, health; if deceased—age, year, and cause of death
    siblings: age, gender, health; if deceased—age, year, and cause of death
    pregnancy/birth complications
    early development (any knowledge of delayed walking/talking)
    childhood (in general)
        quality of family relationships
        religious upbringing
        subcultural values/rituals
    residences
    school: performance, motivation, final educational level
    friends (e.g., none, a few, many, a group)
    intimate relationships (including engagements/marriages/divorces)
    children: gender, age, quality of relationships, frequency of contact
    occupations: type, maximum duration, most recent, reasons for termination
    military service: branch, years, combat exposure, type of discharge
    forensic contacts (e.g., arrests, convictions, incarcerations, parole, probation)
    major events/traumas (e.g., assault, bullying, abuse, best/worst memories, influences)
    past life goals

Current Personal Data
    interests
    religion
    needs/wishes
    current life goals
    contentment
    strengths
    weaknesses/vulnerabilities
    social interaction style
    stressors
    general activity schedule

Attitude Toward Treatment
    goals for treatment/problem list
    motivation for change
    expectations regarding therapy
    views/beliefs about medication
    beliefs about mental illness

(continued)

Observations
    appearance
    alertness
    psychomotor activity
    affect
    attention/interactiveness/eye contact
    speech
    thought processes
    orientation
    general cognition/intelligence
    insight
    judgment

Cognitive Assessment of Psychosis Inventory (CAPI)

Client ID:		Date:		Session #:
Diagnosis:				
Presenting symptom:	☐ Hallucination		☐ Delusion	☐ Bizarre behavior

Type:	☐ Auditory
	   ☐ Inside head
	   ☐ Outside head
	   ☐ Familiar
	   ☐ Unfamiliar
	   ☐ Male
	   ☐ Female
	   ☐ Benevolent
	   ☐ Malevolent
		☐ Visual
		☐ Tactile
		☐ Olfactory
		☐ Gustatory
			☐ Paranoid
			☐ Grandiose
			☐ Somatic
			☐ Erotomanic
			☐ Jealous
			☐ Religious
			☐ Guilt
				Specify:

Intensity:				
Frequency:				
Situation/Activating event(s):				
Beliefs:				
Emotional and behavioral consequences: ☐ Ego syntonic ☐ Ego dystonic				
Compensatory strategies:				
Insight:				
Historical antecedents:				
Core beliefs:				

This inventory is used during sessions as a way to record the sequence of psychological processes involved in a specific occurrence of a psychotic symptom. The information gathered facilitates the development of the case conceptualization. Dennis Given, PsyD, and Karen Shinkle, MSS, contributed to the development of this inventory.

Cognitive Triads for Delusional Beliefs

Type of delusion	View of self	View of others (the world)	View of future
Paranoid	Vulnerable [important] (inferior, defective, socially undesirable)	Powerful, threatening; others are harmful, hostile, and malevolent	Hopeless, uncertain
Jealous	Unworthy, unappealing	Distrustful, exploitative; actions or others are intentional	Hopeless
Control	Weak, powerless, helpless	Powerful, omnipotent, omniscient	Largely determined by others
Somatic	Vulnerable to harm and illness	Dangerous, threatening, infectious	Characterized by suffering
Guilt	Self-loathing	Punishing	Doomed
Grandiose	Special, important (inadequate)	Unrewarding; others are inferior	Optimistic, hopeful
Magical thinking	Capable, possess powers and abilities (inadequate)	Others are vulnerable to powers	Controllable, predictable
Referential (positive form)	Important (inadequate)	Others are powerful, knowledgeable, and "tuned in"	Hopeful

For each category of delusion, hypothesized core beliefs are listed in relation to the components of the cognitive triad—self, others (the world), and the future. [ ] = intermediate core beliefs; ( ) = underlying core beliefs. Dennis Given, PsyD, contributed to this appendix.

Cognitive Distortions
Seen in Patients with Psychosis

Category	Distortion	Explanation	Example
Categorization/ generalization	Dichotomous thinking	Seeing things in terms of two mutually exclusive categories in which no middle ground exists.	"I can't trust anyone."
	Labeling	Attaching global labels to oneself (or others) rather than referring to specific events or actions.	"I'm defective."
	Overgeneralization	A specific event represents life in general rather than being one event among many.	Person believes that because someone was walking behind her down the street, she is always being followed.
Selection bias	Minimization/ mental filter	Treating positive experiences as insignificant or unimportant.	A paranoid individual viewing the goodwill of others as rare exceptions.
	Disqualifying the positive	Positive experiences that conflict with the person's negative views are discounted.	Despite medical tests to the contrary, a person believes he has worms infesting his organs.
	"Should" statements	Believing one way to feel, think, or behave is the only proper way.	"My voices say I should leave the hospital, so I will."
Attribution of responsibility	Personalization/ blame	Believing one (or someone else) is the cause of a particular event to the exclusion of other factors. Can refer to real or imagined situations or events.	Person believes that people on the street are angry at her because she's a Christian.

(continued)

Category	Distortion	Explanation	Example
Arbitrary inference	Jumping to conclusions	Drawing incorrect conclusions about a situation based on a single piece or a few pieces of information.	A friend acts differently so the individual assumes he's an imposter.
	Emotional reasoning	Assuming one's emotional state reflects the true situation.	Because an individual feels like she is being punished, she believes it to be true.
Assumption	Mind reading	Assuming one knows the motives for others' behavior.	"A person coughing is giving me a signal that he doesn't like me."
	Fortune telling	Acting as if future predictions are inevitable truths.	"If I don't wear this aluminum foil hat, then radio waves will destroy my brain."
	Catastrophizing	Seeing negative events as inevitable catastrophes.	Person believes a wrong-number phone call is someone planning to attack her.

Cognitive distortions common to a number of emotional conditions are listed with examples pertaining more specifically to psychotic symptoms. Dennis Given, PsyD, contributed to this appendix.

Cognitive Distortions Specific to Psychosis

Category	Distortion	Explanation	Arbitrary inference
Categorization/ generalization	Magnification of power	Viewing others as all-powerful or all-knowing.	"Others can read my mind."
Selection bias	Discrimination error	Difficulty distinguishing similar aspects of a situation or event.	Person has difficulty recognizing subtle differences in facial cues (e.g., a frown always indicates anger rather than sadness, disappointment, frustration, etc.).
Assumption	Misattribution/ magical thinking	Mistakenly attributing a causal link to a real or imagined stimulus in an attempt to explain a situation or emotional state. Thinking tends to be concrete rather than abstract.	Person concludes her brain was stolen in response to an unfamiliar sensation or emotion.

Cognitive distortions specific to psychotic symptoms are listed with examples. Dennis Given, PsyD, contributed to this appendix.

Thought Disorder Rating Scale (THORATS)

1. Frequency: Formal thought disorder is present:
   0   Less than once a week
   1   Once a week to less than once a day
   2   Once a day to less than once an hour
   3   Once an hour but not almost continuously
   4   Continuously or almost continuously

2. Duration: When present, it lasts:
   0   Never
   1   For a few seconds to less than a minute
   2   For a minute to less than an hour
   3   For 1–2 hours
   4   For more than 2 hours

3. Comprehensibility: Speech is understood:
   0   At all times
   1   67–99% of the time
   2   34–66% of the time
   3   1–33% of the time
   4   Never

4. Amount of distress: When present, thought disorder is distressing:
   0   Never
   1   1–33% of the time
   2   34–66% of the time
   3   67–99% of the time
   4   Always

5. Intensity of distress: This distress is:
   0   Not at all
   1   Mild
   2   Moderate
   3   Marked
   4   Severe

6. Disruption to life: Disruption due to thought disorder is:
   0   Not at all
   1   Mild
   2   Moderate
   3   Marked
   4   Severe

This is a suggested, untested questionnaire to assess the severity of formal thought disorder. It can be used in questioning patients, parents, case workers, or others. The examiner can decide the length of time to assess (e.g., within the last week, month, 3 months).

References

Abi-Dargham, A., Rodenhiser, J., Printz, D., Zea-Ponce, Y., Gil, R., Kegeles, L. S., et al. (2000). Increased baseline occupancy of D_2 receptors by dopamine in schizophrenia. *Proceedings of the National Academy of Sciences of the United States of America*, 97(14), 8104–8109.

Addington, J., Saeedi, H., & Addington, D. (2005). The course of cognitive functioning in first episode psychosis: Changes over time and impact on outcome. *Schizophrenia Research, 78*, 35–43.

Adler, L. E., Freedman, R., Ross, R. G., Olincy, A., & Waldo, M. C. (1999). Elementary phenotypes in the neurobiological and genetic study of schizophrenia. *Biological Psychiatry, 46*(1), 8–18.

Adler, L. E., Olincy, A., Waldo, M., Harris, J. G., Griffith, J., Stevens, K., et al. (1998). Schizophrenia, sensory gating, and nicotinic receptors. *Schizophrenia Bulletin, 24*(2), 189–202.

Akbarian, S., Bunney, W. E., Jr., Potkin, S. G., Wigal, S. B., Hagman, J. O., Sandman, C. A., et al. (1993). Altered distribution of nicotinamide–adenine dinucleotide phosphate–diaphorase cells in frontal lobe of schizophrenics implies disturbances of cortical development. *Archives of General Psychiatry, 50*(3), 169–177.

Akbarian, S., Vinuela, A., Kim, J. J., Potkin, S. G., Bunney, W. E., Jr., & Jones, E. G. (1993). Distorted distribution of nicotinamide–adenine dinucleotide phosphate–diaphorase neurons in temporal lobe of schizophrenics implies anomalous cortical development. *Archives of General Psychiatry, 50*(3), 178–187.

Aleman, A. (2001). *Cognitive neuropsychiatry of hallucinations in schizophrenia: How the brain misleads itself.* Tekst: Proefschrift Universiteit Utrecht.

Aleman, A., Böcker, K., & de Haan, E. (2001). Hallucinatory predisposition and vividness of auditory imagery: Self-report and behavioral indices. *Perceptual and Motor Skills, 93,* 268–274.

Allen, H. A., Liddle, P. F., & Frith, C. D. (1993). Negative features, retrieval processes and verbal fluency in schizophrenia. *British Journal of Psychiatry, 163,* 769–775.

Allendoerfer, K. L., & Shatz, C. J. (1994). The subplate, a transient neocortical structure: Its role in the development of connections between thalamus and cortex. *Annual Review of Neuroscience, 17,* 185–218.

Alpert, M., Shaw, R. J., Pouget, E. R., & Lim, K. O. (2002). A comparison of clinical ratings with vocal acoustic measures of flat affect and alogia. *Journal of Psychiatry Research, 36,* 347–353.

American Psychiatric Association. (1980). *Diagnostic and statistical manual of mental disorders* (3rd ed.). Washington, DC: Author.

American Psychiatric Association. (2000). *Diagnostic and statistical manual of mental disorders* (4th ed., text rev.). Washington, DC: Author.

an der Heiden, W., & Häfner, H. (2000). The epidemiology of onset and course of schizophrenia. *European Archives of Psychiatry and Clinical Neuroscience, 250,* 292–303.

Anderson, S. A., Volk, D. W., & Lewis, D. A. (1996). Increased density of microtubule associated protein 2-immunoreactive neurons in the prefrontal white matter of schizophrenic subjects. *Schizophrenia Research, 19*(2–3), 111–119.

Andreasen, N. C. (1979). Thought, language, and communication disorders: I. Clinical assessment, definition of terms and evaluation of their reliability. *Archives of General Psychiatry, 36*(12), 1315–1321.

Andreasen, N. C. (1984a). *The broken brain: The biological revolution in psychiatry.* New York: Harper & Row.

Andreasen, N. C. (1984b). *The Scale for the Assessment of Negative Symptoms (SANS).* Iowa City: University of Iowa Department of Psychiatry.

Andreasen, N. (1984c). *The Scale for the Assessment of Positive Symptoms (SAPS).* Iowa City: University of Iowa Department of Psychiatry.

Andreasen, N. C. (1989). The Scale for the Assessment of Negative Symptoms (SANS): Conceptual and theoretical foundations. *British Journal of Psychiatry, 155*(Suppl. 7), 53–58.

Andreasen, N. C. (1990a). Methods of assessing positive and negative symptoms. In N. C. Andreasen (Ed.), *Schizophrenia: Positive and negative symptoms and syndromes* (Vol. 24, pp. 73–88). Basel, Switzerland: Karger.

Andreasen, N. C. (1990b). Positive and negative symptoms: Historical and conceptual aspects. In N. C. Andreasen (Ed.), *Schizophrenia: Positive and negative symptoms and syndromes* (Vol. 24, pp. 1–42). Basel, Switzerland: Karger.

Andreasen, N. C. (1999). A unitary model of schizophrenia: Bleuler's "fragmented phrene" as schizencephaly. *Archives of General Psychiatry, 56*(9), 781–787.

Andreasen, N. C., Arndt, S., Alliger, R., Miller, D., & Flaum, M. (1995). Symptoms of schizophrenia: Methods, meanings and mechanisms. *Archives of General Psychiatry, 52*(5), 341–351.

Andreasen, N. C., Carpenter, W. T., Kane, J. M., Lasser, R. A., Marder, S. R., & Weinberger, D. R. (2005). Remission in schizophrenia: Proposed criteria and rationale for consensus. *American Journal of Psychiatry, 162*, 441–449.

Andreasen, N. C., & Grove, W. M. (1986). Thought, language, and communication in schizophrenia: Diagnosis and prognosis. *Schizophrenia Bulletin, 12*(3), 348–359.

Andreasen, N. C., & Olsen, S. (1982). Negative versus positive schizophrenia: Definitions and validation. *Archives of General Psychiatry, 39*, 789–794.

Andreasen, N. C., Olsen, S. A., Dennert, J. W., & Smith, M. R. (1982). Ventricular enlargement in schizophrenia: Relationship to positive and negative symptoms. *American Journal of Psychiatry, 139*, 297–302.

Angrist, B. M., & Gershon, S. (1970). The phenomenology of experimentally induced amphetamine psychosis: Preliminary observations. *Biological Psychiatry, 2*, 95–107.

Arieti, S. (1974). *Interpretation of schizophrenia* (2nd ed.). New York: Basic Books.

Arndt, S., Andreasen, N. C., Flaum, M., Miller, D., & Nopoulos, P. (1995). A longitudinal study of symptom dimensions in schizophrenia: Prediction and patterns of change. *Archives of General Psychiatry, 52*(5), 352–360.

Arnold, S. E. (1999). Neurodevelopmental abnormalities in schizophrenia: Insights from neuropathology. *Developmental Psychopathology, 11*(3), 439–456.

Arnold, S. E., & Trojanowski, J. Q. (1996). Recent advances in defining the neuropathology of schizophrenia. *Acta Neuropathologica (Berlin), 92*(3), 217–231.

Arntz, A., Rauner, M., & van den Hout, M. (1995). "If I feel anxious there must be danger": Ex-consequentia reasoning in inferring danger in anxiety disorders. *Behavior Research and Therapy, 33*, 917–925.

Asberg, M., Montgomery, S. A., Perris, C., Schalling, D., & Sedvall, G. (1978). A comprehensive psychopathological rating scale. *Acta Psychiatrica Scandinavica, 271*(Suppl. 271), 5–27.

Badcock, J. C., Waters, F. A. V., & Maybery, M. (2007). On keeping (intrusive) thoughts to one's self: Testing a cognitive model of auditory hallucinations. *Cognitive Neuropsychiatry, 12*(1), 78–89.

Badcock, J. C., Waters, F. A. V., Maybery, M. T., & Michie, P. T. (2005). Auditory hallucinations: Failure to inhibit irrelevant memories. *Cognitive Neuropsychiatry, 10*, 125–136.

Baddeley, A. D. (1986). *Working memory.* Oxford, UK: Oxford University Press.

Baddeley, A. D. (1990). *Human memory: Theory and practice.* Oxford, UK: Oxford University Press.

Baddeley, A. D. (1992). Working memory. *Science, 255*(5044), 556–559.

Baker, C., & Morrison, A. (1998). Metacognition, intrusive thoughts and auditory hallucinations. *Psychological Medicine, 28,* 1199–1208.

Barber, T. X., & Calverly, D. S. (1964). An experimental study of "hypnotic" (auditory and visual) hallucinations. *Journal of Abnormal and Social Psychology, 63,* 13–20.

Barnes, T. R. E., & Liddle, P. F. (1990). Evidence for the validity of negative symptoms. In N. C. Andreasen (Ed.), *Schizophrenia: Positive and negative symptoms and syndromes* (Vol. 24, pp. 43–72). Basel, Switzerland: Karger.

Barrett, T. R. (1992). Verbal hallucinations in normals: I. People who hear "voices." *Applied Cognitive Psychology, 6,* 379–387.

Barrowclough, C., Tarrier, N., Humphreys, L., Ward, J., Gregg, L., & Andrews, B. (2003). Self-esteem in schizophrenia: Relationships between self-evaluation, family attitudes, and symptomatology. *Journal of Abnormal Psychology, 112,* 92–99.

Beck, A. T. (1952). Successful outpatient psychotherapy of a chronic schizophrenic with a delusion based on borrowed guilt. *Psychiatry, 15,* 305–312.

Beck, A. T. (1963). Thinking and depression: Idiosyncratic content and cognitive distortions. *Archives of General Psychiatry, 9,* 324–333.

Beck, A. T. (1967). *Depression: Clinical, experimental, and theoretical aspects.* New York: Harper & Row. Republished as: Beck, A. T. (1970). *Depression: Causes and treatment.* Philadelphia: University of Pennsylvania Press.

Beck, A. T. (1976). *Cognitive therapy and the emotional disorders.* New York: Meridian.

Beck, A. T. (1996). Beyond belief: A theory of modes, personality, and psychopathology. In P. Salkovskis (Ed.), *Frontiers of cognitive therapy* (pp. 1–25). New York: Guilford Press.

Beck, A. T., Baruch, E., Balter, J. M., Steer, R. A., & Warman, D. M. (2004). A new instrument for measuring insight: The Beck Cognitive Insight Scale. *Schizophrenia Research, 68*(2–3), 319–329.

Beck, A. T., Emery, G., & Greenberg, R. L. (1985). *Anxiety disorders and phobias: A cognitive perspective.* New York: Basic Books.

Beck, A. T., Freeman, A., Davis, D., & Associates. (2003). *Cognitive therapy of personality disorders* (2nd ed.). New York: Guilford.

Beck, A. T., & Nash, J. F. (2005, September). *A conversation with Aaron Beck and John Nash.* Paper presented at the Arthur P. Noyes schizophrenia conference, Philadelphia.

Beck, A. T., & Rector, N. A. (2002). Delusions: A cognitive perspective. *Journal of Cognitive Psychotherapy, 16,* 455–468.

Beck, A. T., & Rector, N. A. (2003). A cognitive model of hallucinations. *Cognitive Therapy and Research, 27,* 19–52.

Beck, A. T., & Rector, N. A. (2005). Cognitive approaches to schizophrenia: Theory and therapy. *Annual Review of Clinical Psychology, 1,* 577–606.

Beck, A. T., Rush, A. J., Shaw, B. F., & Emery, G. (1979). *Cognitive therapy of depression*. New York: Guilford Press.

Beck, A. T., & Steer, R. A. (1993). *Manual for the Beck Anxiety Inventory*. San Antonio, TX: Psychological Corporation.

Beck, A. T., Steer, R. A., & Brown, G. K. (1996). *Manual for Beck Depression Inventory–II*. San Antonio, TX: Psychological Corporation.

Beck, A. T., Ward, C. H., Mendleson, M., Mock, J., & Erbaugh, J. (1961). An inventory for measuring depression. *Archives of General Psychiatry, 4*, 561–571.

Beck, A. T., & Warman, D. M. (2004). Cognitive insight: Theory and assessment. In X. F. Amador & A. S. David (Eds.), *Insight and psychosis: Awareness of illness in schizophrenia and related disorders* (2nd ed., pp. 79–87). Oxford, UK: Oxford University Press.

Beck, J. S. (1995). *Cognitive therapy: Basics and beyond*. New York: Guilford Press.

Beckmann, H., & Lauer, M. (1997). The human striatum in schizophrenia: II. Increased number of striatal neurons in schizophrenics. *Psychiatry Research, 68*(2–3), 99–109.

Beck-Sander, A., Birchwood, M., & Chadwick, P. (1997). Acting on command hallucinations: A cognitive approach. *British Journal of Clinical Psychology, 36*, 139–148.

Behrendt, R. (1998). Underconstrained perception: A theoretical approach to the nature and function of verbal hallucinations. *Comprehensive Psychiatry, 39*, 236–248.

Belger, A., & Dichter, G. (2005). Structural and functional neuroanatomy. In J. A. Lieberman, T. S. Stroup, & D. O. Perkins (Eds.), *Textbook of schizophrenia* (pp. 167–185). Washington, DC: American Psychiatric Association.

Benes, F. M., Kwok, E. W., Vincent, S. L., & Todtenkopf, M. S. (1998). A reduction of nonpyramidal cells in sector CA2 of schizophrenics and manic depressives. *Biological Psychiatry, 44*(2), 88–97.

Benjamin, L. S. (1989). Is chronicity a function of the relationship between the person and the auditory hallucination? *Schizophrenia Bulletin, 15*, 291–310.

Bentall, R. P. (1990). The illusion of reality: A review and integration of psychological research on hallucinations. *Psychological Bulletin, 107*, 82–95.

Bentall, R. P. (2004). *Madness explained: Psychosis and human nature*. London: Penguin Books.

Bentall, R. P., Baker, G., & Havers, S. (1991). Reality monitoring and psychotic hallucinations. *British Journal of Clinical Psychology, 30*, 213–222.

Bentall, R. P. & Kaney, S. (1989). Content specific information processing and persecutory delusions: An investigation using the emotional Stroop test. *British Journal of Medical Psychology, 62*, 355–364.

Bentall, R. P., Kaney, S., & Bowen-Jones, K. (1995). Persecutory delusions and recall of threat-related, depression-related, and neutral words. *Cognitive Therapy and Research, 19,* 445–457.

Bentall, R. P., Kaney, S., & Dewey, M. E. (1991). Paranoia and social responding: An attribution theory analysis. *British Journal of Clinical Psychology, 30,* 13–23.

Bentall, R. P., Rowse, G., Kinderman, P., Blackwood, N., Howard, R., Moore, R., et al. (2008). Paranoid delusions in schizophrenia spectrum disorders and depression: The transdiagnostic role of expectations of negative events and negative self-esteem. *Journal of Nervous and Mental Disease, 196,* 375–383.

Bentall, R. P., Rowse, G., Shryane, N., Kinderman, P., Howard, R., Blackwood, N., et al. (in press). The phenomenology and cognitive structure of paranoid delusions: A transdiagnostic investigation of patients with schizophrenia spectrum disorders and depression. *Archives of General Psychiatry.*

Bentall, R. P., & Slade, P. (1985). Reality testing and auditory hallucinations: A signal detection analysis. *British Journal of Clinical Psychology, 24,* 159–169.

Berenbaum, H., & Oltmanns, T. F. (1992). Emotional experience and expression in schizophrenia and depression. *Journal of Abnormal Psychology, 101,* 37–44.

Berman, I., Viegner, B., Merson, A., Allan, E., Pappas, D., & Green, A. I. (1997). Differential relationships between positive and negative symptoms and neuropsychological deficits in schizophrenia. *Schizophrenia Research, 25,* 1–10.

Berrios, G. E. (1985). Positive and negative symptoms and Jackson: A conceptual history. *Archives of General Psychiatry, 42*(1), 95–97.

Bilder, R. M., Mukherjee, S., Rieder, R. O., & Pandurangi, A. K. (1985). Symptomatic and neuropsychological components of defect states. *Schizophrenia Bulletin, 11*(3), 409419.

Birchwood, M., Mason, R., MacMillan, F., & Healy, J. (1993). Depression, demoralization and control over psychotic illness: A comparison of depressed and non-depressed patients with a chronic psychosis. *Psychological Medicine, 23*(2), 387–395.

Birchwood, M. J., & Chadwick, P. (1997). The omnipotence of voices: Testing the validity of a cognitive model. *Psychological Medicine, 27,* 1345–1353.

Birchwood, M. J., Macmillan, F., & Smith, J. (1992). Early intervention. In M. J. Birchwood & N. Tarrier (Eds.), *Innovations in the psychological management of schizophrenia: Assessment, treatment and services* (pp. 115–145). Oxford, UK: Wiley.

Blakemore, S., Wolpert, D., & Frith, C. (2000). Why can't you tickle yourself? *Neuroreport: For Rapid Communication of Neuroscience Research, 11,* R11–R16.

Blanchard, J. J., Horan, W. P., & Brown, S. A. (2001). Diagnostic differences in social anhedonia: A longitudinal study of schizophrenia and major depressive disorder. *Journal of Abnormal Psychology, 110,* 363–371.

Blanchard, J. J., Mueser, K. T., & Bellack, A. S. (1998). Anhedonia, positive and negative affect, and social functioning in schizophrenia. *Schizophrenia Bulletin, 24,* 413–424.

Bleuler, E. (1950). *Dementia praecox or the group of schizophrenias* (J. Kinkin, Trans.). New York: International Universities Press. (Original work published 1911)

Blood, I. M., Wertz, H., Blood, G. W., Bennett, S., & Simpson, K. C. (1997). The effects of life stressors and daily stressors on stuttering. *Journal of Speech, Language, and Hearing Research, 40*(1), 134–143.

Böcker, K., Hijman, R., Kahn, R., & de Haan, E. (2000). Perception, mental imagery and reality discrimination in hallucinating and non-hallucinating schizophrenic patients. *British Journal of Clinical Psychology, 39,* 397–406.

Boos, H. B. M., Aleman, A., Cahn, W., Hulshoff Pol, H., & Kahn, R. S. (2007). Brain volumes in relatives of patients with schizophrenia: A meta-analysis. *Archives of General Psychiatry, 64,* 297–304.

Bouricius, J. K. (1989). Negative symptoms and emotions in schizophrenia. *Schizophrenia Bulletin, 15*(2), 201–208.

Braff, D. L. (1993). Information processing and attention dysfunctions in schizophrenia. *Schizophrenia Bulletin, 19,* 233–259.

Boydell, J., & Murray, R. M. (2003). Urbanization, migration, and risk of schizophrenia. In R. M. Murray, P. Jones, E. Susser, J. van Os, & M. Cannon (Eds.), *The epidemiology of schizophrenia* (pp. 49–67). Cambridge, UK: Cambridge University Press.

Braff, D. L., Saccuzzo, D. P., & Geyer, M. A. (1991). Information processing dysfunctions in schizophrenia: Studies of visual backward masking, sensorimotor gating, and habituation. In S. R. Steinhauer, J. H. Gruzelier, & J. Zubin (Eds.), *Handbook of schizophrenia* (Vol. 5, pp. 303–334). Amsterdam: Elsevier.

Braver, T. S., Barch, D. M., & Cohen, J. D. (1999). Cognition and control in schizophrenia: A computational model of dopamine and prefrontal function. *Biological Psychiatry, 46*(3), 312–328.

Braver, T. S., & Cohen, J. D. (1999). Dopamine, cognitive control, and schizophrenia: The gating model. *Progress in Brain Research, 121,* 327–349.

Brébion, G., Smith, M. J., & Gorman, J. M. (1996). Reality monitoring failure in schizophrenia: The role of selective attention. *Schizophrenia Research, 22,* 173–180.

Brehm, J. W. (1962). A dissonance analysis of attitude-discrepant behavior. In M. J. Rosenberg, *Attitude organization and change* (pp. 164–197). New York: Gaines Dog Research Center.

Breier, A., Schreiber, J. L., Dyer, J., & Pickar, D. (1991). National Institute of Mental Health longitudinal study of chronic schizophrenia. *Archives of General Psychiatry, 48,* 239–246.

Bremner, J. D. (2005). *Brain imaging handbook.* New York: Norton.

Bresnahan, M., Begg, M. D., Brown, A., Schaefer, C., Sohler, N., Insel, B., et al. (2007). Race and risk of schizophrenia in a U.S. birth cohort: Another example of health disparity? *International Journal of Epidemiology, 36*, 751–758.

Brett, C. M. C., Peters, E. R., Johns, L. C., Tabraham, P., Valmaggia, L., & McGuire, P. (2007). The Appraisals of Anomalous Experiences interview (AANEX): A multi-dimensional measure of psychological responses to anomalies associated with psychosis. *British Journal of Psychiatry, 191*, 523–530.

Brett, E. A., & Starker, S. (1977). Auditory imagery and hallucinations. *Journal of Nervous and Mental Disease, 164*, 394–400.

Brett-Jones, J., Garety, P. A., & Hemsley, D. R. (1987). Measuring delusional experiences: A method and application. *British Journal of Clinical Psychology, 26*, 257–265.

Bromet, E. J., Naz, B., Fochtmann, L. J., Carlson, G. A., & Tanenberg-Karant, M. (2005). Long-term diagnostic stability and outcome in recent first-episode cohort studies of schizophrenia. *Schizophrenia Bulletin, 31*(3), 639–649.

Broome, M. R., Johns, L. C., Valli, I., Woolley, J. B., Tabraham, P., Brett, C., et al. (2007a). Delusion formation and reasoning biases in those at clinical high risk for psychosis. *British Journal of Psychiatry, 191*, s38–s42.

Broome, M. R., Matthiasson, P., Fusar-Poli, P., Woolley, J. B., Johns, L. C., Tabraham, P., et al. (2007b). *Neural correlates of executive function and working memory in the "at-risk mental state."* Manuscript submitted for publication.

Broome, M. R., Woolley, J. B., Tabraham, P., Johns, L. C., Bramon, E., Murray, G. K., et al. (2005). What causes the onset of psychosis? *Schizophrenia Research, 79*, 23–34.

Brown, R. G., & Pluck, G. (2000). Negative symptoms: The "pathology" of motivation and goal-directed behavior. *Trends in Neuroscience, 23*, 412–417.

Brown, S. (1997). Excess mortality of schizophrenia: A meta-analysis. *British Journal of Psychiatry, 171*, 502–508.

Brugger, (2001). From haunted brain to haunted science: A cognitive neuroscience view of paranormal and pseudoscientific thought. In J. Houran & R. Lange (Eds.), *Hauntings and poltergeists: Multidisciplinary perspectives* (pp. 195–213). Jefferson, NC: McFarland.

Buchanan, R. W., & Carpenter, W. T., Jr. (2005). Concept of schizophrenia. In B. J. Sadock & V. A. Sadock (Eds.), *Kaplan and Sadock's comprehensive textbook of psychiatry* (8th ed., pp. 1329–1345). Philadelphia: Lippincott, Williams & Wilkins.

Bunney, B. G., Potkin, S. G., & Bunney, W. E., Jr. (1995). New morphological and neuropathological findings in schizophrenia: A neurodevelopmental perspective. *Clinical Neuroscience, 3*(2), 81–88.

Bunney, W. E., Jr. (1978). Drug therapy and psychobiological research advances in the psychoses in the past decade. *American Journal of Psychiatry, 135*(Suppl.), 8–13.

Bunney, W. E., Jr., & Bunney, B. G. (1999). Neurodevelopmental hypothesis of schizophrenia. In D. S. Charney, E. J. Nestler, & B. S. Bunney (Eds.), *Neurobiology of mental illness* (pp. 225–235). Oxford, UK: Oxford University Press.

Burbridge, J. A., & Barch, D. M. (2007). Anhedonia and the experience of emotion in individuals with schizophrenia. *Journal of Abnormal Psychology, 116,* 30–42.

Burman, B., Medrick, S. A., Machon, R. A., Parnas, J., & Schulsinger, F. (1987). Children at high risk for schizophrenia: Parent and offspring perceptions of family relationships. *Journal of Abnormal Psychology, 96,* 364–366.

Calabrese, J. D., & Corrigan, P. W. (2005). Beyond dementia praecox: Findings from long-term follow-up studies of schizophrenia. In R. O. Ralph & P. W. Corrigan (Eds.), *Recovery in mental illness: Broadening our understanding of wellness* (pp. 63–84). Washington, DC: American Psychological Association.

Cannon, M., Caspi, A., Moffitt, T. E., Harrington, H., Taylor, A., Murray, R. M., et al. (2002). Evidence for early-childhood pan-developmental impairment specific to schizophreniform disorder: Results from a longitudinal birth cohort. *Archives of General Psychiatry, 59,* 449–457.

Cannon, M., Cotter, D., Coffey, V. P., Sham, P. C., Takei, N., Larkin, C., et al. (1996). Prenatal exposure to the 1957 influenza epidemic and adult schizophrenia: A follow-up study. *British Journal of Psychiatry, 168*(3), 368–371.

Cannon, M., Jones, P. B., & Murray, R. M. (2002). Obstetric complications and schizophrenia: Historical and meta-analytic review. *American Journal of Psychiatry, 159,* 1080–1092.

Cannon, M., Kendell, R., Susser, E., & Jones, P. (2003). Prenatal and perinatal risk factors for schizophrenia. In R. M. Murray, P. B. Jones, E. Susser, J. van Os, & M. Cannon (Eds.), *The epidemiology of schizophrenia* (pp. 74–99). Cambridge, UK: Cambridge University Press.

Cannon, M., Tarrant, C. J., Huttunen, M. O., & Jones, P. B. (2003). Childhood development and later schizophrenia: Evidence from genetic high-risk and birth cohort studies. In R. M. Murray, P. B. Jones, E. Susser, J. van Os, & M. Cannon (Eds.), *The epidemiology of schizophrenia* (pp. 100–123). Cambridge, UK: Cambridge University Press.

Cannon, T. D., Kaprio, J., Lonnqvist, J., Huttunen, M., & Koskenvuo, M. (1998). The genetic epidemiology of schizophrenia in a Finnish twin cohort: A population-based modeling study. *Archives of General Psychiatry, 55*(1), 67–74.

Cannon, T. D., Mednick, S. A., & Parnas, J. (1990). Antecedents of predominantly negative and predominantly positive symptom schizophrenia in a high-risk population. *Archives of General Psychiatry, 47,* 622–632.

Cannon, T. D., van Erp, T. G., Rosso, I. M., Huttunen, M., Lonnqvist, J., Pirkola, T., et al. (2002). Fetal hypoxia and structural brain abnormalities in schizophrenic patients, their siblings, and controls. *Archives of General Psychiatry, 59*(1), 35–41.

Cardno, A. G., & Gottesman, I. I. (2000). Twin studies of schizophrenia: From bow-and-arrow concordances to *Star Wars* Mx and functional genomics. *American Journal of Medical Genetics, 97*, 12–17.

Carlsson, A., & Lindqvist, M. (1963). Effect of chlorpromazine or haloperidol on formation of 3-methoxytyramine and normetanephrine in mouse brain. *Acta Pharmacologica et Toxicologica (Copenhagen), 20*, 140–144.

Carpenter, W. T., Jr. (2006). The schizophrenia paradigm: A hundred-year challenge. *Journal of Nervous and Mental Disease, 194*(9), 639–643.

Carpenter, W. T., Jr., Buchanan, R. W., Kirkpatrick, B., Tamminga, C., & Wood, F. (1993). Strong inference, theory testing, and the neuroanatomy of schizophrenia. *Archives of General Psychiatry, 50*(10), 825–831.

Carpenter, W. T., Jr., Heinrichs, D. W., & Wagman, A. M. I. (1988). Deficit and nondeficit forms of schizophrenia: The concept. *American Journal of Psychiatry, 145*(5), 578–583.

Carter, D. M., Mackinnon, A., & Copolov, D. L. (1996). Patients' strategies for coping with auditory hallucinations. *Journal of Nervous and Mental Disease, 184*, 159–164.

Cartwright-Hatton, S., & Wells, A. (1997). Beliefs about worry and intrusions: The meta-cognitions questionnaire and its correlates. *Journal of Anxiety Disorders, 11*(3), 279–296.

Caspi, A., Moffitt, T. E., Cannon, M., McClay, J., Murray, R., Harrington, H., et al. (2005). Moderation of the effect of adolescent-onset cannabis use on adult psychosis by a functional polymorphism in the catechol-O-methyltransferase gene: Longitudinal evidence of a gene X environment interaction. *Biological Psychiatry, 57*(10), 1117–1127.

Caspi, A., Reichenberg, A., Weiser, M., Rabinowitz, J., Kaplan, Z., Knobler, H., et al. (2003). Cognitive performance in schizophrenia patients assessed before and following the first psychotic episode. *Schizophrenia Research, 65*, 87–94.

Cather, C., Penn, D., Otto, M., & Goff, D. C. (1994). Cognitive therapy for delusions in schizophrenia: Models, benefits, and new approaches. *Journal of Cognitive Psychotherapy, 18*, 207–221.

Cather, C., Penn, D., Otto, M. W., Yovel, I., Mueser, K. T., & Goff, D. C. (2005). A pilot study of functional cognitive behavioral therapy (FCBT) for schizophrenia. *Schizophrenia Research, 74*, 201–209.

Chadwick, P., & Birchwood, M. J. (1994). The omnipotence of voices: I. A cognitive approach to auditory hallucinations. *British Journal of Psychiatry, 164*, 190–201.

Chadwick, P., & Birchwood, M. J. (1995). The omnipotence of voices: II. The belief about voices questionnaire (BAVQ). *British Journal of Psychiatry, 166*(6), 773–776.

Chadwick, P., Birchwood, M. J., & Trower, P. (1996). *Cognitive therapy for delusions, voices, and paranoia.* New York: Wiley.

Chakos, M. H., Lieberman, J. A., Bilder, R. M., Borenstein, M., Lerner, G., Bogerts, B., et al. (1994). Increase in caudate nuclei volumes of first-episode schizophrenic patients taking antipsychotic drugs. *American Journal of Psychiatry, 151*(10), 1430–1436.

Chapman, J. (1966). The early symptoms of schizophrenia. *British Journal of Psychiatry, 112*(484), 225–251.

Chapman, L. J. (1958). Intrusion of associative responses into schizophrenic conceptual performance. *Journal of Abnormal and Social Psychology, 56*(3), 374–379.

Chapman, L. J., & Chapman, J. P. (1965). The interpretation of words in schizophrenia. *Journal of Personality and Social Psychology, 95*, 135–146.

Chapman, L. J., & Chapman, J. P. (1973a). *Disorder thought in schizophrenia.* Englewood Cliffs, NJ: Prentice-Hall.

Chapman, L. J., & Chapman, J. P. (1973b). Problems in the measurement of cognitive deficit. *Psychology Bulletin, 79*(6), 380–385.

Chapman, L. J., Chapman, J. P., Kwapil, T. R., Eckbald, M., & Zinser, M. C. (1994). Putatively psychosis-prone subjects 10 years later. *Journal of Abnormal Psychology, 103*, 171–183.

Chapman, L. J., Chapman, J. P., & Miller, E. N. (1982). Reliabilities and intercorrelations of eight measure of proneness to psychosis. *Journal of Consulting and Clinical Psychology, 50*, 187–195.

Chapman, L. J., Chapman, J. P., & Miller, G. A (1964). A theory of verbal behaviour in schizophrenia. *Progress in Experimental Personality Research, 72*, 49–77.

Chapman, L. J., Chapman, J. P., & Raulin, M. L. (1976). Scales for physical and social anhedonia. *Journal of Abnormal Psychology, 85*, 374–382.

Chapman, L. J., & Taylor, J. A. (1957). Breadth of deviate concepts used by schizophrenics. *Journal of Abnormal and Social Psychology, 54*(1), 118–123.

Clark, D. A., Beck, A. T., & Alford, B. A. (1999). *Scientific foundations of cognitive theory and therapy of depression.* New York: Wiley.

Clark, D. M. (1986). A cognitive approach to panic. *Behaviour Research and Therapy, 24*, 461–470.

Clark, D. M., & Wells, A. (1995). A cognitive model of social phobia. In R. G. Heimberg, M. R. Liebowitz, D. A. Hope, & F. R. Schneier (Eds.), *Social phobia: Diagnosis, assessment, and treatment* (pp. 69–93). New York: Guilford Press.

Clark, H. H. (1996). *Using language.* New York: Cambridge University Press.

Close, H., & Garety, P. (1998). Cognitive assessment of voices: Further developments in understanding the emotional impact of voices. *British Journal of Clinical Psychology, 37*, 173–188.

Cohen, J. D., Barch, D. M., Carter, C., & Servan-Schreiber, D. (1999). Context-processing deficits in schizophrenia: Converging evidence from three theoretically motivated cognitive tasks. *Journal of Abnormal Psychology, 108*(1), 120–33.

Cohen, J. D., & Servan-Schreiber, D. (1992). Context, cortex, and dopamine: A connectionist approach to behavior and biology in schizophrenia. *Psychological Review, 99*(1), 45–77.

Collins, A. M., & Loftus, E. F. (1975). A spreading-activation theory of semantic processing. *Psychological Review, 82,* 407–428.

Collins, A. M., & Quillian, M. R. (1969). Retrieval time from semantic memory. *Journal of Verbal Learning and Verbal Memory, 8,* 240–247.

Connell, P. (1958). *Amphetamine psychosis.* London: Chapman & Hall.

Coppens, H. J., Sloof, C. J., Paans, M. J., Wiegman, T., Vaalburg, W., & Korf, J. (1991). High central D_2-dopamine receptor occupancy as assessed with positron emission tomography in medicated but therapy-resistant patients. *Biological Psychiatry, 29,* 629–634.

Corcoran, C., Walker, E., Huot, R., Mittal, V., Tessner, K., Kestler, L., et al. (2003). The stress cascade and schizophrenia: Etiology and onset. *Schizophrenia Bulletin, 29,* 671–692.

Cornblatt, B. A., & Keilp, J. G. (1994). Impaired attention, genetics, and the pathophysiology of schizophrenia. *Schizophrenia Bulletin, 20*(1), 31–46.

Cornblatt, B. A., Lencz, T., & Kane, J. M. (2001). Treatment of the schizophrenia prodome: It is presently ethical? [Special Issue: Ethics of early treatment intervention in schizophrenia]. *Schizophrenia Research, 51*(1), 31–38.

Cornblatt, B. A., Lenzenweger, M. F., Dworkin, R. H., & Erlenmeyer-Kimling, L. (1992). Childhood attentional dysfunctions predict social deficits in unaffected adults at risk for schizophrenia. *British Journal of Psychiatry, 161,* 59–64.

Cotter, D., Kerwin, R., Doshi, B., Martin, C. S., & Everall, I. P. (1997). Alterations in hippocampal non-phosphorylated MAP2 protein expression in schizophrenia. *Brain Research, 765*(2), 238–246.

Cougnard, A., Marcelis, M., Myin-Germeys, I., de Graaf, R., Vollebergh, W., Krabbendam, L., et al. (2007). Does normal developmental expression of psychosis combine with environmental risk to cause persistence of psychosis? A psychosis proneness—persistence model. *Psychological Medicine, 37,* 513–527.

Cowan, N. (1988). Evolving conceptions of memory storage, selective attention, and their mutual constraints within the human information-processing system. *Psychological Bulletin, 104*(2), 163–191.

Cox, D., & Cowling, P. (1989). *Are you normal?* London: Tower Press.

Cozolino, L. (2002). *The neuroscience of psychotherapy: Building and rebuilding the human brain.* New York: Norton.

Creese, I., Burt, D. R., & Snyder, S. H. (1976). Dopamine receptor binding predicts clinical and pharmacological potencies of antischizophrenic drugs. *Science, 192*(4238), 481–483.

Crow, T. J. (1980). Molecular pathology of schizophrenia: More than one disease process. *British Medical Journal, 280,* 66–68.

Crow, T. J. (2007). How and why genetic linkage has not solved the problem of psychosis: Review and hypothesis. *American Journal of Psychiatry, 164,* 13–21.

Csernansky, J. G., Joshi, S., Wang, L., Haller, J. W., Gado, M., Miller, J. P., et al. (1998). Hippocampal morphometry in schizophrenia by high dimensional brain mapping. *Proceedings of the National Academy of Sciences, 95*(19), 11406–11411.

Csipke, E., & Kinderman, P. (2002). *Self-talk and auditory hallucinations.* Manuscript in preparation.

Curtis, C. E., Calkins, M. E., Grove, W. M., Feil, K. J., & Iacono, W. G. (2001). Saccadic disinhibition in patients with acute and remitted schizophrenia and their first-degree biological relatives. *American Journal of Psychiatry, 158,* 100–106.

Cutting, J. (2003). Descriptive psychopathology. In S. R. Hirsch & D. L. Weinberger (Eds.), *Schizophrenia* (2nd ed., pp. 15–24). Malden, MA: Blackwell.

Daniel, D. G., Copeland, L. F., & Tamminga, C. (2004). Ziprasidone. In A. F. Schatzberg & C. B. Nemeroff (Eds.), *The American Psychiatric Publishing textbook of psychopharmacology* (3rd ed., pp. 507–518). Washington, DC: American Psychiatric Publishing.

Danos, P., Baumann, B., Bernstein, H. G., Franz, M., Stauch, R., Northoff, G., et al. (1998). Schizophrenia and anteroventral thalamic nucleus: Selective decrease of parvalbumin-immunoreactive thalamocortical projection neurons. *Psychiatry Research, 82*(1), 1–10.

Davatzikos, C., Shen, D., Gur, R. C., Wu, X., Liu, D., Fan, Y., et al. (2005). Whole-brain morphometric study of schizophrenia revealing a spatially complex set of focal abnormalities. *Archives of General Psychiatry, 62,* 1218–1227.

David, A. S. (1990). Insight and psychosis. *British Journal of Psychiatry, 156,* 798–808.

David, A. S., Buchanan, A., Reed, A., & Almeida, O. (1992). The assessment of insight in psychosis. *British Journal of Psychiatry, 161,* 599–602.

David, A. S., Malmberg, A., Brandt, L., Allebeck, P., & Lewis, G. (1997). IQ and risk for schizophrenia: A population-based cohort study. *Psychological Medicine, 27,* 1311–1323.

Davidson, L., & Stayner, D. (1997). Loss, loneliness, and the desire for love: Perspectives on the social lives of people with schizophrenia. *Psychiatric Rehabilitation Journal, 20*(3), 3–12.

Davidson, L. L., & Heinrichs, R. W. (2003). Quantification of frontal and temporal lobe brain-imaging findings in schizophrenia: A meta-analysis. *Psychiatry Research: Neuroimaging, 122,* 69–87.

Davidson, M., Reichenberg, A., Rabinowitz, J., Weiser, M., Kaplan, Z., & Mark, M. (1999). Behavioral and intellectual markers for schizophrenia in apparently healthy male adolescents. *American Journal of Psychiatry, 156*(9), 1328–1335.

Deane, F. P., Glaser, N. M., Oades, L. G., & Kazantzis, N. (2005). Psychologists' use of homework assignments with clients who have schizophrenia. *Clinical Psychologist, 9*, 24–30.

Delespaul, P., deVries, M., & van Os, J. (2002). Determinants of occurrence and recovery from hallucinations in daily life. *Social Psychiatry and Psychiatric Epidemiology, 37*, 97–104.

Dell, G. S. (1986). A spreading activation theory of retrieval in sentence production. *Psychological Review, 93*(3), 283–321.

DeVries, M. W., & Delespaul, P. A. (1989). Time, context, and subjective experiences in schizophrenia. *Schizophrenia Bulletin, 15*(2), 233–244.

Diamond, M., Rosenzweig, M., Bennett, E., Lindner, B., & Lyon, L. (1972). Effects of environmental enrichment and impoverishment on rat cerebral cortex. *Journal of Neurobiology, 3*(1), 47–64.

Dickerson, S. S., & Kemeny, M. E. (2004). Acute stressors and cortisol responses: A theoretical integration and synthesis of laboratory research. *Psychological Bulletin, 130*, 355–391.

Docherty, N. M., Cohen, A. S., Nienow, T. M., Dinzeo, T. J., & Dangelmaier, R. E. (2003). Stability of formal thought disorder and referential communication disturbances in schizophrenia. *Journal of Abnormal Psychology, 112*(3), 469–475.

Docherty, N. M., Evans, I. M., Sledge, W. H., Seibyl, J. P., & Krystal, J. H. (1994). Affective reactivity of language in schizophrenia. *Journal of Nervous and Mental Disease, 182*(2), 98–102.

Docherty, N. M., Hall, M. J., & Gordinier, S. W. (1998). Affective reactivity of speech in schizophrenia patients and their nonschizophrenic relatives. *Journal of Abnormal Psychology, 107*(3), 461–467.

Dudley, R. E. J., & Over, D. E. (2003). People with delusions jump to conclusions: A theoretical account of research findings on the reasoning of people with delusions. *Clinical Psychology and Psychotherapy, 10*, 263–274.

Dunn, H., Morrison, A. P., & Bentall, R. P. (2002). Patients' experiences of homework tasks in cognitive behavioural therapy for psychosis: A qualitative analysis. *Clinical Psychology and Psychotherapy, 9*, 361–369.

Earnst, K. S., & Kring, A. M. (1997). Construct validity of negative symptoms: An empirical and conceptual review. *Clinical Psychology Review, 17*, 167–190.

Earnst, K. S., & Kring, A. M. (1999). Emotional responding in deficit and nondeficit schizophrenia. *Psychiatry Research, 88*, 191–207.

Eastwood, S. L., Burnet, P. W., & Harrison, P. J. (1995). Altered synaptophysin expression as a marker of synaptic pathology in schizophrenia. *Neuroscience, 66*(2), 309–319.

Eccles, J. S., & Wigfield, A. (2002). Motivational beliefs, values and goals. *Annual Review of Psychology, 53*, 109–132.

Eckblad, M., & Chapman, L. J. (1983). Magical ideation as an indicator of schizotypy. *Journal of Consulting and Clinical Psychology, 51*, 215–225.

Eckbald, M., Chapman, L. J., Chapman, J. P., & Mishlove, M. (1982). *Revised Social Anhedonia Scale*. Madison: University of Wisconsin.

Ellis, A. (1962). *Reason and emotion in psychotherapy*. Oxford, UK: Stuart.

Endicott, J., & Spitzer, R. L. (1978). A diagnostic interview: The Schedule for Affective Disorders and Schizophrenia. *Archives of General Psychiatry, 35*(7), 837–844.

Ensink, B. J. (1992). *Confusing realities: A study on child sexual abuse and psychiatric symptoms*. Amsterdam: VU University Press.

Epstein, S. (1953). Overinclusive thinking in a schizophrenic and a control group. *Journal of Consulting Psychology, 17*(5), 384–388.

Eriksson, P. S., Perfilieva, E., Björk-Eriksson, T., Alborn, A.-M., Nordbor, C., Peterson, D. A., et al. (1998). Neurogenesis in the adult human hippocampus. *Nature Medicine, 4*, 1313–1317.

Erlenmeyer-Kimling, L., Roberts, S. A., Rock, D., Adamo, U. H., Shapiro, B. M., & Pape, S. (1998). Predictions from longitudinal assessments of high-risk children. In M. F. Lenzenweger & R. H. Dworkin (Eds.), *Origins and development of schizophrenia: Advances in experimental psychopathology* (pp. 427–445). Washington, DC: American Psychiatric Association.

Escher, S., Romme, M., Buiks, A., Delespaul, P., & van Os, J. (2002a). Formation of delusional ideation in adolescents hearing voices: A prospective study. *American Journal of Medical Genetics (Neuropsychiatric Genetics), 114*, 913–920.

Escher S., Romme, M., Buiks, A., Delespaul, P., & van Os, J. (2002b). Independent course of childhood auditory hallucinations: A sequential 3-year follow-up study. *British Journal of Psychiatry, 181*, 10–18.

Fadre, L., Wiesel, F. A., Hall, H., Halldin, C., Stone-Elander, S., & Sedvall, G. (1987). No D_2 receptor increase in PET study of schizophrenia. *Archives of General Psychiatry, 44*, 671–672.

Feelgood, S., & Rantzen, R. (1994). Auditory and visual hallucinations in university students. *Personality and Individual Differences, 17*, 293–296.

Feinberg, I. (1982/1983). Schizophrenia: Caused by a fault in programmed synaptic elimination during adolescence? *Journal of Psychiatric Research, 17*, 319–334.

Feinberg, I. (1990). Cortical pruning and the development of schizophrenia. *Schizophrenia Bulletin, 16*(4), 567–570.

Fibiger, H. C., & Phillips, A. G. (1974). Role of dopamine and norepinephrine in the chemistry of reward. *Journal of Psychiatric Research, 11*, 135–143.

First, M. B., Spitzer, R. L., Gibbon, M., & Williams, J. (1995). *Structured Clinical Interview for DSM-IV axis I disorders*. New York: State Psychiatric Institute, Biometrics Research.

Foerster, A., Lewis, S. W., & Murray, R. M. (1991). Genetic and environmental correlates of the positive and negative syndromes. In J. F. Greden & T. R. (Eds.),

Negative schizophrenic symptoms: Pathophysiology and clinical implications (pp. 187–202). Washington, DC: American Psychiatric Association.

Foucher, J. R., Vidailhet, P., Chanraud, S., Gounot, D., Grucker, D., Pins, D., et al. (2005). Functional integration in schizophrenia: Too little or too much? Preliminary results on fMRI data. *Neuroimage, 26*, 374–388.

Foudraine, J. (1974). *Not made of wood: A psychiatrist discovers his own profession* (H. H. Hopkins, Trans.). New York: Macmillan.

Fowler, D. (2007, June). *Studies of associations between trauma and psychotic symptoms in early and chronic psychotic samples in London and East Anglia.* Paper presented at the invitational conference on CBT for psychosis, Amsterdam.

Fowler, D., Freeman, D., Smith, B., Kuipers, E., Bebbington, P., Bashforth, H., et al. (2006). The Brief Core Schema Scales (BCSS): Psychometric properties and associations with paranoia and grandiosity in non-clinical and psychosis samples. *Psychological Medicine, 36*, 1–11.

Fowler, D., Garety, P., & Kuipers, E. (1995). *Cognitive behaviour therapy for psychosis: Theory and practice.* Chichester, UK: Wiley.

Franck, N., Rouby, P., Daprati, B., Dalery, J., Marie-Cardine, M., & Georgieff, N. (2000). Confusion between silent and overt reading in schizophrenia. *Schizophrenia Research, 41*, 357–368.

Freedman, R., Coon, H., Myles-Worsley, M., Orr-Urtreger, A., Olincy, A., Davis, A., et al. (1997). Linkage of a neurophysiological deficit in schizophrenia to a chromosome 15 locus. *Proceedings of the National Academy of Sciences, 94*(2), 587–592.

Freeman, D. (2007). Suspicious minds: The psychology of persecutory delusions. *Clinical Psychology Review, 27*, 425–457.

Freeman, D., Garety, P. A., Bebbington, P., Slate, M., Kuipers, E., Fowler, D., et al. (2005). The psychology of persecutory ideation: II. A virtual reality experimental study. *Journal of Nervous and Mental Disease, 193*, 309–314.

Freeman, D., Garety, P. A., McGuire, P., & Kuipers, E. (2005). Developing a theoretical understanding of therapy techniques: An illustrative analogue study. *British Journal of Clinical Psychology, 44*, 241–254.

Freeston, M. H., Ladouceur, R., Gagnon, F., & Thibodeau, N. (1993). Beliefs about obsessional thoughts. *Journal of Psychopathology and Behavioral Assessment, 15*, 1–21.

Frenkel, E., Kugelmass, S., Nathan, M., & Ingraham, L. J. (1995). Locus of control and mental health in adolescence and adulthood. *Schizophrenia Bulletin, 21*, 219–226.

Frith, C. D. (1979). Consciousness, information processing, and schizophrenia. *British Journal of Psychiatry, 134*, 225–235.

Frith, C. D. (1987). The positive and negative symptoms of schizophrenia reflect impairments in the perception and initiation of action. *Psychological Medicine, 17*(3), 631–648.

Frith, C. D. (1992). *The cognitive neuropsychology of schizophrenia.* Hove, UK: Erlbaum.

Frith, C. D., & Corcoran, R. (1996). Exploring "theory of mind" in people with schizophrenia. *Psychological Medicine, 26,* 521–530.

Frith, C. D., & Done, D. J. (1987). Towards a neuropsychology of schizophrenia. *British Journal of Psychiatry, 153,* 437–443.

Frith, C. D., & Done, D. J. (1989a). Experiences of alien control in schizophrenia reflect a disorder in the central monitoring of action. *Psychological Medicine, 19,* 359–363.

Frith, C. D., & Done, D. J. (1989b). Positive symptoms of schizophrenia. *British Journal of Psychiatry, 154,* 569–570.

Frith, C. D., Leary, J., Cahill, C., & Johnstone, E. C. (1991). Disabilities and circumstances of schizophrenic patients—a follow-up study: IV. Performance on psychological tests. *British Journal of Psychiatry, 159*(Suppl. 13), 26–29.

Fuller, R. L. M., Schultz, S. K., & Andreasen, N. C. (2003). The symptoms of schizophrenia. In S. R. Hirsch & D. L. Weinberger (Eds.), *Schizophrenia* (2nd ed., pp. 25–33). Malden, MA: Blackwell.

Gallagher, A., Dinan, T., & Baker, L. (1994). The effects of varying auditory input on schizophrenic hallucinations: A replication. *British Journal of Medical Psychology, 67,* 67–76.

Gard, D. E., Kring, A. M., Gard, M. G., Horan, W. P., & Green, M. F. (2007). Anhedonia in schizophrenia: Distinctions between anticipatory and consummatory pleasure. *Schizophrenia Research, 93*(1–3), 253–260.

Garety, P., Fowler, D., Kuipers, E., Freeman, D., Dunn, G., Bebbington, P., et al. (1997). London–East Anglia randomized controlled trial of cognitive-behavioural therapy for psychosis: II. Predictors of outcome. *British Journal of Psychiatry, 171,* 420–426.

Garety, P. A., Bebbington, P., Fowler, D., Freeman, D., & Kuipers, E. (2007). Implications for neurobiological research of cognitive models of psychosis: A theoretical paper. *Psychological Medicine, 37,* 1377–1391.

Garety, P. A., & Freeman, D. (1999). Cognitive approaches to delusions: A critical review of theories and evidence. *British Journal of Clinical Psychology, 38,* 113–154.

Garety, P. A., Freeman, D., Jolley, S., Dunn, G., Bebbington, P. E., Fowler, et al. (2005). Reasoning, emotions, and delusional conviction in psychosis. *Journal of Abnormal Psychology, 114,* 373–384.

Garety, P. A., & Hemsley, D. R. (1987). Characteristics of delusional experience. *European Archives of Psychiatry and Neurological Sciences, 236*(5), 294–298.

Garety, P. A., Hemsley, D. R., & Wessely, S. (1991). Reasoning in deluded schizophrenic and paranoid patients: Biases in performance on a probabilistic inference task. *Journal of Nervous and Mental Disease, 179,* 194–202.

Germans, M. J., & Kring, A. M. (2000). Hedonic deficit in anhedonia: Support for the role of approach motivation. *Personality and Individual Differences, 28,* 659–672.

Gilbert, D. T. (1991). How mental systems believe. *American Psychologist, 46,* 107–119.

Gilbert, D. T., & Gill, N. J. A. (2000). The momentary realist. *Psychological Science, 5,* 394–398.

Gilbert, D. T., & Malone, P. S. (1995). The correspondence bias. *Psychological Bulletin, 117,* 21–38.

Gilmore, J. H., & Murray, R. M. (2006). Prenatal and perinatal factors. In J. A. Lieberman, T. S. Stroup, & D. O. Perkins (Eds.), *Textbook of schizophrenia* (pp. 55–67). Washington, DC: American Psychiatric Association.

Glahn, D. C., Ragland, J. D., Abramoff, A., Barrett, J., Laird, A. R., Bearden, C. E., et al. (2005). Beyond hypofrontality: A quantitative meta-analysis of functional neuroimaging studies of working memory in schizophrenia. *Human Brain Mapping, 25,* 60–69.

Goff, D. C. (2004). Risperidone. In A. F. Schatzberg & C. B. Nemeroff (Eds.), *The American Psychiatric Publishing textbook of psychopharmacology* (3rd ed., pp. 495–506). Washington, DC: American Psychiatric Publishing.

Goff, D. C., & Wine, L. (1997). Glutamate in schizophrenia: Clinical and research implications. *Schizophrenia Research, 27*(2–3), 157–168.

Gold, J. M., & Green, M. F. (2005). Schizophrenia: Cognition. In B. J. Sadock & V. A. Sadock (Eds.), *Kaplan and Sadock's comprehensive textbook of psychiatry* (8th ed., pp. 1436–1448). Philadelphia: Lippincott, Williams & Wilkins.

Gold, J. M., Randolph, C., Carpenter, C. J., Goldberg, T. E., & Weinberger, D. R. (1992). Forms of memory failure in schizophrenia. *Journal of Abnormal Psychology, 101*(3), 487–494.

Goldberg, T. E., David, A., & Gold, J. M. (2003). Neurocognitive deficits in schizophrenia. In S. R. Hirsch & D. L. Weinberger (Eds.), *Schizophrenia* (2nd ed., pp. 168–184). Malden, MA: Blackwell.

Gordon, E., Williams, L. M., Haig, A. R., Wright, J., & Meares, R. A. (2001). Symptom profile and 'gamma' processing in schizophrenia. *Cognitive Neuropsychiatry, 6,* 7–19.

Gottesman, I. I. (1991). *Schizophrenia genesis: The origins of madness.* New York: Freeman.

Gottesman, I. I., & Gould, T. D. (2003). The endophenotype concept in psychiatry: Etymology and strategic intentions. *American Journal of Psychiatry, 160,* 636–645.

Gould, R. A., Mueser, K. T., Bolton, E., Mays, V., & Goff, D. (2001). Cognitive therapy for psychosis in schizophrenia: An effect size analysis. *Schizophrenia Research, 48,* 335–342.

Gould, L. (1950). Verbal hallucinations as automatic speech. *American Journal of Psychiatry, 107,* 110–119.

Granholm, E., McQuaid, J. R., McClure, F. S., Auslander, L. A., Perivoliotis, D.,

Pedrelli, P., et al. (2005). A randomized, controlled trial of cognitive behavioral social skills training for middle-aged and older outpatients with chronic schizophrenia. *American Journal of Psychiatry, 162,* 520–529.

Granholm, E., Morris, S. K., Sarkin, A. J., Asarnow, R. F., & Jeste, D. V. (1997). Pupillary responses index overload of working memory resources in schizophrenia. *Journal of Abnormal Psychology, 106,* 458–467.

Grant, P. M., & Beck, A. T. (2005). *Negative cognitions assessment.* Unpublished test.

Grant, P. M. & Beck, A. T. (2008a). *The role of neurocognitive flexibility and cognitive insight in delusions.* Unpublished manuscript.

Grant, P. M., & Beck, A. T. (2008b). *Social disengagement attitudes as a mediator between social cognition and poor functioning in schizophrenia.* Manuscript in preparation.

Grant, P. M., & Beck, A. T. (2008c). *Dysfunctional attitudes, cognitive impairment and symptoms in schizophrenia.* Unpublished raw data.

Grant, P. M., & Beck, A. T. (2008d). *Rejection sensitivity as a moderator of communication disorder in schizophrenia.* Manuscript submitted for publication.

Grant, P. M., & Beck, A. T. (in press). Defeatist beliefs as mediators of cognitive impairment, negative symptoms, and functioning in schizophrenia. *Schizophrenia Bulletin.*

Grant, P. M., Young, P. R., & DeRubeis, R. J. (2005). Cognitive and behavioral therapies. In G. O. Gabbard, J. S. Beck, & J. Holmes (Eds.), *Oxford textbook of psychotherapy* (pp. 15–25). New York: Oxford University Press.

Gray, J. A., Feldon, J., Rawlins, J. N. P., Hemsley, D. R., & Smith, A. D. (1991). The neuropsychology of schizophrenia. *Behavior and Brain Sciences, 14,* 1–84.

Green, M. F. (1996). What are the functional consequences of neurocognitive deficits in schizophrenia? *American Journal of Psychiatry, 153*(3), 321–330.

Green, M. F. (1998). *Schizophrenia from a neurocognitive perspective: Probing the impenetrable darkness.* Boston: Allyn & Bacon.

Green, M. F. (2003). *Schizophrenia revealed: From neurons to social interactions.* New York: Norton.

Green, M. F., Kern, R. S., Braff, D. L., & Mintz, J. (2000). Neurocognitive deficits and functional outcome in schizophrenia: Are we measuring the "right stuff"? *Schizophrenia Bulletin, 26*(1), 119–136.

Greenberger, D., & Padesky, C. A. (1995). *Mind over mood: A cognitive therapy treatment manual for clients.* New York: Guilford Press.

Greenwood, K. E., Landau, S., & Wykes, T. (2005). Negative symptoms and specific cognitive impairments as combined targets for improved functional outcome within cognitive remediation therapy. *Schizophrenia Bulletin, 31,* 910–921.

Grice, H. P. (1957). Meaning. *Philosophical Review, 66,* 377–388.

Gumley, A., O'Grady, M., McNay, L., Reilly, J., Power, K., & Norrie, J. (2003). Early intervention for relapse in schizophrenia: Results of a 12-month randomized controlled trial of cognitive behavioural therapy. *Psychological Medicine, 33*(3), 419–431.

Gur, R. C., & Gur, R. E. (2005). Neuroimaging in schizophrenia: Linking neuropsychiatric manifestations to neurobiology. In B. J. Sadock & V. A. Sadock (Eds.), *Kaplan and Sadock's comprehensive textbook of psychiatry* (8th ed., pp. 1396–1408). Philadelphia: Lippincott, Williams & Wilkins.

Gur, R. E. (1999). Is schizophrenia a lateralized brain disorder? Editor's introduction. *Schizophrenia Bulletin, 25*(1), 7–9.

Gur, R. E., & Arnold, S. E. (2004). Neurobiology of schizophrenia. In A. F. Schatzberg & C. B. Nemeroff (Eds.), *The American Psychiatric Publishing textbook of psychopharmacology* (3rd ed., pp. 765–774). Washington, DC: American Psychiatric Publishing.

Gur, R. E., Cowell, P. E., Latshaw, A., Turetsky, B. I., Grossman, R. I., Arnold, S. E., et al. (2000). Reduced dorsal and orbital prefrontal gray matter volumes in schizophrenia. *Archives of General Psychiatry, 57*(8), 761–768.

Gur, R. E., Mozley, P. D., Resnick, S. M., Mozley, L. H., Shtasel, D. L., Gallacher, F., et al. (1995). Resting cerebral glucose metabolism in first-episode and previously treated patients with schizophrenia relates to clinical features. *Archives of General Psychiatry, 52*(8), 657–667.

Gur, R. E., Nimgaonkar, V. L., Almasy, L., Calkins, M. E., Ragland, J. D., Pogue-Geile, M. F., et al. (2007). Neurocognitive endophenotypes in a multiplex multigenerational family study of schizophrenia. *American Journal of Psychiatry, 164,* 813–819.

Gur, R. E., Resnick, S. M., Alavi, A., Gur, R. C., Caroff, S., Dann, R., et al. (1987). Regional brain function in schizophrenia: I. A positron emission tomography study. *Archives of General Psychiatry, 44*(2), 119–125.

Gur, R. E., Skolnick, B. E., Gur, R. C., Caroff, S., Rieger, W., Obrist, W. D., et al. (1983). Brain function in psychiatric disorders: I. Regional cerebral blood flow in medicated schizophrenics. *Archives of General Psychiatry, 40*(11), 1250–1254.

Guttmacher, M. S. (1964). Phenothiazine treatment in acute schizophrenia: Effectiveness. The National Institute of Mental Health Psychopharmacology Service Center Collaborative Study Group. *Archives of General Psychiatry, 10,* 241–261.

Haddock, G., McCarron, J., Tarrier, N., & Faragher, E. B. (1999). Scales to measure dimensions of hallucinations and delusions: The psychotic symptom rating scales (PSYRATS). *Psychological Medicine, 29,* 879–889.

Haddock, G., Slade, P. D., Prasaad, R., & Bentall, R. (1996). Functioning of the phonological loop in auditory hallucinations. *Personality and Individual Differences, 20,* 753–760.

Haddock, G., Wolfenden, M., Lowens, I., Tarrier, N., & Bentall, R. P. (1995).

Effect of emotional salience on thought disorder in patients with schizophrenia. *British Journal of Psychiatry, 167*(5), 618–620.

Hafner, H. (2003). Prodrome, onset and early course of schizophrenia. In R. M. Murray, P. B. Jones, E. Susser, J. van Os, & M. Cannon (Eds.), *The epidemiology of schizophrenia* (pp. 124–147). Cambridge, UK: Cambridge University Press.

Hafner, H., & an der Heiden, W. (2003). Course and outcome of schizophrenia. In S. R. Hirsch & D. L. Weinberger (Eds.), *Schizophrenia* (2nd ed., pp. 101–141). Malden, MA: Blackwell.

Hampson, M., Anderson, A. W., Gore, J. C., & Hoffman, R. E. (2002, June). *FMRI investigation of auditory hallucinations in schizophrenia using temporal correlations to language areas.* Paper presented at the 8th international conference on functional mapping of the human brain, Sendai, Japan.

Hardy, A., Fowler, D., Freeman, D., Smith, B., Steel, C., et al. (2005). Trauma and hallucinatory experience in psychosis. *Journal of Nervous and Mental Disease, 193*, 501–507.

Harrison, G., Hopper, K., Craig, T., Laska, E., Siegel, C., Wanderling, J., et al. (2001). Recovery from psychotic illness: A 15- and 25-year international follow-up study. *British Journal of Psychiatry, 178*, 506–517.

Harrow, M., & Jobe, T. H. (2007). Factors involved in outcome and recovery in schizophrenia patients not on antipsychotic medications: A 15-year multifollow-up study. *Journal of Nervous and Mental Disease, 195*(5), 406–414.

Harrow, M., & Prosen, M. (1978). Intermingling and disordered logic as influences on schizophrenic "thought disorders." *Archives of General Psychiatry, 35*(10), 1213–1218.

Harrow, M., Silverstein, M., & Marengo, J. (1983). Disordered thinking. *Archives of General Psychiatry, 40*(7), 765–771.

Harvey, P. D., Earle-Boyer, E. A., & Levinson, J. C. (1988). Cognitive deficits and thought disorder: A retest study. *Schizophrenia Bulletin, 14*(1), 57–66.

Harvey, P. D., Howanitz, E., Parrella, M., White, L., Davidson, M., Mohs, R. C., et al. (1998). Symptoms, cognitive function, and adaptive skills in geriatric patients with lifelong schizophrenia: A comparison across treatment sites. *American Journal of Psychiatry, 155*, 1080–1086.

Hatfield, A. B., & Lefley, H. P. (1993). *Surviving mental illness: Stress, coping and adaptation.* New York: Guilford Press.

Hawks, D. V., & Payne, R. W. (1971). Overinclusive thought disorder and symptomatology. *British Journal of Psychiatry, 118*(547), 663–670.

Hazlett, E. A., Buchsbaum, M. S., Byne, W., Wei, T. C., Spiegel-Cohen, J., Geneve, C., et al. (1999). Three-dimensional analysis with MRI and PET of the size, shape, and function of the thalamus in the schizophrenia spectrum. *American Journal of Psychiatry, 156*(8), 1190–1199.

Healy, D. (2002). *The creation of psychopharmacology.* Cambridge, MA: Harvard University Press.

Heaton, R. K., Chelune, G. J., Talley, J. L., Kay, G. G., & Curtiss, G. (1993). *Wisconsin card sorting test manual: Revised and expanded.* Odessa, FL: Psychological Assessment Resources.

Heckers, S. (1997). Neuropathology of schizophrenia: Cortex, thalamus, basal ganglia, and neurotransmitter-specific projection systems. *Schizophrenia Bulletin, 23*(3), 403–421.

Heckers, S., Heinsen, H., Geiger, B., & Beckmann, H. (1991). Hippocampal neuron number in schizophrenia: a stereological study. *Archives of General Psychiatry, 48*(11), 1002–1008.

Heckers, S., Heinsen, H., Heinsen, Y., & Beckmann, H. (1991). Cortex, white matter, and basal ganglia in schizophrenia: A volumetric postmortem study. *Biological Psychiatry, 29*(6), 556–566.

Heckers, S., Rauch, S. L., Goff, D., Savage, C. R., Schacter, D. L., Fischman, A. J., et al. (1998). Impaired recruitment of the hippocampus during conscious recollection in schizophrenia. *Nature Neuroscience, 1*(4), 318–323.

Hegarty, J. D., Baldessarini, R. J., Tohen, M., Waternaux, C., & Oepen, G. (1994). One hundred years of schizophrenia: A meta-analysis of the outcome literature. *American Journal of Psychiatry, 151*, 1409–1416.

Heider, F. (1958). *The psychology of interpersonal relations.* New York: Wiley.

Heinrichs, D. W., Hanlon, T. E., & Carpenter, W. T., Jr. (1984). The Quality of Life Scale: An instrument for rating the schizophrenic deficit syndrome. *Schizophrenia Bulletin, 10*(3), 388–398.

Heinrichs, R. W. (2001). *In search of madness: Schizophrenia and neuroscience.* Oxford, UK: Oxford University Press.

Heinrichs, R. W. (2005). The primacy of cognition in schizophrenia. *American Psychologist, 60*(3), 229–242.

Heinrichs, R. W., & Zakzanis, K. K. (1998). Neurocognitive deficit in schizophrenia: A quantitative review of the evidence. *Neuropsychology, 12*(3), 426–445.

Helbig, S., & Fehm, L. (2004). Problems with homework in CBT: Rare exception or rather frequent? *Behavioural and Cognitive Psychotherapy, 32*, 291–301.

Hemsley, D. R. (1987a). An experimental psychological model for schizophrenia. In H. Hafner, W. F. Gattaz, & W. Janzavik (Eds.), *Search for the causes of schizophrenia* (pp. 179–188). Berlin: Springer Verlag.

Hemsley, D. R. (1987b). Hallucinations: Unintended or unexpected? *Behavioral and Brain Sciences, 10*, 532–533.

Hemsley, D. R. (2005). The schizophrenic experience: Taken out of context? *Schizophrenia Bulletin, 31*, 43–53.

Henquet, C., Murray, R., Linszen, D., & van Os, J. (2005). The environment and schizophrenia: The role of cannabis use. *Schizophrenia Bulletin, 31*(3), 608–612.

Heston, L. L. (1966). Psychiatric disorders in foster home reared children of schizophrenic mothers. *British Journal of Psychiatry, 112*, 819–825.

Heydebrand, G., Weiser, M., Rabinowitz, J., Hoff, A. L., DeLisi, L. E., & Csern-ansky, J. G. (2004). Correlates of cognitive deficits in first episode schizophre-nia. *Schizophrenia Research, 68*, 1–9.

Hirsch, S. R., Das, I., Garey, L. J., & de Belleroche, J. (1997). A pivotal role for glutamate in the pathogenesis of schizophrenia, and its cognitive dysfunction. *Pharmacology, Biochemistry, and Behavior, 56*(4), 797–802.

Ho, B., Nopoulos, P., Flaum, M., Arndt, S., & Andreasen, N. C. (1998). Two-year outcome in first-episode schizophrenia: Predictive value of symptoms for quality of life. *American Journal of Psychiatry, 155*, 1196–1201.

Hoffman, R. E., & Cavus, I. (2002). Slow transcranial magnetic stimulation, long-term depotentiation, and brain hyperexcitability disorders. *American Journal of Psychiatry, 159*, 1093–1102.

Hoffman, R. E., & Dobscha, S. K. (1989). Cortical pruning and the development of schizophrenia: A computer model. *Schizophrenia Bulletin, 15*(3), 477–490.

Hoffman, R. E., & McGlashan, T. H. (1993). Parallel distributed processing and the emergence of schizophrenic symptoms. *Schizophrenia Bulletin, 19*(1), 119–140.

Hole, R. W., Rush A. J., & Beck, A. T. (1979). A cognitive investigation of schizo-phrenic delusions. *Psychiatry, 42*, 312–319.

Hollister, J. M., Laing, P., & Mednick, S. A. (1996). Rhesus incompatibility as a risk factor for schizophrenia in male adults. *Archives of General Psychiatry, 53*(1), 19–24.

Hollon, S. (2007, October). *Cognitive therapy in the treatment and prevention of depression.* Paper presented at the annual meeting of the Society for Research in Psychopathology, Iowa City.

Holzman, P. S. (1991). Eye movement dysfunctions in schizophrenia. In S. R. Stein-hauer, J. H. Gruzelier, & J. Zubin (Eds.), *Handbook of schizophrenia: Vol. 5. Neuropsychology, psychophysiology, and information processing* (pp. 129–145). Amsterdam: Elsevier.

Horan, W. P., Kring, A. M., & Blanchard, J. J. (2006). Anhedonia in schizophrenia: A review of assessment strategies. *Schizophrenia Bulletin, 32*(2), 259–273.

Horan, W. P., Ventura, J., Nuechterlein, K. H., Subotnik, K. L., Hwang, S. S., & Mintz, J. (2005). Stressful life events in recent-onset schizophrenia: Reduced frequencies and altered subjective appraisals. *Schizophrenia Research, 75*, 363–374.

Hughlings Jackson, J. (1931). *Selected writings.* London: Hodder & Stoughton.

Huq, S. F., Garety, P. A., & Hemsley, D. R. (1988). Probabilistic judgements in deluded and nondeluded subjects. *Quarterly Journal of Experimental Psy-chology, 40*(4), 801–812.

Hurn, C., Gray, N. S., & Hughes, I. (2002). Independence of "reaction to hypo-thetical contradiction" from other measures of delusional ideation. *British Journal of Clinical Psychology, 41*, 349–360.

Hustig, H. H., & Hafner, R. J. (1990). Persistent auditory hallucinations and their relationship to delusions and mood. *Journal of Nervous and Mental Disease, 178*, 264–267.

Huttenlocher, P. R., & Dabholkar, A. S. (1997). Regional differences in synapto-genesis in human cerebral cortex. *Journal of Comparative Neurology, 387*(2), 167–178.

Huttunen, M. O., & Niskanen, P. (1973). Prenatal loss of father and psychiatric disorders. *Archives of General Psychiatry, 35*, 429–431.

Ingraham, L. J., & Kety, S. S. (2000). Adoption studies of schizophrenia. *American Journal of Medical Genetics, 97*, 18–22.

Ingvar, D. H., & Franzen, G. (1974). Distribution of cerebral activity in chronic schizophrenia. *Lancet, 2*(7895), 1484–1486.

Inouye, T., & Shimizu, A. (1970). The electromyographic study of verbal hallucina-tion. *Journal of Nervous and Mental Disease, 151*, 415–422.

Janssen, I., Krabbendam, L., Bak, M., Hanssen, M., Vollerbergh, W., de Graaf, R., et al. (2004). Childhood abuse as a risk factor for psychotic experiences. *Acta Psychiatrica Scandinavica, 109*, 38–45.

Jarskog, L. F., & Robbins, T. W. (2006). Neuropathology and neural circuits impli-cated in schizophrenia. In J. A. Lieberman, T. S. Stroup, & D. O. Perkins (Eds.), *Textbook of schizophrenia* (pp. 151–166). Washington, DC: American Psychiatric Association.

Javitt, D. C., & Zukin, S. R. (1991). Recent advances in the phencyclidine model of schizophrenia. *American Journal of Psychiatry, 148*(10), 1301–1308.

Jenkins, R. B., & Groh, R. H. (1970). Mental symptoms in parkinsonian patients treated with L-DOPA. *Lancet, 2*, 177–179.

John, J. P., Khanna, S., Thennarasu, K., & Reddy, S. (2003). Exploration of dimen-sions of psychopathology in neuroleptic-naïve patients with recent-onset schizophrenia/schizophreniform disorder. *Psychiatry Research, 121*, 11–20.

Johns, L. C., Hemsley, D., & Kuipers, E. (2002). A comparison of auditory halluci-nations in a psychiatric and non-psychiatric group. *British Journal of Clinical Psychology, 41*, 81–86.

Johns, L. C., Nazroo, J. Y., Bebbington, P., & Kuipers, E. (2002). Occurrence of hallucinatory experiences in a community sample and ethnic variations. *British Journal of Psychiatry, 180*, 174–178.

Johns, L. C., Rossell, S., Frith, C., Ahmad, F., Hemsley, D., & Kuipers, E., et al. (2001). Verbal self-monitoring and auditory verbal hallucinations in patients with schizophrenia. *Psychological Medicine, 31*, 705–715.

Johnson, M., Hashtroudi, S., & Lindsay, D. (1993). Source monitoring. *Psychological Bulletin, 114*, 3–28.

Johnstone, E. C., Crow, T. J., Frith, C. D., Carney, M. W., & Price, J. S. (1978). Mechanism of the antipsychotic effect in the treatment of acute schizophre-nia. *Lancet, 1*(8069), 848–851.

Johnstone, E. C., & Ownes, D. G. (2004). Early studies of brain anatomy in schizophrenia. In S. M. Lawrie, D. R. Weinberger, & E. C. Johnstone (Eds.),

Schizophrenia: From neuroimaging to neuroscience (pp. 1–19). New York: Oxford University Press.

Jones, P. B., & Done, D. J. (1997). From birth to onset: A developmental perspective of schizophrenia in two national birth cohorts. In M. S. Keshavan & R. M. Murray (Eds.), *Neurodevelopmental and adult psychopathology*. Cambridge, UK: Cambridge University Press.

Jones, P. B., Rodgers, B., Murray, R., & Marmot, M. (1994). Child development risk factors for adult schizophrenia in the British 1946 birth cohort. *Lancet, 344*(8934), 1398–1402.

Kaney, S., Wolfenden, M., Dewey, M. E., & Bentall, R. P. (1992). Persecutory delusions and recall of threatening propositions. *British Journal of Clinical Psychology, 31*, 85–87.

Kapur, S. (2003). Psychosis as a state of aberrant salience: A framework linking biology, phenomenology, and pharmacology in schizophrenia. *American Journal of Psychiatry, 160*(1), 13–23.

Kapur, S., & Seeman, P. (2001). Does fast dissociation from the dopamine D(2) receptor explain the action of atypical antipsychotics?: A new hypothesis. *American Journal of Psychiatry, 158*(3), 360–369.

Kawasaki, Y., Suzuki, M., Maeda, Y., Urata, K., Yamaguchi, N., Matsuda, H., et al. (1992). Regional cerebral blood flow in patients with schizophrenia: A preliminary report. *European Archives of Psychiatry and Clinical Neuroscience, 241*(4), 195–200.

Kay, S. R., Fiszbein, A., & Opler, L. A. (1987). The Positive and Negative Syndrome Scale (PANSS) for schizophrenia. *Schizophrenia Bulletin, 13*(2), 261–276.

Kay, S. R., Opler, L. A., & Lindenmayer, J. P. (1988). Reliability and validity of the Positive and Negative Syndrome Scale for schizophrenics. *Psychiatry Research, 23*(1), 99–110.

Keefe, R. S. E., Bilder, R. M., Davis, S. M., Harvey, P. D., Palmer, B. W., Gold, J. M., et al. (2007). Neurocognitive effects of antipsychotic medications in patients with chronic schizophrenia in the CATIE trial. *Archives of General Psychiatry, 64*(6), 633–647.

Keefe, R. S. E., & Eesley, C. E. (2006). Neurocognitive impairments. In J. A. Lieberman, T. S. Stroup, & D. O. Perkins (Eds.), *Textbook of schizophrenia* (pp. 245–260). Washington, DC: American Psychiatric Association.

Keefe, R. S. E., Poe, M., Walker, T. M., Kang, J. W., & Harvey, P. D. (2006). The Schizophrenia Cognition Rating Scale: An interview-based assessment and its relationship to cognition, real-world functioning, and functional capacity. *American Journal of Psychiatry, 163*(3), 426–432.

Kendler, K. S., Myers, J. M., O'Neill, F. A., Martin, R., Murphy, B., MacLean, C. J., et al. (2000). Clinical features of schizophrenia and linkage to chromosomes 5q, 6p, 8p, and 10p in the Irish study of high-density schizophrenia families. *American Journal of Psychiatry, 157*(3), 402–408.

Kendler, K. S., Thacker, L., & Walsh, D. (1996). Self-report measures of schizotypy as indices of familial vulnerability to schizophrenia. *Schizophrenia Bulletin, 22,* 511–520.

Kerns, J., & Berenbaum, H. (2003). The relationship between formal thought disorder and executive functioning component processes. *Journal of Abnormal Psychology, 112,* 339–352.

Keshavan, M. S., Rosenberg, D., Sweeney, J. A., & Pettegrew, J. W. (1998). Decreased caudate volume in neuroleptic-naive psychotic patients. *American Journal of Psychiatry, 155*(6), 774–778.

Kety, S. S., Rosenthal, D., Wender, P. H., & Shulsinger, F. (1968). The types and prevalence of mental illness in the biological and adoptive families of adopted schizophrenics. *Journal of Psychiatric Research, 6*(Suppl. 1), 345–362.

Kimhy, D., Goetz, R., Yale, S., Corcoran, C., & Malaspina, D. (2005). Delusions in individuals with schizophrenia: Factor structure, clinical correlates, and putative neurobiology. *Psychopathology, 38,* 338–344.

Kimhy, D., Yale, S., Goetz, R. R., McFarr, L. M., & Malaspina, D. (2006). The factorial structure of the schedule for the deficit syndrome in schizophrenia. *Schizophrenia Bulletin, 32*(2), 274–278.

Kinderman, P., & Bentall, R. P. (1996). A new measure of causal locus: The Internal, Personal and Situational Attributions Questionnaire. *Personality and Individual Differences, 20,* 261–264.

Kinderman, P., & Bentall, R. P. (1997). Causal attributions in paranoia and depression: Internal, personal, and situational attributions for negative events. *Journal of Abnormal Psychology, 106,* 341–345.

Kingdon, D., & Turkington, D. (1998). Cognitive behavioural therapy of schizophrenia: Styles and methods. In T. Wykes, N. Tarrier, & S. F. Lewis (Eds.), *Outcome and innovation in psychological treatment of schizophrenia* (pp. 59–79). Chichester, UK: Wiley.

Kingdon, D., & Turkington, D. (2002). *The case study guide to cognitive behaviour therapy of psychosis.* Chichester, UK: Wiley.

Kingdon, D. G., & Turkington, D. (1991). The use of cognitive behavior therapy with a normalizing rationale in schizophrenia: Preliminary report. *Journal of Nervous and Mental Disease, 179,* 207–211.

Kingdon, D. G., & Turkington D. (1994). *Cognitive-behavioral therapy of schizophrenia.* New York: Guilford Press.

Kingdon, D. G., & Turkington, D. (2005). *Cognitive therapy of schizophrenia.* New York: Guilford Press.

Kirkpatrick, B., Buchanan, R. W., McKenny, P. D., Alphs, L. D., & Carpenter, W. T. J. (1989). The Schedule for the Deficit Syndrome: An instrument for research in schizophrenia. *Psychiatry Research, 30*(2), 119–123.

Kirkpatrick, B., Fenton, W., Carpenter, W. T. J., & Marder, S. R. (2006). The NIMH-MATRICS consensus statement on negative symptoms. *Schizophrenia Bulletin, 32*(2), 214–219.

Klosterkotter, J. (1992). The meaning of basic symptoms for the genesis of the schizophrenic nuclear syndrome. *Japanese Journal of Psychiatry and Neurology, 46,* 609–630.

Kosslyn, S. M. (1994). *Image and brain: The resolution of the imagery debate.* Cambridge, MA: MIT Press.

Krabbendam, L., & Aleman, A. (2003). Cognitive rehabilitation in schizophrenia: A quantitative analysis of controlled studies. *Psychopharmacology, 169,* 376–382.

Krabbendam, L., Myin-Germeys, I., Hanssen, M., de Graaf, R., Vollebergh, W., Bak, M., et al. (2005). Development of depressed mood predicts onset of psychotic disorder in individuals who report hallucinatory experiences. *British Journal of Clinical Psychology, 44,* 113–125.

Kraepelin, E. (1971). *Dementia praecox and paraphrenia* (R. M. Barclay, Trans.). Huntington, NY: Krieger.

Krawiecka, M., Goldberg, D., & Vaughan, M. (1977). A standardized psychiatric assessment scale for rating chronic psychotic patients. *Acta Psychiatrica Scandinavica, 55*(4), 299–308.

Kring, A. M., & Neale, J. M. (1996). Do schizophrenic patients show a disjunctive relationship among expressive, experiential, and psychophysiological components of emotion? *Journal of Abnormal Psychology, 105,* 249–257.

Kuipers, E., Garety, P., Fowler, D., Dunn, G., Bebbington, P., Freeman, D., et al. (1997). London–East Anglia randomized controlled trial of cognitive-behavioural therapy for psychosis: I. Effects of the treatment phase. *British Journal of Psychiatry, 171,* 319–327.

Kung, L., Conley, R., Chute, D. J., Smialek, J., & Roberts, R. C. (1998). Synaptic changes in the striatum of schizophrenic cases: A controlled postmortem ultrastructural study. *Synapse, 28*(2), 125–139.

Kwapil, T. R., Miller, M. B., Zinser, M. C., Chapman, J., & Chapman, L. J. (1997). Magical ideation and social anhedonia as predictors of psychosis proneness: A partial replication. *Journal of Abnormal Psychology, 106,* 491–495.

Landa, Y. (2006). *Group cognitive behavioral therapy for paranoia in schizophrenia.* Unpublished manuscript, Weill Cornell Medical College, New York, NY.

Lawrence, E., & Peters, E. (2004). Reasoning in believers in the paranormal. *Journal of Nervous and Mental Disease, 192,* 727–733.

Lawrie, S. M., & Abukmeil, S. S. (1998). Brain abnormality in schizophrenia: A systematic and quantitative review of volumetric magnetic resonance imaging studies. *British Journal of Psychiatry, 172,* 110–120.

Lazarus, R. S. (1966). *Psychological stress and the coping process.* New York: McGraw-Hill.

Lecardeur, L., Giffard, B., Laisney, M., Brazo, P., Delamillieure, P., Eustache, F., et al. (2007). Semantic hyperpriming in schizophrenic patients: Increased facilitation or impaired inhibition in semantic association processing? *Schizophrenia Research, 89*(1), 243–250.

Lencz, T., Smith, C. W., Auther, A., Correll, C. U., & Cornblatt, B. (2004). Non-specific and attenuated negative symptoms in patients at clinical high-risk for schizophrenia. *Schizophrenia Research, 68*(1), 37–48.

Levelt, W. J. M. (1989). *Speaking: From intention to articulation*. Cambridge, MA: MIT Press.

Lewander, T. (1994a). Neuroleptics and the neuroleptic-induced deficit syndrome. *Acta Psychiatrica Scandinavica, 380*, 8—13.

Lewander, T. (1994b). Overcoming the neuroleptic-induced deficit syndrome: Clinical observations with remoxipride. *Acta Psychiatrica Scandinavica, 380*, 64—67.

Lewis, D. A., Glantz, L. A., Pierri, J. N., & Sweet, R. A. (2003). Altered cortical glutamate neurotransmission in schizophrenia. *Annals of the New York Academy of Sciences, 1003*, 102–112.

Liang, M., Zhou, Y., Jiang, T., Liu, Z., Tian, L., Liu, H., et al. (2006). Widespread functional disconnectivity in schizophrenia with resting-state functional magnetic resonance imaging. *Neuroreport, 17*, 209–213.

Liddle, P., & Pantelis, C. (2003). Brain imaging in schizophrenia. In S. R. Hirsch & D. R. Weinberger (Eds.), *Schizophrenia* (2nd ed., pp. 403–417). Maldan, MA: Blackwell.

Liddle, P. F. (1987). The symptoms of chronic schizophrenia: A re-examination of the positive–negative dichotomy. *British Journal of Psychiatry, 151*, 145–151.

Liddle, P. F. (1992). Syndromes of schizophrenia on factor analysis. *British Journal of Psychiatry, 161*, 861.

Liddle, P. F. (2001). *Disordered mind and brain: The neural basis of mental symptoms*. London: Royal College of Psychiatrists.

Liddle, P. F., Friston, K. J., Frith, C. D., Hirsch, S. R., Jones, T., & Frankowiak, R. S. (1992). Patterns of cerebral blood flow in schizophrenia. *British Journal of Psychiatry, 160*, 179–186.

Liddle, P. F., & Morris, D. L. (1991). Schizophrenic syndromes and frontal lobe performance. *British Journal of Psychiatry, 158*, 340–345.

Lieberman, J. A. (2004a). Aripiprazole. In A. F. Schatzberg & C. B. Nemeroff (Eds.), *The American Psychiatric Publishing textbook of psychopharmacology* (3rd ed., pp. 487–494). Washington, DC: American Psychiatric Publishing.

Lieberman, J. A. (2004b). Quetiapine. In A. F. Schatzberg & C. B. Nemeroff (Eds.), *The American Psychiatric Publishing textbook of psychopharmacology* (3rd ed., pp. 473–486). Washington, DC: American Psychiatric Publishing.

Lieberman, J. A., Stroup, T. S., McEvoy, J. P., Swartz, M. S., Rosenheck, R. A., Perkins, D. O., et al. (2005). Effectiveness of antipsychotic drugs in patients with chronic schizophrenia. *New England Journal of Medicine, 353*, 1209–1223.

Lincoln, T. M. (2007). Relevant dimensions of delusions: Continuing the continuum versus category debate. *Schizophrenia Research, 93,* 211–220.

Linden, D. (2006). How psychotherapy changes the brain: The contribution of functional neuroimaging. *Molecular Psychiatry, 11*(6), 528–538.

Linney, Y. M., & Peters, E. R. (2007). The psychological processes underlying thought interference in psychosis. *Behavior Research and Therapy, ?,* xx–xx.

Lippa, A. S., Antelman, S. M., Fisher, A. E., & Canfield, D. R. (1973). Neurochemical mediation of reward: A significant role for dopamine? *Pharmacology, Biochemistry, and Behavior, 1*(1), 23–28.

Llorens, S., Schaufeli, W., Bakker, A., & Salanova, M. (2007). Does a positive gain spiral of resources, efficacy beliefs and engagement exist? *Computers in Human Behavior, 23*(1), 825–841.

Lowens, I., Haddock, G., & Bentall, R. (2007). *Auditory hallucinations, negative automatic and intrusive thoughts: Similarities in content and process?* Manuscript submitted for publication.

Lukoff, D., Nuechterlein, K. H., & Ventura, J. (1986). Manual for the Expanded Brief Psychiatric Rating Scale. *Schizophrenia Bulletin, 12,* 594–602.

Lyon, H. M., Kaney, S., & Bentall, R. P. (1994). The defensive function of persecutory delusions: Evidence from attribution tasks. *British Journal of Psychiatry, 164,* 637, 646.

MacDonald, A. W., & Carter, C. S. (2002). Cognitive experimental approaches to investigating impaired cognition in schizophrenia: A paradigm shift. *Journal of Clinical and Experimental Neuropsychology, 24,* 873–882.

MacDonald, A., Schulz, S. C., Fatemi, S. H., Gottesman, I. I., Iacono, W., Hanson, D. et al. (n.d.). *What we know . . . What we don't know about schizophrenia.* Retrieved August 21, 2008, from Schizophrenia Research Forum Website. www.schizophreniaforum.org/whatweknow.

Maher, B. A. (1983). A tentative theory of schizophrenic utterance. In B. A. Maher & W. B. Maher (Eds.), *Progress in Experimental Personality Research: Vol. 12. Personality* (pp. 1–52). New York: Academic Press.

Maher, B. A. (1988). Anomalous experience and delusional thinking: The logic of explanations. In T. F. Oltmanns & B. A. Maher (Eds.), *Delusional beliefs. Wiley series on personality processes* (pp. 15–33). Oxford, UK: Wiley.

Malla, A. K., Cortese, L., Shaw, T. S., & Ginsberg, B. (1990). Life events and relapse in schizophrenia: A one year prospective study. *Social Psychiatry and Psychiatric Epidemiology, 25,* 221–224.

Malla, A. K., & Norman, R. M. (1992). Relationship of major life events and daily stressors to symptomatology in schizophrenia. *Journal of Nervous and Mental Disease, 180,* 664–667.

Mancevski, B., Keilp, J., Kurzon, M., Berman, R. M., Ortakov, V., Harkavy-Friedman, J., et al. (2007). Lifelong course of positive and negative symptoms in chronically institutionalized patients with schizophrenia. *Psychopathology, 40,* 83–92.

Manschreck, T. C., Maher, B. A., Milavetz, J. J., Ames, D. Weinstein, C. C., & Schneyer, M. L. (1988). Semantic priming in thought disordered schizophrenic patients. *Schizophrenia Research, 1*(1), 61–66.

Marder, S. R., & Fenton, W. (2004). Measurement and treatment research to improve cognition in schizophrenia: NIMH MATRICS initiative to support the development of agents for improving cognition in schizophrenia. *Schizophrenia Research, 72*(1), 5–9.

Marder, S. R., & Wirshing, D. A. (2003). Maintenance treatment. In S. R. Hirsch & D. L. Weinberger (Eds.), *Schizophrenia* (2nd ed., pp. 474–488). Malden, MA: Blackwell.

Marder, S. R., & Wirshing, D. A. (2004). Clozapine. In A. F. Schatzberg & C. B. Nemeroff (Eds.), *The American Psychiatric Publishing textbook of psychopharmacology* (3rd ed., pp. 443–456). Washington, DC: American Psychiatric Publishing.

Marengo, J. T., Harrow, M., & Edell, W. S. (1993). Thought disorder. In C. G. Costello (Ed.), *Symptoms of schizophrenia* (pp. 27–55). Oxford, UK: Wiley.

Margo, A., Hemsley, D., & Slade, P. (1981). The effects of varying auditory input on schizophrenic hallucinations. *British Journal of Psychiatry, 139*, 122–127.

Margolis, R. L., Chuang, D. M., & Post, R. M. (1994). Programmed cell death: Implications for neuropsychiatric disorders. *Biological Psychiatry, 35*(12), 946–956.

Mathew, R. J., Duncan, G. C., Weinman, M. L., & Barr, D. L. (1982). Regional cerebral blood flow in schizophrenia. *Archives of General Psychiatry, 39*(10), 1121–1124.

McCabe, R., Leudar, I., & Antaki, C. (2004). Do people with schizophrenia display theory of mind deficits in clinical interactions? *Psychological Medicine, 34*, 401–412.

McCarley, R. W., Wible, C. G., Frumin, M., Hirayasu, Y., Levitt, J. J., Fischer, I. A., et al. (1999). MRI anatomy of schizophrenia. *Biological Psychiatry, 45*(9), 1099–1119.

McEvoy, J. P., Apperson, L. J., Appelbaum, P. S., Ortlip, P., Brecosky, J., Hammill, K., et al. (1989). Insight in schizophrenia: Its relationship to acute psychopathology. *Journal of Nervous and Mental Disease, 177*(1), 43–47.

McGlashan, T. H., Heinssen, R. K., & Fenton, W. S. (1990). Psychosocial treatment of negative symptoms in schizophrenia. In N. C. Andreasen (Ed.), *Schizophrenia: Positive and negative symptoms and syndromes* (Vol. 24, pp. 175–200). Basel, Switzerland: Karger.

McGlashan, T. H., & Hoffman, R. E. (2000). Schizophrenia as a disorder of developmentally reduced synaptic connectivity. *Archives of General Psychiatry, 57*, 637–648.

McGlashan, T. H., Zipursky, R. B., Perkins, D., Addington, J., Miller, T., Woods, S. W., et al. (2006). Randomized, double-blind trial of olanzapine versus placebo in patients prodromally symptomatic for psychosis. *American Journal of Psychiatry, 163,* 790–799.

McGrath, J. (2005). Myths and plain truths about schizophrenia epidemiology: The NAPE lecture 2004. *Acta Psychiatrica Scandinavica, 111,* 4–11.

McGrath, J., Saha, S., Welham, J., Saadi, O. E., MacCauley, C., & Chant, D. (2004). A systematic review of the incidence of schizophrenia: The distribution of rates and the influence of sex, urbanicity, migrant status and methodology. *BMC Medicine, 2,* 13.

McGuigan, F. (1978). *Cognitive psychophysiology: Principles of covert behavior.* New Jersey: Prentice Hall.

McKenna, P. J. (1994). *Schizophrenia and related syndromes.* Oxford, UK: Oxford University Press.

McKenna, P. J., & Oh, T. M. (2005). *Schizophrenic speech: Making sense of bathroots and ponds that fall in doorways.* New York: Cambridge University Press.

McNeil, T. F., Cantor-Graae, E., & Cardenal, S. (1993). Prenatal cerebral development in individuals at genetic risk for psychosis: Head size at birth in offspring of women with schizophrenia. *Schizophrenia Research, 10*(1), 1–5.

McNeil, T. F., Cantor-Graae, E., Nordstrom, L. G., & Rosenlund, T. (1993). Head circumference in "preschizophrenic" and control neonates. *British Journal of Psychiatry, 162,* 517–523.

Meares, R. (1999). The contributions of Hughlings Jackson to understanding dissociation. *American Journal of Psychiatry, 156,* 1850–1855.

Mednick, S. A., Machon, R. A., Huttunen, M. O., & Bonett, D. (1988). Adult schizophrenia following prenatal exposure to an influenza epidemic. *Archives of General Psychiatry, 45*(2), 189–192.

Meehl, P. E. (1962). Schizotaxia, schizotypy, schizophrenia. *American Psychologist, 17,* 827–838.

Meehl, P. E. (1990). Toward an integrated theory of schizotaxia, schizotypy, and schizophrenia. *Journal of Personality Disorders, 4,* 1–99.

Melinder, R. D., & Barch, D. M. (2003). The influence of a working memory load manipulation on language production in schizophrenia. *Schizophrenia Bulletin, 29,* 473–485.

Milev, P., Ho, B., Arndt, S., & Andreasen, N. C. (2005). Predictive values of neurocognition and negative symptoms on functional outcome in schizophrenia: A longitudinal first-episode study with 7-year follow-up. *American Journal of Psychiatry, 162*(3), 495–506.

Miller, E., & Karoni, P. (1996). The cognitive psychology of delusions: A review. *Applied Cognitive Psychology, 10,* 487–502.

Miller, P., Byrne, M., Hodges, A. N., Lawrie, S. M., Owens, D. G. C., & Johnston, E. C. (2002). Schizotypal components in people at high risk of developing schizophrenia: Early findings from the Edinburgh high-risk study. *British Journal of Psychiatry, 180,* 179–184.

Mintz, S., & Alpert, M. (1972). Imagery vividness, reality testing, and schizophrenic hallucinations. *Journal of Abnormal and Social Psychology, 19,* 310–316.

Miyamoto, S., Stroup, T. S., Duncan, G. E., Aoba, A., & Lieberman, J. A. (2003). Acute pharmacological treatment of schizophrenia. In S. R. Hirsch & D. L. Weinberger (Eds.), *Schizophrenia* (2nd ed., pp. 442–473). Malden, MA: Blackwell.

Monroe, S. M. (1983). Major and minor life events as predictors of psychological distress: Further issues and findings. *Journal of Behavioral Medicine, 6,* 189–205.

Moore, M. T., Nathan, D., Elliott, A. R., & Laubach, C. (1935). Encephalographic studies in mental disease: An analysis of 152 cases. *American Journal of Psychiatry, 92* 43–67.

Moran, L. J. (1953). Vocabulary knowledge and usage among normal and schizophrenic subjects. *Psychological Monographs, 67,* 1–19.

Moritz, S., & Woodward, T. S. (2006). A generalized bias against disconfirmatory evidence in schizophrenia. *Psychiatry Research, 15,* 157–165.

Morrison, A. P. (2001). The interpretation of intrusions in psychosis: An integrative cognitive approach to hallucinations and delusions. *Behavioral and Cognitive Psychotherapy, 29,* 257–276.

Morrison, A. P. (2004). The use of imagery in cognitive therapy for psychosis: A case example. *Memory, 12*(4), 517–524.

Morrison, A. P., & Baker, C. A. (2000). Intrusive thoughts and auditory hallucinations: A comparative study of intrusions in psychosis. *Behavior Research and Therapy, 38,* 1097–1107.

Morrison, A. P., French, P., Walford, L., Lewis, S. W., Kilcommons, A., Green, J., et al. (2004). Cognitive therapy for the prevention of psychosis in people at ultra-high risk. *British Journal of Psychiatry, 185,* 291–297.

Morrison, A. P., & Haddock, G. (1997). Cognitive factors in source monitoring and auditory hallucinations. *Psychological Medicine, 27,* 669–679.

Morrison, A. P., Renton, J. C., Dunn, H., Williams, S., & Bentall, R. P. (2004). *Cognitive therapy for psychosis: A formulation-based approach.* Hove, UK: Brunner-Routledge.

Morrison, A. P., Wells, A., & Nothard, S. (2000). Cognitive factors in predisposition to auditory and visual hallucinations. *British Journal of Clinical Psychology, 39*(Pt. 1), 67–78.

Mortensen, P. B., Pedersen, C. B., Westergaard, T., Wohlfahrt, J., Ewald, H., Mors, O., et al. (1999). Effects of family history and season of birth on the risk of schizophrenia. *New England Journal of Medicine, 340,* 603–608.

Muller, B. W., Sartory, G., & Bender, S. (2004). Neuropsychological deficits and concomitant clinical symptoms in schizophrenia. *European Psychologist, 9,* 96–106.

Myin-Germeys, I., Delespaul, P., & van Os, J. (2005). Behavioral sensitization to daily life stress in psychosis. *Psychological Medicine, 35,* 733–741.

Myin-Germeys, I., Krabbendam, L., & van Os, J. (2003). Continuity of psychotic symptoms in the community. *Current Opinion in Psychiatry, 16,* 443–449.

Myin-Germeys, I., van Os, J., Schwartz, J. E., Stone, A. A., & Delespaul, P. A. (2001). Emotional reactivity to daily life stress in psychosis. *Archives of General Psychiatry, 58,* 1137–1144.

Nash, J. F. (2002). Autobiography. In H. Kuhn, *The essential John Nash* (pp. 5–12). Princeton, NJ: Princeton University Press.

Nasrallah, H., & Smeltzer, M. (2002). *Contemporary diagnosis and management of the patient with schizophrenia.* Newtown, PA: Handbooks in Health Care Company.

Nayani, T. H., & David, A. S. (1996). The auditory hallucination: A phenomenological survey. *Psychological Medicine, 26,* 177–189.

Nelson, H. E. (1997). *Cognitive behavioural therapy with schizophrenia: A practice manual.* Cheltenham, UK: Stanley Thornes.

Nelson, H. E. (2005). *Cognitive-behavioural therapy with delusions and hallucinations: A practice manual* (2nd ed.). Cheltenham, UK: Nelson Thornes.

Neuroscience Education Institute. (2010). *Psychosis and schizophrenia: Thinking it through.* Carlsbad, CA: Author.

Ngan, E. T., & Liddle, P. F. (2000). Reaction time, symptom profiles and course of illness in schizophrenia. *Schizophrenia Research, 46*(2–3), 195–201.

Nicol, S. E., & Gottesman, I. I. (1983). Clues to the genetics and neurobiology of schizophrenia. *American Scientist, 71,* 398–404.

Norman, D. A., & Shallice, T. (1986). Attention to action: Willed and automatic control of behavior. (Center for Human Information Processing Technical Report No. 99, rev. ed.). In R. J. Davidson, G. E. Schartz, & D. Shapiro (Eds.), *Consciousness and self-regulation: Advances in research* (pp. 1–18). New York: Plenum Press.

Norman, R. M. G., & Malla, A. K. (1991). Subjective stress in schizophrenic patients. *Social Psychiatry and Psychiatric Epidemiology, 26,* 212–216.

Norman, R. M. G., Malla, A. K., Cortese, L., Cheng, S., Diaz, K., McIntosh, E., et al. (1999). Symptoms and cognition as predictors of community functioning: A prospective analysis. *American Journal of Psychiatry, 156*(3), 400–405.

Novaco, R. W. (1994). Anger as a risk factor for violence among the mentally disordered. In J. Monahan & H. Steadman (Eds.), *Violence and mental disorder: Developments in risk assessment* (pp. 21–60). Chicago: University of Chicago Press.

Nuechterlein, K. H., & Dawson, M. E. (1984). Information processing and attentional functioning in the developmental course of schizophrenic disorders. *Schizophrenia Bulletin, 10,* 160–203.

Nuechterlein, K. H., Edell, W. S., Norries, M., & Dawson, M. E. (1986). Attentional vulnerability indicators, thought disorder, and negative symptoms. *Schizophrenia Bulletin, 12,* 408–426.

Nuechterlein, K. H., & Subotnik, K. L. (1998). The cognitive origins of schizophrenia and prospects for intervention. In T. Wykes, N. Tarrier, & S. Lewis (Eds.), *Outcomes and innovations in psychological treatment of schizophrenia* (pp. 17–41). Chichester, UK: Wiley.

O'Callaghan, E., Larkin, C., Kinsella, A., & Waddington, J. L. (1991). Familial, obstetric, and other clinical correlates of minor physical anomalies in schizophrenia. *American Journal of Psychiatry, 148,* 479–483.

O'Donnell, P., & Grace, A. A. (1998). Dysfunctions in multiple interrelated systems as the neurobiological bases of schizophrenic symptom clusters. *Schizophrenia Bulletin, 24*(2), 267–283.

O'Donnell, P., & Grace, A. A. (1999). Disruption of information flow within cortical–limbic circuits and the pathophysiology of schizophrenia. In C. A. Tamminga (Ed.), *Schizophrenia in a molecular age* (pp. 109–140). Washington, DC: American Psychiatric Association.

O'Donovan, M. C., & Owen, M. J. (1996). The molecular genetics of schizophrenia. *Annals of Medicine, 24,* 541–546.

O'Flynn, K. O., Gruzelier, J., Bergman, A., & Siever, L. J. (2003). The schizophrenia spectrum personality disorders. In S. R. Hirsch & D. L. Weinberger (Eds.), *Schizophrenia* (2nd ed., pp. 80–100). Malden, MA: Blackwell.

O'Leary, D. S., Flaum, M., Kesler, M. L., Flashman, L. A., Arndt, S., & Andreasen, N. C. (2000). Cognitive correlates of the negative, disorganized, and psychotic symptom dimensions of schizophrenia. *Journal of Neuropsychiatry and Clinical Neuroscience, 12*(1), 4–15.

Olney, J. W., & Farber, N. B. (1995). Glutamate receptor dysfunction and schizophrenia. *Archives of General Psychiatry, 52,* 998–1007.

Oltmanns, T. F. (1978). Selective attention in schizophrenic and manic psychoses: The effect of distraction on information processing. *Journal of Abnormal Psychology, 87*(2), 212–225.

Oltmanns, T. F., & Neale, J. M. (1978). Distractibility in relation to other aspects of schizophrenic disorder. In S. Schwartz (Ed.), *Language and cognition in schizophrenia* (pp. 117–143). Hillsdale, NJ: Erlbaum.

Overall, J. E., & Gorham, D. R. (1962). The Brief Psychiatric Rating Scale. *Psychological Reports, 10,* 799–812.

Owen, M. J., Craddock, N., & O'Donovan, M. C. (2005). Schizophrenia: Genes at last? *Trends in Genetics, 9,* 518–525.

Owens, D. G. C., & Johnstone, E. C. (2006). Precursors and prodromata of schizophrenia: Findings from the Edinburgh high-risk study and their literature context. *Psychological Medicine, 36,* 1501–1514.

Pakkenberg, B. (1990). Pronounced reduction of total neuron number in mediodorsal thalamic nucleus and nucleus accumbens in schizophrenics. *Archives of General Psychiatry, 47*(11), 1023–1028.

Palmer, B. A., Pankratz, V. S., & Bostwick, J. M. (2005). The lifetime risk of suicide in schizophrenia: A reexamination. *Archives of General Psychiatry, 62*(3), 247–253.

Palmer, B. W., Heaton, R. K., Paulsen, J. S., Kuck, J., Braff, D., Harris, M. J., et al. (1997). Is it possible to be schizophrenic yet neuropsychologically normal? *Neuropsychology, 11,* 437–446.

Pearlson, G. D., Petty, R. G., Ross, C. A., & Tien, A. Y. (1996). Schizophrenia: A disease of heteromodal association cortex? *Neuropsychopharmacology, 14*(1), 1–17.

Pedrelli, P., McQuaid, J. R., Granholm, E., Patterson, T. L., McClure, F., Beck, A. T., et al. (2004). Measuring cognitive insight in middle-aged and older patients with psychotic disorders. *Schizophrenia Research, 71,* 297–305.

Pelton, J. (2002). Managing expectations. In D. Kingdon & D. Turkington (Eds.), *A case study guide to cognitive behaviour therapy of psychosis* (pp. 137–157). Chichester, UK: Wiley.

Penades, R., Boget, T., Lomena, F., Bernardo, M., Mateos, J. J., Laterza, C., et al. (2000). Brain perfusion and neuropsychological changes in schizophrenia patients after cognitive rehabilitation. *Psychiatry Research: Neuroimaging, 98,* 127–132.

Peralta, P. V., Cuesta, M. J., & de Leon, J. (1991). Premorbid personality and positive and negative symptoms in schizophrenia. *Acta Psychiatrica Scandinavica, 84,* 336–339.

Peralta, P. V., Cuesta, M. J., & de Leon, J. (1992). Formal thought disorder in schizophrenia: A factor analytic study. *Comprehensive Psychiatry, 33*(2), 105–110.

Peralta, V., de Leon, J., & Cuesta, M. J. (1992). Are there more than two syndromes in schizophrenia? A critique of the positive–negative dichotomy. *British Journal of Psychiatry, 161,* 335–343.

Perivoliotis, D., Morrison, A. P., Grant, P. M., French, P., & Beck, A. T. (2008). *Negative performance beliefs and negative symptoms in individuals at ultra high risk of psychosis: A preliminary study.* Manuscript submitted for publication.

Peters, E. R., Joseph, S. A., & Garety, P. A. (1999). Measurement of delusional ideation in the normal population: Introducing the PDI (Peters et al. Delusions Inventory). *Schizophrenia Bulletin, 25,* 553–76.

Peters, E. R., Pickering, A. D., Kent, A., Glasper, A., Irani, M., David, A. S., et al. (2000). The relationship between cognitive inhibition and psychotic symptoms. *Journal of Abnormal Psychology, 109,* 386–95.

Peuskens, J. (2002). New perspectives in antipsychotic pharmacotherapy. In M. Maj & N. Sartorius (Eds.), *Schizophrenia* (2nd ed.). West Sussex, UK: Wiley.

Phillips, M. L., & David, A. S. (1997). Viewing strategies for simple and chimeric faces: An investigation of perceptual bias in normals and schizophrenic patients using scan paths. *Brain and Cognition, 35,* 225–238.

Phillips, W. A., & Silverstein, S. M. (2003). Convergence of biological and psychological perspectives on cognitive coordination in schizophrenia. *Behavioral and Brain Sciences, 26,* 65–137.

Pilling, S., Bebbington, P., Kuipers, E., Garety, P., Geddes, J., Orbach, G., et al. (2002). Psychological treatments in schizophrenia: I. Meta-analysis of family intervention and cognitive behavioral therapy. *Psychological Medicine, 32,* 763–782.

Pinninti, N. R., Stolar, N., & Temple, S. (2005). 5-minute first aid for psychosis. *Current Psychiatry, 4*, 36–48.

Portas, C. M., Goldstein, J. M., Shenton, M. E., Hokama, H. H., Wible, C. G., Fischer, I., et al. (1998). Volumetric evaluation of the thalamus in schizophrenic male patients using magnetic resonance imaging. *Biological Psychiatry, 43*(9), 649–659.

Posey, T., & Losch, M. (1983). Auditory hallucinations of hearing voices in 375 normal subjects. *Imagination, Cognition and Personality, 2*, 99–113.

Post, R. M., Fink, E., Carpenter, W. T., Jr., & Goodwin, F. K. (1975). Cerebrospinal fluid amine metabolites in acute schizophrenia. *Archives of General Psychiatry, 32*(8), 1063–1069.

Practice Guideline for the Treatment of Patients with Schizophrenia, Second Edition. (2004). *American Journal of Psychiatry, 161*(2).

Pretzer, J., & Beck, A. T. (2007). Cognitive approaches to stress and stress management. In D. H. Barlow, P. M. Lehrer, R. L. Woolfolk, & W. E. Sime (Eds.), *Principles and practice of stress management* (3rd ed., pp. 465–496). New York: Guilford Press.

Ralph, R. O., & Corrigan, P. W. (2005). *Recovery in mental illness: Broadening our understanding of wellness.* Washington, DC: American Psychological Association.

Ramachandran, V. S., & Blakeslee, S. (1998). *Phantoms in the brain.* New York: Morrow.

Rankin, P., & O'Carroll, P. (1995). Reality monitoring and signal detection in individuals prone to hallucinations. *British Journal of Clinical Psychology, 34*, 517–528.

Read, J., Perry, B. D., Moskowitz, A., & Connolly, J. (2001). The contribution of early traumatic events to schizophrenia in some patients: A traumagenic neurodevelopmental model. *Psychiatry: Interpersonal and Biological Processes, 64*, 319–345.

Read, J., van Os, J., Morrison, A. P., & Ross, C. A. (2005). Childhood trauma, psychosis and schizophrenia: A literature review with theoretical and clinical implications. *Acta Psychiatrica Scandinavica, 112*, 330–350.

Rector, N. A. (2004). Dysfunctional attitudes and symptom expression in schizophrenia: Differential associations with paranoid delusions and negative symptoms. *Journal of Cognitive Psychotherapy: An International Quarterly, 18*(2), 163–173.

Rector, N. A. (2007). Homework use in cognitive therapy for psychosis: A case formulation approach. *Cognitive and Behavioural Practice, 14*(3), 303–316.

Rector, N. A., & Beck, A. T. (2001). Cognitive behavioral therapy for schizophrenia: An empirical review. *Journal of Nervous and Mental Disease, 189*, 278–287.

Rector, N. A., & Beck, A. T. (2002). Cognitive therapy for schizophrenia: From conceptualisation to intervention. *Canadian Journal of Psychiatry, 47*, 41–50.

Rector, N. A., Beck, A. T., & Stolar, N. (2005). The negative symptoms of schizophrenia: A cognitive perspective. *Canadian Journal of Psychiatry, 50,* 247–257.

Rector, N. A., Seeman, M. V., & Segal, Z. V. (2002). *The role of the therapeutic alliance in cognitive therapy for schizophrenia.* Paper presented at the annual meeting of the Association for the Advancement of Behavior Therapy, Reno, NV.

Rector, N. A., Seeman, M. V., & Segal, Z.V. (2003). Cognitive therapy for schizophrenia: A preliminary randomized controlled trial. *Schizophrenia Research, 63,* 1–11.

Rees, W. J. (1971). On the terms "subliminal perception" and "subception." *British Journal of Psychology, 62,* 501–504.

Reichenberg, A., & Harvey, P. D. (2007). Neuropsychological impairments in schizophrenia: Integration of performance-based and brain imaging findings. *Psychological Bulletin, 153*(5), 833–858.

Reichenberg, A., Weiser, M., Rapp, M. A., Rabinowitz, J., Caspi, A., Schmeidler, J., et al. (2005). Elaboration on premorbid intellectual performance in schizophrenia: Premorbid intellectual decline and risk for schizophrenia. *Archives of General Psychiatry, 62,* 1297–1304.

Riley, B. P., & Kendler, K. S. (2005). Schizophrenia: Genetics. In B. J. Sadock & V. A. Sadock (Eds.), *Kaplan and Sadock's comprehensive textbook of psychiatry* (8th ed., pp. 1354–1371). Philadelphia: Lippincott, Williams & Wilkins.

Robins, C. J., Ladd, J., Welkowitz, J., Blaney, P. H., Diaz, R., & Kutcher, G. (1994). The Personal Style Inventory: Preliminary validation studies of new measures of sociotropy and autonomy. *Journal of Psychopathology and Behavioral Assessment, 16,* 277–280.

Robinson, D. G., Woerner, M. G., McMeniman, M., Mendelowitz, A., & Bilder, R. M. (2004). Symptomatic and functional recovery from a first episode of schizophrenia or schizoaffective disorder. *American Journal of Psychiatry, 161*(3), 473–479.

Roffman, J., Marci, C., Glick, D., Dougherty, D., & Rauch, S. (2005). Neuroimaging and the functional neuroanatomy of psychotherapy. *Psychological Medicine, 35*(10), 1385–1398.

Romer, D., & Walker, E. F. (2007). *Adolescent psychopathology and the developing brain: Integrating brain and prevention science.* New York: Oxford University Press.

Romme, M., & Escher, D. (1989). Hearing voices. *Schizophrenia Bulletin, 15,* 209–216.

Romme, M., & Escher, D. (1994). Hearing voices. *British Medical Journal, 309,* 670–670.

Rosenfarb, I. S., Goldstein, M. J., Mintz, J., & Nuechterlein, K. H. (1995). Expressed emotion and subclinical psychopathology observable within the transactions between schizophrenic patients and their family members. *Journal of Abnormal Psychology, 104*(2), 259–267.

Rosenheck, R. A., Leslie, D. L., Sindelar, J., Miller, E. A., Lin, H., Stroup, T. S., et al. (2006). Cost-effectiveness of second-generation antipsychotics and perphenazine in a randomized trial of treatment for chronic schizophrenia. *American Journal of Psychiatry, 163*(12), 2080–2089.

Rosenthal, D., Wender, P. H., Kety, S. S., Schulsinger, F., Welner, J., & Ostergaard, L. (1968). Schizophrenic's offspring reared in adoptive homes. In D. Rosenthal & S. S. Kety (Eds.), *The transmission of schizophrenia* (pp. 377–391). Oxford, UK: Pergamon.

Rosoklija, G., Toomayan, G., Ellis, S. P., Keilp, J., Mann, J. J., Latov, N., et al. (2000). Structural abnormalities of subicular dendrites in subjects with schizophrenia and mood disorders: Preliminary findings. *Archives of General Psychiatry, 57*(4), 349–356.

Rosvold, H. E., Mirsky, A. F., Sarason, I., Bransome, E. D., & Beck, L. H. (1956). A continuous performance test of brain damage. *Journal of Consulting Psychology, 20,* 343–350.

Rund, B. R. (1990). Fully recovered schizophrenics: A retrospective study of some premorbid and treatment factors. *Psychiatry: Journal for the Study of Interpersonal Processes, 53*(2), 127–139.

Saha, S., Chant, D., & McGrath, J. (2007). A systematic review of mortality in schizophrenia: Is the differential mortality gap worsening over time? *Archives of General Psychiatry, 64*(10), 1123–1131.

Sajatovic, M., & Ramirez, L. F. (2003). *Rating scales in mental health* (2nd ed.). Hudson, OH: Lexi-Comp.

Salomé, F., Boyer, P., & Fayol, M. (2002). Written but not oral verbal production is preserved in young schizophrenic patients. *Psychiatry Research, 111*(2–3), 137–145.

Sapolsky, R. M. (1992). *Stress, the aging brain, and the mechanisms of neuron death.* Cambridge, MA: MIT Press.

Satel, S. L., & Sledge, W. H. (1989). Audiotape playback as a technique in the treatment of schizophrenic patients. *American Journal of Psychiatry, 146*(8), 1012–1016.

Satorius, N., Jablensky, A., Korten, A., Ernberg, G., Anker, M., Cooper, J., et al. (1986). Early manifestations and first contact incidence of schizophrenia in different countries. *Psychological Medicine, 16,* 909–928.

Saykin, A. J., Gur, R. C., Gur, R. E., Mozley, P. D., Mozley, L. H., Resnick, S. M., et al. (1991). Neuropsychological function in schizophrenia: Selective impairment in memory and learning. *Archives of General Psychiatry, 48*(7), 618–624.

Schneider, K. (1959). *Clinical psychopathology.* New York: Grune & Stratton.

Schultz, S. K., & Andreasen, N. C. (1999). Schizophrenia. *Lancet, 353*(9162), 1425–1430.

Schulz, S. C., Olson, S., & Kotlyar, M. (2004). Olanzapine. In A. F. Schatzberg & C. B. Nemeroff (Eds.), *The American Psychiatric Publishing textbook of psychopharmacology* (3rd ed., pp. 457–472). Washington, DC: American Psychiatric Publishing.

Schürhoff, F., Szöke, A., Méary, A., Bellivier, F., Rouillon, F., Pauls, D., et al. (2003). Familial aggregation of delusional proneness in schizophrenia and bipolar pedigrees. *American Journal of Psychiatry, 160*, 1313–1319.

Seckinger, S. S. (1994). Relationships: Is 1-900 all there is? *The Journal of the California Alliance for the Mentally Ill, 5*, 19–20.

Seeman, P. (1987). Dopamine receptors and the dopamine hypothesis of schizophrenia. *Synapse, 1*(2), 133–152.

Seeman, P., Chau-Wong, M., Tedesco, J., & Wong, K. (1975). Brain receptors for antipsychotic drugs and dopamine: Direct binding assays. *Proceedings of the National Academy of Sciences, USA, 72*, 4376–4380.

Seeman, P., Ulpian, C., Bergeron, C., Riederer, P., Jellinger, K., Gabriel, E., et al. (1984). Bimodal distribution of dopamine receptor densities in brains of schizophrenics. *Science, 225*, 728–731.

Seikmeier, P. J., & Hoffman, R. E. (2002). Enhanced semantic priming in schizophrenia: A computer model based on excessive pruning of local connections in association cortex. *British Journal of Psychiatry, 180*, 345–350.

Selten, J. P., Brown, A. S., Moons, K. G., Slaets, J. P., Susser, E. S., & Kahn, R. S. (1999). Prenatal exposure to the 1957 influenza pandemic and non-affective psychosis in The Netherlands. *Schizophrenia Research, 38*(2–3), 85–91.

Sensky, T., Turkington, D., Kingdon, D., Scott, J. L., Scott, J., Siddle, R., et al. (2000). A randomized controlled trial of cognitive-behavioral therapy for persistent symptoms in schizophrenia resistant to medication. *Archives of General Psychiatry, 57*(2), 165–172.

Shahzad, S., Suleman, M-I., Shahab, H., Mazour, I., Kaur, A., Rudzinskiy, P., et al. (2002). Cataract occurrence with antipsychotic drugs. *Psychosomatics, 43*, 354–359.

Shallice, T. (1982). Specific impairments of planning. *Philosophical Transactions of the Royal Society London, Series B, Biological Sciences, 298*(1089), 199–209.

Shallice, T., & Evans, M. E. (1978). The involvement of the frontal lobes in cognitive estimation. *Cortex, 14*(2), 294–303.

Shergill, S. S., Cameron, L. A., & Brammer, M. J. (2001). Modality specific neural correlates of auditory and somatic hallucinations. *Journal of Neurology, Neurosurgery, and Psychiatry, 71*, 688–690.

Silbersweig, D. A., Stern, E., Frith, C., Cahill, C., Holmes, A., Grootoonk, S., et al. (1995). A functional neuroanatomy of hallucinations in schizophrenia. *Nature, 378*(6553), 176–179.

Slade, P. D. (1976). An investigation of psychological factors involved in the predisposition to auditory hallucinations. *Psychological Medicine, 6*, 123–132.

Slade, P. D., & Bentall, R. (1988). *Sensory deception: A scientific analysis of hallucination*. Baltimore: Johns Hopkins University Press.

Smith, B., Fowler, D. G., Freeman, D., Bebbington, P., Bashforth, H., Garety, P., et al. (2006). Emotion and psychosis: Links between depression, self-esteem, negative schematic beliefs and delusions and hallucinations. *Schizophrenia Research, 86*, 181–188.

Smith, E., & Jonides, J. (2003). Executive control and thought. In L. R. Squire, F. E. Bloom, S. K. McConnell, J. L. Roberts, N. C. Spitzer, & M. J. Zigmond (Eds.), *Fundamental neuroscience* (2nd ed., pp. 1353–1394). San Diego: Academic Press.

Smith, N., Freeman, D., & Kuipers, E. (2005). Grandiose delusions: An experimental investigation of the delusion as defense. *Journal of Nervous and Mental Disease, 193*, 480–487.

Spauwen, J., Krabbendam, L., Lieb, R., Wittchen, H., & van Os, J. (2006). Impact of psychological trauma on the development of psychotic symptoms: Relationship with psychosis proneness. *British Journal of Psychiatry, 188*, 527–533.

Speilberger, C. D., Gorusch, R. L., Lushene, R. E., Vagg, P. R., & Jacobs, G. A. (1983). *Manual for the State–Trait Anxiety Inventory*. Palo Alto, CA: Consulting Psychologists Press.

Spence, S. A., Hirsch, S. R., Brooks, D. J., & Grasby, P. M. (1998). Prefrontal cortex activity in people with schizophrenia and control subjects: Evidence from positron emission tomography for remission of "hypofrontality" with recovery from acute schizophrenia. *British Journal of Psychiatry, 172*, 316–323.

Spitzer, M., Braun, U., Hermle, L., & Maier, S. (1993). Associative semantic network dysfunction in thought-disordered schizophrenic patients: Direct evidence from indirect semantic priming. *Biological Psychiatry, 34*(12), 864–877.

Spitzer, M., Weisker, I., Winter, M., Maier, S., Hermle, L., & Maher, B. A. (1994). Semantic and phonological priming in schizophrenia. *Journal of Abnormal Psychology, 103*(3), 485–494.

Stahl, S. M. (1999). *Psychopharmacology of antipsychotics*. London: Dunitz.

Starker, S., & Jolin, A. (1982). Imagery and hallucination in schizophrenic patients. *Journal of Nervous and Mental Disease, 170*, 448–451.

Starker, S., & Jolin, A. (1983). Occurrence and vividness of imagery in schizophrenic thought: A thought-sampling approach. *Imagination, Cognition, and Personality, 3*, 49–60.

Startup, H., Freeman, D., & Garety, P. (2007). Persecutory delusions and catastrophic worry in psychosis: Developing the understanding of delusion distress and persistence. *Behaviour, Research and Therapy, 45*, 523–537.

Steen, R. G., Mull, C., McClure, R., Hamer, R. M., & Lieberman, J. A. (2006). Brain volume in first-episode schizophrenia: Systematic review and meta-analysis of magnetic resonance imaging studies. *British Journal of Psychiatry, 188*, S10–S18.

Steer, R. A., Kumar, G., Pinninti, N. R., & Beck, A. T. (2003). Severity and internal consistency of self-reported anxiety in psychotic outpatients. *Psychological Reports, 93*, 1233–1238.

Stefanis, N. C., Hanssen, M., Smirnis, N. K., Avramopoulos, D. A., Evdokimidis, I. K., Stefanis, C. N., et al. (2002). Evidence that three dimensions of psychosis have a distribution in the general population. *Psychological Medicine, 32*, 347–358.

Stern, Y. (2002) What is cognitive reserve? Theory and research application of the reserve concept. *Journal of the International Neuropsychological Society, 8*, 448–460.

Stolar, N. (2004). Cognitive conceptualization of negative symptoms in schizophrenia. *Journal of Cognitive Psychotherapy: An International Quarterly, 18*, 237–253.

Stolar, N., Berenbaum, H., Banich, M. T., & Barch, D. M. (1994). Neuropsychological correlates of alogia and affective flattening in schizophrenia. *Biological Psychiatry, 35*, 164–172.

Strauss, J. S. (1969). Hallucinations and delusions as points on continua function: Rating scale evidence. *Archives of General Psychiatry, 21*, 581–586.

Strauss, J. S. (1989). Mediating processes in schizophrenia. *British Journal of Psychiatry, 155* (5), S22—S28.

Strauss, J.S., & Carpenter, W. T., Jr. (1972). The prediction of outcome in schizophrenia: I. Characteristics of outcome. *Archives of General Psychiatry, 27*(6), 739–746.

Strauss, J. S., Carpenter, W. T., Jr., & Bartko, J. J. (1975). Speculations on the processes that underlie schizophrenic symptoms and signs: III. *Schizophrenia Bulletin, 11*, 61–69.

Strauss, J. S., Rakfeldt, J., Harding, C. M., & Lieberman, P. (1989). Psychological and social aspects of negative symptoms. *British Journal of Psychiatry, 155*, 128–132.

Stroup, T. S., Kraus, J. E., & Marder, S. R. (2006). Pharmacotherapies. In J. A. Lieberman, T. S. Stroup, & D. O. Perkins (Eds.), *Textbook of schizophrenia* (pp. 303–325). Washington, DC: American Psychiatric Association.

Sullivan, P. F., Kendler, K. S., & Neale, M. C. (2003). Schizophrenia as a complex trait. *Archives of General Psychiatry, 60*, 1187–1192.

Sullivan, P. F., Owen, M. J., O'Donovan, M. C., & Freedman, R. (2006). Genetics. In J. A. Lieberman, T. S. Stroup, & D. O. Perkins (Eds.), *Textbook of schizophrenia* (pp. 39–53). Washington, DC: American Psychiatric Association.

Susser, E., Neugebauer, R., Hoek, H. W., Brown, A. S., Lin, S., Labovitz, D., et al. (1996). Schizophrenia after prenatal famine: Further evidence. *Archives of General Psychiatry, 53*(1), 25–31.

Szeszko, P. R., Bilder, R. M., Lencz, T., Pollack, S., Alvir, J. M., Ashtari, M., et al. (1999). Investigation of frontal lobe subregions in first-episode schizophrenia. *Psychiatry Research, 90*(1), 1–15.

Tamminga, C. A. (1998). Schizophrenia and glutamatergic transmission. *Critical Reviews in Neurobiology, 12*(1–2), 21–36.

Tarrier, N. (1992). Psychological treatment of positive schizophrenia symptoms. In D. Kavanaugh (Ed.), *Schizophrenia: An overview and practical handbook* (pp. 356–373). London: Chapman & Hall.

Tarrier, N., Yusupoff, L., Kinney, C., McCarthy, E., Gledhill, A., Haddock, G., et al. (1998). Randomised controlled trial of intensive cognitive behaviour therapy for patients with chronic schizophrenia. *British Medical Journal, 317,* 303–307.

Taylor, J. L., & Kinderman, P. (2002). An analogue study of attributional complexity, theory of mind deficits and paranoia. *British Journal of Psychology, 93,* 137–140.

Tien, A. Y. (1991). Distributions of hallucinations in the population. *Social Psychiatry and Psychiatric Epidemiology, 26,* 287–292.

Tienari, P., Sorri, A., Lahti, I., Naarala, M., Wahlberg, K. E., Moring, J., et al. (1987). Genetic and psychosocial factors in schizophrenia: The Finnish Adoptive Family Study. *Schizophrenia Bulletin, 13,* 477–484.

Tienari, P., Wynne, L. C., Sorri, A., Lahti, I., Laksy, K. Moring, J., et al. (2004). Genotype–environment interaction in schizophrenia-spectrum disorder: Long-term follow-up study of Finnish adoptees. *British Journal of Psychiatry, 184,* 216–222.

Tompkins, M. A. (2004). *Using homework in psychotherapy: Strategies, guidelines, and forms.* New York: Guilford Press.

Torrey, E. F., Bowler, A. E., Taylor, E. H., & Gottesman, I. I. (1994). *Schizophrenia and manic–depressive disorder: The biological roots of mental illness as revealed by the landmark study of identical twins.* New York: Basic Books.

Turkington, D., Sensky, T., Scott, J., Barnes, T. R. E., Nur, U., Siddle, R., et al. (2008). A randomized controlled trial of cognitive-behavior therapy for persistent symptoms in schizophrenia: A five year follow up. *Schizophrenia Research, 98*(1–3), 1–7.

Valmaggia, L. R., Freeman, D., Green, C., Garety, P., Swapp, D., Antley, A., et al. (2007). Virtual reality and paranoid ideations in people with an at-risk mental state for psychosis. *British Journal of Psychiatry, 191,* 563–568.

van Kammen, D. P., van Kammen, W. B., Mann, L. S., Seppala, T., & Linnoila, M. (1986). Dopamine metabolism in the cerebrospinal fluid of drug-free schizophrenic patients with and without cortical atrophy. *Archives of General Psychiatry, 43*(10), 978–983.

van Os, J., & Krabbendam, L. (2002, September). *Cognitive epidemiology as a tool to investigate psychological mechanisms of psychosis.* Paper presented at the annual meeting of the European Association for Behavioural and Cognitive Therapies, Maastricht, the Netherlands.

van Os, J., & Selton, J.-P. (1998). Prenatal exposure to maternal stress and subsequent schizophrenia: The May 1940 invasion of the Netherlands. *British Journal of Psychiatry, 172,* 324–326.

van Os, J., & Verdoux, H. (2003). Diagnosis and classification of schizophrenia: Categories versus dimensions, distributions versus disease. In R. M. Murray, P. B. Jones, E. Susser, J. van Os, & M. Cannon (Eds.), *The epidemiology of schizophrenia* (pp. 364–410). Cambridge, UK: Cambridge University Press.

van Os, J., Verdoux, H., Bijl, R., & Ravelli, A. (1999). Psychosis as a continuum of variation in dimensions of psychopathology. In H. Hafner & W. Gattaz (Eds.), *Search for the causes of schizophrenia* (Vol. IV, pp. 59–80). Berlin: Springer.

Vaughan, S., & Fowler, D. (2004). The distress experienced by voice hearers is associated with the perceived relationship between the voice hearer and the voice. *British Journal of Clinical Psychology, 43*(2), 143–153.

Velakoulis, D., Wood, S. J., Wong, M. T. H., McGorry, P. D., Yung, A., Phillips, L., et al. (2006). Hippocampal and amygdala volumes according to psychosis stage and diagnosis: A magnetic resonance imaging study of chronic schizophrenia, first-episode psychosis, and ultra-high-risk individuals. *Archives of General Psychiatry, 63,* 139–149.

Velligan, D. I., Mahurin, R. K., Diamond, P. L., Hazleton, B. C., Eckert, S. L., & Miller, A. L. (1997). The functional significance of symptomatology and cognitive function in schizophrenia. *Schizophrenia Research, 25,* 21–31.

Ventura, J., Nuechterlein, K. H., Green, M. F., Horan, W. P., Subotnik, K. L., & Mintz, J. (2004). The timing of negative symptom exacerbations in relationship to positive symptom exacerbations in the early course of schizophrenia. *Schizophrenia Research, 69*(2–3), 333–342.

Versmissen, D., Janssen, I., Johns, L., McGuire, P., Drukker, M., Campo, J. À., et al. (2007). Verbal self-monitoring in psychosis: A non-replication. *Psychological Medicine, 37,* 569–576.

Vita, A., De Peri, L., Silenzi, C., & Dieci, M. (2006). Brain morphology in first-episode schizophrenia: A meta-analysis of quantitative magnetic resonance imaging studies. *Schizophrenia Research, 82,* 75–88.

Vita, A., Dieci, M., Silenzi, C., Tenconi, F., Giobbio, G. M., & Invernizzi, G. (2000). Cerebral ventricular enlargement as a generalized feature of schizophrenia: A distribution analysis on 502 subjects. *Schizophrenia Research, 44,* 25–34.

Volkow, N. D., Wolf, A. P., Van Gelder, P., Brodie, J. D., Overall, J. E., Cancro, R., et al. (1987). Phenomenological correlates of metabolic activity in 18 patients with chronic schizophrenia. *American Journal of Psychiatry, 144*(2), 151–158.

Walder, D. J., Walker, E. J., & Lewine, R. J. (2000). Cognitive functioning, cortisol release, and symptom severity in patients with schizophrenia. *Biological Psychiatry, 48,* 1121–1132.

Walker, E. F. (1994). Neurodevelopmental precursors of schizophrenia. In A. S.

David & J. C. Cutting (Eds.), *The neuropsychology of schizophrenia.* Hove, UK: Erlbaum.

Walker, E. F. (2002). Risk factors and the neurodevelopmental course of schizophrenia. *European Psychiatry, 17*(Suppl. 4), 363–369.

Walker, E. F., Baum, K. M., & Diforio, D. (1998). Developmental changes in the behavioral expression of vulnerability for schizophrenia. In M. F. Lenzenweger & R. H. Dworkin (Eds.), *Origins and development of schizophrenia: Advances in experimental psychopathology* (pp. 469–491). Washington, DC: American Psychological Association.

Walker, E. F., & Diforio, D. (1997). Schizophrenia: A neural diathesis–stress model. *Psychological Review, 104,* 667–685.

Walker, E. F., Grimes, K. E., Davis, D. M., & Smith, A. J. (1993). Childhood precursors of schizophrenia: Facial expressions of emotion. *American Journal of Psychiatry, 150,* 1654–1660.

Walker, E., & Harvey, P. (1986). Positive and negative symptoms in schizophrenia: Attentional performance correlates. *Psychopathology, 19*(6), 294–302.

Walker, E., Kestler, L., Bollini, A., & Hochman, K. M. (2004). Schizophrenia: Etiology and course. *Annual Review of Psychology, 55,* 401–430.

Walker, E., Lewine, R. J., & Neumann, C. (1996). Childhood behavioral characteristics and adult brain morphology in schizophrenia. *Schizophrenia Research, 22,* 93–101.

Walker, E., McMillan, A., & Mittal, V. (2007). Neurohormones, neurodevelopment and the prodrome of psychosis in adolescence. In D. Romer & E. F. Walker (Eds.), *Adolescent psychopathology and the developing brain: Integrating brain and prevention science* (pp. 264–283). New York: Oxford University Press.

Warman, D. M., Lysaker, P. H., & Martin, J. M. (2007). Cognitive insight and psychotic disorder: The impact of active delusions. *Schizophrenia Research, 90,* 325–333.

Warner, R. (2004). *Recovery from schizophrenia: Psychiatry and political economy* (3rd ed.). Hove, UK: Brunner-Routledge.

Warner, R., & de Girolamo, G. (1995). *Epidemiology of mental disorders and psychosocial problems: Schizophrenia.* Geneva: World Health Organization.

Waters, F. A. V., Badcock, J. C., Maybery, M. T., & Michie, P. T. (2004). *The role of affect in auditory hallucinations of schizophrenia.* Unpublished doctoral dissertation, University of Western Australia, Crawley.

Waters, F. A. V., Badcock, J. C., Michie, P. T., & Maybery, M. T. (2006). Auditory hallucinations in schizophrenia: Intrusive thoughts and forgotten memories. *Cognitive Neuropsychiatry, 11,* 65–83.

Watts, F. N., Powell, G. E., & Austin, S. V. (1997). The modification of abnormal beliefs. *British Journal of Medical Psychology, 46,* 359–363.

Wegner, D. M., Schneider, D. J., Carter, S. R., & White, T. L. (1987). Paradoxical effects of thought suppression. *Journal of Personality and Social Psychology, 53,* 5–13.

Weinberger, D. R. (1987). Implications of normal brain development for the pathogenesis of schizophrenia. *Archives of General Psychiatry, 44,* 660–669.

Weinberger, D. R. (1996). On the plausibility of "the neurodevelopmental hypothesis" of schizophrenia. *Neuropsychopharmacology, 14*(Suppl. 3), 1S–11S.

Weinberger, D. R., Berman, K. F., & Zec, R. F. (1986). Physiologic dysfunction of dorsolateral prefrontal cortex in schizophrenia: I. Regional cerebral blood flow evidence. *Archives of General Psychiatry, 43*(2), 114–124.

Weingarten, R. (1994). The ongoing processes of recovery. *Psychiatry, 57,* 369–375.

Weiser, M., van Os, J., Reichenberg, A., Rabinowitz, J., Nahon, D., Kravitz, E., et al. (2007). Social and cognitive functioning, urbanicity and risk for schizophrenia. *British Journal of Psychiatry, 191,* 320–324.

Weissman, A. N., & Beck, A. T. (1978, November). *Development and validation of the Dysfunctional Attitudes Scale.* Paper presented at the annual meeting of the Advancement of Behaviour Therapy, Chicago.

West, A. R., Floresco, S. B., Charara, A., Rosenkranz, J. A., & Grace, A. A. (2003). Electrophysiological interactions between striatal glutamatergic and dopaminergic systems. *Annals of the New York Academy of Sciences, 1003,* 53–74.

West, A. R., & Grace, A. A. (2001). The role of frontal–subcortical circuits in the pathophysiology of schizophrenia. In D. G. Lichter & J. L. Cummings (Eds.), *Frontal–subcortical circuits in psychiatric and neurological disorders* (pp. 372–400). New York: Guilford Press.

West, D. (1948). A mass observation questionnaire on hallucinations. *Journal of Social Psychiatry Research, 34,* 187–196.

Wieselgren, I. M., Lindstrom, E., & Lindstrom, L. H. (1996). Symptoms at index admission as predictor for 1–5 year outcome in schizophrenia. *Acta Psychiatrica Scandinavica, 94,* 311–319.

Wilk, C. M., Gold, J. M., McMahon, R. P., Humber, K., Iannone, V. N., & Buchanan, R. W. (2005). No, it is not possible to be schizophrenic yet neuropsychologically normal. *Neuropsychology, 19*(6), 778–786.

Wilkaitis, J., Mulvihill, T., & Nasrallah, H. A. (2004). Classic antipsychotic medications. In A. F. Schatzberg & C. B. Nemeroff (Eds.), *The American Psychiatric Publishing textbook of psychopharmacology* (3rd ed., pp. 425–442). Washington, DC: American Psychiatric Publishing.

Williamson, P. (2006). *Mind, brain, and schizophrenia.* New York: Oxford University Press.

Wing, J. K., & Agrawal, N. (2003). Concepts and classification of schizophrenia. In S. R. Hirsch & D. L. Weinberger (Eds.), *Schizophrenia* (2nd ed., pp. 3–14). Malden, MA: Blackwell.

Wing, J. K., Babor, T., Brugha, T., Burke, J., Cooper, J. E., Giel, R., et al. (1990). SCAN. Schedules for Clinical Assessment in Neuropsychiatry. *Archives of General Psychiatry, 47*(6), 589–593.

Wing, J. K., Cooper, J. E., & Sartorius, N. (1974). *Measurement and classification* of psychiatric symptoms: An introduction manual for the PSE and Catego Program. London: Cambridge University Press.

Winterowd, C., Beck, A. T., & Gruener, D. (2003). Cognitive therapy with chronic pain patients. New York: Springer.

Wong, A. H. C., & Van Tol, H. H. M. (2003). Schizophrenia: From phenomenology to neurobiology. Neuroscience and Biobehavioral Reviews, 27, 269–306.

Wong, D. F., Wagner, H. N., Tune, L. E., Dannals, R. F., Pearlson, G. D., & Links, J. M. (1986). Positron emission tomography reveals elevated D_2 dopamine receptors in drug-naive schizophrenics. Science, 234, 1558–1563.

Woodward, T. S., Moritz, S., Cuttler, C., & Whitman, J. C. (2006). The contribution of a cognitive bias against disconfirmatory evidence (BADE) to delusions in schizophrenia. Journal of Clinical and Experimental Neuropsychology, 28, 605–617.

World Health Organization. (1973). International pilot study of schizophrenia. Geneva: Author.

World Health Organization. (1993). International statistical classification of diseases and related health problems (10th ed.). Geneva: Author.

Wright, J. J., & Kydd, R. R. (1986). Schizophrenia as a disorder of cerebral state transition. Australian and New Zealand Journal of Psychiatry, 20, 167–178.

Wyatt, R. J., Alexander, R. C., Egan, M. F., & Kirch, D. G. (1988). Schizophrenia, just the facts: What do we know, how well do we know it? Schizophrenia Research, 1(1), 3–18.

Young, H., Bentall, R., Slade, P., & Dewey, M. (1987). The role of brief instructions and suggestibility in the elicitation of auditory and visual hallucinations in normal and psychiatric subjects. Journal of Nervous and Mental Disease, 175, 41–48.

Young, J. E., & Brown, G. (1994). Young Schema Questionnaire. In J. E. Young (Ed.), Cognitive therapy for personality disorders: A schema-focused approach. Sarasota, FL: Professional Resource Press.

Zhou, Y., Liang, M., Jiang, T., Tian, L., Liu, Y., Liu, Z., et al. (2007a). Functional dysconnectivity of the dorsolateral prefrontal cortex in first-episode schizophrenia using resting-state fMRI. Neuroscience Letters, 417, 297–302.

Zhou, Y., Liang, M., Wang, K., Hao, Y., Liu, H., et al. (2007b). Functional disintegration in paranoid schizophrenia using resting-state fMRI. Schizophrenia Research, 97, 194–205.

Zimmermann, G., Favrod, J., Trieu, V. H., & Pomini, V. (2005). The effect of cognitive behavioral treatment on the positive symptoms of schizophrenia spectrum disorders: A meta-analysis. Schizophrenia Research, 77, 1–9.

Zipursky, R. B., Lim, K. O., Sullivan, E. V., Brown, B. W., & Pfefferbaum, A. (1992). Widespread cerebral gray matter volume deficits in schizophrenia. Archives of General Psychiatry, 49(3), 195–205.

Zubin, J., & Spring, B. (1977). Vulnerability: A new view of schizophrenia. Journal of Abnormal Psychology, 86, 103–126.

Index